Hunting Shadows
A Family's War

By

Carole McEntee-Taylor & Brian Corbin

First published 2023 by Carole McT Books

Copyright © Carole McEntee-Taylor & Brian Corbin

The right of Carole McEntee-Taylor & Brian Corbin as the Authors of the Work has been asserted by them in accordance with the Copyright, Designs and Patents Act, 1988. Apart from any use permitted under UK copyright law, this publication may only be reproduced, stored or transmitted, in any form, or by any means, with prior permission in writing of the author or, in the case of reprographic production, in accordance with the terms of licences issued by the Copyright Licensing Agency.

Every effort has been made to obtain the necessary permissions with reference to copyright materials, both illustrative and quoted. We apologise for any omissions in this respect and will be pleased to make the appropriate acknowledgement in any future editions.

Edited by Jules Davies
Cover by Flintlock Covers https://www.flintlockcovers.com/

Other books by Carole McEntee-Taylor

Carole McEntee-Taylor Books https://carolemctbooks.info

Non Fiction

Pen and Sword Books Ltd:
Herbert Columbine VC
Surviving the Nazi Onslaught
A Battle Too Far Military Detention Colchester from 1947
The Battle of Bellewaarde June 1915
From Colonial Warrior to Western Front Flyer
The History of Coalhouse Fort
A History of Women's Lives in Scunthorpe

The Weekend Trippers
My War and Peace
Biography of John Doubleday: The Work

The Re-Enlightenment
The Holiday From Hell

Fiction
Secrets
Betrayed
Lives Apart: A WW2 Chronicle – 5 book series
Obsession – 5 book series
Secret Lives – 6 books
A One Way Ticket – 4 book series
Love, Resistance, Betrayal

Dedication

To the Corbin family past, present and future.

To my wife Belinda for simply everything. To my children Andrew and Emma for inspiring me in so many ways.

May your hands always be busy
May your feet always be swift
May you have a strong foundation
When the winds of changes shift
May your heart always be joyful
May your song always be sung
May you stay
Forever young

Bob Dylan

Acknowledgment

I started researching and eventually writing a family history during the Covid-19 lockdown in 2020. This was when I realised two things. One, I can't write and two there was a story worthy of being told within this history.

Thanks go to Belinda for her patience and understanding. To Jeff for encouraging me. To my sisters for their support. To Graham, Rodney and Sally.

Special thanks to Carole, the most energetic, highly professional, caring, intelligent and knowledgeable partner one could hope to have. Working with Carole has been a constant education and Hunting Shadows would not be without her.

Everything in this book is true… well almost!

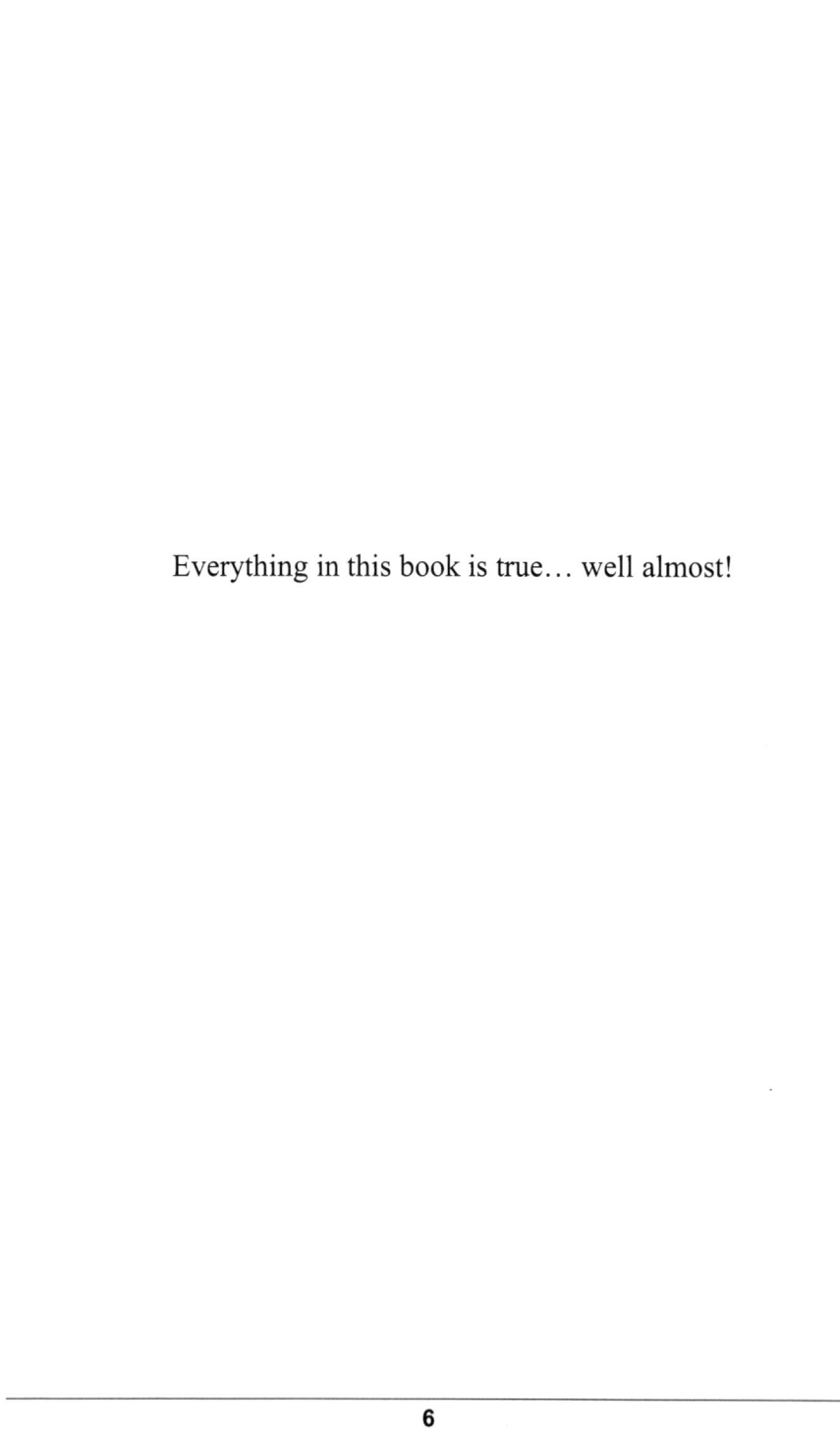

Characters

Jimmy Corbin
Walter Corbin – Jimmy's dad and **Fred Corben**'s uncle
Daisy Lizzie – Jimmy's Mum

John Periman – Elsie's husband
Elsie Periman (nee Corbin) – Jimmy's sister
Rodney Periman – Elsie's son

Fred Corben – Daisy Irene's husband
Daisy Irene Corben (nee Corbin) – Jimmy's sister
Jack - evacuee
Lucy – evacuee
Mick - evacuee
Sandie - evacuee
Jane - evacuee

Lilly – Jimmy's sister
Colonel Simon Sinclair – RSS (Radio Security Service)
Madeline Cartwright – Jimmy's girlfriend
Peregrine Thompkin-Cartwright – Madeline's father

Frederick Farmer
Alice Farmer – Frederick's wife
Betty – Frederick's daughter
Margaret – Frederick's daughter
Jeanne - Frederick's daughter
Ruth Maund – Fredrick's half sister
Geoffrey Maund – Ruth's husband
Li Kang

Charlotte Mason
Rebecca Mason – Charlotte's sister
Maj (Ret'd) Adrian Mason – Charlotte's father
Josephine Mason (deceased) – Charlotte's mother
Anthony Hallett SOE Operative – Charlotte's trainer

Clarisse SOE Operative
Mathew Hart
Patrick O'Brien
Keith Burns/ Stanley Cruickshank

Germany
Kristian von Klotz
Otto von Klotz – Kristian's father; Frederick's half-brother.

Eric Hoffer – Brandenburg Detachment - German Special Forces
Kriminalkommissar Werner Fischer - Gestapo

1955

Prologue

The White Cliffs of Dover came slowly into view and the middle-aged man standing on the deck gave a wry smile. The last time he'd been here his whole being had been on high alert, his attention focused anywhere but on the iconic cliffs. This time was very different, there was no welcoming committee. But there wouldn't be because this time no one knew he was coming.

As the ship edged closer he thought back to the last time he'd arrived on these shores and how he owed his life to something that had happened so long ago. How much that event had affected the future, not just his but that of the world, he had no way of knowing. In the great scheme of things he wasn't important, but he could only hope the small contribution by his family had made some difference.

He turned away from the wind to light his cigarette, exhaled slowly and watched the smoke curling skywards. There was so much pinned on this journey, all his hopes for a new start as there was nothing left of his previous life. But what if he was wasting his time? He had no idea how much they knew, so much would have been hidden and might have continued to remain secret even though the war was now over. The man who had saved his life might not have survived and if he hadn't, the family might not want to know him, they might not be able to see past the atrocities committed by his country to the truth. He had heard the sly comments by the occupying forces in his own country about how strange it was that no German had ever been a Nazi. He understood why the majority of Germans would want to deny their past, but he didn't. How could he? There were certain things he was actually proud of, because he and his family were not the same as those men and women who had caused such chaos in the world.

The cliffs came closer, and he inhaled deeply. This time the nicotine helped to calm his nerves and he began to feel more optimistic. He was worrying about nothing. Even if the worse happened and they doubted his word, once he explained everything he was sure they would accept him and then he would be able to start again. Whether *he* would ever be able to forget the past was another matter, but he owed it to those he had loved to try.

The man finished the cigarette, threw the stub into the swirling waters of the harbour and stared up at the cliffs, so close now he could almost reach out and touch them. The thought made him smile. Years ago, knowing these cliffs were behind him, had been something to celebrate because it meant he had survived another day. His thoughts returned to that fateful day and the time that had followed. So many things had happened in the intervening years that it was surprising he could actually remember his feelings the last time he'd been here. But the memories were surprisingly clear and for a brief moment he had to fight down the rising panic that threatened to overwhelm him as he remembered how close he had come to dying here.

The next few moments passed in a blur and he was barely aware of them. Then a voice over the loud speaker reminded him that the ship would dock in another hour. His fears resurfaced, he clenched his fists and closed his eyes.

'Are you alright?' The voice was gentle and for a split second the traveller forgot everything as he opened his eyes and gazed at the woman staring at him with such concern.

'Yes, yes I am fine, thank you.' He was immediately aware of his accent, and he waited for the reaction. But there was none, her expression hadn't changed, then her lips parted and a smile lit up her face.

'I'm sorry, you must think me very forward, I was just a little concerned…' The words tailed off and she flushed with embarrassment.

He shook his head and, without thinking, reached out a hand to took hers. 'I am very grateful for your concern Fraulein.' As soon as the word escaped his lips he froze but again, there was still no adverse reaction. She made no attempt to pull away so before he could change his mind he was speaking, the words tumbling out seemingly without recourse to his brain. 'It will be a while before we dock, would you like to take some tea with me?' He realised he was holding his breath and all the fears he had successfully buried for most of the journey began to resurface.

'I'd love to, thank you.' Her eyes hadn't left his and his heart soared. For the first time in ages he was no longer afraid of rejection, for some reason the future didn't seem to matter anymore, at least not as much as it had. He knew he had only just met her, but she seemed vaguely familiar for some reason. He smiled. He was probably just getting old and she had a pretty face.

As the woman turned away, the smile faded, her eyes were no longer warm and inviting, her expression cold. Fortunately, it had been much easier than she thought to pick him up although he seemed younger than she'd expected and kinder. She frowned. What was the matter with her? There was no room for compassion. He was the enemy, the man she had been searching for, never really expecting success but then... then suddenly everything had changed. She was so close now she owed it to herself not to get complacent. She wasn't there yet. But she would be. The answers to her questions would soon be within her grasp and then she could have her revenge. She just had to be patient.

Bower Street Maidstone

Part 1

1940

Chapter 1

RAF Cranfield, Bedfordshire, England
The low, insistent, irritating buzzing in his brain was growing louder. Jimmy Corbin shook his head and then wished he hadn't as the pain intensified, but the buzzing didn't stop. It was now louder than the relentless pounding in his head that he had been trying to ignore since he'd dragged himself out of bed earlier that day. With hindsight it hadn't been one of his better ideas to celebrate finally achieving his pilot's wings the previous day by drinking copious amounts of alcohol, not when he had to fly this morning. Somehow, he had managed to pass the air to ground firing tests although he had no idea whether he'd hit any of the fixed targets with his head pounding and his stomach complaining bitterly at every movement of the aeroplane. But the temptation to paint the town red had been too much. Gaining his wings had taken so long that surely he was entitled to enjoy the moment? He'd been determined to fly ever since he was

twelve years old when he'd stood in a field in Maidstone with hundreds of other people watching Sir Alan Cobham's Flying Circus entertaining the public. He had been fascinated by flying before, but after that day it was all he wanted to do, and despite being a working class boy born in Maidstone, and having been turned down by the RAF once before, he had persevered and yesterday, at the age of 22, he'd finally succeeded. Flying was quite a change from teaching at Shoreditch College, but he had no intention of looking back. He had finally achieved his life's dream and, having overcome so much, Jimmy had been sure he was justified in celebrating so after the parade he and his friends had headed to the local pub to show off their wings and have a party. Champagne had flowed freely and wanting to treasure every moment he had kept the cork from the first bottle, it was in his pocket now, a good luck charm.

While it was nice to reminisce about the previous evening, what he could remember anyway, Jimmy knew he really needed to find out what that bloody noise was so he tried to focus his attention on the present. It was ridiculous but he was sure it was getting louder. His frown deepened as he shook his head yet again, but the buzzing continued… it was definitely getting louder, there was no doubt about that.

Jimmy stared through the cockpit window of the Miles Magister aircraft and breathed a sigh of relief. Thank God. Not long now and he would be able to land, find some aspirin and get some much needed sleep, anything to get rid of the dreadful foggy feeling in his head, the cramps in his stomach and that bloody awful buzzing. He just needed to hang on a little longer and he would be down. The runway was coming rapidly towards him and Jimmy tried to concentrate. 'For heaven's sake, I don't mind having the hangover, but can you at least wait for me to land before filling my head with that dreadful noise…' He muttered irritably. The words had only just left his mouth when the truth suddenly dawned on him and the nausea that had been threatening throughout the flight rose up into his mouth. The noise wasn't coming from his head but from the cockpit.

'Oh shit…' Jimmy couldn't think of anything else to say as he realised that the buzzing that had been driving him mad was not a result of his hangover. It was the warning signal telling him he hadn't let down the undercarriage. He was about to land the aeroplane on a hard runway without lowering the wheels and there was absolutely nothing he could do about it because it was much too late. As the ground came rapidly up to meet him Jimmy wondered briefly whether landing belly up on tarmac would be worse than doing the same thing in a grassy field before bracing himself. His last thought as the aeroplane hurtled towards the runway was that maybe the champagne cork wasn't a lucky charm after all. Perhaps it was jinxed?

****

67 College Road, Maidstone
Frederick entered the Territorial Army's Headquarters and made his way to the Home Guard Office he was using until they found their own building. He still couldn't believe things had deteriorated so much, the Germans had forced the British Army back across the Channel without most of their weapons and France had fallen. There was a real danger of invasion, and without the heavy equipment the Army had left behind and the woeful state of their static defences, they would struggle to defend themselves. X11 Corps had been formed in 1940 as part of the Home Defence and their main formations consisted of two infantry divisions and three artillery regiments under the control of Lt General Andrew Thorne, Commander in Chief Home Forces. Based at 10 Broadwater Down in Tunbridge Wells, it was expected to defend Kent and Sussex. A wry smile crossed Frederick's face, with the help of the Home Guard of course. Hopefully General Sir William Edmund Ironside, Commander-in-Chief, General Headquarters (GHQ), Home Forces would be successful in preparing Britain's anti invasion defences in time to fight off the enemy or they would soon all be speaking German.

Frederick shook his head and gave into the anger bubbling just below the surface. How on earth could the government have left everything so late. It wasn't as if they hadn't known what that maniac was planning. Presumably they had given into complacence, assuming the Armed Forces could hold back the relentless tide, but their carelessness was unforgivable. No doubt it would be left to the ordinary man and woman to fight for their country while the politicians made their usual hash of things. The Great War was supposed to have been the war to end all wars, killing on an industrial scale that was meant to stop any future generations having to repeat the carnage. He had hoped his own three daughters, twenty-one-year-old Betty, seventeen year old Margaret Mary and ten year old Jeanne Ursula, would grow up in a peaceful world but it seemed that fate had other ideas. He had also hoped that he wouldn't be leading the fight this time, that was a job for younger men, but after the catastrophe in France it might only be a short time before Kent became the front line and he ended up in the thick of the fighting again, even if it was as a Captain in the Home Guard this time.

****

Yelsted, Kent
'His eyes are definitely too close together Becca. I'd give him a wide berth if I were you.' Charlotte Mason watched her twin getting ready for the night out with her new boyfriend. The girls were both around five foot four, long-haired brunettes with almost identical soulful eyes. The only real visible difference was that Rebecca had curled her hair leaving it wavy and shimmering in the dim light of the bedroom, while Charlotte's was tied back neatly.

'Rubbish, you're just jealous Charlotte. He's gorgeous.' Rebecca gave an exaggerated sigh making her sister laugh, reached over to the radio and turned up the volume. Tommy Dorsey's *I'll never smile again* filled the room.

'Well don't say I didn't warn you.' Charlotte stood up and glanced at her watch. 'I'd better go. Daddy promised to drive me to the station.'

'Good luck with the interview.' Rebecca still couldn't understand why her sister wanted to join the First Aid Nursing Yeomanry (FANY). She'd never shown any interest in nursing and even when Charlotte had explained that she wouldn't be a nurse, she was enlisting to be either a clerk or a driver, it still didn't really make sense. Being stuck in a clerk's job in some office in London or even a driver was hardly exciting. Charlotte would be bored stiff in no time, but it seemed her father knew better as he had suggested she join them. That meant the interview was probably only a formality, but it still seemed a strange choice to her. However, both he and Charlotte had made it clear it was nothing to do with her so she would keep her nose out. Thank goodness she'd joined the Women's Royal Navy Service (WRNS), it had to be much more exciting than some boring office job, and she couldn't wait to start.

Rebecca glanced at the clock on the wall and continued to put the finishing touches to her make-up. Mathew Hart was meeting her in twenty minutes at the local pub and despite her sister's warning she couldn't wait. They were only going to the Nag's Head for lunch but if things went well… Rebecca grinned. She was getting carried away. So far she'd only spoken a few words to him, when he'd asked her out. She might discover he was really boring or had bad breath or something. Her plans for the future could wait until she'd at least had a drink with him.

'You worry too much Charlotte. He's only meeting her in the pub for lunch, perfectly safe.' Major Adrian Mason took his eyes off the road briefly and smiled at her.

'Sorry Dad, there's just something about him.' Charlotte fell silent unable to put her feelings into words.

'Sure you're not just jealous?' His smile broadened at the expression on her face. 'That he chose to ask Rebecca out and not you?'

Charlotte looked horrified. 'You are joking, aren't you?'

Adrian patted her hand. 'Yes of course I am. Rebecca's your twin. She's just like you. If you think there's something wrong with this Mathew character then I'm sure she'll feel the same way.'

'Becca is more trusting than me, you know she is.' Charlotte retorted. 'That's why you suggested me for this job and not her.'

'True, but it wasn't just that. You are more like me. Becca takes after your mother, God rest her soul.'

'Gentle, sensible.' Charlotte smiled at him. Their French mother had died three years earlier of cancer and they all missed her terribly.

Adrian nodded. 'Yes. She was always the better person. Me… well I'm just an old soldier.'

'Not *just* an old soldier Daddy. You and men like you will be needed to win this war.'

'And people like you.' Adrian fell silent. When he'd suggested Charlotte apply for the FANY he'd had mixed feelings, given their secret involvement in intelligence activities. Although in the Great War they had mainly provided nursing services they had been in the forefront of the action, driving their own ambulances, collecting casualties from the front line and some of their number had been involved in spying.

It was only because of his own connections that he knew their role had been expanded prior to this war and now included radio operators, encryption specialists, drivers and cooks as well as clerks. He didn't want to put his daughter in danger, but she would be wasted in any of the regular services. Not only was she exceptionally bright, she also had a quiet courage and was prepared to act on her instincts. Although they were twins Rebecca was different, which was why he hadn't suggested she too join. Rebecca was better suited to something more ordinary and he'd been delighted when she'd enlisted in the WRNS, even if she did claim it was because they had the best uniform. 'You will be careful won't you Charlotte?'

Charlotte laughed. 'Of course, I will Daddy. The most dangerous thing I'm likely to be doing is driving around London!'

Adrian shook his head. 'Yes, I know. I suppose I am just going to miss you.' He was sure they would find her something else to do because driving would be a waste of her skills, but it wasn't for him to say. Once they had decided on her role she would have to sign the Official Secrets Act and then she wouldn't be able to tell him anything, but perhaps it would be better not to know what his daughter was doing anyway, he would only worry.

'Well, we're here.' He pulled over and parked the car at the entrance to the station. Charlotte leaned over and kissed him on the cheek before climbing out and heading inside. Adrian watched her go with mixed feelings. He was proud of Charlotte and he knew she would be an asset to the FANY, but a part of him almost hoped she would be turned down so he had her back home and safe. He shook his head. The country was at war and they all had to do something to stop the Nazis. Fate would see that Charlotte served in the most suitable place and if it was FANY, then he was sure she would make him proud.

****

'South Moor', Maidstone, Kent

The large staff car pulled up outside Fred Corben's house, the driver remained in the car while the passengers, an older man with military bearing and two burly, heavy-set men climbed out and approached the front door. Having been told to expect a visit Fred had been watching out of the window so he opened the door almost immediately and indicated the way to his sitting room. The smaller of the men seemed to be in charge and he led the way, the other two followed close behind, their eyes seemingly on swivels as they checked all around. Fred licked his lips nervously before entering and closing the door behind him. Almost immediately he was struck by how small the room suddenly seemed and once again he licked his lips in apprehension.

'Can I get you some tea?'

The man in charge shook his head. 'No thank you Mr Corben. We won't be long. No doubt you are wondering why we are here, so we won't keep you in suspense.'

Fred nodded and indicated they sit down. 'How can I help you gentlemen?'

'We need your skills but before we go any further, we need you to sign some paperwork.'

Fred frowned. 'I don't understand…'

'The Official Secrets Act.' While he was speaking one of the other men took out a sheaf of papers from his briefcase and handed them to Fred with a pen. 'If you'd like to read the documents first and then sign, sir.'

Fred was feeling even more nervous now. One of the men was standing by the window, his eyes watching the street while the man who'd given him the paperwork moved back to the door and he guessed they were policemen of some sort. 'Can't I ask what this is about before I sign?'

The first man eyed him thoughtfully before shaking his head. 'No, other than your country is at war and we need everyone to play their part in defeating our enemies. There are several ways of winning a war…' He stopped and indicated the paperwork. 'If you'd like to sign sir then we can explain.'

Fred stared at him in consternation for several seconds then mentally shrugged. It looked like he didn't have much choice. He glanced at the clock and made up his mind. Daisy Irene would be back soon and the brief message he'd had from these men was that they wanted to conclude their business while he was alone in the house. He took the papers and began to read through carefully even though he had already decided to sign. Curiosity had now replaced concern and he signed his name with a flourish before handing everything back.

'Thank you, Mr Corben. You don't mind if I call you Fred, do you? Obviously everything you are about to hear is top secret and any breach of that security to anyone, including your wife, family or friends will result in you being arrested, imprisoned and charged with treason.' The man stopped and stared into Fred's eyes. Fred stared back, unsure whether he was meant to comment or not, then realised that he was probably meant to acknowledge that he had apparently just signed his life away.

'Yes, I understand.' He frowned. 'But what about my wife? I can't just…' He fell silent realising he had no idea what they were asking him to do. 'Yes, I understand.' He finally repeated.

The man smiled. 'Thank you. It will all become clear I promise, we just need to go through the formalities.' He glanced up at the clock on the mantlepiece and then returned his attention to Fred. 'I'm Colonel Simon Sinclair, and I am in charge of something called the Radio Security Service – the RSS. Put simply, it's our job, using radio intercepts, to find German spies operating in this country and see if we can turn them, identify members of the German Secret Service wherever they are, and if possible, use them to provide false information to the enemy. We also need to work out what the enemy knows, how much they are prepared to believe and whether the information they are acting upon is guesswork or if there are agents supplying them with allied plans. The reason we want you is because of your role at the General Post Office (GPO) and your skills in signals from your years in the Royal Navy. We've identified that the Germans are using groups of five letters in their short wave signals. We need someone to break those codes so we can read their messages.'

Fred stared at him in growing excitement, his misgivings forgotten and he began to relax for the first time since they'd notified him of their visit. 'I'm honoured you think I can help.' He said eventually.

Simon smiled back. He hadn't really thought the man in front of him would refuse to help but it was always good to know his hunches were correct. Fred Corben ticked all the boxes, even to the extent that although he lived near his family he was treated very much as an outsider so was unlikely to have trouble keeping his work secret. They had looked into his background very carefully. His father had been discharged from the Navy after going mad and had died in a mental institution when Fred was young. His mother had left him in a strict Navy boarding school while she moved to South Moor in Durham and married a man from Naval Pensions. Obviously, this had a long lasting effect on Fred as he had named his house after that area. From the little they could find out about him Fred had grown into a quiet lonely boy, who preferred his own company to being part of a crowd. He had joined the Navy in 1917 where he had developed into a very talented signaller before leaving in 1925 and joining the GPO where he had done very well. The only concerns they had were around his wife. The two were obviously close and he was wondering how much of a temptation it would be for Fred to confide in Daisy Irene. 'You do know that you can't tell your wife anything.'

Fred looked confused. He thought they had already covered that. 'Yes, I know, you said that...' He stopped abruptly, suddenly realising he was sounding impertinent. 'I'm sorry sir, that sounded rude.'

Simon laughed. 'No, you're right Fred, I did mention it but it's not easy to keep secrets from our wives. I just wanted to make sure you understood.'

Fred nodded and thought for a second. 'What do I tell her then? I can't just disappear.'

'You won't have to. You'll just tell her that you can't tell her what you are doing other than its very important for the war effort. Most people will understand that so it shouldn't be a problem. If you do have to go away we'll give you an address where she can write to you, but most of the time you'll be working within a reasonable distance so you'll be able to come home regularly.' He looked at the man holding the signed paperwork and nodded imperceptibly. The man took some more papers out of his pocket and handed them to Fred. 'These are your travel documents and a special note to say you are on government business. This will allow you to travel around as and when necessary and prevent you having any problems because you are in civilian clothes.' Simon stood up. It was time to go. He held out his hand. 'Goodbye Fred, and welcome to RSS.'

He saw them to the front door, watched them climb into the staff car and drive off before closing the door and leaning back against the wall. It had been a very eventful morning but it appeared this was just the beginning. Now he had to tell Daisy Irene that he was off to do his bit. His face darkened slightly. He had never kept secrets from his wife before. Unfortunately, he had no choice. Hopefully she would understand.

****

RAF Cranfield, Bedfordshire, England

The plane hit the ground with a horrendous crunch and skidded forwards, lurching and screeching violently all the way down the runway. Jimmy clenched the control column and fought desperately to keep the aircraft straight as it seared the tarmac at 60 mph on its belly. Eventually he switched the engines off and braced himself as the machine carried on for some distance before finally coming to a shuddering halt. Jimmy stared ahead in shock, unable to believe that he seemed to be unhurt. Everything was suddenly quiet, even his hangover had gone and somehow he found the strength to haul himself out of the aeroplane. That too didn't seem to have suffered too much and as he stood shaking beside it the ground crew approached. The only damage he could see was that the propeller had been mangled on impact. It crossed his mind that perhaps the champagne cork had worked after all. He was still pondering that when the ground crew came rushing up.

Jimmy waved sheepishly and watched their expressions of sympathy fade away as they realised that he wasn't hurt.

'What the hell happened?'

'I just forgot…' Jimmy shrugged and hoped no one would get too close as he was sure he reeked of alcohol and the last thing he needed was to lose the wings he'd spent so long gaining. He had not even had them for twenty four hours for heaven's sake. Before they could answer Jimmy staggered off towards the Mess wondering how long it would be before the CO called for him and his life unravelled. He would go down in history as the man who had not even had his wings for a full day.

Chapter 2

45 College Road, Maidstone, Kent

Jeanne watched her parents saying goodbye and tried to keep her tears at bay. It wouldn't do to upset her mum who was already unhappy enough. She wished Betty was there to comfort her but she had left her job at the General Accident Insurance Company when war started and joined the Women's Auxiliary Air Force (WAAF). She was currently based on one of the air force bases and Jeanne hadn't seen her for ages. Her other sister, Margaret, was still at Maidstone Girls Grammar School (MGGS) although she would be leaving soon. Jeanne was due to leave Brunswick House County Primary and start at MGGS the following year, if the invasion didn't happen of course and the school was still open. Things were changing so much she was beginning to realise that she couldn't rely on anything.

The dog fights in the skies above them and the fears of invasion which seemed to grow each day had unsettled her mother, making her anxious and nervous, even though her father hastened to reassure them that it wouldn't happen, and she believed him. Frederick Farmer was her hero so she was sure he was right about everything. She found it difficult to understand why her mum couldn't see that, especially as she had been so brave in the last war. Jeanne smiled as she remembered the family story about how her father had been wounded, shot in the arm in the Great War and how her mother had lied so she could go to him. She had claimed to be his wife to get a passport, sewn some gold sovereigns into the lining of her corset in case of emergency, and travelled all the way through war torn France to Le Petit Trianon, the hospital in Versailles, on her own. On arrival she had seen that Fred had a tag on his toe which stated they were going to amputate his arm. A horrified Alice had removed the tag and so her beloved father hadn't had his arm amputated. Instead, he had returned home on Number 2 Hospital Ship, the *Astonia*, spent six months in hospital in Aberdeen, then moved to Southwold where he was discharged on 24th August 1916. He had then returned to Detling and his old job as a clerk with Charles Arckoll Ltd and married Alice on 22nd December of that year.

Jeanne sighed and brought her thoughts back to the present. It seemed hardly any time since the whole world had gone mad but in those ten months life had changed out of all recognition. When she remembered how life had been before the war she often wondered if things would ever return to normal. One of the things she missed most of all were the summer picnics. Her parents had belonged to a tennis club, situated on farmland at the top of Postley Road, and every Saturday in summer they had all walked to the farm carrying everything they needed including their picnic teas. Her parents had played tennis and she had spent her time climbing trees in the orchard with the other children. The farm was owned by Mr Sankey who had also delivered their milk every day in a big metal churn, scooping it out with a metal measure into their own milk jug. He drove a horse and cart and it had been her job to pay him. The weekly bill was 2/11 ¾ d and she was always given 3s and allowed to keep the change. They had a second milkman each day as well, but he drove a proper milk float which wasn't half as much fun. The groceries were delivered twice a week by Mr Esland who also brought them a rabbit every Tuesday so they always had rabbit pie for lunch on Wednesdays with the vegetables he had brought the day before. The baker and butcher also delivered so there was no need to go out to shop until the war started and then, because food was rationed, they had to go out with their books to get certain things.

The family always had their summer holiday during the last two weeks of August, and they had embarked on their vacation in the same spirit as previous years, at least she had, totally unaware of the momentous events that were about to turn her world upside down. Everything had been fine until the final Friday, a time she now thought of as the moment life altered completely. She could clearly remember her Uncle Dreyfus arriving at the beach in Broadstairs where they had been playing. He was driving her grandfather's car, a large vehicle with lots of seats and a huge box like boot at the back called an Essex. She recalled her parents and uncle, heads together, discussing something heatedly and then their holiday was over. From what she could understand the Germans had invaded Poland and for some reason this was making everyone nervous. She'd not had time to ask why as the family had immediately hurried home, their belongings still covered in sand and then, on their arrival home they had put on all the lights, only for their next door neighbour to tell them there was supposed to be a complete blackout. That had been Friday 1st September.

On the Sunday they had attended All Saints Church as usual and Jeanne had begun to wonder what all the fuss had been about when the vicar suddenly announced that war had been declared. The gasps of horror followed by hushed silence finally got through to her and she realised something terrible was happening. The family had returned home and as the air raid sirens went off outside they had sat in the living room with their gas masks on wondering what would happen next. The siren had turned out to be a false alarm and for months nothing had happened although the war was the only thing people were talking about. At that time it wasn't the fear of war that had really worried her. Unlike her parents who had experienced the previous conflict Jeanne had no idea what she should be scared of, so her concerns had been more selfish. She had seen pictures in the newspapers showing thousands of children being evacuated, a word she hadn't really understood until it was explained to her. But once she did understand she was terrified that her parents would decide to send her away. So far it hadn't happened and despite the worsening war news her fear had gradually receded, especially as some of the children who had been evacuated had returned home when the expected bombing hadn't happened. Jeanne was relieved her fears had been groundless, but she sensed her parents weren't relaxing and she soon realised that things must be getting worse when her father joined the local branch of the Home Guard. Originally set up as the Local Defence Volunteers in May 1940 to protect Britain in the event of an invasion, over a million men had soon volunteered including her father and although they didn't have proper uniforms or weapons to start with she soon grew used to seeing them about the town.

But this wasn't the only change. Because Maidstone was the centre of county administration and had vital road, rail and river links it had become something called a Nodal Point and was heavily fortified. The town now had huge ditches around the edge to stop tanks and there were concrete obstacles along many of the roads, not to mention pill boxes, road blocks and checkpoints everywhere.

Jeanne had listened carefully as her father had explained that Nodal points were intended to defend London and the industrial heartlands of the Midlands by slowing up any German advance, but she didn't really understand how people like her father were meant to stop thousands of German soldiers and deep down she was sure he was just trying to stop her feeling frightened. Fortunately, the town was also home to the Queen's Own Royal West Kent Regiment and 13 Infantry Training Centre, and now the British Expeditionary Force had been evacuated from France the town was full of soldiers. They were also surrounded by airfields so she no longer felt quite as scared, but she still wished the war would end and things would go back to normal.

The only real constant in her life had been school but she sensed even that was becoming different as they held frequent shelter drills. Jeanne didn't like the claustrophobic feel of the underground shelter and the thought of spending hours in there, having lessons in the dark dingy space with only a couple of light bulbs or candles if the electricity went out, wasn't something she was looking forward to. She could only hope that it wouldn't happen and that her father was right and everything would be fine. She had been sure her father's view of the war was correct until he had suddenly told them he had to go away and that he couldn't tell them where which seemed ridiculous to her. As if she would tell anyone anything that could put her wonderful father in danger. But it was more than ridiculous, it was frightening. Some of her friends had already had to say goodbye to their fathers who had been conscripted, but Jeanne had clung onto the hope that because her father was older and was a Captain in the Home Guard, he would not have to go away at all, and everything would continue as normal. But now everything had changed. The war had suddenly come home and she was scared.

****

Magdeburg, Germany

The scream sounded remarkably like that of a todesfee (banshee), or at least what Kristian von Klotz imagined one must sound like. He pulled out of the dive, adjusted the controls of the aeroplane and she slowly straightened up. Kristian listened carefully, the screaming had stopped but he could hear what sounded like moaning. His face darkened and his stomach churned as the horrible thought crossed his mind that there was someone else on board the aeroplane, someone who shouldn't be there. Even worse was the realisation that the stowaway might have fallen out while he was busy doing acrobatics, and that he could now be in serious trouble because of the stupidity of some idiot who was on board when he shouldn't be. Acrobatics were not allowed under any circumstances. He swallowed nervously and headed back to the airfield. He needed to land quickly, find out exactly who else was on the aeroplane and pray they weren't injured.

The aircraft circled the Fliegerschule Magdeburg, the new training school located on the eastern outskirts of the city on land adjoining the main municipal airport. He could just make out the main road leading to Potsdam and Berlin and then the ultra-modern accommodation blocks, apparently based on Italian fascist architecture, completely different from the normal Prussian military barracks which invariably resembled brick built fortresses. The rooms were comfortable, light, spacious and perfect for long periods of study which was fortunate as alongside flying lessons the pilots also spent hours studying various other subjects that went alongside aviation.

There were two parallel runways in the grassy field, one for take offs, the other for landing with a neutral area between the two to enable aircraft to turn off at the end of their landing run and taxi back to the take-off runway in safety. During the day it was easy to see what he was doing but night flying was different. The runway marker flags had been replaced by portable lamps and any obstacles were also supposed to be illuminated, but there was no proper approach lighting. Although he had landed here several times in the dark Kristian was unnerved by fears of an unexpected guest aboard the aeroplane so he was finding it hard to concentrate and he found his thoughts wandering. How on earth could he explain injury or the death of a fellow pilot when he wasn't even meant to be up in the air, let alone performing acrobatic stunts.

He finally came into land and slowly taxied to a halt, his heart pounding uncomfortably against his ribs. He had worked hard since he'd come to the flying school, hours of flying, studying, passing every exam, determined to prove to his father that the Luftwaffe was right for him and now... now it was all about to fall apart because of someone else. Suddenly feeling furious Kristian leapt out and peered at the aircraft.

'You could have killed me...' The voice came from one of the students who was carefully extracting himself from the aircraft. 'I didn't have my parachute on and I wasn't strapped in. I nearly fell out...' He fell silent as he suddenly noticed the anger on Kristian's face.

'What the hell were you doing?' Kristian could barely contain his rage.

The student swallowed nervously. 'I'm sorry Herr Oberleutnant. I thought I'd get a lift back to the hangers… rather than walk after we'd finished training. I wasn't expecting you to take off again.'

Kristian continued to glare at him as recognition slowly came. 'You're Schmidt… Arnold Schmidt?'

'Jawohl Herr Oberleutnant.' Schmidt was now standing stood rigidly to attention and Kristian could see the embarrassment on his face and something else that Kristian belatedly recognised as fear. As he wondered briefly if it was from his near death experience, or concern that he was going to be court martialled, Kristian began to calm down. By rights he should report the man but if he did he would be in trouble too so it was probably safer to just yell at him and then forget all about it. There was no one else about so the only real problem was if the stowaway was going to report him.

Kristian took a breath. 'Yes, I could have killed you but we're both at fault. You shouldn't have been on my aeroplane, and I shouldn't have been performing… practising fighter tactics at this time of night.' He decided at the last minute not to use the word acrobatics. No point giving the man ammunition.

'Jawohl Herr Oberleutnant.' Schmidt eyed him warily. Was he really going to get away with this? He hesitated and then decided to be honest. 'I'm really sorry Herr Oberleutnant. I only climbed aboard because I wanted a lift back to the accommodation. If I'd known you weren't finished…'

Kristian suddenly grinned. 'You frightened the bloody life out of me. I had no idea where that noise was coming from.'

Arnold relaxed slightly. 'I was terrified…' He grinned, 'although I probably wouldn't have been if I'd been strapped in. I know I shouldn't ask this but is there any chance you could teach me those manoeuvres?'

Kristian eyed him for several seconds before answering. 'I don't see why not. It might come in useful in the future.'

'That's what I thought Herr Oberleutnant.'

Kristian nodded. 'Alright. Let's just forget all about this. Good night Schmidt.' He watched as the man hurried across the runways and disappeared into the darkness then shook his head. In future he would check before taking his aircraft up. Fortunately, no one had been hurt this time but he would never forgive himself if he lost his wings, not least because it would give his father great satisfaction to find him a place in the Kriegsmarine instead and that wasn't how Kristian intended to fight this war. His face darkened as he wondered yet again how his father could reconcile his hatred of Hitler and his regime with his apparent support for the war. Kristian was trying hard not to think about the time he would have to fight, flying was his love but the longer he stayed here training other pilots the better.

****

RAF Cranfield, Bedfordshire
Jimmy lay on his bed and read the letter he'd started writing to his parents.
Dear Mum and Dad
Just to let you know I finally got my wings. I couldn't believe it, after trying for so long. Me, the lad from the working class background, had finally been accepted into the RAF. Unfortunately, that's the good news. The bad news is that I was so pleased with myself that I went out to celebrate with my friends and had a little too much to drink. I've blown it. I've wasted all those years and now I'm a complete failure. I woke up this morning with such a hangover that I tried to land the aeroplane with the undercarriage down. They weren't very pleased with me for smashing up one of their planes so it was all for nothing. I've lost my wings again and will probably be on my way home soon. I'm so sorry to let you both down and my country, Still I'm sure the army will have me so I won't be home for long.

He read the words several times, wondering what else he could add to his spectacular failure, before sinking even further into depression. It was a shame he didn't have any alcohol in his room he could really do with a drink and he didn't fancy going down the local pub and putting up with the ribbing and sarcastic comments from the other pilots. He wouldn't have minded if he had made a genuine mistake, he could have lived with that. But this was done through sheer stupidity. He'd known he had to fly the next day but his desire to celebrate had taken precedence over his common sense. He'd spent years trying to achieve this and then thrown it all away.

Suddenly furious with himself he tore the letter into pieces and threw it towards the bin, but it missed. Jimmy stared at the bits of paper on the floor, shook his head and then suddenly smiled. Perhaps that was a sign it was time to stop feeling sorry for himself. The ground crew hadn't said anything about courts martial so maybe he was worrying about nothing. He would see what tomorrow brought and then, if the worst happened, he would try and find a way to stay in, even if he had to start from the beginning. There was no way he would let them throw him out, not now. He'd fought so hard to get this far, he wouldn't give up now. It wasn't as if he would ever do anything that stupid again. He'd learnt his lesson. There was a war on, they were desperate for pilots. They needed him.

****

'South Moor', Maidstone, Kent
Fred Corben had spent most of the day staring out of the sitting room window, his mind going over the morning's meeting. He was still uneasy about keeping secrets from Daisy Irene but if he was honest he couldn't wait to get started. He enjoyed working at the GPO but this would be a lot more interesting, and he would feel that he was doing something useful. Fortunately, the rest of the family left them alone, uneasy by the fact that they were closely related, so at least he didn't have to worry about them wanting to know what he was doing. He also knew they found him difficult to get on with because he was so quiet and not one for family socialising, probably a result of a lonely childhood with no one to talk to which had left him very self-reliant. A smile crossed his face as his thoughts returned to Daisy Irene. Despite their family's misgivings about them being first cousins they had been married nearly three years now and he could honestly say they had been the happiest of his life. He was still congratulating himself on his luck at finding such a perfect wife when he heard the front door open and his heart beat quicker.

'Hello Fred, did your meeting go alright?' Daisy Irene put her head around the sitting room door and smiled.

Fred wondered briefly if he was meant to have even mentioned the meeting, but it was much too late now and anyway it gave him the perfect excuse to tell her that he had to go away.

'Yes, thank you. It was fine. I have to go away though, well I might have to... They have some work for me. I can't tell you anything else. I'm sorry.' Fred gabbled, completely forgetting the carefully prepared statement he had worked out.

Daisy Irene stared at him in astonishment. 'Going away? What do you mean? Have you been conscripted?' Even as she asked she knew that was unlikely given his age.

'No, yes, I mean...' Fred took a deep breath and this time spoke more calmly. 'I can't tell you anything except I have been accepted as a volunteer so I may need to work away occasionally. Nothing very exciting but I have to do my bit don't I?'

Daisy Irene looked totally confused. Her shy husband had volunteered for something that had needed a special meeting. Surely volunteers just went somewhere and offered their services. She stared at him for so long that he began to flush and she suddenly realised he was lying to her. She was about to remark on that when she changed her mind. Fred was highly intelligent and from the little she had gathered from his few friends, had been very good at his job which was something to do with signals. Presumably this new job he had volunteered for or, more likely had been picked for, was something to do with that. The news from the war was dreadful, the evacuation from Dunkirk and now the constant battles above their heads as the Luftwaffe fought to control the skies, not to mention the continued threat of invasion meant the country needed everyone and if her husband could do something useful who was she to stand in his way? She knew Fred well enough to know he would hate lying to her so if he couldn't tell her about it then she wouldn't push him. Life was hard enough without making it more difficult and she was proud of him for being needed, whatever it was he was doing. Anyway, she had some news of her own.

****

Yelsted, Kent

Charlotte arrived back later that day filled with enthusiasm for her new job. As she'd suggested earlier she was to train as a driver and would be assigned to one of the officers. She would also work as his clerk which meant she would have access to secret documents. At least she assumed that was why she'd had to sign the Official Secrets Act.

'How did you get on?' Adrian poured them both some whisky in an attempt to hide his feelings.

'I leave to start training tomorrow.'

'What are you doing, or shouldn't I ask?' He handed her the drink and Charlotte sipped it thoughtfully.

'No, probably best not to, but it's not dangerous. Its pretty much what I said this morning before I went.' She smiled. 'And that is all I can say on the subject to you or Becca.' She frowned. 'Is she back yet?' She had barely asked the question when Becca came flying through the door.

'So, are you going to be working in London? Or don't you know yet?'

'Yes, I've been accepted so I'll be leaving tomorrow.'

'Congratulations then, although I am surprised. I can't see you stuck behind a desk.'

Charlotte grinned. 'Well, the FANY do all sorts of things, so who knows what I'll be doing.' She changed the subject. 'How was your lunch? Is Mr Hart as wonderful as you thought?'

Becca immediately forgot about Charlotte's job and launched into a long description about their lunch.

'Why hasn't he been conscripted?' Adrien eventually interrupted.

Becca shrugged. 'He's a farm labour so until they find someone to take his place he can't join up. He's very fed up about it as he wants to join the army now.'

Charlotte didn't answer but she and her father exchanged glances.

Becca frowned. 'I saw that. It's the truth, you can ask him yourself when he brings me home tomorrow.'

'You're seeing him again tomorrow. Doesn't he have any work to do?'

'Of course he does. I really don't know why you don't like him.'

Charlotte sighed. 'I just think there's something odd about him.'

'Oh for goodness sake, you're just jealous.' Becca snapped.

'No, I'm not...' Charlotte began to explain but she didn't get the chance, her sister had already stormed out of the room.

Chapter 3

RAF Biggin Hill

Betty Farmer finished her shift in the Sector Station Operations Room of the airbase and headed slowly back to her hut. She was exhausted but that wasn't the only thing worrying her. She had reached the maximum requisite age for a plotter and she was concerned they would move her elsewhere. Although the job was stressful she had never felt so alive as she did when seated at the ops table tracking the size and direction of the incoming raiders, taken from the information received from radar stations and observation posts manned by the Observer Corps around the coast. The information she plotted was used to direct the RAF into the path of incoming Germans, the only means they had of intercepting them. She only wished they were more successful in stopping the raids but given the size of the opposition they were somehow managing to hold their own.

'Letter for you.' Her friend Janet handed her an envelope and she smiled. Judging from the handwriting it was from Margaret.

Dear Betty

I hope this letter finds you well. No doubt you are very busy unlike me. I can't wait to leave school and start working. It's so frustrating being treated like a child, stuck at school during the day and at home every night babysitting Jeanne while Dad is busy with the Home Guard and Mum frets about the bombing. The bloody Germans are continually bombing us but no doubt you know that. I heard on the radio that they are aiming for the airfields so I hope you are safe. It must be scary being the target. I know they keep dropping them on us instead but that's because they're bloody useless and keep missing the targets. I was going to say I thought I would be scared if I knew they were aiming at me but maybe not. Perhaps being a target is safer ha ha. Yes I know it's not really funny but I have learnt that it is better to laugh than to cry. Unfortunately Mum doesn't appreciate my sense of humour and Dad says it's because of my age. I think it's just because I feel useless and think I should be doing something to help.

Anyway, enough of my moaning and on to more important things. Have you met anyone interesting yet? It must be wonderful being surrounded by all those dishy RAF chaps. I do envy you. Perhaps I'll join the WAAF too when I leave school. Do you think they'll take me?

Talking of dishy chaps Maidstone is full of interesting men, and not just English soldiers. I can't wait to be old enough to go out in the evening. Christine, my friend, tells me there are parties every night and not enough girls to go around!!!

Yes, I know what you're going to say. Be careful or I'll get a reputation but given the way the war is going we could all be dead soon and I want to enjoy myself before that happens. I don't see anything wrong with that and I'm sure you don't either. It's a different world to the one our parents grew up in so they'll just have to accept that we are not going to behave the same as them. Its 1940, not 1910 after all. Anyway Mum can't really say too much, not after the way she behaved when Dad was injured. Maybe I've inherited her sense of adventure!

*Well, I suppose I'd better go so I can catch the post. Write soon and tell me all your news and I mean **all** your news.*

Your loving sister
Margaret

Betty grinned, folded the letter up and placed it back in the envelope. Margaret was already becoming a handful, once she left school she would probably be worse. Her parents should probably get her signed up to one of the services as soon as possible. He smile widened as she tried to imagine Margaret taking orders. On the other hand, perhaps a good steady job would be better!

****

Highworth, Wiltshire
Frederick Farmer stared out of the window as the train slowed before its arrival at Highworth Station, the end of the branch line, about three miles from Coleshill, his thoughts on his family. He wasn't happy about leaving Alice and Jeanne alone, but he had no choice. It seemed fate had dealt him a more important role in this war than just Captain of the local Home Guard, unfortunately it meant keeping secrets from his family, but he had been doing that for the last couple of years, ever since he'd heard from his half-brother. A wry smile crossed his face as he remembered how shocked he'd been when Otto had first contacted him. His birth had always been shrouded in mystery, his mother had rarely mentioned his real father, just that he had been a Prussian diplomat, something no one had really believed.

Why would they? His mother, Frances Histed, was the daughter of farm labourers. It was most unlikely she had ever been to London in the late 1880s let alone met some Prussian officer who had then made her pregnant. The whole thing was ridiculous, at least it would have been if his stepfather, James Samuel Farmer, hadn't suddenly been able to buy a public house on marrying his mother. Frederick had often wondered about his parentage, mainly because he couldn't stand his stepfather, a bully who had removed him from school aged twelve so he could work in the pub, the Cock Horse Public House in Detling. If it had been an important role Frederick wouldn't have minded, but it was just to hold the heads of the horses while the drivers refreshed themselves in the pub and then stable them afterwards. He also found him other more arduous jobs, none of which he was paid for. Frederick had finally come to the conclusion that the truth lay somewhere between his father being a Prussian diplomat and a local married man. The most likely explanation was that his mother had somehow been impregnated by someone with money who had then bought her silence with a husband who had settled for a pub in lieu of bringing up an illegitimate child. At least that was what he'd thought until he'd finally found out the truth.

His thoughts drifted back to the Great War. Because of the possibility that he might be German Frederick had enlisted almost immediately war had been declared to prove his patriotism, not that it had made any difference to his stepfather who still treated him with disdain. Attesting on 9th September at 15a Farringdon Road, the headquarters of the 6th London Regiment, Frederick smiled as he remembered the satisfaction he felt after enlisting with his friends into the 'Cast Iron Sixth' as the Sixth (City of London) Battalion, the London Regiment (City of London Rifles) was known. His satisfaction was only briefly dented by James Samuel's sarcastic quip, in front of a large group of the Cock Horse's drunken regulars, that Frederick had only gone to London because the local regiments didn't want him. Frederick had initially been tempted to defend himself and argue that his stepfather's comment was untrue. He hadn't joined the local regiments because they weren't taking volunteers leaving him no choice but to go elsewhere. However, he suddenly realised that he didn't really care what this ignorant man thought so instead Frederick shrugged, turned his back on his stepfather and continued talking with the friends who had enlisted with him. To his amusement, judging by

James Samuel's furious expression, his nonchalant attitude seemed to have had more effect than if he'd argued. Now he thought about it he realised that had been the start of his independence, of no longer needing to seek the approval of his stepfather. In any case he was soon too busy to worry about James Samuel.

Frederick had initially joined the 2/6th Battalion which had been formed to take all the volunteers, but he was then transferred to the 1/6th three weeks before they sailed for France on 28th February 1915. After that the self-doubts that had beset him in England faded into insignificance as he came to terms with life in the trenches. In August they were holding the line in sector W3, just west of Loos, and although things were reasonably quiet while the British and French prepared for the Battle of Loos, there were still casualties from snipers and heavy shell fire as the working parties constructed new trenches. It was while providing cover to the overnight working parties on 1st September that Frederick was shot in the wrist, the bullet travelling to his elbow before exiting.

The next few months had been hard as he fought back against his injury, but they would have been much worse without Alice to keep him going. Would he have done things differently if he'd known enlisting had made no difference to how his stepfather saw him? Frederick smiled, the answer clear as daylight. No. He had long since let go of how his stepfather had treated him. Quite frankly it was no longer important, a decision helped by James Samuel not leaving him anything in his will, all his savings going to his legitimate children. Not that Frederick had ever wanted anything from him, other than love of course and once he'd realised that wasn't going to happen, James Samuel's material possessions had become irrelevant. Frederick had realised that he was perfectly capable of making his own way in the world with his loving wife Alice who had proved so resourceful. It still amazed him that she had forged a passport and then travelled through a country at war to see him. He could see how difficult the journey had been by the number of stamps on the back of the passport but each time she had kept going, determined to reach him. And thank God she had, or he would have lost an arm unnecessarily.

The train pulling up abruptly jolted Frederick out of his thoughts. He alighted quickly, made for the exit and followed the instructions he'd received to the Post Office, a double fronted building located on the High Street. He checked there was no one else with him as he entered the building and saw the Post Office on the left of the long central corridor. Frederick walked quickly to the end of the corridor and took in the walled garden before returning to the Post Office and walking up to the counter where he quickly spoke the password he had been given.

The lady behind the counter stared up at him for a couple of seconds before responding. 'If you'd like to wait over there.' She indicated some seats and then disappeared into her office.

As he waited Frederick again considered the wisdom of what he was about to do. He had signed the Official Secrets Act a couple of years earlier when this journey had begun and although he had taken it seriously, there was something about the complete secrecy of his latest instructions that had driven home to him that his life was no longer his own. He could not tell anyone what he was doing, but that wasn't new, that had applied since the beginning. It was the new instructions that were worrying him. These stated that anyone who knew about him or his base when he'd set it up was to be considered a legitimate target because they were a threat to the mission. On return to Maidstone and the setup of his Operating Base (OB) Frederick would be given a sealed envelope with the names of local people who were considered a threat and it was this that concerned him more than anything. The idea of having to kill people he knew who had done nothing to deserve death, people like the Chief Constable who would probably oppose the invasion with as much force as him, was something he was having considerable trouble coming to terms with. Unfortunately, he'd agreed the terms and conditions of the job, so he had no choice. But it was one thing passing on messages from a foreign country, quite another to kill in cold blood.

****

Chatham, Kent

John Perriman glanced up at the skies where the RAF and Luftwaffe were battling it out above him yet again and wondered if his brother-in-law was up there. It was ages since he'd seen Jimmy, not since he'd helped John dig the Anderson shelter in their garden. Fortunately, they hadn't had to use it very much so far but given the damage done to European cities he couldn't see it being much longer before the Luftwaffe started bombing towns and cities, not just airfields. John didn't envy Jimmy, alone in a Spitfire fighting off the enemy. He couldn't understand the attraction of flying, he'd much rather keep his feet on the ground, well on a ship. There was nothing like being at sea, being with his mates and knowing he had the entire weight of the British Royal Navy behind him. Jimmy would be on his own, taking part in a very individual combat, something that felt completely alien to him, a man who loved company.

John had joined the Navy in 1921 and married Elsie Corbin, Jimmy's oldest sister, in 1934. They had one child Rodney and John was becoming increasingly concerned about having to leave his family. A part of him couldn't wait to get back to sea, to be in action, doing something, anything to stop the threat from the Nazis, but if he was at sea he would be worrying about Elsie and Rodney so perhaps it was a good thing he had a shore posting at the moment and was based in Chatham, but he couldn't see that continuing. He was convinced he would eventually return to sea and then who would look after them? Maybe he could persuade them to move somewhere else. Even as he thought that John snorted with derision. Elsie would never move away from her family, certainly not while they were at war, not unless it was with him but unfortunately he wasn't in control of his life. That belonged to the Navy.

The shrieking of a dying engine broke into his thoughts and he watched as one of the aeroplanes dived headfirst into the waves. Judging by the cheers around him it was an enemy aircraft, not the RAF. John smiled. Jimmy lived to fight another day then. He had no idea if it was Jimmy up there, but it comforted him to think his brother-in-law had survived another battle.

****

Coleshill House, Berkshire

Frederick was just about to speak to the Post Mistress again when she reappeared and indicated the front door of the Post Office. He breathed a sigh of relief, hurried to the door and climbed aboard a blacked out 1500cwt truck which had pulled up outside. He was barely seated on the uncomfortable bench when the truck sped off almost unseating him. Frederick grabbed hold of the bench and tried to guess in which direction they were heading, but it was impossible. He wasn't even sure if the truck was driving a direct route or a more convoluted way so eventually he gave up, closed his eyes and tried to make the most of the quiet time he was sure he wouldn't experience again until he'd left wherever it was they were going. He was still wondering where that was when the car finally drew up at what sounded like some kind of checkpoint. Fred was aware of muffled talking then the truck began climbing up a slight incline, he heard pigeons in the distance and then they stopped, someone pulled up the back and he was told to get out. He was by a large stable block. The light was fading and he could hardly see anything now so he headed quickly inside and up the stairs to the first floor. It was even darker now and Fred groped around for something to sit on. He would have a quick smoke then get some sleep. He lit a cigarette and exhaled gratefully. As the smoke curled upwards he began to relax.

'No smoking mate.' The voice was hoarse with sleep, but Fred could identify what sounded like a Yorkshire accent.

'Are you sure? I can't see any signs.'

'That's because it's too bloody dark.' The voice sounded rather irritated now.

'Well, there's no one here.' Fred took another quick drag. 'I'll be finished in a minute.'

'No, there's no fucker about.' This was another voice with a London accent. 'But another minute might be too late. You're sitting on a box of TNT so perhaps you could put the fag out so we all get to wake up tomorrow!'

Chapter 4

Wormwood Scrubs, London

Fred climbed into the staff car that had called to pick him up and settled into the back seat. He had no idea where he was going but the destination didn't worry him that much. He was more interested in what he was going to do. Unfortunately, he wouldn't know until he arrived so he turned his attention back to Daisy Irene and a brief smile crossed his face. He had always thought that it was a shame they couldn't have had children, not for him particularly as he wasn't that interested in children, but Daisy Irene would have made a wonderful mother. It was strange that the war that had driven so many people apart and caused so much misery was about to provide his wife with some happiness. She wouldn't have time to miss him, she would be too busy looking after evacuees. She was going to collect them later that afternoon. She had volunteered to take two children which was fine with him as they had the required number of bedrooms. He was wondering idly if they would be boys or girls when the car drew up outside Wormwood Scrubs Prison.

Fred paled. What on earth… Had he done something wrong? His eyes met those of the driver who was watching him in the driver's mirror with some amusement.

'It's alright sir, you're not in trouble. The boss thought this was a good place to work from.'

Fred grinned and began to relax. 'It's certainly the last place I would have expected.'

The car pulled up by the large doors, the driver jumped out, opened the door and indicated that Fred ring the bell. 'Just tell them your name and they'll take you to the boss. I'll see you later sir… to run you back home when you've finished.'

Fred rang the bell and gave the officer his name through the small opening and waited. Within minutes the large door opened and Fred stepped inside.

****

RAF Cranfield, Bedfordshire

Much to Jimmy's relief nothing else was said about his landing. He found out later that pilots often forgot to lower their undercarriages at the training school and the RAF couldn't afford to ground them all so it was easier to overlook it and hope the pilots had learned their lessons. Relieved he had survived Jimmy vowed to concentrate on his training and not make any more mistakes. He had worked too hard to ruin everything because of a moment of stupidity.

A few days later he joined his fellow pilots as they crowded into a large room on the station where Jimmy was surprised to find they were allowed some choice in which branch of the RAF they would be sent to.

'Well Jimmy, old boy, what's it to be?' Pete asked.

Jimmy thought for a moment then replied. 'No contest. It's got to be Coastal Command.'

His friend looked confused. 'Why? I thought you'd plump for Fighter Command.'

Jimmy shook his head. 'No, Coastal Command has those beautiful Sunderlands, and you have twelve crew members. Bit like being in charge of your own ship.' He grinned. 'And if I get hit I won't have to die alone!'

As his companion laughed and they took their seats the Station Commander appeared in front of them and within minutes was asking who was interested in Coastal Command. Jimmy stood up immediately as did several others and then waited patiently as the Wing Commander chose several men, but not Jimmy who resumed his seat in disappointment, his brain frantically working out the pros and cons of the remaining three Commands: Fighter, Bomber and Balloon. He didn't know much about Balloon Command, but it didn't take him long to realise that his choice had been made as he wasn't interested in Bomber Command at all. Bomber aircraft were heavy, unwieldy machines that were good at dropping bombs but not at protecting themselves from enemy attack, either from the air or the ground. At least in a fighter aeroplane he would be able to defend himself and fight back. He was just congratulating himself on having made his decision quickly when he realised that the Wing Commander was asking for volunteers for Fighter Command. Jimmy shot up, his heart beating faster and then it was over. He had been chosen. In his humble opinion his life expectancy had probably lengthened. Now all he needed to know was what aircraft he would be flying.

The following day he was told he was being posted to No 7 Operational Training Unit in Hawarden in Flintshire, Wales. Jimmy smiled. He didn't know much about Hawarden except they only flew Spitfires. His conversion course would be to the iconic Spitfire and he couldn't wait.

That night they all hurried down to the pub where they celebrated the end of 14 APTS with numerous sherries. Just before they finished one of the pilots stood up.

'Before we all go our separate ways I want to make a few awards.'

Jimmy put his glass down and listened with interest.

'Now we all like to see what our machines can do, but perhaps trying to land without wheels may not be the best idea a person could have. I'd like to present Jimmy with a little memento to remind him what happens when one doesn't lower the undercarriage.'

Jimmy watched in astonishment as he pulled out a smooth triangular block of dark wood bearing a small brass plate with the words 14 AFTS etched on it. Jimmy recognised it immediately. It was the tip of the propellor that had once belonged to the Master he had tried to land without wheels. He grinned and downed his sherry. Another lucky charm to add to his champagne cork.

****

45 College Road, Maidstone, Kent

Jeanne stood in the garden watching the aeroplanes flying towards London, their vapor trails filling the sky.

'Jeanne, come into the shelter at once.' Alice sounded anxious and not wanting to upset her Jeanne reluctantly turned away and then smiled as she spotted another lady with her mother. 'Aunty Ruth. I didn't know you were here.'

'Hello my beautiful niece. I thought I would come and see you all, but I didn't expect your dad to be out.'

'It's the Home Guard.' Alice spoke apologetically. 'He's on duty most nights and when we have daylight raids too.' She led the way into the shelter. 'How's Geoffrey?'

Ruth Maund sighed. 'I've not heard very much other than he's alright, at the moment. Fortunately he's a long way from the fighting, being stationed in the Far East.' Ruth, Frederick's half-sister, had married Geoffrey Maund, a handsome, debonair man who had been in the Royal Navy and the Flying Corps during the Great War and then dabbled in numerous dangerous sports once the war had finished.

According to her parents', whose conversations Jeanne had overheard, Ruth and Geoffrey didn't appear to have a home of their own and Jeanne's grandfather, James Samuel, was not in favour of the match. While Geoffrey was away Ruth was forced to live in the pub as a housekeeper and general dogsbody. Jeanne was fascinated by her Aunt Ruth who swore like a trooper, wore leather trousers and owned a motorcycle.

'That's certainly a blessing...' Alice began but she didn't get any further as Ruth continued.

'Although they may decide to bring some of them back here if things get worse. Not much point keeping the Far East safe if Britain goes under.'

Alice paled. 'You don't really think that's going to happen, do you?'

Ruth suddenly realised Jeanne was staring at her in horror and she forced a smile. 'Of course not. I'm just being a silly so and so.' She reached down and tickled Jeanne. 'Don't take any notice of your batty Aunt, Jeanne.' She sighed and turned toward Alice. 'I'm just missing Geoffrey. I know we've spent a lot of our married life apart but somehow this is different. You're lucky to have Frederick around most of the time.' She fell silent.

Alice was about to say something when there was a massive explosion and the ground shook violently causing them to almost lose their balance.

'What on earth...?' Ruth was already leaving the shelter, ignoring Alice's exhortation to remain in safety. A few seconds later she put her head back in the entrance. 'I think they must be bombing the town.' She had barely finished speaking when there was another massive explosion and everything shook.

Jeanne wriggled out of her mother's arms and hurried towards her aunt. In the distance she could see smoke rising into the sky and then there was the sound of more bombs dropping. Jeanne trembled and huddled closer to her aunt as several loud explosions followed. She felt her mother's arms around her and held her breath as the ground shook again.

'Come back in here Jeanne for heaven's sake.' Alice's voice rose in panic as the bombing grew nearer. This time neither Ruth nor Jeanne argued, both following her back into the safety of the Anderson shelter. The bombing continued for several minutes, dull thuds growing louder until the whole shelter was shaking violently. Jeanne could hear her mother praying and she closed her own eyes and clasped her hands together. 'Dear God, please don't let my father die.' She muttered repeatedly.

Ruth reached out and put her arm around her niece, trying not to let the bombing affect her, hoping her stoicism would rub off on Alice and Jeanne. Instead she concentrated her thoughts on her brother and the rest of the Home Guard who she assumed would be trying to help those affected.

Then, as suddenly as it began it was over. The skies above were full of aircraft heading back towards the coast leaving behind them a trail of destruction, fires, dense palls of smoke, the pungent aroma of broken sewage and gas pipes mingling together and in the background they could hear the urgent jangling of fire engines and ambulances. Although the all-clear siren had not yet gone Jeanne followed Ruth back outside, curiosity overcoming her fear. She wasn't tall enough to see much but she could see the houses opposite and she gasped in horror. One had taken a direct hit, its jagged outline stark against the sky, possessions strewn everywhere, flames still creeping upwards despite the water from the fireman's hosepipe. She reached out and took Ruth's hand.

'It's alright Jeanne, they aren't hurt... look they were in their shelter.' Ruth pointed to the shocked woman leading two children away from the house. Jeanne recognised Mrs Jenkins, her oldest boy was in the same class as Jeanne. His father was away fighting with the army somewhere. Jeanne wondered what he would say when he came home to find his house bombed. Jeanne shivered despite the warm day and began to pray that her house wouldn't get bombed. It would be horrible not to have anywhere to live.

'Where will they live?' Her voice was barely a whisper and she realised her aunt couldn't hear her above the noise. She took a deep breath and repeated her question. 'Where will they go?'

'They'll be alright Jeanne. Don't worry. The most important thing is that they weren't hurt.' Ruth realised that Jeanne was worrying about herself and her own family and she smiled. 'I expect they have family they can live with, just like you do.' She hugged Jeanne closer and was rewarded by feeling her niece's body relax.

Jeanne stared up at the sky, terrified the aeroplanes would come back despite the fact she could see the German aeroplanes fleeing the scene of their terror. Then she heard the familiar sounds of Spitfires and Hurricanes chasing them across the sky, followed by the rattle of machine guns and then a puff of smoke as one of the marauders was hit. She jumped in the air with delight and was about to cheer when she realised that it was headed towards the town, nose down as it spiralled out of control, smoke pouring from its tail.

Despite the obvious danger Jeanne watched in fascination until she realised her mother was dragging her back towards the shelter again.

'But I want to watch...' Jeanne had barely reached the entrance when the ground shook again, the intense vibration knocking her over. She jumped up and scanned the sky in the direction she'd seen the aircraft, finally spotting a new source of smoke in one of the fields outside the town. This time she gave into her delight. 'Yes!' She yelled. 'They got him.'

Alice was about to admonish her for crowing over the death of a fellow being when she saw the satisfaction on Ruth's face and stopped. 'Yes, they did. We should say a prayer for our brave pilots... and for the man who was killed.' *And for your father that he has survived* she continued under her breath. But Jeanne wasn't listening. She was staring at Ruth who was frowning.

'I have no problem praying for our pilots but I'm not praying for the bloody Nazis.' She ignored Alice's disapproving look. 'If you want to use the bible how about we remember that they started this war, let them reap what they've sown. I can't believe you care that much about them, not after the last lot.'

Alice shook her head, not knowing how to explain. She hated the Hun with a passion, but her church upbringing made it hard for her to cheer the killing of another human being.

Jeanne glanced from her mother to her aunt and wondered what she'd done wrong. She was sure if her father had been there he would have cheered the death of the German, he certainly wouldn't have felt sorry for him. Jeanne knew whose side she was on. Let her mother pray for the enemy. She would only use her prayers for the men and women defending them. As she said the words under her breath Jeanne suddenly remembered her father was somewhere out there. In her fear she had forgotten that. She paled and looked at Ruth. 'What about Daddy?'

Ruth exchanged glances with Alice and put her arm around Jeanne. 'I'm sure he's absolutely fine Jeanne. It would take a lot more than a few Nazis to get him. Don't forget he has already survived war with the Germans.'

Jeanne nodded and tried to take comfort from her aunt's words but an annoying little voice in the back of her head kept whispering 'But what if he isn't alright…?'

****

RAF Hawarden, Flintshire, Wales

Jimmy's first thought as he arrived at the aerodrome just outside Chester was confusion as it was right next to another airfield, Sealand, which meant they would have to fly a right handed circuit on take-off or risk colliding with aeroplanes taking off from there. His second surprise was that it still had grass runways which he would later discover flooded when it rained heavily. Work was underway to build a new runway but from what he could see the workmen spent most of their time dodging incoming aircraft. He looked round hoping to see Spitfires but as there was also a maintenance unit there were all types of aeroplanes around the field, even a large factory on the east side making Wellington bombers. As he made his way further in he finally spotted six Mark 1 Spitfires alongside two Miles Masters Trainers. There was also a brand new Spitfire standing on its own which he soon learnt was for the Chief Flying Instructor's use if the airfield came under attack.

To his disbelief 7 OTU was housed in a large crate that had once been home to a Lockheed Hudson. It was dark and dingy with a tarpaulin for a door and also housed the instructors, many of whom were Hurricane pilots from 77 Squadron, veterans of the Battle of France. His own accommodation was in a large camouflaged bell tent and he was grateful it was summer.

A few days later Jimmy was playing cards when one of the more experienced pilots interrupted him. Joe was on leave from the frontline and Jimmy had met him the previous day when Joe had taken him up in one of the Master II to check what he could do before being let loose on the Spitfires because they were more precious than the Masters, even if they were the cast offs the RAF weren't using in frontline action. 'Put the cards down Mr Corbin. I have a treat for you.' He pointed to a rather tatty looking Spitfire on its own in the middle of the runway. 'Think you're ready to handle her?'

Jimmy's heart skipped a beat and he felt the familiar mixture of fear and excitement. 'I certainly am, sir.' He spoke with more confidence than he felt. This was his big chance and he was determined not to ruin it. He collected his parachute, put on his helmet and hurried over to the aircraft. While he watched Joe leave the crate and head in his direction he fastened his parachute, clambered onto the wing, lowered the side flap in the Perspex hood that covered the cockpit and climbed in. He could smell glycol and there was mud on the floor, but Jimmy didn't care. He was about to fly a Spitfire and nothing was going to put him off. Joe climbed up on the wing and took him through the instruments. They were more advanced than anything he'd flown previously but he'd had time to study the manual so they were not that unfamiliar. Joe finished with a lecture about how to raise and lower the undercarriage, a complicated manoeuvre which involved ensuring he did things in the right order and finally he was told to zigzag down the runway because the nose cone was so long he wouldn't be able to see where he was going otherwise.

'If you have a taxiing accident it will cost you 5s. Get off the ground as quickly as you can or the glycol engine coolant will boil and that will cost you another 5s. If you get stuck in the mud don't use too much throttle or you'll tip up on your nose…'

'And that will cost me another 5s.' Jimmy finished.

Joe grinned and climbed off leaving Jimmy on his own trying to remember all the instructions. Somehow he managed the take-off, even remembering the right hand turn to avoid aircraft taking off from Sealand, and then he was at 25,000 feet and he started to relax. The engine was far more powerful than anything he had flown before and he was soon soaring above the North Wales countryside, everything else forgotten as he familiarised himself with every aspect of the aircraft. Time literally flew by until eventually he glanced at his watch, realised he had been up for nearly two hours and his fuel was running low. Reluctantly he turned back towards Hawarden and began to prepare for landing, coming in on a curved approach so he could keep sight of the airfield. Then it was all over. The aircraft was on the ground and taxiing gently to a halt. There was a sudden silence and Jimmy climbed stiffly out.

'Ah Sgt Corbin, I was beginning to think you weren't coming back.'

Jimmy grinned. 'Sorry sir, got a bit carried away.' He was still on cloud nine, unable to believe he had finally flown the iconic Spitfire. He could now understand why pilots loved that aircraft. He had felt invincible and was convinced that nothing the enemy could throw at him would be enough to defeat such an amazing aeroplane.

Chapter 5

Yelsted, Kent

'Well goodbye Becca.' Charlotte hugged her sister tight. 'Look after yourself and Daddy.'

'I wish you had a few more days here. I don't understand why you have to go away on a course just to work in an office.'

Charlotte shrugged. 'I think a lot of the stuff I will be dealing with is secret, so I need to know background information, that kind of thing. At least that's what they've said.'

'I'll miss you... even if you don't like Mathew.'

Charlotte grinned. 'It's probably a good job I don't or I might be jealous.'

'True, but it's important to me that you like him.'

'I do Becca, he's just not my type.' Charlotte lied. There was something seriously odd about Mathew, but she couldn't put her finger on it. However, she didn't want to fall out with her sister over him so she would leave it to her father to keep an eye on things and reserve judgement.

'How long will you be gone?' Becca was suddenly conscious of how much she would miss her twin. They had never been apart before.

'I don't know. Once I've finished the training I'll probably start working straight away so it might be a while.'

'Well, I can aways come and visit you. You're only in London after all.'

'There was also talk of moving around a bit too, so I won't necessarily be in the capital.' Charlotte improvised quickly before leaning forward and hugging her. 'I'll miss you Becca.'

'Oh.. alright...' Becca blinked back the tears that were pricking her eyelids and forced a smile. 'We'll have to be content with writing to each other then.'

She watched as Charlotte disappeared into the station before climbing back into the passenger seat.

'I'm sure she'll be back before we know it.' Adrian patted her arm, started the engine and they drove in silence back to the house.

****

Singapore

Geoffrey Maund finished reading the latest letter from Ruth and sighed. He was missing her desperately, but his work would have been much harder if she'd been there with him. He would have hated lying to her so perhaps it was best this way. He stared out across the water, his attention returning to the message he had just decoded. It sounded urgent so perhaps now was the time to finally trust his protégé with the intelligence they had. He was almost one hundred percent satisfied the man was everything he claimed to be, so it was time to take a chance. He had only been waiting for the last layer of information and he would have brought him in anyway, but the Colonel's message implied that the situation was starting to deteriorate so he needed the help now, not at some time in the future.

Geoffrey stood up, grabbed his jacket and hat and headed purposefully for the door. He still found it astonishing that he had been recruited for something so important and that being in the Marine Craft Section of the RAF was just a cover for his real role. He had been preparing himself for transfer to the Far East when he had been contacted by the security services who had suggested he could help by doing a little more than rescuing downed aircraft crews. The meetings that had followed with Colonel Simon Sinclair had been exciting and worrying in equal measure. There had been enough concern about Germany trying to start another war, but he had been unaware that there was also a threat from Japan. Since then he had realised just how much danger there was in the Far East, but even worse in his opinion, no one appeared to be paying attention. Geoffrey had no qualms about getting involved, but as the months had passed he had begun to wonder if he was wasting his time as no one appeared to be listening.

****

RAF Hawarden, Flintshire, Wales

The next few days were spent putting the finishing touches to their flying abilities including formation flying which Jimmy hated and lost no time in moaning about. 'This is bollocks. I'm going to spend all my time trying not to fly into you while the Germans pick us off one by one.'

His companion sighed. 'Don't you ever stop binding Jimmy? The RAF know what they're doing.'

Jimmy didn't bother answering, he was sure he was right, but it was probably an argument he wasn't going to win. The next part of the course was learning how to attack and then air to ground firing where he learnt that the Spitfire only had about eleven seconds of ammunition under continuous firing so they were encouraged to fire in short two second bursts or risk running out of ammunition. The final lesson was on aerobatics and this was the one Jimmy had been dreading. They had not been allowed to carry out aerobatics in the Magister and he had never tried in the Master which meant his first attempt would be in a Spitfire, an aircraft with a maximum speed in excess of 300mph.

Stomach churning, his heart thudding uncomfortably against his ribs, Jimmy decided to go as high as possible so he had plenty of room. He climbed to 20,000 feet and then made the decision to stick to a slow roll. He pulled the nose above the horizon and started to bank, then the nose began to drop and in order to roll over he had to apply top rudder and forward pressure. He could feel the sweat forming on his upper lip as he tentatively carried out the procedure. To his horror the aircraft shook wildly from side to side and he was struggling to control it. After what seemed like hours, but was probably only a few seconds, Jimmy got the aircraft back under control and with relief he reported that he was on his way back. There was no answer from the radio and he was about to repeat his message when the cockpit was suddenly filled with the sound of heavenly choirs singing *The Lord is My Shepherd.* Jimmy tapped his headset, but the music continued, and he paled. Maybe he had botched up the roll after all, had died and was on his way to heaven. He was still pondering this when he remembered that the TR9 sets they used were rather unreliable, it was Sunday morning, and he was in fact listening to the BBC Choir.

After landing safely he wandered slowly over to the crate where he intended to carry on playing cards, but on the way he was met by one of the other pilots who told him the Wing Commander wanted to see him. Jimmy blanched and thought hard. He hadn't done anything wrong had he? His acrobatics might not have been the best, but he'd brought the aeroplane back down safely. He was still running through every possibility when he entered the office.

'Good afternoon, Sergeant Corbin. Your posting has come through. 66 Squadron, currently at Coltishall, Norfolk so you'll be busy.'

Jimmy relaxed. He wasn't in trouble after all, then he took in the number of the Squadron he'd been posted to and nodded uneasily. 'Yes sir.' He didn't know how he felt. He was relieved he wasn't in trouble, but he was finally about to enter the war on a day when the Luftwaffe had bombed Liverpool and Manchester, shot down nine RAF planes, killed two pilots and with the knowledge that the enemy continued to outnumber the RAF two to one.

****

Coleshill House, Berkshire

Frederick ate his lunch in what he assumed was the servant's hall and kitchen and prepared himself mentally for the final part of the course before returning home and putting some of the things he had learnt into action, starting with setting up his Observation Base (OB). The weekend had passed quickly, and he was feeling quite optimistic as he recalled all the skills he had learnt. Conversation was mute as the men were not encouraged to get to know each other but he didn't mind. He quite liked his own company and not having to chatter about inconsequential things meant he could make plans. His first job was to find a suitable place for his OB. It had to be somewhere easily accessible so he didn't draw attention to himself, but at the same time hidden completely from view. He had already worked out that it would probably have to be in the woods near where he lived. It would take him some time to dig down deep enough so the sooner he was home the better and then he could get started.

That morning had been spent learning how to boobytrap tanks and aircraft. The grounds were full of a mixture of damaged and dummy tanks and aircraft specifically for that task. The previous day had been spent learning how to build an OB followed by classes in close combat, map reading, stealth movements across the countryside at night, and on how to use various explosives as well as how to make their own with easily acquired ingredients. Fred was surprised how much he remembered about using firearms and was surprised how accurate he still was, although grenades were new to him. To his surprise one of the things he excelled at was waiting for a target and firing a rifle at long distance. Being a sniper was a useful skill for someone who was being trained to attack the enemy wherever they were and he much preferred that to blowing things up. Frederick was surprised to realise that he had more or less forgotten his reservations about killing in cold blood, especially after listening to some of the stories of his fellow students who had witnessed various bombings in their home cities. They were not allowed to say where they came from or where they lived, but none of the men were stupid and could easily identify regional accents.

He was due to return to Maidstone tomorrow and for the first time since the evacuation from Dunkirk Frederick was feeling confident about their chances. He had never mentioned his fears to Alice about a Nazi invasion because she was already worried enough, but having listened to their instructions which stated they were expected to go underground if it looked like the Nazis were going to make a successful invasion he now realised that it might be a good idea to send both her and Jeanne away for a while, at least until the danger passed. It would be much easier to disappear if he was living on his own. In any case if the worst happened he wanted Alice and Jeanne as far away from the south coast as possible. Fred frowned. He was assuming they would invade through the English Channel, but it was always possible they would use East Anglia. He would need more details before he arranged evacuation for his wife and daughter. He would never forgive himself if he sent them closer to the danger.

****

Luftflotte 2, Pas-de-Calais
Oberleutnant Kristian von Klotz taxied to a halt and breathed a sigh of relief. He couldn't believe he had survived yet again. It was becoming more and more dangerous over the south coast of Britain. The RAF were improving and they had the advantage of flying over their own country so if they had to bail out they would be rescued. Kristian's abiding fear was of having to ditch his aeroplane in the English Channel.

He remained motionless in the cockpit for several minutes while he thought about the colleagues he had seen shot down and he wondered how many had survived. Not for the first time he wished he could just go home and forget the war, but he couldn't. He would be shot as a deserter if he even let anyone hear his thoughts, let alone run away. But its wasn't just his life that was at risk. It was important for his father's sake that he continued to play the part of a committed Luftwaffe officer. It wouldn't protect Otto indefinitely, especially if he came to the attention of the Intelligence services but Kristian could only do his best. He clenched his fist in a mixture of fear and anger as he wondered how much longer he could get away with flying into battle and avoiding any engagement with the enemy, only really getting involved when he was attacked. Sooner or later he would be noticed and there was no feasible explanation he could come up with for not trying to kill the enemy. He closed his eyes, thought hard for a few moments and then made his decision. On the next raid he would have to make sure he shot down at least one pilot or he would be in trouble and that wouldn't help anyone, least of all his father.

Kristian shook his head as he remembered the last conversation he'd had with Otto when his father had told him exactly what he had been doing through the past few years. Kristian had been shocked but that had almost immediately been replaced with admiration as he finally realised how his father was able to live with the Nazis. He was spying on them and passing on information to his half-brother in Britain. Otto had then given him the address of the Englishman and told Kristian he could go there if the worst happened and he was shot down or had to bail out over England. Kristian hoped he wouldn't have to use the information, but the name and address were seared into his memory anyway.

'Are you injured Oberleutnant?'

'No Karl, I'm fine, just getting my breath back.' Kristian forced a smile at the lead member of the ground crew who was watching him in concern.

'Looks like you were lucky.' Karl continued to examine the aircraft.

Kristian frowned, forgot all about his father and the Englishman and climbed wearily out. Karl pointed out several bullet holes. 'A bit closer...' He didn't need to say more as Kristian could see for himself. Obviously trying to stay neutral wasn't going to keep him alive.

****

C Wing, Wormwood Scrubs Prison

Fred had been reading through the latest reports for several hours when he suddenly spotted something. The hundreds of volunteers were based all around the country and their logs were placed in double envelopes, sealed and posted to PO Box 485, Howick Place, London, SW1 before being passed onto Fred and others who spent hours decoding them.

'Look at this.' He had decoded the brief message and then passed the log to his colleague, Ron. 'What do you make of that?'

Ron read it quickly then grinned. 'Looks like we are going to have a visitor.' He frowned. 'We need to find out more.'

'We've found that so let's hope our volunteers have picked up on any subsequent messages.' There was several minutes silence as the two men worked feverishly through all the messages that had come in on the days after the original report.

'Got it.' Fred waved a piece of paper triumphantly in the air and then began decoding. 'He's coming in by parachute, into Kent.' He frowned as he read more. 'The Maidstone area by the looks of it. That's a bit close to home.'

Ron stood up. 'He'll probably come in under cover of one of the Luftwaffe bombing raids then. We'd better notify the Home Guard and the local garrison there.'

'It's still a bit vague though, isn't it?' Fred was rereading the information, double checking he'd decoded it properly. 'Shouldn't we wait until we have something more concrete?'

Ron grinned. 'Like time and co-ordinates?' He realised Fred was about to say yes and hurried on. 'Look it's unlikely they'll send any more. It would be too difficult to be that accurate if they are coming in by parachute. They'll probably have been given an address and they'll make their way to that on their own.'

Fred thought for a moment and then nodded. 'Yes, I suppose that makes sense. Will we know if they pick him up?'

Ron shrugged. 'Possibly. If they turn him they'll want to know if he's communicating properly so our volunteers will be monitoring him. Whether we'll recognise that information of course is another matter.' He indicated the remaining logs. 'Better get back to work. You never know what else is hiding in there.'

Fred smiled. 'Point taken.' He sighed. 'Just how many spies do you think there are here?'

'Impossible to say although I think we've probably picked most of them up and a large percentage are working for us now, but there's always the possibility that the odd one has slipped though.' He gave an encouraging smile. 'But the harder we work, the less chance there is of that happening.'

Fred thought for a moment. 'And the bombers. Do you believe they are being guided in?'

'No, probably not... although I suppose anything is possible. They confiscated all the amateur radio transmitters before the war started and just left the receivers. It's those that many of our volunteers are using and they have all been carefully vetted.' He glanced at his watch. 'I'm going to pass this on and then I'll be back. Do you want some tea?'

Fred nodded. 'Yes please.' He thought about Daisy Irene for a moment and wished he could warn her, but he couldn't, not without breaking the Official Secrets Act. Sighing loudly he turned his attention back to the remaining logs and began reading.

****

Coleshill House, Berkshire

Charlotte sat in the carriage and wondered where she was going. She had arrived in London expecting to be assigned as a driver, but instead she had been given instructions to go to somewhere called Highworth where she would be met and taken to her training base. She had wanted to ask what she was being trained to do but decided that the secrecy might be part of the selection process and she didn't want to be turned down because she asked too many questions.

The train eventually arrived at the end of the branch line, she took down her suitcase from the luggage rack and alighted. It was a short walk to the street where a car was waiting. Charlotte hesitated and glanced around but the driver was already climbing out and beckoning her.

'Miss Charlotte Mason?'

'Yes, that's me.'

'Good, if you'd like to get in I'll take you to your billet.'

He took her case and put it in the boot while Charlotte climbed into the back seat and wondered where she was going. She didn't have long to wait, the car journey was quite short and she was soon pulling up at a large country house. After passing through the checkpoint at the gate she had a few moments to take in the extensive grounds and then she was at the house and the driver was getting her suitcase back out of the boot.

'Thank you. Where do I go now?'

He grinned. 'If you go through the front door someone will meet you. Goodbye Miss.'

Charlotte walked up to the front door and rang the bell.

'Miss Mason? We've been expecting you.' The man was tall with dark hair, hazel eyes and well-built with a pleasant face. 'If you'd like to follow me I'll explain everything.'

He led her along a corridor, through a door at the end and indicated she sit down at the table. Charlotte did as she was told. The room was surprisingly sparse, only a table and two chairs and she started to feel uncomfortable. Perhaps she'd done something wrong and was in trouble.

As if he'd read her thoughts he smiled. 'It's alright Miss Mason, you aren't in any trouble. Far from it. You're here because we think you might have the skills we are looking for. I'm Major Hallet by the way, Anthony Hallet.'

Charlotte stared across the table at him. 'I'm intrigued.' She said eventually.

He smiled. 'Before I tell you anything I have to remind you that you've signed the Official Secrets Act so if you tell anyone anything we discuss here you will be tried for treason.'

Charlotte paled and he relaxed slightly. 'Sorry, that's just the formal part. Would you like some tea?'

Charlotte shook her head. 'No... not yet. Can you tell me what I'm doing here?'

Major Hallet stood up and lit a cigarette. 'This is a training base for men who have volunteered to be part of the Auxiliary Force. I know you won't have heard of them so let me explain briefly.'

Chapter 6

Over Kent
Kristian fired the last of his ammunition, then cursed loudly before soaring upwards, searching for cover in the few clouds in the summer skies over the Kent, at least he thought that was where he was going, hoping to escape the Spitfire that had suddenly appeared in front of him, guns firing short bursts which thankfully missed him. Kristian could feel the panic rising inside him, there was no escape, he was low on fuel, out of ammunition and lost. The word reverberated through his brain as he realised it was true. He had been so busy trying to lose the enemy fighters he had lost track of the terrain below. Not knowing what else to do Kristian continued to climb before spinning over and falling like a stone. He waited until the last minute and then pulled out, levelled up and glanced frantically around. To his relief there was no sign of any enemy aircraft, not in any direction but nothing below him looked familiar. He peered through the cockpit window, searching for the coastline, but all he could see were fields, trees and in the distance, what appeared to be a town. Perhaps that was Maidstone or it might be Aylesford or even Sittingbourne. Kristian cursed in frustration and then the engine cut out.

****

Near Yelsted, Kent
Becca raced through the undergrowth, heart pounding. That was the last time she spent any time with Mathew Hart. She couldn't believe he wouldn't take no for an answer. Her sister had warned her, told her he wasn't to be trusted, but she hadn't believed her thinking Charlotte was jealous of her latest conquest. Becca cursed her stupidity. She rarely argued with her twin, but if they did have words it was normally over a boy. Their arguments never lasted long; they were too close for that. Charlotte was like another part of her. It had always been like that, they knew what each other was thinking and feeling, something they had always believed was to do with being twins. But now Charlotte had gone away and Becca was on her own. If she hadn't been on her own she would never have agreed to go walking through the countryside with Mathew. Even though she had been out with him twice now she would have kept to public places for

a bit longer. As much as she didn't want to accept that Charlotte might be right her own instincts had begun to warn her that something wasn't quite right. But with Charlotte gone she had been lonely so she'd decided to ignore the nagging voice in her head and let him persuade her to do something slightly reckless. It wasn't that risky, only walking through the woods, but then it had all gone wrong. Mathew had stopped abruptly and was suddenly kissing her. Becca hadn't minded that and she had responded with a certain amount of passion until his hands had begun wandering. Becca wasn't that inexperienced, so she told him to stop, fully expecting him to comply but he hadn't. Instead, he had become very aggressive and she'd had to fight him off.

Somehow, she had to get home without going past him but he knew the countryside around here much better than she did. She stopped, leaned back against the large oak tree and tried to get her breath back. She could hear him crashing through the undergrowth in the distance and her heart began to beat faster. What on earth had possessed her to go walking out with him during an air raid? Even here she could hear the distant crump of bombs as the German planes bombed the RAF airfields relentlessly.

She suddenly realised she couldn't hear Mathew anymore and her heart leapt into her mouth. She summoned up all her courage and peered around the tree but there was no one there. Taking a deep breath she turned back and began walking, trying her utmost not to tread on anything that would give her position away.

She had travelled some distance and was beginning to think she might have escaped him, when she heard wood cracking and she cursed under her breath. Perhaps she should find something to defend herself with. There were plenty of branches around. She looked around frantically and then saw a long thick branch lying on the ground. That would do. She reached out, picked it up, then carrying it carefully she continued on her way, hoping to find some way of circling around him and reaching the safety of her home.

****

Singapore

'You can work from here Kang.' Geoffrey Maund settled his protégé in a small office down the corridor from his own.

'Thank you, Geoffrey. You won't regret this lah.'

Geoffrey smiled. 'I know I won't.' He indicated the equipment he would need to listen in to signals and messages being transmitted by the Japanese. 'Get used to everything and keep me informed. Anything that seems slightly off, however small let me know. And don't forget to monitor all our bases as well.'

Kang frowned. 'You really think there are British people spying for the Japanese?'

Geoffrey shrugged. 'Anything's possible Kang. People do the strangest things, often because they believe they are morally right, but more often it's just for money.' He sighed. 'But you probably know that don't you?'

'Yes, I have seen this with my own eyes.' Kang's face was impassive and Geoffrey cursed himself for reminding the young man of things he knew Kang would much rather forget.

'I'm sorry, I didn't mean to remind you…'

Kang gave a wry smile. 'I never forget Geoffrey. You no need to apologise. You have given me way of paying back and for that I am eternally grateful.'

Suddenly embarrassed, Kang turned back towards his desk and began fiddling with the morse code transmitter while Geoffrey let himself out quietly.

Li Kang had been recruited by Geoffrey a year earlier, not long after he'd escaped China. He had tried to settle into life in Malaya after his arrival in Penang but everything he'd witnessed and experienced had continued to haunt him. Even now he had trouble sleeping so he was more than happy to know he could work his own hours. He stared at the new equipment and thought how much he owed Geoffrey.

Geoffrey stared out of the window of his own office and lit a cigarette, his thoughts on what he knew about the young Chinese man. Li Kang had initially been arrested after getting into a fight with a Korean when he'd accused him of being Japanese. The police had broken up the brawl and taken both men to the Police station where they had subsequently discovered that Li Kang was correct. At the time Geoffrey had been searching for possible Japanese spies and had asked the police to keep their eyes open for Japanese masquerading as Chinese or Korean and using forged papers so one of the policeman contacted him to say they had just arrested someone who might be useful. After a short while talking with him Geoffrey discovered that Li Kang was intelligent, articulate, could write and speak good English, Japanese and Mandarin and hated the Japanese with a passion, although he wouldn't elaborate on why, other than he couldn't stand the way they treated his people. Geoffrey was sure there was more to it, something personal, but he decided not to push it too much. There was plenty of time for him to get to know Li Kang better if he chose to take a chance on him and he had already decided to do that. Having persuaded the police to release Kang into his custody Geoffrey had then spent time getting to know him, a process that had eventually led to him finding out exactly why Kang hated the Japanese so much.

******

London

As Mark had a new Rover Jimmy and his three friends, the four replacement pilots for 66 Squadron, had decided to drive to Surrey via London and have some fun on the way. It was early afternoon when they arrived in Oxford Street and much to their surprise everything seemed unnaturally quiet.

'Where is everyone?' Jimmy stared around in disbelief. He had expected the famous street to be packed with shoppers, hopefully young women but the streets were deserted.

'Goodness only knows.' Mark Sweaton answered as he pulled the car over and parked up. Then he frowned. 'What the hell is that awful noise?'

'Air raid siren.' Jimmy recognised it immediately and his heart sank. He climbed out of the car and stared up at the sky, searching for enemy aircraft.

'Over there!' Pete Carlton pointed into the distance where they could just make out around twenty aircraft darting across the sky as if they were in some kind of bizarre mating ritual, but Jimmy knew exactly what was going on.

'They're Messerschmitt 109s and Spitfires.' He swallowed nervously. In a few hours that would be him and his friends up there. He shielded his eyes from the sun and watched in awe as the pilots dipped and turned, twisting in all directions leaving curly white contrails in their wake. They came closer, and Jimmy could hear the engines screaming as the pilots threw them around the sky, pushing them to their limit, diving and climbing as they tried to avoid each other. One in particular caught his eye, the Spitfire climbing high to gain the advantage, he could hear short bursts of machine gun fire and then one of the aircraft burst into flames and disintegrated, the debris tumbling from the sky onto the ground. Jimmy shook his head. Where were the tight flying formations they had spent weeks learning, the ones he'd complained about as unworkable. The planes were a jumble, he could barely tell who the enemy was. Then it hit him again. In a few hours this would be him.

The distant crump of bombs indicated that despite the best efforts of the RAF the Luftwaffe had again managed to find their targets. Heinkel HE111s must have broken through the air defences and dropped their cargo over London. He was to find out later that the oil tanks at Tilbury Docks in the East End of London had taken a direct hit, the fires raging so intensely that night that the glow could be seen from as far away as Piccadilly Circus. But at that moment he had no idea where the bombs had dropped and he could only pray that casualties were light.

Eventually the all-clear sounded and they climbed back into the car to continue their journey. The earlier joking and camaraderie had long gone as they sat there, lost in their own thoughts. For the first time Jimmy realised that the Squadron must have taken heavy casualties to need four new replacement pilots, but it wasn't until they arrived at Kenley in Surrey that they learned the aircraft they had seen in action were from 66 Squadron, the same Squadron they had been posted to.

****

Somewhere in Kent

The parachute floated lazily down to earth, Kristian hanging on tightly while his eyes searched for enemy planes, not that were likely to shoot him out of the air. The RAF didn't do that, but they would radio through to their headquarters and the police or some other organisation would be waiting for him. For a brief moment he accepted that the war was over for him, he would spend it in a prisoner of war camp, no more fighting, no more killing… then his sense of duty kicked in. His father needed him, he couldn't give up, much as he might want to.

The ground suddenly seemed a lot closer and then he was down, knees bent, rolling to one side as he'd been taught. He stood up quickly and pulled out his pistol but there was no one around, he was completely alone on the edge of a field. Kristian unfastened the parachute and began folding it up quickly. He would have to hide it, no point leaving it around for someone to find.

He headed towards the nearby trees, crossed a small stream and found a hollow by the side of an oak tree. He dug deeper with his hands and buried the parachute. It wasn't very well hidden but would do in the short term. It should give him time to put some distance between him and the field anyway.

He glanced around, there was still no sign of anyone so he looked at his compass and began walking. If he kept going in this direction he should eventually reach the coast, providing he avoided being arrested of course.

He had only been walking for a few moments when he heard the sound of voices ahead and he froze.

****

Coleshill House, Berkshire
'Would you like a cigarette?

Charlotte shook her head. 'No, thank you. I don't smoke.'

Major Hallet lit his own and sat back. 'Right. The simple explanation is that the Auxiliary Force was set up to carry out spying, sabotage and guerrilla warfare behind the lines.' He saw her expression change and smiled. 'If the Germans succeed in invading Britain the idea is for isolated units to disrupt their operations and cause them as much trouble as possible. They are split into three main forces: fighting patrols, special duties and signals. To put it briefly the fighting patrols will be an offshoot of the Home Guard. Their remit is to come out at night and attack enemy airfields, fuel dumps, railway lines, supply dumps and convoys. Anything in fact that can hinder the enemy's progress. Special duties refer to spying, intelligence gathering and observing enemy troop movements, insignias and formations. Signals will transmit this information to Headquarters and will be used to supply the fighting patrols with targets. As you can imagine this work will be incredibly dangerous.'

Charlotte stared at him. 'I'm assuming you don't want me to run around the countryside blowing up things?'

Major Hallet smiled. 'No, you would be helping with special duties. If you were interested of course.'

'Spying on them you mean?'

'Yes, gathering information so we can provide our fighting units with targets that will make a difference. You'll pass that information on using dead letter drops so that you don't have any contact with anyone else.' He saw her confusion. 'You will leave coded information at a location that has been agreed and it will be picked up at a later date when you aren't there.'

Charlotte nodded. 'So no one knows who I am.' She thought for a moment. 'Would I do this in my own area or go somewhere else?'

'I think it depends on where you come from. You live near Maidstone which is a very important communication hub so I would imagine we'll want you to stay there. We would find you a job that allows you to move around and would reduce the chances of the Germans becoming suspicious of you.'

Charlotte was silent. Half of her was terrified, but the rest of her couldn't wait to start training. She was about to say so when the Major spoke again. 'Don't give me your answer yet. Go back to your room and sleep on it. It's a big commitment and once you agree you can't back out. Think about the effect this could have on your father and sister.'

Charlotte paled. 'You mean I would be putting them in danger?'

'Yes. I'm not going to lie to you. If the Germans find out you are spying they are unlikely to believe that your family weren't involved.' He hesitated. 'And you will be tortured to make you give up anyone else you work with.'

'But I'll be working on my own, you just said so.'

'That won't stop them trying to get information from you.' He finished his cigarette and stood up. 'Get some sleep and come back and see me in the morning.'

Charlotte stood up and walked slowly to the door. She had no idea how she was going to sleep, not with such an enormous decision to be made.

****

Near Yelsted, Kent
'Come on Becca. Don't be stupid. I'm not going to hurt you. Why are you running away from me?' Mathew stopped and listened hard. She couldn't be far away, not in those shoes she was wearing anyway. Remembering how she looked in her new summer dress, stockings and heeled shoes and how she'd felt in his arms Mathew felt his body reacting and his anger resurfaced. Why the hell had she run off? Stupid cow. She obviously wanted it or why dress like that? His dad was right, she was just a little tease. 'Come on Becca.' He took a deep breath. 'Let me walk you home. It's not safe with those bloody Nazis flying around.' He stopped and waited and was about to try again when he caught sight of something moving ahead.

****

Outside Maidstone, Kent
'There's been several reports of a parachute coming down.' The constable handed the sheaf of papers to the Desk Sergeant who sighed. It wasn't the first time they'd been informed about parachutists, he blamed the Ministry of Information and their numerous propaganda posters warning about fifth columnists and spies. It was bound to spark panic that he and his colleagues had to sort it out. They had a rash of bogus reports every time there was a raid, including several citing groups of nuns falling out of the sky. He had no idea whose bright idea it had been to suggest the Nazis might be dressed as nuns, but he'd like to get them alone in a dark room… He switched off his wandering thoughts and returned his attention to the constable. 'Where abouts?'

'Most of them say over towards Yelsted, although this one,' the constable sorted through quickly, 'seems to think it was nearer Maidstone.'

The Sergeant sighed. 'Probably nothing, you know how they panic every time the krauts come over.'

'Should we go and search though?' The constable looked concerned. Most of the witnesses had been adamant they had seen a parachute coming down and for once they all cited the same time and area, well all of them except that woman. He didn't think it was very likely that they were all lying but it wasn't his place to say.

The sergeant read through the reports quickly and then nodded. 'Yes, alright, take some of the men and go towards Yelsted. Ignore the other one as it's in the opposite direction.'

The constable breathed a sigh of relief and hurried off to do as he'd been instructed. The sergeant was probably right, the woman who'd said she'd seen one near Maidstone was elderly and had seemed quite confused.

****

Near Yelsted, Kent

Rebecca stepped cautiously out from behind the tree, Mathew breathed a sigh of relief and forced himself to smile pleasantly. 'What did you run for you silly goose? I'm not going to hurt you.'

She approached him warily, the branch still in her hand. 'I said no, but you didn't stop.'

Mathew's smile widened. 'That's because you're so gorgeous Becca. I couldn't keep my hands off you.' He raised both hands in supplication. 'But I promise to behave… honestly.' The last thing he needed was her telling stories about him to her father. Mathew wasn't afraid of many people, but Becca's father was something else. Major Mason had a reputation for not taking any nonsense off anyone and he idolised his twin daughters. If he thought anyone had hurt one of them he would be more than happy to take the law into his own hands, whatever the cost.

Becca relaxed slightly. 'You promise to take me home?'

'Yes of course I will.' He frowned and peered at her right hand. What was she carrying? 'What's the branch for?'

Becca didn't answer and Mathew could feel his anger rising again. Somehow, he managed to sound calm and even amused. 'You won't need the weapon, Becca. Anyone would think you don't trust me.'

'I don't.' Rebecca snapped and then wondered if that had been wise. There was something in his face…

'Put the branch down then and let's go home.' He could hardly let her go home carrying that massive branch, not if he wanted to walk away from her house with both his legs intact.

She shook her head, but she did move closer. Mathew waited patiently until she was within touching distance then deciding he had no choice he suddenly lunged at her.

Chapter 7

Near Yelsted, Kent
Kristian stood silently, debating whether he should make his way towards the sound of the voices he could hear or whether he should go in the other direction. Common sense dictated that he get as far away as possible. They were the enemy and unless he was prepared to overpower them in some way or even kill them they would be bound to hand him over to the authorities. He was still hesitating when the voices grew louder and curiosity overcame his caution.

He stepped carefully forward until he was close enough to hear what they were saying before relaxing and allowing himself a wry smile. It was just a young couple having an argument. It must be nice to have nothing to worry about but making love in the countryside. It was such a long time since he'd seen Ulrike or spent any time with her. He missed her terribly and he knew she missed him because she told him in every letter. Damn the war, keeping him away from those he loved. He had barely seen his son since his birth. Manfred had been born six months earlier and Kristian had only seen him twice. For a brief moment he was back in Bavaria, in the family home with his wife and son. He could see them so clearly. If he was captured he would spend the rest of the war, however long that was, in a camp. It could be years before he saw Ulrike and Manfred again. At least if he escaped back to the continent he would have leave and could go home.

Kristian made up his mind and was about to turn away when he heard an ear piercing scream. For a split second he thought they were just playing around, but there was something about the noise… Kristian shook his head. He was sure he could hear fear in the young woman's voice and without really thinking about the consequences he forgot about his family and began making his way through the trees towards them.

****

Coleshill House, Berkshire
Charlotte sat on her bed in the room that had been allocated to her and thought over everything the Major had told her. Whilst the concept of the Auxiliary Force horrified her, she understood the point. What was absolutely terrifying though was that the authorities really

believed the Germans would invade before the end of the year. Up until then she hadn't believed it could actually happen, but hearing the truth from the Major and seeing the extensive preparations that were being made to defend Britain had brought the truth home to her. Her thoughts travelled to the men who had volunteered. They had done so knowing their life expectancy was only a couple of weeks, knowing they were completely expendable. *And so are you* the voice in her head interrupted her thoughts. *You are just as expendable because your role is to act as their eyes and ears, to find targets and pass information.* She lay back on her bed and thought about the conversation with the Major. She had until the following morning to make a decision. If she decided she didn't want to be involved she would be driven back to the station and put on a train for London. If she agreed to be involved she would begin her training. She wondered if her father knew about this place and whether this was what he was worried about and then decided that he probably didn't. Although he wanted her to play her part she was sure he wouldn't have condemned her to a life expectancy of under two weeks if the Nazis actually invaded.

She was about to sit up when she had a sudden pain in her head. Her first thought was that her sister had banged her head and then she smiled. Nobody believed that she and Becca could actually feel each other's pain and it was so bizarre that she barely accepted it herself. She closed her eyes and focused on Becca, but the pain had gone now and she felt completely at peace. Charlotte frowned, perhaps she was lightheaded because she was hungry. It was hours since she'd eaten. She finished the remains of her tea and stood up. There was no point dragging this out. She had already made up her mind so she might as well tell the Major now.

****

Near Yelsted, Kent
Mathew stared down at Rebecca's prone body in horror. There was blood seeping out onto the ground behind her and for a moment he felt sick. Then he shook his head. It wasn't his fault, it was hers. If she'd just given him the branch instead of struggling... He hadn't meant to hurt her, he just wanted to take the branch away. But for some reason she wouldn't let go and instead had fought against him.

Mathew peered down at her. She was very quiet and he was just starting to worry that she was badly hurt when he realised how peaceful she looked, angelic almost. He couldn't stop himself leaning closer, breathing in the fragrant aroma of her perfume. Mathew could see the curves of her body against her dress and almost trance like he placed his hand on her breast. It was soft to his touch and he squeezed gently. His heart beat faster and his body began to react, his breathing coming in short, ragged gasps. He knew he should stop but she was unconscious so she wouldn't know anything about it, and anyway he was much too excited to walk away. It wouldn't take very long; she would never know....

Mathew could barely control himself as he lifted her skirt and quickly removed her knickers, throwing them into the undergrowth. Oblivious to anything else he undid his trouser buttons, freeing his erection, before plunging inside, thrusting violently against her. Within minutes it was all over and he collapsed forward, breathing heavily. As his breath gradually returned he eased himself up on his elbow and stared down at her. To his disappointment there was still no response so eventually Mathew pulled out and began doing up his buttons. He waited a few more minutes but she still appeared to be unconscious and he was starting to feel irritated. It was a shame she wouldn't remember the good time he had given her. Perhaps he should bring her round and then he could make love to her again. He leant forward and slapped her face. There was no reaction so he tried again. He was starting to grow angry. How dare she? She was deliberately ignoring him. His mood darkened and he raised his hand to hit her again when a voice shattered the silence.

'What the hell have you done?' It was a long time since Kristian had spoken English, but he was sure he'd used the right words. The boy in front of him jumped away from the girl and stared at him in shock.

Kristian pointed his pistol at him, indicating he back away from her. There was something about the way she was laying that was bothering him. He waited until the boy was several feet away before leaning forward and placing his finger against her neck, his eyes still on Mathew. He moved his finger around but there was definitely no pulse. Then he straightened up and stared at the boy in shock. 'She's dead. You've killed her.' Even as he spoke the image of the boy making love to her came back into his mind and he felt sick. 'You were… he couldn't think of the word he needed. Making love wasn't something you did to a dead body. Eventually the right words came to him. 'You were having sex with a dead woman.'

Mathew paled. 'No… no… You're lying… you filthy fucking Nazi.'

Kristian shook his head. 'No, I am not. She is dead and you were having sex with her.'

There was a brief silence then Mathew suddenly sputtered. '*You killed her.*'

Kristian stared at him in shock and disbelief. He was about to deny the ridiculous accusation when the danger of the situation he was in suddenly struck him. No one would believe him. He was the enemy, he'd been a member of the Luftwaffe who had been dropping bombs on their country a few hours ago. Why would anyone take his word over that of a British boy. Kristian wouldn't be treated as a POW, allowed to sit out the war in peace, he would be tried and hanged because he couldn't prove that this disgusting pig was lying.

Mathew watched the realisation dawn on the Nazi and he suddenly smiled. 'I'd get the fuck out of here if I was you. They hang people for murder here and it's my word against yours.' His smile widened. 'And they'll see that you raped her too. I'll tell them I was out for a walk and I found her like this and you running off.'

Kristian was rooted to the spot. Part of him wanted to avenge the poor dead girl even if he didn't know her and even if she was the enemy, but common sense told him he had no chance of being believed. The girl was a casualty of war. If he hadn't been here the boy might have been arrested but as things were there was nothing he could do. Well, there was one thing he could do… He raised the pistol, aimed at the boy and his finger tightened on the trigger. He could see the fear in his eyes and then he became aware of how quiet it was. There were no more aeroplanes dogfighting above them, just the sounds of the countryside. A gunshot would be heard for miles. It would bring people to them and, when they found the dead bodies, they would assume he'd killed both of them. Kristian slowly lowered the Luger. The fear left Mathew's eyes, he raised his hand and grinned. 'Bye bye Nazi.'

Kristian knew he was beaten and he started to turn away. Then an idea came to him and he turned back. 'Which way to Sittingbourne?' It was too risky telling the boy where he was making for even though it was in the boy's interests for him not to be found. But if he found out where Sittingbourne was he could find the way to the address his father had given him. It was time he followed Otto's instructions and asked for help. He would be taking a chance but he had no choice.

****

Coleshill House, Berkshire

'Are you quite sure?' Major Hallet stared at her. 'You don't have to decide until tomorrow.' She was standing in his room, a mirror of her own only slightly bigger.

Charlotte smiled. 'Of course I want to be involved, so why waste time? I do have one condition though.'

The Major frowned. 'Condition?'

'That if I work in Maidstone my father and sister are sent somewhere else to live so there's no immediate connection to me.'

'I'm not sure that's possible. What reason would they have to move?'

'My father could be given a job somewhere further north and my sister could receive her posting details for the WRNS. That way they should be safe, at least for a while.'

The Major considered her request for a few second and then nodded. 'I can't see that would be a problem.'

Charlotte breathed a sigh of relief. 'Good. When do I start training then?' She laughed at his expression. 'Yes, I know I'm probably mad, but you obviously need me or you wouldn't have brought me here.'

'You will be completely on your own apart from the dead letter contact with the Auxiliary you are assigned to and any contact via Headquarters. You can't tell anyone anything.'

Charlotte nodded. 'Understood.'

Major Hallet relaxed and smiled back. 'Well, in that case, welcome to the team. Oh… and you can call me Anthony when we're on our own. If we meet at all once this is live it will be safer for you not to address me as Major.'

Charlotte nodded. 'Yes, I can see the sense in that *Anthony*.'

He turned away briefly, opened the cupboard in the corner of the room and took out a bottle of whisky. 'Would you like a drink?'

Charlotte smiled. 'I'd love one, thank you. Although I haven't eaten since this morning so I'd better not have too much.'

Anthony looked horrified. 'Good heavens I'm so sorry.' He reached for the telephone by his bed. 'I'll order us something to eat. You don't mind eating in my room? Obviously you can't mix with any of the men here, not until you've finished your training and the other women aren't due to arrive until tomorrow morning.' It was the fifth group of men to have completed their training, but Charlotte was in the first group of women.

'Are there many of us?' Charlotte sipped her drink while he was ordering them some food and waited for him to replace the receiver before asking.

'More then you would expect.'

Charlotte raised an eyebrow and Anthony looked embarrassed. 'I'm sorry. I didn't mean to imply that women were any less courageous than men.'

'Yes you did, but I won't hold it against you.' Perhaps she should put her drink down, it was going to her head, and she was starting to sound like she was flirting. She was saved from having to say anything else by a knock at the door.

'Ah, that's probably the food.' Anthony hurried to the door leaving Charlotte to compose herself.

****

Near Yelsted, Kent

Mathew waited for the German to leave before sinking to the ground in relief. It took him a few moments to realise he was safe and then he stood up and begun running back to Rebecca's house, his brain going over and over his story. He hadn't gone far when he pulled up abruptly as a better idea came to him. He had to get it right first time. That Nazi must have been on the parachute they had seen coming down earlier. Becca had spotted it first and that was when she'd tried to stop him, saying they needed to get help, to find someone to capture the German. Mathew had been more intent in making love to her than worrying about Luftwaffe pilots so he hadn't taken much notice of where the parachute was heading for. Then Becca had pulled away from him, shouted at him and run off.

Mathew had been furious. If he hadn't been so intent on chasing her he would probably have gone to investigate. But she had distracted him, stopped him from catching an enemy pilot. The thought briefly crossed his mind that if only he had gone after the Nazi, Becca would still be alive. Mathew cursed loudly and brought his thoughts back the present. Becca was dead because of that Nazi and he needed everyone to know that. If he could find the parachute he could leave it near the body. That way they would believe him without asking too many questions. He retraced his steps until he was back with Rebecca's body then headed off in the direction the Nazi had come from. The time lapse between them seeing the parachute floating down was quite short and he had to have been quite close or he wouldn't have seen them at all because of the trees.

It took Mathew over an hour to find where Kristian had buried the parachute and it was getting dark. He had been on the verge of giving up when he finally spotted it by the tree. He pulled it clear, hurried back to the body, and left it under a bush just before the clearing. He didn't dare leave it in the open or they might get suspicious because the Nazi was bound to have made some attempt to conceal it.

He then resumed his run back to the Major's house on the edge of the village where he quickly rang the bell before taking a deep breath.

'Yes? What is it?' Major Mason opened the door himself taking Mathew by surprise.

'Rebecca… I'm so sorry…' Mathew was surprised to find tears soaking his cheeks and for a moment he couldn't speak. What if the Major wouldn't believe him? He took another breath. 'I'm so sorry. I couldn't stop him.'

'Couldn't stop who? What the hell are you talking about boy? And where's my daughter?'

'The Nazi, the pilot…'Mathew was fighting to breathe he was so terrified.

'Where's Rebecca? What Nazi pilot?' By now the Major was looking more anxious than angry and Mathew relaxed slightly and his words flowed more freely.

'I found her in the woods… she's dead… there was one of those Nazi flyers… he ran off when I arrived. I'm so sorry I didn't get there in time.' He fell silent, dropped his head and prayed the Major would believe him.

Adrian grabbed him by the shoulders. 'What the hell do you mean? Rebecca… she can't be dead…'

'I'll take you to her. I didn't want to move her.' Mathew began crying openly.

The Major yelled at his housekeeper to telephone the police and then he grabbed Mathew's arm and dragged him down the drive.

****

Coleshill House, Berkshire
Charlotte lay on her bed and thought about the evening. She had just signed her life away but that wasn't what she was thinking about. Instead of thinking about the momentous decision she had made her brain kept replaying snatches of conversation with the handsome Major. It was obviously the alcohol. She would keep off the whisky next time then she would be able to concentrate on the important things, like her training and how to avoid being arrested by the invading German Forces. It was that thought that brought her back to reality. This wasn't a game. She and all those men staying in the stable block had volunteered to die rather than let the Nazis over run the country. She couldn't afford to let them down by acting like a silly girl. They would be relying on her and, in any case, she wanted her father to be proud of her.

****

Near Yelsted, Kent
Adrian stared down at the body of his dead daughter, tears streaming down his cheeks. He knelt down and checked for a pulse but there was nothing. She looked so peaceful, as if she was asleep, He touched her hair gently and then realised the state of her dress. Blind rage began to take hold and he turned his head towards Mathew. 'She was in your care.' His voice was deceptively quiet and it was a few seconds before Mathew realised the danger he was in.

'I trusted you with her.' Adrian stood up and took a menacing step towards Mathew. 'I trusted you with her. Charlotte said there was something wrong with you. I should have listened, made Becca listen…'

'I didn't do anything.' Mathew shouted. 'It was the Nazi… look his parachute is over there.'

Adrian stopped and stared in the direction he was pointing before walking slowly towards it. Mathew breathed a sigh of relief.

Adrian stared down, there was no doubt the parachute was German, perhaps this weasel was telling the truth and Charlotte had been wrong. Oh God! He shook his head and felt sick. How on earth was he going to tell Charlotte?

****

Outside Maidstone, Kent

Frederick finished digging and leaned on the spade breathing heavily. It had taken him a little while, but he'd finally identified the right place for his OB. Buried deep in some trees, off the normal walking paths he had settled down to watch the area for a couple of days first to make sure he would not be disturbed. In the time he'd spent watching he hadn't seen anyone, the only visitors foxes, badgers and rabbits which suited him fine as at least he would have a ready source of food if he had to remain there for any length of time. There was a small slow flowing stream not far away which would provide fresh drinking water and the odd fish so he had begun his excavation.

It had taken him several hours to make a decent start and he still had plenty of work to do, not to mention his normal Home Guard duties which had increased dramatically since the defence plan had been submitted to the Home Office in June. Fortress Maidstone, as it was known, was coming on apace. From the original outdated static defences, the town now had over 463 large shell proof pillboxes, 1,788 small bullet proof pill boxes, 50 miles of concrete anti-tank obstacles, and 43 miles of anti-tank ditches. A further 1840 pill boxes were under construction with another 2200 being planned. Bridge crossings were heavily defended with demolition charges attached in case they needed to blow them up. Meanwhile the Maidstone and Malling battalions of the Home Guard had been given responsibility for manning part of the Newhaven to Hoo General Head Quarters (G.H.Q.) Line which meant covering 55 Observation Posts (OP) and the 115 pill boxes. As Home Counties HQ recommended that each OP needed a minimum of eight men with five per pill box they were continually trying to recruit new members. Fortunately, the anti-tank pill boxes were manned by the regular units of the Royal Artillery or they would have struggled to find enough manpower. If the invasion did happen he would find it difficult to be in two places at once and he hoped that he didn't have to choose between staying with his men or disappearing underground. His instructions were to only disappear if the Germans occupied the area so he assumed he would fight for as long as he could and then if the worst happened he would abandon his post and escape to his OB. Well, he would if he ever finished it.

Frederick glanced at his watch, he needed to leave the woods before it became too dark or he might draw attention to himself.

He was just about to move away when he heard the distinctive sound of a branch cracking. Frederick froze. Someone was out there.

Chapter 8

C Wing, Wormwood Scrubs Prison
'Anything on that German spy? The one coming in near Maidstone.'

Fred looked up in surprise. It wasn't often Colonel Sinclair visited them. 'No sir. Nothing at all.'

'Damn!' Sinclair cursed. He saw Fred's curiosity and sighed. 'There's been a sighting of a parachutist near a place called Yelsted. I expect you know it.'

Fred nodded. 'Yes, it's not that far from where I live. Is that our man then?'

'Could be, well it probably is. How many Germans are there likely to be parachuting into Kent?' He smiled then almost immediately his face darkened. 'Only this one is not exactly trying to avoid attention. He's killed some girl in the woods. Spotted by a farm labourer.'

Fred looked horrified. 'That's awful.' He should have warned Daisy Irene. What if something happened to her… He realised the Colonel was talking and he tried to put his fears aside and concentrate.

'Yes it is. But hopefully it will provide some clues that will lead us to him.'

'I'm worried about my wife,' Fred suddenly blurted out. 'I mean I am doing this job, what if they know?'

Colonel Sinclair stared at him. 'Why on earth should they know about you? This organisation is secret and our operatives certainly are.' His eyes narrowed. 'Unless you've said something.'

Fred shook his head. 'No, of course I haven't.' He snapped before a horrified expression appeared on his face. He took a breath. 'I'm so sorry sir. I didn't mean… It's probably knowing I can't say anything and I'm here and she's on her own.'

Colonel Sinclair eyed him thoughtfully. 'I understand that. But there's no reason for the German spy to go after your wife. He'll go to the address he's been given and then collect whatever information he's been sent to get. Then he'll start to transmit to Abwehr Intelligence and then, God willing, we'll have him.'

Fred looked more relaxed. 'You're right of course sir.' He indicated the latest pile of logs. 'I'll make a start on these then?'

'You do that Fred and don't worry.' He thought for a moment. 'I'll have a word with the local Home Guard, get them to run some patrols near where you live, just to make sure.'

'Thank you, sir. I'd appreciate that.' Fred looked much happier.

Colonel Sinclair sat in the back of his staff car and thought about Fred Corben. He was very good at his job and had already spotted several things that his other people had missed. He needed him concentrating on the job, not worrying about his wife. 'Take me to Maidstone Chapman.'

****

Outside Yelsted, Kent
Mathew finally arrived back at the family farm. It was in darkness and he breathed a sigh of relief. The last thing he needed was to have to explain where he'd been until now. He let himself in, crept up to his bedroom, threw himself on the bed, stared up at the ceiling and allowed himself to relax. A smile spread across his face as he realised he was probably over the worst, well as far as the girl was concerned anyway. He wasn't out of the woods yet, but it seemed that once they'd found the parachute the police had believed his story. The Major hadn't seemed quite so convinced but it was the police he was more worried about. He needed to make sure they didn't hear anything to make them suspicious. Not that they should as he'd covered his tracks quite well over the years. He was still congratulating himself when he remembered the other problem and his spirits plummeted. Patrick would be furious…

'Where the hell have you been to this hour?' The door burst open interrupting his thoughts. His father, Bill, stood there in his pyjamas, a furious expression on his face.

Mathew sighed. 'Rebecca is dead. She was killed by a Nazi pilot. I couldn't…' He didn't get any further. His father took several steps towards the bed, leaned over, grabbed him by the shoulders and started shaking him. 'Don't fucking lie to me boy…'

'What on earth are you doing Bill? Leave Mathew alone.' Mildred Hart barely raised her voice but Bill immediately let go and turned to her.

'You don't understand Mildred. He's killed that girl…'

'Don't be so ridiculous Bill. Mathew wouldn't hurt a fly would you son?'

'No Mum. It wasn't me. A Nazi pilot killed her.' Mathew let out a convincing sob. 'They found his parachute near the body. You ask the police or the Major. It is all my fault though. If I'd been there I could have protected her.'

Bill snorted. 'You're fucking useless, you couldn't protect anyone.'

'Don't talk to him like that!' Mildred snapped. 'Don't listen to him Mathew. I know you're telling the truth.'

Mathew gave a surreptitious glance at his father and then focused on his mother. 'It was awful. I saw him running off but I thought she was hurt so I didn't follow him. I stopped…' He took a breath for effect, 'but she was dead. By the time I realised that the bastard was gone.' He put his hands over his eyes and began sobbing loudly.

Mildred pushed her husband out of the way, sat on the bed and hugged him. Bill watched silently. He would never understand why Mildred always believed everything Mathew said. He was sure the boy was lying, but even worse, he was sure it wasn't the first time. This wasn't the first girl who'd come to harm after going out with his son. Bill suddenly realised what he was thinking and cut the idea off abruptly. Now he was being stupid. Mathew was a weak spineless excuse for a son but he wasn't a killer. He'd never have the bottle for that. Those other girls had just been making trouble. Mathew wasn't a popular lad. It had always been the same, ever since school. He watched his wife hugging him and turned away in disgust. Mildred had ruined the boy, always stuck up for him, never let Bill punish him, whatever he'd done. Always finding excuses for him. No wonder he'd turned out like he had.

Mathew watched his father out of the corner of his eye. It looked like he'd succeeded in persuading them all that he was innocent. Now he just had to hope they wouldn't find the pilot, not that they would believe him if they did, but he could cast doubts on Mathew's story, just enough to make them look at him more closely. He shivered suddenly as he remembered that the pilot was the least of his worries. He had failed to do what he'd been paid for and he had a horrible feeling the people who were paying him would not be very forgiving.

****

Outside Maidstone, Kent

Frederick listened carefully for several minutes but he could no longer hear any noise, no crackling of twigs, no voices, nothing at all. When he'd first heard the branches breaking his initial thought had been to hide until he found out what was going on, that would avoid having to make unnecessary explanations to whoever it was tramping through the woods, so he'd climbed up the nearest tree. It would have been much easier to have just asked, especially when he realised that it was the police trudging thought the undergrowth, but the last thing he needed was to let anyone know he had been in this part of the woods or he would have to find somewhere else for his OB. When he'd spotted the police he had been tempted to show himself but caution had won and he'd remained where he was. Now he was grateful he hadn't revealed himself. The police had come close enough for him to hear some of their conversation and he had finally gathered that there had been a murder and they were hunting for the perpetrator. If he'd revealed himself he might have been a suspect, especially as he couldn't explain what he was doing there. There were no Home Guard manoeuvres in this area and although he could probably have made something up, it didn't pay to lie to the police and given the secrecy of the operation he had signed up to, the last thing he needed was to draw attention to himself.

Frederick climbed cautiously down from the tree, stood silently for several seconds to make sure the police had definitely gone, then slowly made his way back home.

****

Coleshill House, Berkshire

Charlotte was eating buttered toast and drinking tea in the kitchen on her own when Anthony appeared. She couldn't wait to get started on her training and she hoped at least some of the other women would be arriving that day. She looked up and smiled. 'Morning Anthony. Am I going to start training now?'

There was no answering smile and she started to feel uncomfortable. Perhaps she was supposed to call him Major… although she was sure he'd said to call him by his first name. She was about to ask when he sat down at the table opposite her, took a deep breath and spoke.

'I'm really sorry Charlotte. I have some very bad news for you.'

Charlotte stared at him in confusion. *Bad news... oh Christ... her father. He must have had an accident... or maybe it was a heart attack?* Her imagination ran away with her for several seconds and she was about to ask if something had happened to her father when everything suddenly fell into place, she turned the colour of chalk, her eyes glazed over and he could see the shock etched on her face. He was about to explain when she suddenly burst out. 'Oh God, its Becca isn't it? My sister. She's dead?'

Anthony was so astonished he couldn't speak for a moment then finally he nodded. 'Yes... yes it is. I'm so sorry.' He frowned. 'I don't understand. How could you possibly know? I mean...'

'We're twins...' Charlotte interrupted him. 'We *were* twins. If one of us is... *was* injured the other always knew. I felt a dreadful pain in my head last night but then it was gone and everything was peaceful. I guessed Becca must have banged her head but as I wasn't in pain anymore I mistakenly assumed she was alright, but she wasn't was she? That must have been when it happened.' Anthony realised that Charlotte was talking more to herself rather than him, although he was fascinated by what she was saying.

'Yes, it did happen yesterday evening, but I'm not sure of the time.'

Charlotte sighed. 'I am. It was just before I came to see you, but that doesn't matter now does it?' She stopped muttering to herself and fixed him with a piercing glare. 'How did she die?'

Before he could answer her face darkened. 'Was it that farm labourer... Mathew Hart?'

Anthony looked confused and shook his head. 'No, that wasn't what I was told. Apparently it was a German, a pilot. He parachuted out of his plane and killed her. She must have seen him and he was frightened she'd tell the authorities.'

Charlotte looked even more shocked. 'You're sure?' That didn't make sense at all. Surely if Becca had seen a German pilot she would have been terrified, so scared that Charlotte would have felt something. But she hadn't. Just the pain in her head and then nothing. She tried to concentrate on what Anthony was saying.

'Yes, that's what the police said. They spent all night searching but couldn't find him I'm afraid. But I'm sure he won't get away.' He glanced at his watch. 'There's a train leaving in an hour or I could drive you home?' It was against all the rules but she had just suffered a terrible bereavement, he could hardly leave her to make her own way to Maidstone.

Charlotte nodded. 'Would you mind? It's such a long way.' Her voice cracked with emotion and Anthony was about to answer when he realised she was crying, tears falling silently down her cheeks.

He pulled a handkerchief from his top pocket, handed it to her and waited until she'd wiped her eyes and blown her nose before speaking again. 'Come on, let's get you packed and home. Your father will need you.'

******

45 College Road, Maidstone, Kent

'Daddy!' Jeanne flung herself into his arms and was rewarded with a bearlike hug.

'Hello Jeanne. No need to ask if you've missed me then?' Frederick put his suitcase down and smiled down at her. 'Where's Margaret?'

'She's at school. There's a letter for her from Betty. There's one to me too and you.' She handed him the letter and sighed. 'You won't have to go away again, will you?'

Frederick didn't answer, instead he put the letter in his pocket to read later and changed the subject. 'Where's your mother?'

'She's gone to the shops. She said she wouldn't be long unless there were lots of queues.'

'I'll have to make my own tea then.' Frederick laughed and Jeanne joined in.

'I'll make it. Mum says I am getting much better at making tea now.'

'Alright, I'll unpack while you're doing it. Did Mum get a newspaper?'

Jeanne gave a theatrical sigh. 'You've been away three days and all you're interested in is the news!' She pointed to the kitchen. 'It's on the table.' She frowned. 'Mum said there had been a murder but she wouldn't tell me anything else.'

'Quite right too.' Frederick headed towards the kitchen. 'Now you put the kettle on, I'll unpack later.' The newspaper was on the table, the murder on the front page. Frederick skimmed the article quickly, wondering if it was only front page news because the murderer was suspected of being a Luftwaffe pilot. Although the first paragraph was dedicated to the victim, a young girl with the name of Rebecca Mason, the next paragraph was about the pilot and the fact that so far he had evaded their attempts to apprehend him. The population was exhorted to take keep their eyes peeled, not to approach him because he was dangerous and to report anything suspicious to the police, Home Guard, or the military authorities, whoever was nearest. Frederick sighed. That meant he would probably spend all day chasing ghosts. He wanted to catch the man as much as anyone, but telling the public there was a Nazi on the run and one who had already killed once, without any form of description, was enough to cause total panic.

'Fred, you're home. Thank goodness.' Alice hurried into the kitchen, put the shopping basket on the table and put her arms around him. 'I've missed you and what with that maniac on the loose...'

Frederick kissed her forehead and hugged her back. 'Yes I saw. He's probably long gone now though. He's hardy likely to stick around is he, not after what he's supposed to have done. However, you should warn Margaret to come straight home after school and not hang around with her friends for the next few days.'

Alice frowned. 'She's becoming impossible Fred. I hardly recognise her sometimes. She's completely wild.'

Frederick grinned. 'Must take after her mother than... that wild streak.' He smiled at her but then realised Alice wasn't really listening.

'What do you mean supposed to? Don't you think he did kill her then? If he didn't who did?'

Frederick shrugged and went back to reading the article. 'I have no idea love, but if I had just jumped out of my aeroplane and been lucky enough to land safely I'm not sure I would stop to kill some girl.' He stopped as he reached the line which stated that it was believed the man had sexually assaulted the girl before killing her and shook his head. If you were on the run in a foreign country would you really stop to force yourself on some innocent girl? Wouldn't you be concentrating on getting away?

'Well, the police know what they're doing and no one else is likely to have killed her are they?' Alice pursed her lips and Frederick sighed. Alice still hadn't forgiven the Germans for the Great War, there was no point arguing with her as she would believe anything the newspapers said about the enemy, especially if it was derogatory. That was one of the reasons he hadn't mentioned having contact with his half-brother.

'Here's your tea Daddy.' Jeanne placed the cup and saucer carefully on the kitchen table and he smiled at her, grateful to change the subject. 'Thank you, Jeanne. That looks lovely.' He folded the newspaper, pushed it to one side and sat down. 'Now what have you both been up to while I've been away?' He was about to drink his tea when there was a loud knock at the front door.

Chapter 9

RAF Kenley, Surrey

Jimmy's brief introductory tour of the airbase by Claude, who had worked with Supermarine, the makers of the Spitfire, before enlisting into the RAF, was interrupted by the distant hum of Spitfires and he joined several other men watching members of 66 Squadron's A Flight as they touched down intermittently, the stragglers finally appearing in dribs and drabs after the first Spitfires had landed. They had been scrambled again since the dog fight he had witnessed over London earlier and as the pilots climbed wearily out of their cockpits Jimmy could see the exhaustion and strain on their faces.

Claude waved to a couple of the men before leading them to the Dispersal Hut where B Flight were preparing to take over from A Flight. Jimmy was surprised to find the atmosphere so calm, with pilots sitting around playing cards or chatting quietly. All were wearing variations of the RAF regulation flying gear topped by their yellow Mae West life jackets. The Flight Commanders were seated next to the duty telephone operator in a corner at a table with a black telephone on.

Claude introduced them to the few pilots who had shown an interest in their arrival. 'Right, that's Bobby, or Oxo as he's known. That's Durex... don't ask. Pretending to read a book is Pickles.' The names continued and Jimmy wondered vaguely if he would remember them.

'Ah, more sprogs, just what we need.'

'Welcome to the show boys, front seats available daily.' Various facetious remarks greeted them and then they were introduced to the Flight Commander, Flt Lt Hubert Allen or 'Dizzy' Allen as he was more popularly known. Jimmy swallowed nervously. Flt Lt Allen had red hair and freckles and looked tough and menacing. Jimmy was soon to learn that he took his job seriously but off duty had a limitless capacity for having fun.

He looked them over before asking. 'Are you boys operational?'

Jimmy answered for them. 'No sir, but we have had a few hours on Spitfires.'

Dizzy sighed and tried to look enthusiastic. 'Well, that's something I suppose. Don't worry we'll have you operational in no time. We have allocated you your flights anyway. Corbin you will be in Flight B.'

'Bad luck!' someone shouted and several other pilots laughed.

Dizzy continued. 'All squadrons are divided into either A or B Flights. Each is normally made up of twelve pilots divided into four sections each having three pilots. They are identified by a colour, red, blue, yellow or green. Your Flights always remain the same, but you have to check the noticeboard every day to find out which section you're in. Is that clear?'

'Yes sir.' Jimmy and the others spoke in unison.

'Good, spend the rest of the day getting to know your way around. Any questions about Spits ask Claude, he's the expert. You need to pick up your life jackets and get them painted pronto.'

The four of them left the hut, picked up their life jackets and spent the rest of the day painting them with yellow dope so they would be more conspicuous if they came down in the sea. They didn't find out until much later that the yellow dope made the life jackets highly inflammable.

When he'd finished Jimmy strolled out onto the airfield to watch what was left of the Squadron returning from the latest fight, many badly shot up, their tails and wings peppered with bullet holes. He watched the planes trundle into their parking bays, the pilots climb carefully out of the cockpits, jump to the ground and hold brief conversations with the ground crew. The pilots looked exhausted and unkempt, many sporting bandages. One pilot appeared to have oil over his face, it was only when he came closer that Jimmy realised it was blood.

'What happened?' One of the other pilots asked.

'I got hit in the reflector sight, the bloody thing exploded and a load of glass shot into my face.' The pilot sounded more irritated than concerned.

'Get yourself patched up and we'll take you for a drink.'

'You're on.' He raised a weary hand and headed towards the dispersal hut to get cleaned up and debriefed. Jimmy shivered. Welcome to 66 Squadron.

****

Yelsted, Kent

Charlotte was barely aware of most of the journey back home, her thoughts on her beautiful gentle sister. She couldn't understand why Becca had been walking around the woods in the first place. It was hardly something she normally did. She was about to voice her thoughts aloud when she realised they had reached her home. Anthony climbed quickly out and opened the door for her.

'I won't come in as I'm sure you don't want strangers intruding at this time.'

'No, please come in, at least have some tea before you drive back.' Charlotte managed a small smile. 'Anyway I'd like you to meet my father.'

Anthony shrugged and followed her to the front door, waited while she opened the door and stepped in behind her. The hall was dark after the bright daylight and he almost bumped into her. He was about to ask if there was a light switch when she spoke.

'Daddy?'

'Charlotte? I wasn't expecting you to come home.' Adrian looked awful, the strain in his eyes piercing her heart. Charlotte ran to him and he engulfed her in his arms.

'Of course, I came home. What else could I do? She was my sister. I can't believe she's dead.' They stayed like that for several minutes until Charlotte suddenly remembered Anthony.

'This is Major Anthony Hallet, he's..' She hesitated.

'I'm in charge of the unit your daughter has been recruited to sir, I'm very sorry to meet you in such awful circumstances. I wasn't going to come in, but Charlotte insisted.'

'It's a long journey, the least we could do is to offer him some tea.'

'Yes, of course. I agree.' Adrian shook his hand. 'Come through, I'll arrange something.' He headed back in the direction from which he'd appeared while Anthony followed Charlotte into what turned out to be the sitting room and sat down in one of the armchairs. He glanced around the room, taking in the comfortable décor and numerous photos of the girls on the mantlepiece.

'I really don't want to be in the way Charlotte.'

'You're not Anthony. I'm grateful for the company to be honest. I think I'm still in shock. It doesn't seem real. I don't even know what she was doing walking alone in the woods.'

'She was with that bloody farm labourer.' Adrian came back into the room in time to hear the end of the conversation.

'And it's him who says he saw a German parachutist?' Charlotte was immediately suspicious.

Adrian sighed. 'I thought exactly the same but they found the parachute, and since then they have found other witnesses who thought they saw a plane coming down during the bombing.'

There was a brief silence before Anthony spoke. 'I don't want to interfere but would you like me to ask my contacts… see if there is any other information?'

Adrian nodded. 'I would be very grateful Major.'

'Anthony please.' He turned to Charlotte. 'I'll give you my telephone number so you can contact me as soon as you are ready to come back.'

Charlotte nodded. 'Thank you. We need to arrange the funeral and once that's over I will be in touch.'

The sitting room door opened and the housekeeper entered with a tray. 'I'll leave it here shall I sir?' She glanced at Adrian before placing the tray on the table and approaching Charlotte. 'I'm so sorry Miss Charlotte. Such a dreadful thing to happen.'

'Thank you Mrs Jenkins.' Charlotte reached for one of the cups, her hands trembling.

'Here let me.' Anthony poured some tea into her cup and added some sugar. 'It's good for shock I'm told.'

Adrian watched him paying attention to his daughter and some of his distress momentarily lifted. It was good that Charlotte had someone to lean on. He reached for his own tea his thoughts on Rebecca. Someone was going to pay for the death of his daughter. Despite evidence to the contrary, he still blamed Mathew Hart for her death. If she hadn't been out there with him she wouldn't have been attacked. He frowned as he realised one of the things that had been bothering him. 'Why was she on her own?'

Charlotte looked confused. 'She wasn't. You said Mathew was with her.'

Adrian shook his head. 'No, he said he saw the German assaulting her, but by the time he got there she was dead.'

Charlotte paled. 'Assaulted?'

Adrian sighed and cursed himself for speaking without thinking. 'I'm sorry. I was hoping not to have to tell you but I expect you would have found out eventually.' He took a deep breath, closed his eyes and said the words he'd hoped not to have to say out loud. 'Mathew said the Nazi was raping her but ran off when he appeared. He stopped to help her but discovered she was dead and by the time he'd realised that the bastard had gone.'

He opened his eyes and stared at Charlotte. Tears were streaming down her cheeks. He was about to stand up and go to her but Anthony was already putting his arms around her so Adrian sat back and tried to ignore the sudden surge of jealousy that Charlotte didn't seem to need him anymore. He knew he was being ridiculous, that feeling slightly superfluous was childish and he should be grateful that the Major was so attentive, but he couldn't help himself.

****

45 College Road, Maidstone, Kent
'And you really think this Nazi spy could be meeting someone in Maidstone?' Frederick sounded incredulous.

'Yes, we see no other reason for him to parachute here. He would want to get as close as he could to wherever he was going.' Colonel Sinclair drank his tea slowly.

'And you don't have any idea who he is meeting?' Frederick thought about all the defences now in place and wondered how on earth a German agent could get around without being spotted.

The Colonel put the cup down, opened his briefcase and pulled out a roll of paper. As he unrolled it Frederick could see it was a large scale map of Maidstone and he leaned forward to get a better look. 'None at all unfortunately. I can't tell you the reason why but I'd like you to do some patrols around this area.' He indicated several streets near where Fred Corben lived. 'Just make your presence felt for a couple of weeks. I'll keep you informed as to whether we've caught him or not.'

'And you really think he raped and killed that poor girl?' Frederick was still sceptical about the whole thing. 'I'm sorry sir but if I was engaged in espionage the last thing I'd do on arrival in the country I was going to spy on was to draw attention to myself by attacking and killing the first female I came across.'

The Colonel eyed him thoughtfully. 'I'm inclined to agree with you Captain Farmer, but I can only go with the facts as they are presented to me. It seems highly unlikely that we have two Nazis parachuting into the Kent countryside at the same time doesn't it?' Fredrick could see a twinkle in the Colonel's eyes as he continued 'Although I suppose anything is possible. They do say fact is stranger than fiction.' He sighed and stood up. 'I will keep you informed as to whether we have found him, but I can rely on you to do your bit?'

'Yes sir, of course. We'll start patrolling around there tonight.'

'Thank you, Captain Farmer. I'll see myself out. Thank your daughter… Jeanne isn't it?... for the lovely tea. A very nice brew if I may say so.'

Frederick smiled. 'I'll tell her Colonel.' His smile faded as he watched the Colonel go and wondered what he wasn't being told. Surely if they really believed the spy was in the area they would flood it with personnel, not leave it to the Home Guard? But he knew there was at least one Nazi in the area, and he had killed a young woman, at least he had according to that young farm labourer.

****

RAF Kenley, Surrey

'Come on let's go for drink.' Jimmy was physically tired; it had been a long day but his brain wouldn't shut down and he didn't feel sleepy. As there wasn't much night flying those on duty the next morning were resting in their rooms while those on standby or on rest days had already left for the local pubs.

Mark shook his head and yawned widely. 'Sorry mate, think I'm going to have to turn in.'

'It'll give us the chance to familiarise ourselves with the local hostelries.' Jimmy sighed and tried again to persuade him, but Mark stretched, yawned again and waved an arm as he left to go to his hut.

Jimmy watched him in frustration and then Pete took pity on him and stood up. 'Go on then. I'm in. What about you Dave?'

Dave shook his head and yawned loudly. 'No, I'm going to get some shut eye. I'm done in. Don't get into trouble!'

Jimmy grinned. 'Me? Trouble? Never!'

They set out for a pub in nearby Purley that was apparently a popular pub with the other pilots. It was Saturday night so by the time they arrived it was already packed with local lads and their girls, all enjoying a few drinks. Jimmy ordered a couple of pints of Bass at the bar while he and Pete began chatting about their first impressions.

Halfway through the evening the air raid siren went off, immediately followed by ack ack, the sound of the guns signalling that the German bombers were probably overhead. Within minutes they could hear the crump of bombs landing in the distance. All around them people were debating the likely target, but then the thuds suddenly grew louder. It was too late to find an air raid shelter; the bombers were much too close. They were still trying to decide what to do when there was a terrific crash and the pub door flew open. The walls shook, dust sifted down from the rafters, Jimmy jumped and then glanced around him. Everyone had disappeared and it took him a minute or two to realise that the floor was a carpet of bodies lying face down with their hands over their ears. Only Jimmy and Pete were still standing, both clutching their pints. The two men exchanged glances, put their beers down and threw themselves on the ground with everyone else.

It was Jimmy's first encounter with air raid etiquette and, although it was a thoroughly unpleasant experience, it did have its upside. Lying on his stomach with bombs raining down did seem to make it easier to strike up conversations with some of the local ladies.

****

67 College Road, Maidstone

Frederick finished reading through the latest instructions which outlined the increased civil defence services for Nodal points. Maidstone had been designated a category B Nodal Point because several trunk roads ran through the centre of town, it was an important crossing over the River Medway and was on both the mainline railway from London to Ashford and the Medway Valley railway line from Strood to Paddock Wood. Category A Nodal Points were reserved for villages and towns near the coast which could be cut off for six days whereas category B Nodal Points were further inland and should only be isolated for up to three days. Frederick gave a wry smile, at least the authorities hoped that was the case. Maidstone would therefore be allocated more drinking and firefighting water, firefighting apparatus and personnel, extra ARP (Air Raid Personnel), shelters or trenches for the whole population, petrol for the fire-fighting appliances and a sufficient food supply. Frederick shook his head as he wondered how they could calculate water, food and petrol accurately. Thank goodness it wasn't his job.

He continued reading and his expression became more troubled. The civilian population would not be evacuated under any circumstances, they would be told to go to their shelters or basements like they did in an air raid and remain there during any battles. The Ministry of Information was already producing posters telling people to Stay Put. Frederick shook his head. How would he feel knowing that Alice, Betty, Margaret Mary and Jeanne were hiding in their Anderson shelter with battles raging all around? He knew he should set an example but he also knew he couldn't do his job with the Home Guard or the Auxiliaries properly if he was worrying about his family. Somehow he would have to ensure they left the area in plenty of time. He had no idea how he would manage that, so he put it to the back of his mind and continued reading. A Triumvirate would be formed to ensure proper liaison between the civilian and military authorities. This would consist of a local military commander, a police representative and a civilian representative of the Local Authority, either the Mayor, Chairman of the District Council, or Chairman of the Emergency Committee. Frederick sighed again. If everything went wrong it was possible that these were the people he would have to remove because they would know too much. He would just have to hope it didn't happen.

He sat back and wondered how on earth he was going to juggle all his commitments. He still had his OB to dig out and it was beginning to feel like time was running out.

****

Outside Maidstone, Kent

Kristian was starving. He had spent the day walking towards Maidstone, somehow managing to avoid the numerous checkpoints and observation posts that seemed to be dotted around everywhere. He guessed there were other defences he hadn't seen and he was impressed. If Hitler thought his forces were just going to walk into Britain he was likely to get a rude awakening. It wouldn't be like France. He had finally reached the outskirts of the town, at least he hoped it was. By keeping to the countryside during the day he was sure he had managed to avoid being seen by anyone, but he knew his luck couldn't hold indefinitely. He needed help. He had initially headed in the opposite direction before breaking into an isolated farmhouse and stealing some clothes and food the previous night. He had then changed direction and headed back towards Maidstone, but he couldn't risk breaking in anywhere again, it would be like leaving a trail for them to follow.

If it hadn't been for that poor girl he would have handed himself in to the authorities but he was terrified they would shoot him on sight. Even if they didn't he was sure they wouldn't believe that he hadn't harmed her. He finally reached the street he had been searching for, leant back against a large oak tree and peered at the row of houses in front of him. It was pitch black, the heavy clouds blocked out the moon and there were no street or house lights because of the blackout. He peered into the darkness, there was no movement that he could discern but he knew that if he was to find the right address now was the time to look, when everyone was asleep. He had memorised the address and its position on the map so it was just a case of finding out exactly where he was and then searching for the house. He stepped away from the tree and, after offering up a brief prayer, began trudging quietly into the town.

Chapter 10

45 College Road, Maidstone, Kent

Frederick hurried home from his Home Guard duty, hoping to get some breakfast before he went to work. It had been a busy night again, mainly thanks to some vandals who had broken into one of the mini Nissen huts which had been set up in various places and filled with ammunition in case of invasion. The one that had been broken into was on the tow path of the River Medway and the area around it was strewn with live 303 rounds, hand grenades (Mills bombs) and large calibre shells. But even worse they had then received reports that some children had helped themselves to the ammunition, presumably to play with. Fortunately, they'd had the sense to throw the mills bombs in the river after a neighbour who had served in the Great War recognised them and called the police. He had also arrived in time to stop the kids prizing out the ball caps of the bullets and shells to get the cordite so they could make their own fireworks. To Frederick's relief no one had been hurt but precious resources had been lost and he hoped the police soon found the idiots who had caused the problem in the first place.

Fredrick entered the back yard through the back gate and headed wearily into the privy, his thoughts on Betty's letter. His oldest daughter was a credit to them and he was very proud of her. Her life must be even more precarious than his at the moment with all the raids on the airfields. He had been delighted when she'd joined the WAAF, but there were times he wished she'd chosen something less dangerous. Jeanne was also growing up well. It was only Margaret who gave them any concerns. Alice was right, his middle daughter was becoming a bit of a handful, but he didn't know what to do about it. It was probably just high spirits. Once she left school and found some work she would be too busy to cause them worry, at least he hoped so. As he closed the door behind him, the hairs on the back of his neck stood up and he was suddenly convinced that someone was watching him. He stood still for several moments before dismissing it as his imagination playing tricks. He'd had a long night and he wasn't as young as he used to be. Why would anyone be hiding in his back yard? He shook his head, smiled ruefully and closed the toilet door.

****

Outside Yelsted, Kent

Eyes closed, cigarette in his hand, Mathew was enjoying the late summer sunshine. He had positioned himself next to the large stack of hay bales piled in the corner of the field waiting to be moved to the barn for the winter. He inhaled deeply and then…

'Telling the cops that there was a Nazi on the loose wasn't very bright was it?' Patrick O'Brien spat loudly in his ear. Mathew nearly jumped out of his skin, opened his eyes in shock and tried to ignore the frantic beating of his heart against his ribs.

'Well? What have you got to say for yourself?'

The Irish accent was always more pronounced when Patrick was angry, Mathew blanched and stared back at him for a couple of seconds before finally answering. 'I had to tell them something…' he started before changing direction. 'I didn't have any choice. They found the parachute so I told them it was a pilot.'

'And that makes a difference?' Patrick sounded furious. 'The bastards are running around the place hunting for a Nazi. It won't matter to them whether he's a fucking pilot or any other type of German. For Jesus' sake…' He shook his head in disgust. 'The poor chump's only just landed and he's already the most wanted person in the country.' Mathew could see the pulse in Patrick's neck vibrating wildly and he found himself fixated on it and struggling to look away.

'Well? I'm talking to you, you fucking idiot!' Patrick was inches from his face, his breath hot on Mathew's cheek but he still couldn't make himself answer.

'I'm sorry…' he spluttered eventually. 'I had no choice. They would have found the parachute anyway; it wasn't very well hidden.'

'But you didn't need to help them, did you?' Patrick leaned forward menacingly.

Mathew shrank back against the straw bale and wondered if it was worth trying to run away. He was still thinking about how far he would get when Patrick suddenly sat down on the ground next to him and lit a roll up. Mathew stared at him in confusion and Patrick shrugged. 'What's done is done Mathew. We need to salvage what we can.' He drew deeply on his cigarette and Mathew started to breathe again. Perhaps Patrick wouldn't kill him after all. They smoked in companionable silence for several minutes and finally Mathew decided it was safe to broach the question that he was dying to ask.

'Will I be able to meet him?'

'Why? So you can tell him it's your fault the whole fucking country is looking for him?'

Mathew paled again. 'No... I mean it's not my fault, I told you that. It's that fucking German pilot's fault. If he hadn't killed that girl no one would have known your spy was in the country would they?'

Patrick suddenly grabbed him around the throat making Mathew choke. 'He's not my spy you bloody idiot!'

Mathew struggled against him, his face turning slowly blue until Patrick suddenly let go and sat back. Mathew grabbed his throat, gasping frantically as he tried to replace the air that had been squeezed out of his lungs.

Patrick ignored him. 'You can meet him later. I was planning on bringing him to the pub but given that every policeman and soldier in Kent is probably looking for him I don't think that's a very good idea.' He frowned, took another deep drag on his cigarette and frowned. 'What the hell actually happened?'

Mathew repeated his story while Patrick sat in silence. He was beginning to worry the Irishman didn't believe him when he finally spoke.

'Alright, this is what we're going to do. I'll take him somewhere else for a while, give the dust time to settle.' He changed the subject abruptly. 'Have you found somewhere to live yet or are you still living at home?'

Mathew flushed and shook his head. 'No, I'm a bit short of cash to be honest.'

'For fuck's sake Mathew, you really are a useless bastard.' Patrick reached into his pocket and pulled out a piece of paper. 'Good job I've done all the work for you then isn't it? This is a small holding outside Liverpool, the last tenant has been called up so you can take over the farming too, that should keep you out of the Forces and the landlady isn't too fussy, she just wants a new tenant.' He saw Mathew's confusion and sighed. 'We don't want her asking too many questions about your friend when he moves in do we? Its reasonably isolated too so no one will see you coming and going.'

'You want me to move to Liverpool?' Mathew looked horrified.

'Our friends need information about ships, they want to stop the Atlantic convoys. We have received information that the HQ of the Naval department in charge of escorting the Atlantic Convoys is being moved from Plymouth to Liverpool next year so that's where he needs to be. Furthermore, by moving up north he's out of the way. They won't be looking for him up there… or you.' He added. Patrick was reasonably sure Mathew was lying about what had happened to the girl but he wasn't interested. As long as Mathew behaved himself and didn't draw attention to their activities he didn't care what he did.

Mathew was about to argue that he didn't want to move north when he realised it was the answer to his problems. No one would know him up there.

****

RAF Kenley, Surrey

The morning after his arrival Jimmy met his new Commanding Officer, Sqn Ldr Rupert Leigh, a man he was soon to realise was kind and charming and very popular with his men. 'Well, you've had a little time to get used to the way we do things round here. What are your thoughts.'

Jimmy was about to answer when Mark interrupted.

'It's definitely a busy place sir.'

The Squadron Leader smiled. 'You can say that again. We certainly need new pilots but we need you alive. I know you've all flown Spits, but you have a long way to go which is why I've decided not to put you on operational duty, not just yet...' He could see they were disappointed, but things were too precarious to throw inexperienced pilots at the Nazi onslaught. They would just be cannon fodder and it took too long to train them to lose them on their first flight. 'You need more experience before you face the Hun. Get in as much practice as you can. You're going to need it.'

Jimmy stared at him in disbelief, unable to work out whether he was relieved or disappointed. Then he realised that as much as he wanted to be up there, doing his bit and fighting the enemy, a part of him was quite happy that it wouldn't be just yet. Perhaps he should take the opportunity to take a few hours leave and go and see his parents.

****

45 College Road, Maidstone, Kent

Kristian had spent a cold night in the small shed unsure how to make contact. He could hardly knock on the front door. He was still thinking about it when the back gate opened and a middle-aged man came in and headed towards the outside toilet. Kristian peered through the window in the door and wondered if this was him. He would only get one chance, if he was wrong he would be chased through the town and… he closed off his chaotic thoughts and waited for the man to emerge from the privy.

'Mr Farmer…' His voice sounded horribly loud in the early morning quiet.

Frederick jumped and spun around. The voice had come from his shed and he squinted in the early sunlight. 'Yes? Who are you?'

The man appeared in the doorway and Frederick gasped. The ill-fitting clothes suggested a tramp, but the pistol suggested something else. The unshaven man was fit with cropped blonde hair and he could see the strain in his eyes. This had to be the pilot everyone was looking for which begged the question. Why was he hiding in Frederick's shed and how did he know his name. 'Who are you?' He repeated.

'Kristian von Klotz.' The man muttered softly and Frederick saw the fear in his eyes.

He gasped. 'You're the pilot that killed the girl?' Then he registered the name and he paled. He was about to say something when Kristian snapped.

'No of course not. What do you think I am? The boy that was with her killed her. They were arguing then I heard her scream so I went to intervene, but I was too late.' He shook his head as the images flooded his mind. 'The sick bastard was fucking her, even though she was dead.' He ignored the horror on Frederick's face and continued. 'He threatened me, said he would tell everyone that I had done it, but I didn't. I swear, but no one is going to believe me are they? I need your help to get away. Father said you would help me.'

'That was before you killed and raped a young woman.' Frederick forgot his own doubts and snapped back.

Kristian's voice rose an octave and his grip tightened on the pistol. 'I didn't do it I tell you. I swear on my father's life, your half-brother's life.'

Frederick stared at him in shock and realised that he had no choice. Even if he didn't believe Kristian he would have to help. He couldn't have anyone knowing this was his nephew, not all the time they believed he had killed that young woman. He would have to find some solution but meanwhile he needed to hide him. 'Alright... alright... Wait in the shed until I come back and for God's sake, stay out of sight.'

'You aren't going to hand me over to the authorities?' Kristian hadn't moved.

Frederick shook his head. 'Of course not. You're my nephew.' He saw the relief in the man's eyes and he watched as Kristian lowered the pistol.

'Then you do believe me?'

Frederick hesitated a second too long and Kristian's expression clouded over. 'I didn't do it. I swear. But no one is going to take my word, are they?'

'We'll worry about that later. Have you eaten?' Frederick was stalling for time but a part of him was beginning to believe his nephew.

Kristian shook his head and slowly lowered the pistol. 'Not since yesterday morning. I broke into a farmhouse and stole these clothes and some cheese and bread.'

Frederick frowned. 'Where did you break in?'

'Not here, it was near Sittingbourne I think. I wanted them to think I had gone that way. I even told that boy that was where I was heading... well I asked him for directions anyway.' He saw Frederick's expression and he was confused. 'What is it?'

Frederick shook his head. 'There's not time now, get back inside and I'll bring you some food out.' He turned away and headed towards the house, his mind going over everything Colonel Sinclair had said. There had been no mention of the pilot asking directions to Sittingbourne. Mathew Hart had lied to the authorities. The question was why? It could only be because he didn't want them to find the pilot, presumably because Kristian was telling the truth. He was still thinking about that with a sense of relief when an even more heinous idea occurred to him. Was Mathew Hart the contact for the German spy who was supposed to have parachuted in or was his nephew the German agent? Frederick allowed the ghost of a smile to cross his face. Now he was probably letting his imagination run away with him but he would definitely ask Kristian why he had jumped out over Kent. Not that he was likely to tell him the truth if he was a German agent.

Frederick thought back over the few conversations he'd had with Kristian's father and mentally shook his head. No, it didn't make any sense. Otto was virulently anti-Nazi so presumably he had brought his son up the same way. He disappeared back inside the house and closed the back door.

Kristian slid to the floor of the shed feeling slightly better. He wasn't out of the woods yet but at least his uncle hadn't dismissed him out of hand. He closed his eyes and for the first time in two days he began to drift off into a restless sleep.

Chapter 11

133 Bower Street, Maidstone

Jimmy arrived at the family home and stood outside for a few moments letting the memories flood back. It seemed like ages since he'd been home. Having three sisters he had been spoiled rotten and his memories were nearly all happy. He had spent all his life in this house until he'd finally joined the RAF. But his family had originally come from Ramsgate. His grandfather, William, a butcher who lived at 16 Brunswick Street in Ramsgate with his wife Ann had been rather an entrepreneur; he was also a general labourer, jobbing bricklayer and a painter as well as taking in lodgers. His son, Jimmy's father, Walter Corbin had left Ramsgate in 1900, family rumours suggested a falling out which had resulted in Jimmy's branch of the family changing the spelling of their name to *Corbin* while his cousins spelt it *Corben*. Jimmy didn't know if that was true or whether someone had just made a spelling mistake when filling in the various census and other forms, but the disagreement sounded more interesting. Maybe if he had time one day he would try to find out. He smiled. If he survived the war of course.

His thoughts drifted back to his parents. Having moved to Maidstone Walter met Daisy Lizzie, a local girl from Yalding who had left school at twelve. She married Walter when she was twenty three. A broad smile crossed his face. His mother might only be five feet one inch tall but she certainly wasn't frail. She had an inner strength that Jimmy often thought was the backbone of the family. Walter and Daisy Lizzie had married in 1905, then rented 133 Bower Street for 9s a week from Sharp's toffee company. The house was a two up, two down terraced house and as the family quickly outgrew their space, Walter and Daisy Lizzie slept in the front bedroom, the three daughters, Elsie, Daisy, and Lilly shared a room at the back of the house while Jimmy slept on a wooden board that hung over the bath in the upstairs room in the extension built by Walter. The bathroom led off from the girl's room so Jimmy had grown up not really knowing what privacy meant.

Cooking was done on the wood fire in the scullery; the same fire heated the huge copper saucepan with a wooden lid that contained five gallons of water. The Sunday joint was ten pounds of Argentine sirloin from Fletcher's butchers at the bottom of Bower Street and was kept in the meat safe. His mother made the meat last four days, including the beef hash on Wednesdays. In another corner were grey flagstones where the milk jug stood. It was the sound of the horses pulling the milk cart that was the alarm call for the start of the day. Within moments of stopping an orderly queue of women formed, each holding a large ceramic jug. Bread was delivered three times a day. Washing clothes was a three day effort that Jimmy was delighted not to be involved in. It had been enough hard work ladling the hot water into the bath upstairs in the extension for Sunday baths. The washing had been for his mother and sisters to do before his two elder sisters had married and left home, Elsie to John Perriman and Daisy to their cousin Fred Corben. Lilly was still living at home although he guessed she would probably be at work now.

He was still standing there thinking about the past when his father appeared. 'Jimmy?' Walter's face lit up. 'You do look very smart in your uniform. I hardly recognised you. Why didn't you tell us you were coming?' Before Jimmy could answer he turned back to the house. 'Daisy! Quick, look who's come to visit?' He spun back and then frowned. 'There's nothing wrong is here?'

Jimmy shook his heads. 'No Dad, it's just a flying visit.' He grinned at the unintended pun.' I can only stay a few hours but I'm not that far away now so I should be able to come more often.'

'Jimmy!' Daisy Lizzie came running out of the house and threw her arms around him. Jimmy hugged her back and then felt her shaking. He pulled away slightly and stared at her in consternation. 'What on earth is it Mum?'

'It's nothing Jimmy. I'm just so please you're alright.' She wiped her eyes and grabbed his arm. 'Don't let's waste time standing out here. Come in and I'll put the kettle on.'

Jimmy grinned and followed them both back into the house. 'What about work Dad? I don't want to stop you…'

'Don't be daft boy I can spare you a few moments can't I? No point employing others to work for you if you can't be late on the odd occasion is there?'

Jimmy nodded. His father was a plumber and at five feet nine with broad shoulders he was a very strong man. Once, for a bet, he had climbed the Style and Winch brewery chimney, which was 80' high, carrying a hundred weight and three quarters of lead. He was also a good business man, always charging London rates of 1s and 3d per hour so although they weren't rich, money had never been short. 'Anyway, I've got some news too. I've just been employed to design sinks for Detling Aerodrome, for developing reconnaissance photographs. The way they keep moving you around our paths will probably cross one day!'

Jimmy laughed. 'I don't have anything to do with reconnaissance Dad. I'm a fighter pilot now, or I will be when they finally let me fly operations.' He fell silent.

'You're not flying yet then?' Daisy sounded relieved and he bit back the angry retort he had been about to make. Of course, his mother wouldn't want him flying in combat. She would probably be happier if he spent the war hiding in an aircraft hangar. He forced a smile. 'No not yet. The CO thinks we need more practice. Probably a good thing.'

'Of course it is lad.' Walter joined in. 'They want to make sure you're the best you could be before letting you loose, and then the Krauts won't know what's hit them will they?'

Jimmy was about to answer when the air raid siren went and he found himself being hurried towards the Anderson shelter in the garden. Above him he could hear the now familiar sound of the Spitfires, Hurricanes and Me109s fighting it out above them.

'I suppose you see this often?' He said eventually. No wonder his mother was relieved that he wasn't flying yet.

'It's an almost everyday occurrence…' Daisy Lizzie winced as she recognised the scream of an aeroplane heading for the ground, followed by the sounds of bombing in the distance.

'Sounds like they're after the airfields again.' His father glanced in the direction of West Malling and sighed. 'Hope that's not Detling again.'

Jimmy didn't answer. He'd come to visit his parents to escape watching other pilots risking their lives to protect the country while he did nothing, and he still couldn't get away from it.

****

Bower Street, Maidstone Kent

Elsie Periman watched the latest incursion into the skies over Maidstone, cursed loudly, picked Rodney up and hurried towards the Anderson shelter. Bloody Germans. If she hadn't had Rodney to look after she would have joined one of the women's services. Anything to fight against the enemy who had ruined their peaceful lives for the second time in this century. Elsie had worked at Alabaster Passmore Printing Firm for several years before marrying John and having Rodney, and as much as she loved them both very much she was bored. She'd always been very intelligent and not having anything to keep her brain occupied was driving her mad. It was alright for John, as a telegraphist he had work every day at Chatham docks, knowing he was doing something to fight back. At the moment he was busy using his considerable skills to train others, but she didn't think it would be long before he would be either sent back to sea or moved elsewhere. Meanwhile she was stuck at home doing nothing of any use.

As she settled Rodney into the shelter Elsie thought back to their conversation the previous night. John wanted her to move somewhere inland, away from the constant threat of bombing, but if she did that she would be even more isolated, especially if John did go back to sea. At least being in Maidstone meant she could spend time with her parents and sisters. It would be nice to see Jimmy again but from what she could gather the RAF kept moving him around and he wasn't the best letter writer. On the other hand perhaps she should write to him? It wasn't as if she had anything else to do while the aeroplanes fought to the death in the skies above her. Except she'd left her writing paper and pen inside the house.

Elsie checked Rodney, he was dozing in his pushchair, thankfully oblivious of the danger above and she made a decision. It wouldn't take a minute to go back into the house and fetch them.

****

282 Boxley Road, Maidstone, Kent

Ruth double checked her father was nowhere in sight before sitting down at the kitchen table with her tea and toast and slowly opening the letter from Geoffrey. Letters were few and far between so she tried to savour every moment. The last thing she needed was her father ruining her precious time with her husband with his sarcastic comments.

My darling Ruth

It's been so long since I've seen you, it feels like forever. I hope you are keeping well and that you and your family are safe, well everyone except your father of course! I'm sorry I probably shouldn't have said that but the old bugger, as you so charmingly describe him, isn't exactly the nicest person I've ever met. If there was any justice he'd have been locked up by now but I suppose I should know by now that justice doesn't seem to follow the truth so I'll just change the subject instead.

Thank you for the photograph. I loved seeing you on your motorbike, those leather trousers are really something. If I didn't miss you before, which of course I did, I am now really pining for you desperately.

Ruth smiled. He was right about her father, he treated her like a skivvy and completely ignored poor Frederick although that probably suited her half-brother who had made a success of his life despite his stepfather. The family had originally come from Sussex, but James Samuel had moved from Crowborough to Tunbridge Wells sometime after her stepbrother was born. Her mother, Frances Elizabeth Salina Novis Histed, was also from Sussex, having been born in May 1860 at Rotherfield. Her father, Thomas James Histed was a shoe and boot maker who died when he was only 31 and her mother Mary Anna Novis, a widow at the age of 30 had married George Sawyers a farm labourer, eight years later.

James Samuel had apparently been a coffee trader and owner of a coffee house in Tunbridge Wells before suddenly moving to Detling after 1899 where he took ownership of the Cock Horse Inn. He had gradually developed a bit of a reputation and was what other people called a bit of a wheeler dealer, buying and selling property and collecting the rents. At one time he'd also had a pig farm on the Pilgrims Way, bought and sold cattle, built houses brick by brick with his own hands before employing others to do it for him including Dreyfus. He attended the cattle auctions at Maidstone Market every week, was known by all the auctioneers as a real fly boy and carried a black swordstick everywhere with him which was probably useful as he was also a money lender. From what Ruth could see her father liked living on the edge of the law, after all his own mother had been convicted for larceny at the age of 18, serving three months hard labour and three weeks solitary confinement in 1855 and her father had been convicted of the same thing back in 1912. Presumably he considered himself to be following in his family footsteps.

They had recently moved to this house at Boxley Road and her father now spent most of his time in his greenhouses. Ruth only hoped that he wouldn't use the war to make himself money as she would never forgive him for profiteering.

Ruth sighed. Obviously the rogue gene had missed her as although she often escaped into the countryside, walking for miles around Boxley and Detling recapturing the romantic episodes of her youth to avoid spending time with him, she wouldn't have dreamt of doing anything illegal. She made a conscious effort to stop thinking about him, finished her toast and brushed the crumbs off the letter before continuing reading.

So, for some family news, brother Arthur is still Air Marshall and no doubt very busy given the dreadful newsreels we are seeing. It must be very frightening for you all and I wish I was there to protect you, and before you tell me that you don't need anyone to protect you I know that, but you must allow a chap to want to be the rock for his wife to lean on. Seeing what you are going through while I sit here in relative peace and calm is very unsettling and definitely not the way things should be.

Anyway, enough of my guilt and back to family news. Brother Loben is now the Captain of the Ark Royal, not sure where it is currently and obviously I couldn't tell you even if I did but I am sure, like Arthur, he is also in the thick of it. My only consolation is that brother Hugh is with 210sq RAF in the wilds of Scotland somewhere so maybe I am not the only one sitting the war out. I'm sorry, this letter is turning into one long moan, but you have no idea how frustrating it is to be so far away from any action while you and my brothers are experiencing the war first-hand.

Probably time to change the subject and talk about something else otherwise my letter will only depress you and that is not my attention. If I can do nothing else at least I can try and cheer you up and give you something to look forward to.

As you know the Marine Craft Section is based near Singapore, a place you would love. I'll have to bring you here when the war is over and you can have fun shopping and just generally enjoying yourself. I'll be able to take you to all the places I know and we can pretend we were never separated. And there I go, back to my misery again. I can imagine you reading this wondering if your darling husband has anything cheerful to say, judging by this letter, the answer is no. I miss you too much and most of the funny things that do happen here are probably covered by the Official Secrets Act so I can't tell you. It's very frustrating. And on that miserable note I am going to finish now as I want to catch the post or you will have to wait even longer to hear from me. I think I will have to try and make notes of the more cheerful things happening here, ready to tell you in my next letter.

Meanwhile take care of yourself my darling Ruth, I am with you in spirit if not in person and God willing we will be together soon.

All my love darling

Geoffrey

Ruth finished the last of her tea at the same time as she reached the end of his letter and sighed heavily. She missed him so much. She had grown used to him travelling around the word and getting involved in all sorts of dangerous sports, but this was different. If only she had gone with him when he was first posted. At the time it had not seemed to be a good idea and she had elected to remain at home to look after her mother, but now she would give anything to be with him, away from the constant invasion scares and relentless Luftwaffe incursions over the county, not to mention the scares about some lunatic German pilot running amok in the countryside killing young women.

****

Bower Street, Maidstone

'Elsie?' Jimmy arrived at his sister's house not long after the Germans had turned tail and were being chased back to France. He tried the front door but there was no answer so after a few seconds he hurried around the back. They must still be in the shelter. Perhaps they hadn't heard the all-clear.

'Jimmy!' He frowned at the sound of a loud shout behind him, spun around and looked askance at the back door. It had fallen off its hinges and was blocking the doorway, presumably a result of one of the explosions.

'Elsie what on earth…'

'Can you get me out?'

'Yes of course. Are you hurt?'

Now he was closer he could see she wasn't injured, but she did look pale. He began to pull the door out of the way and as soon as there was a gap Elsie forced her way through and ran towards the shelter. Jimmy stared after her in confusion.

'*Thanks Jimmy.*' He muttered to himself before following her. Elsie disappeared inside the shelter and reappeared with a sleepy looking Rodney. She was looking very sheepish and Jimmy grinned as he realised the reason for her panic. 'I don't think you're meant to leave him alone in there.'

Elsie looked horrified. 'Don't tell John will you? He'll go spare. I only went back to get some writing paper to drop you a line as I hadn't heard from you in ages and the bloody Germans dropped a bomb close enough to damage the door and then I couldn't get back out.' She stopped, took a breath to calm herself down and grinned. 'Goodness, was I pleased to see you!'

Jimmy shook his head. 'No, I won't say anything but please don't risk your life again to write to me. I'm probably not worth it!'

Elsie looked more relaxed now and she smiled. 'Have you got time for a cup of tea?'

'When have you ever known me turn down a cup of tea?' He smiled at Rodney who was now waking up. 'Hello young Rodney. Had a good sleep then?'

****

Maidstone, Kent

Frederick spent the day carrying out his Home Guard duties, checking on the men manning the pill boxes, all the time wondering what he could do about his nephew. Eventually he had decided to make him some false papers, if nothing else it would give him some practice. One benefit of Frederick's new role in the Auxiliaries was having access to the necessary documents and stamps needed to create forgeries, hence being able to provide Kristian with new documents but the question was what should the papers say? The country was full of numerous other nationalities fleeing the occupation of their countries so perhaps he could make him French or Belgium… Frederick shook his head. No, Kristian looked very German and although he spoke English his accent was also German. Then he smiled. Of course. He could pass as a Norwegian, that would explain the accent and maybe with Norwegian papers he could find a fishing boat and leave the country that way. Unfortunately, he had no idea how but he would worry about that once he'd taken the first step which was to draw him up some documents. Frederick glanced at his watch. Another couple of hours and he could get back to the house and start work. He knew it wasn't ideal to use the shed in his garden to hide his Auxiliary equipment but until his OB was complete he had nowhere else. He certainly couldn't use the Home Guard premises. At least he didn't have to worry about Alice, or the girls snooping around.

Chapter 12

RAF Kenley, Surrey

Although he was pleased to have had time to visit his family Jimmy was growing increasingly bored as they spent the next couple of weeks practicing while they watched the Squadron flying sortie after sortie. To Jimmy it felt like being in a cinema watching a film and munching popcorn when all he really wanted was to be part of the action. They listened as the other pilots shared their stories: flying into gaggles of Messerschmitt 109s as they swarmed across the Channel, watching enemy aircraft flash vertically downwards right in front of them, so close they could see the rivets and streaks of oil on the fuselage and he struggled to contain their impatience. They were part of the airbase but separate and it was beginning to drive Jimmy mad.

'How much flaming longer do we have to wait?' He slammed his fist into his hand in frustration.

Mark shrugged. 'Perhaps we should be grateful for the time to practise. No doubt they'll have us up there sooner or later.'

Jimmy sighed. 'I know, but I just feel like a fraud. They're taking a right hammering up there, surely they need us now, not some time in the bloody future?' He was about to say more when one of the men arrived and told them Jimmy and Pete had been summoned to the CO's office.

'One of ours has crash landed in a field near Sevenoaks. I want you to go and fetch him.'

'Yes sir.' Despite the circumstances Jimmy was delighted to finally be doing something he considered useful. But then the CO continued. 'Oh... one other thing. We don't know yet if the pilot survived or not.' Jimmy paled and his good mood immediately dissipated.

They climbed into the CO's staff car and headed off in the direction of where the aeroplane had last been seen, trying to push thoughts that they might find a dead pilot strapped into his aircraft to one side. Instead they concentrated on discussing the numerous pilots who had bailed out or crash landed and still returned to the airfield in one piece.

Eventually they arrived at the location, turned into a country lane and immediately spotted the Spitfire lying on its belly in the middle of a small field. There were numerous people clustered around it including one wearing the distinctive yellow life jacket. Jimmy and Pete cheered up. The jacket belonged to Fl Off Crelin Bodie, known as Bogle, a scruffy looking individual who liked to wear a pullover full of holes, was always smiling and full of boundless energy. He glanced across at them as they approached and grinned.

'What took you so long?'

As they travelled back Bogle explained what had happened. As one of the best pilots he was often used as a weaver, a hazardous role that involved flying a few thousand feet above the rest of the Squadron hunting for enemy planes. Each operation normally had two weavers and when they spotted the enemy they radioed through their position to the rest of the crew. They were highly vulnerable to attack if they were spotted first because they didn't have the protection of the rest of the squadron. 'We were set upon unexpectedly and then I heard bullets hitting the side of the aeroplane. When I opened the throttle the aircraft didn't respond at all then it suddenly seized up completely. I found myself at 15,000 feet with no power and I knew I couldn't make it back to Kenley so I scouted around for a field to land in.' Bogle shrugged. 'Just my luck, I saw one below me but the farmer had filled it with concrete blocks, old cars and trip wires intended to stop enemy planes landing. A great idea but not for friendly aircraft.' He grinned. 'Unfortunately, I didn't have any option. It was too late to go anywhere else so I banked steeply, whipped up the undercarriage and tried to slow her down. We were still going too fast when we hit the ground. The Spit slid along the grass, tipped forward on its nose, crashed back and then stopped. I jumped out quickly, half expecting it to burst into flames but fortunately nothing happened. Looks like lady luck was with me today, not even a scratch!'

Jimmy listened in awe, wondering if he would be quite so calm and collected in the same situation. Perhaps Mark was right after all. They really weren't ready yet.

****

C Wing, Wormwood Scrubs

Fred finished going through the last of that day's logs and sat back, his thoughts on the missing German agent. Despite an extensive search they hadn't found any sign of him, other than a report of him apparently killing some woman which didn't seem to make a lot of sense. They were no nearer finding his contact either. There had been no more radio traffic in that area, which meant that either the agent had made contact with the traitor, the traitor no longer needed to make contact with the agent because he knew where to go or he thought they might be listening in and was just laying low. Fred frowned. There was nothing to say the traitor was a man of course, it could just as easily be a woman. But until his listeners picked up some more radio signals in that location they were effectively blind, and with nothing they could use to advise the authorities, the agent could escape completely.

He glanced at the clock, stood up and headed for the door. At least he could go home tonight so he would know Daisy Irene was safe. Perhaps he would have better luck tomorrow.

****

Yelsted, Kent

The day of Rebecca's funeral was sunny and bright which seemed completely wrong to Charlotte. Her heart was broken, and she would have preferred it to be wet and miserable to suit her mood. The service was well attended, probably because of the circumstances. Neighbours she hadn't seen in years all turned out to watch the coffin file past and the church was full, although she was sure many of them were members of the press wanting to milk the story of the girl killed by a Nazi pilot who the authorities had failed to capture. Charlotte couldn't believe they still hadn't found him and she agreed with her father that someone must be helping him.

She was finding it hard to concentrate on the service, her mind filled with so many memories of her sister. If only she hadn't gone out with that stupid farm labourer she would still be alive. Charlotte realised she was clenching her fists and she tried to relax but couldn't. Instead of praying for her sister's soul she spent most of the service cursing Mathew Hart and imagining what she would say or do to him if their paths crossed. She found it impossible to concentrate on her beautiful sister and, in an attempt to break the cycle of her thoughts she glanced around the church again and she was horrified to see him hovering at the back by the door. How dare he come to the funeral? She was sure her father had made it clear he wasn't welcome.

Charlotte was just about to get up and confront him when she realised that would ruin her sister's funeral and she wouldn't give him the satisfaction of doing that so somehow she remained seated.

'Are you alright?' Anthony was sitting on her left side and he could feel her shaking. 'Sorry, stupid question.' He fell silent not sure how to comfort her and then instinctively reached out and took her hand.

Charlotte was taken aback but his hand felt comforting and for a moment she forgot about Mathew hovering at the back of the church. She squeezed his hand in return and tried to concentrate on the vicar instead.

Adrian stared stonily ahead, his thoughts on Rebecca and how he had failed to save her. He was her father and should have been able to stop this happening, but he hadn't. He had promised Josephine that he would look after their girls, but he had let her down too. Rebecca was dead and Charlotte was in danger thanks to him. Adrian glanced briefly to one side and was grateful to see Anthony was holding Charlotte's hand then he frowned. He couldn't risk losing her as well, it wasn't too late. Somehow he would have to persuade her to leave the FANY before they trained her for anything dangerous. He should never have recommended her to them in the first place, he had put duty to his country numerous times above the safety of his girls, well not anymore. Let someone else take the risks.

****

45 College Road, Maidstone, Kent
'You don't mind?'

Alice shook her head. 'Of course not. We can't leave the poor boy on his own after everything he has already gone through.'

Frederick breathed a sigh of relief. He had already provided Kristian with some identity papers in the name of Olaf Aaberg, but he didn't want to just arrive at the house with him without checking with Alice first. 'Right, I'll collect him from the hostel and bring him home.'

Jeanne held out her hand and gave their guest a shy smile. 'Hello, I'm very pleased to meet you.' He was very handsome, Margaret would love him. In fact she couldn't wait to see her sister's face, but unfortunately she had to go to Woolworths and line up for the broken biscuits which weren't on ration. At least that was better than collecting horse manure off the road to use as compost on the vegetables.

Margaret stared in astonishment as her father introduced the young Norwegian airman to his family. 'Olaf has just escaped from Norway and needs somewhere to stay while he finds some work or begins training for the new Norwegian Brigade that is being formed in London. He doesn't speak much English yet, but I'm sure that will soon come.'
Alice shook Olaf's hand and spoke briefly, welcoming him to their house. Margaret was still staring until she suddenly realised her father was watching her. She smiled and held out her hand. 'Hello Olaf. I can help you with your English if you like.'
'Thank you.' Kristian smiled back and tried to withdraw his hand. 'It's very kind of you.'
'Not at all. I would love to help.' Margaret finally let go his hand and blushed slightly. 'You must be missing your own family so much.'
Kristian hesitated, wondering whether he should answer or pretend he didn't understand, but Frederick had impressed on him not to say too much so he eventually just nodded.
Alice watched her middle daughter with misgivings. It looked like Olaf already had an admirer. She would have to speak to Frederick to get him moved on as soon as possible. It wasn't that she had anything against Norwegians, but Margaret was only seventeen and very impressionable. With hindsight perhaps it wasn't such a good idea to have a young attractive man sharing the house with them.

****

RAF Acklington, Northumberland
Much to Jimmy's disgust they had suddenly been transferred north to 610 Squadron. Jimmy was placed into B Flight and spent the first few days practising tight formation flying which mainly entailed ensuring they didn't hit any of their own aircraft. Having spent weeks binding about how useless it was Jimmy was feeling extremely

disgruntled. He couldn't understand why they had suddenly been transferred north when 66 Squadron had lost five pilots in two days, many of them sprogs like him who were killed without even firing a shot. There was no action *up north,* what was the point of sending them up there.

On 10th September that suddenly changed. He was woken at 05.10hrs and as he was *on readiness* he made his way to the dispersal hut with the intention of going back to sleep. It was too early for banter, especially as he and some of his new friends has travelled into Newcastle the previous night for a boozy session in the local pub, the Turk's Head, so he settled down into a comfy chair and watched his companions finding their own ways of surviving the tedium and tension of the dispersal hut. He was still thinking about how boring it was when the telephone suddenly rang and he almost jumped out of his skin. He was instantly alert, watching closely as the telephone operator nodded solemnly into the receiver then spoke to the flight commander who shouted 'Scramble Blue Section. Angels 20.'

Jimmy was already on his feet, his half-drunk mug of tea and open magazine abandoned as he raced towards the Spitfires waiting in their dispersal pens, propellors already turning, engines roaring in anticipation as the fitters and riggers made last minute checks. Jimmy jumped into the cockpit, adrenaline coursing through him. At last he was going up, all that preparation, months of training and rehearsals would now be put into practice. Without giving a second thought as to what he was likely to be flying into Jimmy plugged in his R/T lead and oxygen mask and released the brakes. The chocks were removed, the CO glanced across from his own machine and they exchanged the thumbs up sign. Jimmy opened the throttle and slowly moved off.

The CO took off first followed closely by Blue Two and then Jimmy who was Blue Three. Once airborne they reformed into their normal V shape, dawn was beginning to break and the half-light cast an unwelcome haze that Jimmy realised would make spotting the enemy that much harder.

They continued to climb until they reached 20,000 feet and then flew flat out through the morning mist towards the shipyards where the intention was to head off the German bombers. It was imperative to stop them before they could find their target as a decent hit could set the war at sea back for several months.

Now he was finally up Jimmy's nerves returned with a vengeance and he tried talking to himself in an attempt to calm his fears. *'This is it Jimmy old boy, your turn to join the fight.'* He could feel his stomach fluttering with fear and as he glanced across at the other two pilots he wondered if they too felt frightened or whether it was just him.

They finally reached the shipyards and below him, through the patchy grey cloud, Jimmy could make out neat rows of terraced streets leading to the yards where gantries lined the docks like giant steel horses standing guard over the half-built ships. They circled cautiously, searching for any sign of the enemy, but it was hard to see anything through the columns of cumulus clouds. Jimmy's nerves grew worse as he continued to scour the horizon, squinting at every possible speck he imagined he could see. The bandits must be here somewhere, so why couldn't he see them? The clouds cleared momentarily and he squinted towards the sun, searching for any sign of the enemy before twisting around in the cockpit, but there was still nothing.

They flew out over the North Sea, still searching and then the CO ordered them to reduce their height to below the cloud level. Jimmy swallowed nervously. He was already a bundle of nerves and now they were being told to fly through cloud, dangerous at the best of times.

The Spitfire slid through the banks of grey restricting his vision to virtually nothing and then he had cleared the clouds and was flying out the other side. Jimmy took a deep breath and was just starting to relax when the R/T crackled into life. 'Boys I think we've got ourselves a bandit. Take a look on the ground. I reckon he might have engine trouble.'

Jimmy stared down at the calm waters of the North Sea and there it was, a Heinkel 115 seaplane, used for reconnaissance and laying mines. It appeared undamaged and had probably been forced to land through engine problems. The three aircraft swooped and circled above him menacingly to ensure he didn't take off until a Naval warship appeared and took the crew prisoner.

As Jimmy landed back at Acklington he felt a rush of euphoria. He had survived to fight another day. He was unlikely to be that lucky next time but he was grateful that his first encounter with the enemy had been a gentle one. He felt into his trouser pocket and smiled as he felt the champagne cork. Perhaps it really was lucky after all.

That night Jimmy and his friends went to the Eldon Grill, a superb restaurant in the city where they dined on mixed grills at 3s and 6d each and then headed towards their favourite pub, the Turk's Head. The barmaid asked what they wanted to drink but before the others could answer Jimmy spoke. 'This lot will have pints, but I'll have a vodka.'

The barmaid smiled. 'Anything with it?'

Jimmy grinned. 'A bit of rum?'

'And some sherry,' Pete chipped in.

The barmaid frowned but Jimmy had no intention of backing down, he was too busy celebrating his survival, so he just nodded. 'Better do as he says love.'

'You'd better add some gin too.' Someone else added.

The barmaid eventually presented him with a cloudy liquid which Jimmy eyed warily for several minutes before finally picking it up and somehow downing it in one. The drink seared the back of his throat making him gasp and tears appeared in his eyes while everyone else laughed. He cleared his throat. 'Wow that's got quite a kick!'

This was greeted with more laughter and then a question from Pete. 'So what's it called Jimmy?'

Jimmy grinned. 'A Spitfire of course!' The Spitfire cocktail was born, a cloudy concoction of just about anything they could get their hands on. It tasted dreadful but its virtue was that it got them drunk very quickly. [1]

****

45 College Road, Maidstone, Kent

Providing Kristian with an alternative identity was only a short term solution to their problem. Unfortunately, the area was still overrun with the authorities searching for his nephew who now believed he wasn't only a murderer but also a spy, and Frederick was wary of trying to move him until he had found a way of getting him back across the Channel. He wasn't the only one who was becoming frustrated.

---

[1] At the end of the war the Turk's Head was still serving Spitfire cocktails.

'I'm never going to escape am I?' Kristian looked distraught. The family had gone for a walk and he had finally found some time alone with his uncle. If he could have just handed himself over and been treated as a POW he wouldn't have minded that much, but because of the murdered girl it wasn't that simple. He also had another problem, one he didn't want to bother his uncle with. He was sure his cousin, Margaret, was developing feelings for him. She always seemed to appear when he least expected it, leaning towards him, her eyes sending him secret messages that he daren't respond to, but that he couldn't ignore for much longer either. So far he had managed to be polite to her, pretending his English didn't stretch that far when she suggested things he daren't agree to like going for a walk or a drink in the local pub. But he couldn't keep putting her off, not without upsetting her or making her suspicious and he couldn't tell his uncle either for fear of causing unnecessary problems with the only man who could help him out of the mess he was in.

Frederick didn't answer straight away then spoke his thoughts out loud. 'If the woman hadn't been killed and they weren't also searching for a German spy as well, it would be much easier.'

'German spy?' Kristian looked confused and then even more concerned. As if he didn't have enough to worry about.

Frederick cursed under his breath. He hadn't meant to say anything about the spy but it was too late now. 'On the night you bailed out our security services intercepted a message saying a German spy was parachuting into Kent.' Frederick sighed. He shouldn't have given Kristian that information, but he was already in enough trouble, and the boy needed to know why it was proving so hard to move him.

Kristian looked thoughtful. 'Maybe I could help find him?'

'How are you going to do that?' Frederick looked sceptical.

'I don't know.' Kristian continued to think hard, then sighed in exasperation. 'Or maybe not. It was just an idea. Maybe I should just give myself up?'

'If you do that you'll land me in it too.' Frederick snapped then raised his hand in apology. 'I'm sorry, I didn't mean to lose my temper with you.' He took a breath and eyed Kristian thoughtfully. 'If you can think of a way of finding the spy it might help.' He didn't know how, but he would listen to anything that could get them out of the mess they were in.

Kristian stared at him for several long silent minutes, then finally spoke. 'I can't think how I could do that to be honest, but it doesn't matter as I've had a much better idea.'

Frederick looked sceptical. 'Go on?'

'They're looking for a spy, yes?'

Frederick nodded impatiently.

'Then we could give them one.'

'I don't understand…'

'Me. We could say I am the spy but that I want to work for the British, which is why I am coming forward.'

Frederick shook his head. 'It wouldn't work. They might still lock you up and hang you for killing that girl or they might not believe you want to work for us and execute you anyway. Not to mention that I will also be arrested and hanged for treason for harbouring you. And even if they did believe you, the real spy would still be out there somewhere doing all sorts of damage.'

Kristian leaned forward. 'I can't change that although I might be able to find out more when I get back to Germany. But even if I can't your people will find him eventually. Can we leave that for a moment and go back to my idea?' He waited until Frederick nodded and then carried on. 'I don't see why it won't work, not if we plan it carefully. The first problem is that I have to prove that I have only just arrived, yes?'

'How are you going to do that?'

'You can vouch for me. I arrived the day after the girl was killed, that's when you introduced me to your wife and daughters. The secret is to keep to the truth as much as possible yes? That I am your nephew and my father sent me. I know he didn't actually send me but he did tell me to come to you if I was in trouble over here, so it's not much of a lie.' Kristian took a breath. 'They already know you were in contact with my father before the war don't they, so I can say I have come over with a message from my father and that I want to work for the British too. He couldn't find a safe way of contacting either you or them, not with such an important message, so that's why I'm here… so I can pass the message on and we can work out a way of me passing additional information back from Germany.'

Fredrick eyed him thoughtfully, his brain racing. 'But what about the message they intercepted about the spy? Who was it for? If the spy is you the message could only be for me which makes me even more of a traitor than I already am!'

Kristian thought for a moment. 'My father risked contacting you once to say I was coming because it was really important you met me and took me to meet your superiors.'

'Why would he do that?'

'Because my message is so important it has to reach the right people and if I just came on the off chance, without any way of actually making contact, it might not reach the right people.'

'I don't know....' He saw Kristian's exasperation and sighed. 'Alright, I suppose it might work. But we would have to make sure there were no holes in your story, it would have to be airtight.'

'I agree and I know it's a risk but I can't see any other way. I hate this war. I have spent most of it trying to avoid killing anyone and I am still in the shit. I want to do something to end the war, get rid of the Nazis and save my country before they completely destroy it.'

Frederick was going over things in his head looking for flaws. 'The message would have to be worth you risking your life for. Is there anything you do know that would be worth that?'

Kristian hesitated and then nodded. 'Yes I do know something I could use. My father told me something he overheard. If we decide to go ahead I'll tell you then.'

Frederick allowed himself a wry smile. 'Don't you trust me?'

Kristian grinned. 'Yes, I do.'

'Then you'd better tell me as I need to know if it will be enough.'

Kristian hesitated then instinctively lowered his voice. 'Hitler is planning on invading the Soviet Union next year, once he's invaded and subdued Britain. He doesn't want a war on two fronts so once Britain is out of the war, he'll turn his eyes eastward.'

Frederick stared at him in disbelief. 'But he has a pact with Stalin?'

'He only signed that to keep them out of the war, that's why he gave them half of Poland, to keep them happy and unsuspecting.'

Frederick's brain was rushing through the ramifications. 'That's madness. The Soviet Union is massive, how on earth does he expect to control it?'

'Exactly.' Kristian sighed. 'It will be the end of Germany which is why he has to be stopped.'

Frederick was still stunned. If Kristian was right the war could be over more quickly than expected, but if it depended on Britain losing the war then was there really any change? With difficulty he turned his attention back to the present.

'Alright, I agree that's big enough for you to risk your neck but even if British intelligence believe you and we get you back to Germany, or at least to Europe, how are you going to explain your escape to your own people? If they don't believe how you escaped they'll execute you!'

Kristian shrugged, his expression bleak. 'I don't have any choice Uncle. I can't keep pretending I support the regime without knowing that I am doing something to fight against it. This is my opportunity.'

Frederick didn't answer for several seconds while he tried to work out whether it could work. Eventually he decided that they needed to at least plan for that option as he had no other ideas, not ones that would stand any chance of success anyway.

Chapter 13

Yelsted, Kent

'I don't understand?' Charlotte stared at her father in shock. She had been trying to subdue her grief and get ready to return to her training when he'd dumped the bombshell on her. 'You want me to leave the FANY? Why?'

'Because I don't want you to be in danger.'

Charlotte shook her head in disbelief and began to laugh. 'You don't want me in danger? That's ridiculous Dad, we're fighting a war. Of course, I am in danger. Becca was just out for a walk with her boyfriend and she was killed by the enemy, so how do you think you're going to protect me?'

Adrian glared at her. 'You don't understand…'

'Yes I do. You couldn't protect Becca so now you think you can wrap me up in cotton wool and I'll be safe. Well, it won't work Daddy. I…'

'I promised your mother I would look after you both.' Adrian snapped, his interruption making her jump. 'And I failed.'

Charlotte sighed. 'I understand that Daddy, but Mummy would have wanted me to have a life, she would have wanted me to fight for what's right, not to hide away indoors. You know that's true.' She hesitated before continuing. 'And you have always wanted the same. That's why you recommended me for the FANY in the first place.' She had no intention of sitting out the war but she would prefer to have her father's blessing. 'Anthony is picking me up in an hour's time. I don't want to argue with you but I need to do this, for Becca as much as anyone.'

Adrian stared at her for several seconds then finally lowered his eyes. 'Yes of course, I know you're right.' He sighed and reached out his arms. 'Please look after yourself. I don't think I could bear to lose you as well.'

'I'll be fine Daddy.' Charlotte felt his arms engulf her and fought back tears. 'I'm indestructible, you'll see!' She wiped her eyes and smiled. 'I'll finish packing.'

****

RAF Gravesend, Kent

Jimmy took off and soon reached 30,000 feet. Things had been quiet so with no enemy to fight the CO had decided to give them some combat practice. The idea was to dive down on each other and then climb back up again. Jimmy engaged in the pretend battle, peeling off in plenty of time to avoid a collision, his movements controlled, measured and planned, knowing it was nothing like the real thing. As he moved away, he watched while two other planes prepared to undertake a similar manoeuvre and then everything suddenly went wrong. One of the aircraft misjudged the distance and instead of careering past each other there was a sickening bang followed by a bright yellow flash and debris shooting out from the explosion. Jimmy watched in horror as both planes dropped like stones, trailing black smoke before smashing into the ground.

He woke with a start, his limbs still trembling, his body covered in sweat, his breathing coming in short, ragged gasps. It was several days now since he'd watched two of his friends crash into each other and although one had miraculously survived, having somehow managed to bail out, the other had died and he was still struggling to come to terms with such a pointless death.

Jimmy had been separated from Mark and his other friends several days earlier. While Mark and Pete had gone to Southend, and Dave had remained at Acklington, Jimmy had been posted back to 66 Squadron which was now operating out of Gravesend. He had been delighted to see some of his old friends again although the Squadron had a new CO, Sqn Ldr Athol Forbes who had been Flight Commander at 303 Squadron which was largely made up of Polish pilots who had fled Europe earlier in the summer.

Jimmy sat up and took several deep breaths, trying to get rid of the nightmarish image of the two planes crashing in mid-air. It took some time and by the time he felt better he was wide awake. Not wanting to risk having any more bad dreams he decided he might as well get up. It was just before dawn, a dull miserable day with low cloud and a cold irritating drizzle. He made his way to the mess, dozed until breakfast and then had a good fry up of bacon and eggs before heading towards the dispersal hut and sitting down. As he waited his thoughts returned to his dream. Maybe it was an omen? He felt in his pocket for his lucky champagne cork and turned it over and over and then the telephone rang. Everyone jumped as the operator answered it.

'It's for you Johnny, some little WAAF says you were supposed to meet her last night.' Everyone laughed, grateful for the diversion, however small, and the officer blushed. Silence resumed until the telephone rang again and the Commander shouted, 'Scramble base, angels one-six.'

Chairs scraped along the bare floor and the pilots leapt to their feet. Outside Spitfires belched blue clouds of smoke and roared into life, Jimmy sprinted to his plane, grabbed the parachute resting on the wing and climbed into the cockpit while the erk (slang for aircrew) who had prepared the aircraft stood on the wing to one side. Once Jimmy was inside he fastened his straps and closed the cockpit flap. As the man wished him good luck Jimmy pulled on his helmet, clipped the oxygen-mask-cum-microphone across his mouth and pushed home the R/T plug. The other erk disconnected the battery plug and slammed the aircraft's nose shut. They exchanged the thumbs up signal and Jimmy looked across at the rest of his section in the half light of dawn. Red One and Red Three were already moving across the grass. Jimmy was Red Two so he hurriedly waved the chocs away, released the handbrake, bumped after them and took up his position to the right of Red One, the Flight Commander. They opened throttles and took off, followed closely by Yellow, Green and Blue Sections, the whole process being completed in two minutes.

The radio fizzed and buzzed, noisy with atmospherics and then the Squadron Leaders voice came through loud and clear.

'Are you in position Green, Red and Yellow leaders?'

The replies were fed back including Jimmy's section leader and they were given a new course. The pilots turned to follow the new instructions, spreading out so they could search the sky for the enemy. By now they had climbed to 15,000 feet and the cold began to seep through his clothing. Jimmy shivered, pulled down his oxygen tube from its clip and fitted it to his mask before switching it on. No point taking chances.

They flew towards the familiar skies of Maidstone and Dover to intercept the bombers but it wasn't those Jimmy was worried about, it was the scores of Me 109s protecting them that would be the real danger.

'Bandits! At two o'clock.'

Jimmy swivelled around but couldn't see anything, then his eyes fastened onto the horizon. Several miles away he could see a line of black dots like a swarm of flies spread out across the sky. They were heading away from him, hundreds of them. As they drew closer Jimmy could make out the Me109s more clearly and then they were ordered to break up and begin the attack. Jimmy was on his own.

****

45 College Road, Maidstone, Kent

Colonel Sinclair sat quietly in the armchair in Frederick's front room and listened to the Captain of the local Home Guard, a mixture of disbelief and growing fury on his face. Several times he wanted to interrupt, but somehow he managed to keep quiet and make himself listen. Eventually Frederick finished speaking, glanced at the man sitting next to him, who he had introduced as his nephew, and waited. He had watched the Colonel carefully while he was explaining everything and he guessed they were not going to have an easy ride.

'You really expect me to believe this?' The Colonel eventually spoke.

'It's the truth sir. Kristian is my nephew; you can verify that. His father, Otto, has helped us with information, through me, since before the war. Kristian arrived after the girl was killed, in fact it was the day after you came to see me. You can verify that too by asking my wife who believes him to be a Norwegian pilot. He risked his neck to come here and warn us about something important and to offer his services to us from behind German lines. I had lost contact with Otto after the war started and we've had no information from him since then, but this way we can resume that link.' Frederick had not mentioned the message they had intercepted saying the spy was on his way and he hoped the Colonel wouldn't think of it because he was sure their explanation would not hold up to too much questioning.

'Why has it taken you so long to contact me?'

Frederick resisted the temptation to cross his fingers. This was one of the dangerous bits. If Kristian was genuine why hadn't they come forward immediately? 'Because you were looking for a German spy who had allegedly murdered a young woman. Kristian was terrified you wouldn't believe him, that he would either be shot on sight or tried and hanged.'

'Why shouldn't we believe him if he arrived after the event?'

'Would you in his position? He's an enemy agent.'

'What's this information?' Colonel Sinclair changed the subject.

'Hitler is intending to attack the Soviet Union next year.' Kristian spoke for the first time.

Colonel Sinclair burst out laughing. 'That's ridiculous. Why on earth would he do something so suicidal?'

'Because he's insane.' Kristian was not smiling. 'He thinks he is invincible. His forces have overrun Europe in record time. Why should anyone doubt him? His intention is to knock Britain and her Empire out of the war, either by defeating her or coming to some kind of agreement. That way he gets rid of the danger of a war on two fronts. Then he will turn his war machine eastwards so he can take Soviet resources, their oil, their factories and their manpower, to be used as slave labour of course.'

There was silence. 'How do you know this?'

'My father is still a respected member of the Reich, he has very important contacts. But you will know that when you investigate him as I am sure you will.'

'Why does he want to help us defeat his country?'

'Because he is a patriotic German. If Hitler attacks the Soviet Union we will eventually lose and then Germany will be torn apart, completely ruined. He wants to stop that.'

'He wants a negotiated settlement?' The Colonel was watching Kristian speculatively.

'Yes, I believe so, a settlement with the Generals, not the regime.'

'And what if that's not on the table?'

Kristian glanced at Frederick and then back at the Colonel. 'Maybe not now, but if we can help you enough the British government may change its mind?'

The Colonel sat back and closed his eyes for a second. Churchill would never agree to anything other than unconditional surrender, but this man didn't need to know that. 'I can't make a decision without consulting other people. You understand that?'

'Yes, yes of course.' Frederick began to relax slightly. At least he seemed to be taking them seriously.

The Colonel suddenly stood up and Frederick swallowed nervously. This was the crunch point, if they were to be arrested it would be now.

'You are to come with me Herr von Klotz.' Colonel looked at Kristian and then turned to Frederick. 'You will remain here and carry on whatever tasks have been allocated to you. You will not speak of this to anyone, including your wife. Is that clear?'

Frederick nodded as relief flooded through him. 'Yes, yes sir, of course.' They obviously weren't in the clear yet but the Colonel seemed to believe them, enough not to arrest him anyway and he didn't appear to have noticed the discrepancy. He watched them leave, closed the door behind them and wondered how long it would take the Colonel to realise that there was another spy out there, that the radio traffic his men had picked up referred to someone else, not his nephew, someone infinitely more dangerous. He was tempted to go after the Colonel and tell him, but he needed to wait until Kristian was on his way home first. He had no idea how he would let the Colonel know the truth, but he would find a way. He had to. Meanwhile, with Kristian gone he would continue to prepare his OB and once that was done he would search for the real spy himself. He had no idea how he could find him but he had no option. No one else was going to be looking for him and God only knew what damage he could inflict on the Allies if he was allowed to carry on his activities without interference. If he could only identify the spy himself he might yet escape being tried for treason, but even more important he might be able to sleep at night.

****

Over Kent

Jimmy stared out of his cockpit at complete chaos. An Me 109 shot past, closely followed by a Spitfire, another dived past Jimmy's wing. Overhead several planes swooped and climbed and Jimmy had a brief moment of panic as he couldn't tell what was going on. He was vaguely aware of the CO's voice 'He's on you Red Two...' and then 'I've got him.'

Jimmy's training finally kicked in. He checked his rear mirror, all was clear. He searched for a target but couldn't see one. He checked his mirror again and there it was, an Me109 locked on his tail, bullets streaming from his wing.

Jimmy pulled the Spitfire into a tight evasive turn and rolled into a dive, somehow managing to avoid the gunfire. As the aircraft plummeted the blood drained from his head and he blacked out.

****

Arkley View, near Barnet

Fred had finally settled into their new address. Those in charge had eventually decided that it was too dangerous to carry on working at Wormwood Scrubs while the Germans were bombing London so heavily and they had moved to Arkley View, a large country house on a site two miles north of Barnet on 3rd October. The volunteers now sent their logs to PO Box 25. It was already being used by the Post Office as an intercept station and now housed various huts used for analysis, intelligence, direction finding and various other administrative duties as well as a teleprinter terminal. The communications side of the RSS for which Fred worked had been given the name Special Communications Unit 3 (SCU3).

Fred read the message from Colonel Sinclair in astonishment. It appeared they had found the German spy so he no longer needed to look out for radio traffic relating to him. Fred stared down at the instructions in confusion, checked the time the message had been written and shook his head. That didn't make any sense. He had already come across one log sheet that reported information that he was sure was related to the German spy and separated it out. He reread the form and shook his head again. The code had been broken and stated clearly that the agent had arrived safely and was moving north with the contact as directed. Unfortunately, there were no more details about the contact, so he was no nearer finding out who it was. But it was the time of the message that was bothering him. It had come in several hours after the log report so either Colonel Sinclair was lying to him for some reason which didn't seem very likely or they had intercepted one German agent and there was another spy on the loose.

Fred sat back in his chair, stared at the bare walls of the office and wondered what he should do. He could hardly question Colonel Sinclair, but what if he was right and there really was another Nazi agent in the country, one that was moving north.

****

RAF Gravesend, Kent

By the time Jimmy came to again the Spitfire had dropped several thousand feet and after several anxious glances out of the cockpit he realised he was close to the coast of Calais. He searched around but there was no sign of the enemy, in fact the skies were empty, there was no one about at all. Jimmy flew around for several minutes, looking frantically for any signs of the battle but there was nothing so eventually he turned for home.

As he approached Gravesend Jimmy began to slowly relax. He was almost home; the champagne cork had protected him again. As he landed safely and taxied slowly along the field Jimmy realised he wasn't the first pilot back, several Spitfires already lined the field, bullet holes clearly visible and as he came to a halt Jimmy wondered about the other pilots who hadn't yet returned. He knew it sometimes took days, depending on where the pilot had bailed out or crash landed. The aircraft taxied to a halt, he climbed out, had a brief conversation with the aircrew and trudged to the dispersal hut, his nerves still jangling.

With his feet firmly back on the ground Jimmy finally allowed himself to accept that he had survived his first real taste of battle. He was briefed by the intelligence officer, not that he could remember much and then he sat quietly sipping hot sweet tea and munching toast, the adrenaline gradually seeping away leaving him calm and relaxed.

****

RAF Biggin Hill

It was the first opportunity she'd had to read the letter from Margaret that had arrived that morning. Betty stepped outside away from the noisy control room, lit a cigarette and began reading.

Dear Betty

The most amazing thing has happened. I'm madly in love with a Norwegian pilot who is staying with us. He's absolutely smashing, really good looking and very polite. I couldn't believe it when he suddenly appeared with Dad. All my dreams come true! He doesn't say very much and Dad says he won't be staying here that long but that doesn't matter. He can write to me from wherever he is going can't he! I'm so excited and I can't wait for you to meet him.

Betty sighed and wondered if her parents knew about her sister's crush on their house guest. Perhaps she should warn them?

Chapter 14

London

Colonel Sinclair stared out of the office window at the River Thames below and hoped he had done the right thing. Something was nagging at him but he didn't know what it was, just that he had missed something important. He had gone over his conversation with Captain Farmer and his nephew repeatedly but he couldn't place what was bothering him. After consultation with his colleagues he had eventually decided to trust Kristian von Klotz, and the German was currently on his way back to Europe. They had thought long and hard about how to send him back as he had been missing for several days and they couldn't afford to make the German Intelligence agencies suspicious, not if they wanted Kristian to survive long enough to send them information. They had eventually decided to smuggle him aboard a Norwegian vessel whose Captain was known to be pro-Nazi. Once in Norway he would have little trouble getting back to Germany. It was a long journey but that would help muddy the time frame and make his escape more plausible.

He was still thinking about it when the telephone rang. 'Yes… ah Mr Corben. Did you get my message?' He listened carefully and frowned. 'What do you mean?'

Fred repeated his concerns, that a log citing radio traffic about a new arrival had been received, that the spy was going north with the contact and that the signal had been intercepted before the Colonel's message.

'Are you sure?' Colonel Sinclair cursed under his breath. Fred had found the missing piece, the thing that had been nagging at him. If the man was correct there was a real German spy on the loose, one that wasn't Frederick Farmer's nephew. He had allowed himself to be distracted by Kristian von Klotz when the real danger was still out there. He took a breath. 'Right Fred, keep me informed of anything else that comes in relating to this and ignore my earlier message. As you say the spy is still out there.' He replaced the receiver before Fred could ask any questions and cursed again, this time out loud. It was time to pay Captain Frederick Farmer another visit.

****

RAF West Malling, Kent

Having taken off from Gravesend that morning Jimmy was instructed to fly to West Malling which had been the home of the Maidstone Flying Club before the war. Somehow he became separated from the rest of the patrol and by the time he reached the airfield it was already dark. Jimmy touched down as normal but because there was no moon he couldn't see the numerous small bomb craters from various previous German attacks that pockmarked the field.

He gently eased the brakes on but to his horror one of the oleo legs became stuck in a bomb hole that had been badly filled. The leg wedged itself in the mud and began acting as an axis so the aeroplane began to spin round and round in tight circles. Jimmy was unable to do anything except try to prevent himself from throwing up all over the cockpit until eventually the aircraft came to halt leaving him badly shaken but thankfully unhurt. Unfortunately, his mishap had been witnessed by several men of the Squadron who nicknamed it Corbin's merry go round and teased him mercilessly for his remaining time there.

****

Outside Maidstone, Kent

Frederick moved the spade, placed the wooden boards carefully over the hole before covering them with more soil. From a distance the area looked undisturbed. Hopefully it would remain so as this was his escape route, a way out if the Germans found the main entrance which he would dig later when he had more time. If they had found his OB he probably didn't stand much chance of getting away but it was worth planning anyway. He glanced at his watch, just time to read Betty's letter before he needed to go back.

He read the short letter from his eldest daughter and cursed. No wonder Kristian had been in such a hurry to get away. It hadn't just been fear of the authorities, the poor lad had been terrified of Margaret. It would have been funny if it hadn't been so serious. The problem was who else had Margaret told about Kristian? Fortunately, his daughter believed that Kristian was Norwegian, at least he assumed she did, but it would only take the wrong person to put two and two together… Damnation! The question was what to do about it now? Kristian was long gone, probably even back in Germany by now. Was it worth telling Colonel Sinclair about it or should he just leave it?

****

Outside Yelsted, Kent
'He's gone!' Mildred wailed.

Bill slurped the rest of his tea and slammed the cup down on the table. 'What do you mean he's gone?'

'His suitcase has gone, the one on the top of the wardrobe, there's clothes missing and underwear, socks, pants...' She burst into noisy tears.

Bill stood up, a frown on his face. 'Surely he's left a note or something...'

Mildred blew her nose and shook her head. 'Not that I can see.'

Bill sighed and stepped towards the door. Mildred watched him, irritation flooding her body. Why on earth didn't he hurry? As if he'd read her thoughts Bill turned towards her.

'No point rushing is there, not if he's gone.' He ignored her sobs but took the stairs two at a time anyway.

He knew immediately that Mildred was right, the room had an empty feel as if the spirit had left it. The wardrobe was partially open and he could see it was empty. His son had few clothes and none of them were there. He looked around carefully before checking the drawers of the bedside cupboard and it was then he saw the letter.

Dear Mum and Dad

I've moved out, gone away for a while to take up a job in Wales. It will get me away from here and all the gossip, you know what people are like. I'll send you my address once I'm settled so don't worry about me.

Mathew

Bill read the short note again and sighed heavily. Was his son running away because he had killed that girl or because he had told the truth and was upset that people thought he might be lying? It probably didn't matter that much. By running away he had made himself look guilty. Bill knew he wouldn't really miss his son, the boy was nothing but trouble, but Mildred would be devastated. He turned around, letter in hand and headed for the stairs.

****

45 College Road, Maidstone, Kent

Jeanne had hurriedly shut the front gate to keep the cows and sheep out of the garden as they were taken to the weekly cattle market before going out into the back garden to play. She was engrossed in her game, pretending to be her mother visiting the poor families in the new council houses as a District Visitor, only in her game she was allowed to actually speak and play with the children, unlike normally when her mother wouldn't let her have anything to do with them. Jeanne frowned as she thought about her mother's restrictions on her walking on her own in Stone Street or other areas where lodgings houses and pubs were as well. It was very strange perhaps she should ask why she couldn't walk there or mix with poor children. She was still thinking about that when she suddenly heard the familiar noise, looked up and saw a formation of German aircraft coming towards the town. Her first thought was to go into the shelter as she'd been instructed, but before she could move the bombs started dropping and everything shook with the force of the massive explosions. It was several seconds before she realised she was lying on the ground.

'Jeanne!' Alice yelled, her voice barely loud enough to be heard above the sound of the bombs falling.

'I'm alright Mum.' Jeanne struggled to her feet and ran towards her.

'Come on, into the shelter in case they come back.'

'What about Dad?'

'He's at work love. Don't worry, I'm sure he's safe.'

The shelter was cold and damp, Jeanne settled back on to the bench seat and examined her clothes which were covered in dust.

'Alice? Jeanne? Thank goodness you're both alright.' Frederick peered into the shelter and breathed a sigh of relief. He had left his men helping to dig out the casualties from the damage to Brenchley Gardens which had taken a direct hit with several people dead.

'Have they killed anyone?' Jeanne asked.

Frederick sighed. He wanted to lie to her but there was no point, she would find out the truth soon enough. 'Yes, love. Just stay here with Mum until I get back alright?'

'You're going out again?'

He could hear the panic in her voice and he forced a smile. 'I won't be long. I just have to make sure we've got everyone out. You wouldn't like me to leave anyone behind would you?'

Jeanne shook her head. 'No, of course not.' She watched as he left the shelter and looked at her mother. Alice was fighting back tears so Jeanne moved closer, put her arms around her mother and muttered softly. 'Dad will be safe Mummy. He'll be back soon.'

Alice didn't answer. She hugged her daughter closer and wondered if they could go away for a few weeks, anything to escape the constant fear.

****

'South Moor', Maidstone, Kent

Daisy Irene and her two evacuees, a brother and sister, five year old Jack and three year old Lucy came out of the shelter and back into the house as soon as the all clear went. She made them some lunch and then returned to the urgent problem that needed resolving within the next few days. Daisy Irene had joined the committee in charge of resettling evacuees in an attempt to help settle the vast numbers being sent out of London. They had managed the first batch reasonably easily but they had just received word that a further eight and a half thousand were due to arrive that month. She was perfectly happy to take a few more herself, it was lovely to have the house filled with children, but she couldn't take all of them. This meant redoubling her efforts to persuade other families to take them. She waited for them to finish their lunch and then helped them put their coats on.

'Where are we going?' Jack enquired.

'Are we going to the park?' Lucy asked before Daisy Irene could answer.

'We can go to the park on the way home but first we need to go to the library.'

Jack frowned. 'The library?'

Daisy Irene was about to encourage them to hurry up when she had a thought. 'Yes, that's right. You've been to the library before, haven't you?'

Jack exchanged glances with Lucy and shook his head. 'No, what is it? Do they do food?'

Daisy Irene laughed. 'No, they lend books.' She saw his disappointment and smiled. 'I can see you don't think that's very exciting but I'll get you some books and then we can read them tonight. I bet you'll be surprised how much fun that is.'

John stared at her and then shrugged. He was missing his mum, but this lady was very nice and so far she had told them the truth about everything so maybe she was right about books too.

Daisy Irene left the house, locked the front door, took their hands, and headed in the direction of the library. She had intended searching for the addresses of the local country houses, those that she might not know and also checking the electoral roll to find new places to take the evacuees, but she would also get the children some books and read to them before bed. It would give her something to do in the evening as Fred was often away now with his secret work. It was a good job she had the children or she would be very bored without Fred to talk to. The next question would be how many extra children could she fit in. Jack and Lucy had settled in very well and she didn't want to disrupt them, but they needed more accommodation and the best way was to set an example. She would look for a brother and sister around the same ages so they would have some company. She smiled. Fred would get a shock when he came home next time.

****

Singapore

Geoffrey glanced down at the file he'd made up after he'd recruited Li Kang and reread the notes he'd made. Even in their abbreviated form the horror of Li Kang's story jumped off the pages like something out of a film and he had to keep reminding himself that this had really happened, that human beings could really behave in such an appalling way. He could still hear the details, repeated in a monotone as if Kang was trying to take away the emotion.

Li Kang had been twenty three when his world had fallen apart. A native of Manchuria he, like the vast majority of Chinese citizens of the area, had grown increasingly fed up with Japanese rule and their support of Chinese warlord Zhang Zuolin. Although Manchuria was legally Chinese much of the south of the region was controlled by the Japanese through its railways, its leasehold on the Liaodong Peninsula and in various other ways that compromised

Chinese sovereignty. In an attempt to reassert their jurisdiction, the Chinese began building railways to encircle the Japanese, and when Zhang Zuolin was murdered by the Japanese his son allied himself to the Chinese Nationalists. The anti-Japanese movement became so strong that the communists and the nationalists even agreed to stop fighting and join forces to throw the Japanese out of Manchuria.

By July 1937 the Japanese had occupied Fengtai which was a railway junction close to Marco Polo Bridge and on 7th July a small Japanese force demanded entry to the tiny walled town of Wanping to search for one of their soldiers who had allegedly gone missing. The Chinese garrison refused the Japanese entry, then a shot was heard, and both sides started firing. Both Chinese and Japanese refused to make any concessions and the conflict grew. The Second Sino-Japanese war had begun.

'When the fighting spread I decide to take my wife, Ah Lum, and my two beautiful daughters, Bo and Chin, to Nanking. We thought we would be safe in the capital. What we didn't know was that our enemy was determined to break us and General Matsui Iwane had ordered the city to be destroyed.' Li Kang closed his eyes and fell silent. Eventually Geoffrey interrupted.

'I have read several reports of what happened in Nanking, you don't need to repeat everything they did, just tell me about your family.' Geoffrey hated having to push Kang for what he knew must be very painful memories, but he needed to know whether Kang was a nationalist or a communist before he could fully trust him and the only way to do that was to spend lots of time speaking to him, finding out why he'd fled China and why he hated the Japanese so much. Geoffrey was pleased with the intercepts Kang had already picked up, however, the signals had already been decoded by him, mere tests to ensure the man was genuine, but the situation was deteriorating and his workload accelerating so although he was almost entirely convinced that the man was not a Japanese spy he still needed to know exactly what had happened before he could make a final decision about whether to let him loose on the most important stuff.

Geoffrey had done his own research after finding out that Li Kang and his family had fled to the capital and what he'd discovered had sickened him. Nanking had been burned to the ground, over 150,000 male prisoners of war had been massacred as well as more than 50,000 male civilians whilst over 20,000 women and girls had been raped, many of them mutilated. As horrific as the figures sounded Geoffrey was convinced in his own mind that they had probably been underestimated which made his job even harder, but he needed to be sure Kang wasn't a communist. He was about to prompt him again when Kang began speaking.

'I initially hid my family outside the city, but we soon ran out of supplies and I did not know what to do. My daughters were starving, my wife terrified... Eventually I decided that the only option was to take them to the safety zones set up by the international community and leave them there. I would then go and join the Chinese who were fighting back. Not the communists, I couldn't fight with them, I hate them almost as much as the Japanese.' Kang fell silent again wondering if he should explain why but that wasn't what the British officer had asked so he resumed speaking. 'I left them in the wooded area outside the city and went back in to get them some false papers. I'd had an idea that if I could get Ah Lum documents declaring she was a mistress of one of the top Japanese Generals and that the two children were his, it might be just enough to get them all to safety.' Tears rolled down his cheeks. 'But it took me over two days to get the right documents and when I hurried back to where I'd left them they weren't there.'

Geoffrey didn't really know what had happened next except what Kang had surmised. Ah Lum and the children had run out of food before he left them so he could only assume she had waited some time and then, presuming he must have been killed because he hadn't returned, had decided to risk taking the children into the city herself. It was several days before Kang found her mutilated body in a mass grave in the city but there was no sign of the children. He had continued to search and eventually been told that his daughters had been rescued by another Chinese family but their house had been burned to the ground as the marauding soldiers set fire to the city. He had never found their bodies.

Geoffrey had been unable to speak for several minutes after Kang told him his story. Eventually he'd poured them both some whisky and after both men had emptied their glasses he spoke.

'I can't think of anything to say Kang, nothing can bring your family back and I'm so sorry.' Kang didn't answer, his eyes wore the far away stare of a man who had seen too much and would never recover. Geoffrey refilled their glasses. 'All I can do is continue to give you a way to get some kind of revenge by intercepting their signals, finding their spies and ruining their plans. It will never be enough but it's better than nothing.' He would still need to check out as much of Kang's story as he could, but he had little doubt now that Li Kang was telling the truth.

Kang refocussed his gaze. 'I would do anything.'

'Good, then keep listening to Japanese radio traffic and decoding their messages. I know it doesn't sound very much but we could stop them repeating their atrocities if their plans are known about in advance.'

Kang nodded and fixed Geoffrey with a piercing stare. 'I know the importance of what we're doing and I am very honoured that you have asked me to help you.'

Geoffrey smiled. He would have like do leave it there, but he needed one last answer. 'I'm sorry to keep prying, but you said you hate the communists almost as much as the Japanese. Can I ask why?'

Kang stared at him. 'It was because of them I was away from my family for such a long time. They stopped me, wanted to know what I was doing, wanted me to leave my family and fight with them. If they hadn't held me up I might have got back in time to save them.'

Chapter 15

45 College Road, Maidstone, Kent

'What do you mean he's gone?' Margaret pouted. 'Where's he gone?'

'Back to the war I think.' Jeanne smiled at her sister.

'Did he leave me any messages?'

Jeanne looked confused. 'No. I don't think so. Why were you expecting him to?'

Margaret shook her head. 'He might have stayed long enough to say goodbye.' She sighed. 'He was very dishy wasn't he?'

Jeanne smiled, she'd seen her sister's attempts to get Olaf to ask her out, none of which had worked. She tried to be tactful. 'Yes, but he was only here while he got ready to go back to the war.'

Margaret looked even more miserable. 'Yes, I suppose so.' She looked at Jeanne, shrugged and smiled. 'Oh well, plenty more fish in the sea!'

Jeanne looked completely confused and Margaret laughed. 'Don't worry, you'll understand when you get older.' She hurried out of the door and Jeanne sighed. It was very odd that he hadn't said goodbye but living through a war was odd. He probably just hadn't had time. Hopefully Margaret would see that as Jeanne didn't like seeing her sister unhappy.

****

'South Moor', Maidstone, Kent

Fred arrived home, let himself in and stared in astonishment at the two children who appeared in the kitchen door. Surely he hadn't been away that long, he could have sworn Jack and Lucy were only five and three, but the two children facing him looked considerably older.

'Fred, you're home.' Daisy Irene rushed past the children and flung her arms around him. 'I'm so pleased to see you. Come and meet the children.'

'I thought I already had.' Fred was becoming even more confused. 'Jack and Lucy isn't it?' He was rather proud of himself for remembering their names.

Daisy Irene burst out laughing. 'These aren't Jack and Lucy, goodness what do you think I've been feeding them on?' She hurried on before he could say anything. 'This is Mick and Sandie. Mick is ten and Sandie is eleven. They are staying here too.'

Fred was about to ask how many more children there were in the house when Jack and Lucy came flying out of the living room. 'Uncle Fred. You're home.' To his amazement Lucy ran up to him and put her arms around him while Jack held out his hand. Fred grinned, gave Lucy a hug and shook Jack's hand. 'Hello Lucy, Jack. I'm very pleased to see you too.' He was about to say more when he saw another face peering out from behind the living room door.

'This is Jane. She's six.' Daisy Irene took the small child by the hand and led her out into the now crowded hall. 'This is Uncle Fred, my husband, Jane.' She turned to Fred. 'Jane is an orphan, her parents were killed a few weeks ago. She travelled down with Mick and Sandie so I thought it was best she stayed with them.' She hesitated. 'You don't mind, do you?'

Fred grinned. 'Hello Jane. It's nice to meet you. Of course I don't mind although you'll have to forgive me if I don't remember all your names and get you mixed up. I'm getting old!' He winked and all the children laughed.

'You must be hungry, come into the kitchen and I'll do you something to eat. How long are you staying?'

Fred followed them all back into the kitchen and watched in amusement as Sandie helped his wife prepare some food.

'I'm surprised you managed to find room for them all.' He remarked later that evening when the children had all gone to bed and it was just him and Daisy Irene.

Daisy Irene laughed. 'It's a bit of a squeeze but they all get on so well and Sandie and Mick help with the younger ones. Its company for me too. You really don't mind, do you?'

'Of course not. I'm pleased to see you so happy' He put his arm around her, pulled her closer and kissed her gently. 'I've missed you.'

'I've missed you too.' Daisy Irene kissed him back.

Fred grinned. 'I'm surprised you have the time.'

She looked concerned and then realised he was joking and punched him gently on the arm. 'I would have been so lonely with you gone that it's nice to have them here.' She changed the subject. 'Did you know that Jack and Lucy had never been to a library?'

'Really? Fred looked shocked.

'I don't think education and fun was very high on the list of things they did in London. I suppose if you're very poor libraries aren't that important. Do you remember how their clothes were falling apart when they arrived?'

'I think you've done a very good job with them Love, they are like different children.' It was true. They had been very quiet, unlike now. They hadn't stopped chatting since he'd arrived home and to be hugged by Lucy had been very gratifying, and it was all thanks to his special wife.

'Do you think that will cause them a problem when they finally go back home?'

'I don't see why?' Fred looked more closely at her. 'More importantly, how will you manage when they go home?'

Daisy Irene shrugged. 'I'll be fine. I have no choice. I know they aren't my children Fred, so I'll just make the most of them while they're with me.' She snuggled into his arms and hoped it would be that easy. The children had filled a void she hadn't realised was there.

****

RAF West Malling, Kent

The intensity of the Battle of Britain was finally waning, there were still incursions by the enemy but nothing like the intensity they had experienced in the summer and early autumn. They still went up on regular patrols but often returned empty handed which suited Jimmy who was just grateful to survive every patrol.

It was now late September and the Squadron was returning from yet another abortive sortie over the Channel. Having failed to sight the enemy again Jimmy was feeling in a good mood and he decided it was time for some fun so, without really thinking it through, he suggested to the Squadron Leader that they *'beat up'* Maidstone. *Beating up* was common practice among pilots and involved flying as low as possible over an area to frighten the inhabitants. It wasn't meant as anything other than a joke, a way of releasing tension, but unfortunately it wasn't very often seen that way by those on the receiving end. Afterwards Jimmy wondered why the Squadron Leader had agreed but at the time the only thing in all their minds was to celebrate that they had all survived another day and sensible, rational thinking didn't really come into it.

The section approached the town at speed, then they dropped rapidly from thousands of feet to just a few hundred, opened their throttles and flew low over the chimneys and rooftops at 300mph.

Having finished their joke, the pilots flew back to West Malling where, to their horror, a reception committee awaited them.

'What the bloody hell did you think you were doing?' The CO was furious, his face puce with rage. 'My telephone hasn't stopped ringing.' Even as he yelled at them the telephone began ringing again.

'It was just a bit of fun sir…' Jimmy began.

'Maidstone was bombed this morning you fucking idiot!' The CO yelled, interrupting Jimmy's lame attempt at an apology. 'Do you really think they needed you to terrify them when you're supposed to be protecting them?'

Jimmy paled. The CO rarely swore. He must be absolutely fuming. 'I had no idea sir.'

'It makes no bloody difference Corbin whether you knew that or not. Even if they hadn't been bombed this morning you knew they had been bombed at other times. What the bloody hell possessed you to be so *fucking* stupid?'

Jimmy was now beginning to panic. He and the other pilots in his section could be court martialled for something that they had intended as a joke, something intended to let off a bit of steam after months of stress.

'I'm really sorry sir.' He swallowed nervously.

There was silence except the relentless ringing of the telephone.

'It won't happen again sir, ever.'

'We didn't intend any harm sir.'

The other pilots joined in and, after glaring at them for several more seconds, too angry to even speak, the CO turned away. The telephone stopped briefly and then started again, no doubt more furious towns folk wanting to vent their fury at him, and while he understood his men's need to let off steam, this time his sympathy was entirely with the citizens of Maidstone. The last thing he wanted was to court martial his men, incursions into their airspace might be waning but they still needed every pilot they had, especially the experienced ones. Unable to think of anything else to say he finally dismissed them before sitting down at his desk and reaching for some forms.

A few days later Jimmy was moved to Biggin Hill.

****

Chatham, Kent

John rushed out of the hut where he was teaching the latest recruits and began searching the sky for bombers, but there was no one there so why were there anti-aircraft guns firing? As the men poured out behind him John glanced around confused and then realised where the noise was coming from. He began laughing.

'Is it a raid sir?' The recruit looked barely eighteen and John could see the fear in his eyes. He shook his head and grinned. 'No, look over there.' He indicated *HMS Atherstone* which had been damaged in the English Channel by enemy bombing and towed into Chatham to have the damage repaired. 'They're having some new 4.5 inch high angle anti-aircraft guns installed fore and aft, looks like they were testing them out. Which wouldn't have been so bad if *HMS Arethusa* hadn't been close by and decided to test their new guns at the same time.' John's grin widened. Obviously, they hadn't bothered warning anyone first so no one in the vicinity had been expecting them to start firing and panic had ensued. The nearby buildings had been filled with workers who had streamed out of their workshops in fear only to find the gunners on both ships laughing.

John grinned, shook his head and turned around. 'Come on, let's get back to work.'

John headed back to the teaching hut followed by the men, most of whom also seemed to have found it quite funny. Personally, he agreed, a welcome break from the monotony, but he could understand why some of his colleagues were not so amused. Personally, he was just grateful that it was a false alarm.

****

45 College Road, Maidstone, Kent

'What the hell were you doing?' Colonel Sinclair shouted, his face red with anger. 'You have let a spy, a real German spy, sent over her to do God knows what, get away. We have no fucking idea where he is because thanks to you the trail has gone cold. He's gone north. That's all we know. What the hell were you thinking?'

'I needed to get Kristian away. He's my nephew. And he will provide you with intelligence, good information, I know he will.'

'That's not the bloody point! He could have done that without us losing the other one, the real spy.'

Frederick kept his eyes down and prayed he wasn't about to be arrested.

'I should have you arrested for treason.'

'Yes you should.' Frederick decided there was little point in arguing. He was guilty… he only wished there was some way he could keep Alice and Jeanne from finding out what he'd done. He was just wondering if he should mention Betty's letter or whether that would cause even more problems for his family when he realised the Colonel was speaking.

'But that won't really help will it?' The Colonel sighed. 'I know you've joined the Auxiliaries, it's a shame to waste that. We might still need you.'

Frederick was amazed the Colonel knew but then he realised that it wasn't so surprising. He looked thoughtful. 'You think the danger of invasion is over?'

'It would seem so, certainly until the spring. So other than your Home Guard duties that leaves you at a loose end doesn't it?'

Frederick gave a wry smile, relaxed slightly and nodded. If he was still useful he might be off the hook after all.

'Good then you can work for me. I want to know anyone from the area who has suddenly moved elsewhere.' He saw the change in Frederick's expression. 'What is it?'

'It's probably nothing but the boy that was with the murdered girl, Mathew Hart. He's gone to Wales. For a fresh start according to his father.'

'You don't sound convinced.'

Frederick took a breath and hoped he wasn't about to get himself into even more trouble. 'Kristian said that Mathew killed the girl. He caught him having sex with her afterwards…' He saw the confusion on the Colonel's face, '…after she was dead.' The confusion changed to disgust. Fredrick carried on. 'He threatened Kristian that he would tell the police he'd seen him kill her. That was why he was so scared. Kristian knew he wouldn't stand a chance…'

The Colonel sighed. That made a lot more sense. 'I'll ask the police to visit the parents, get an address. If he is something to do with the Nazi agent the police asking questions won't alert him. He'll think it is about the girl that was killed. Anything else?'

Frederick shook his head. 'No, that was as far as I had got. I didn't want to ask Bill, his father, too many questions in case I made him suspicious, but I don't think they know where he is. From the little I did get out of Bill, Mathew just left a note saying he was going to Wales and would be in touch with his address. They hadn't heard anything since.'

The Colonel thought for a moment. He would send Frederick to question the boy once they knew exactly where he was.

****

133 Bower Street, Maidstone, Kent
'Jimmy it's good to see you boy!' Walter greeted him with a hearty pat on the back, grabbed his arm and led him towards the kitchen. 'Got time for a cup of tea?' Jimmy was about to answer when Daisy Lizzie appeared and flung her arms around him.

'Hello Mum, Dad, thought I'd call in to let you know I'm being transferred again, to Biggin Hill this time.' He didn't get any further.

'You don't want to let the townsfolk see you in that uniform.' Lilly appeared at the kitchen door. She waved briefly. 'Sorry I can't stop. I'm on the way to work.'

'You still working at the Ministry of Labour?' Jimmy asked before he really registered what she'd said.

'Yes, that's right.' She stepped towards him, gave him a kiss on the cheek, a quick hug then moved back and glared at him. 'I know it's not your fault. You wouldn't be that stupid. But can you tell your idiot playboy friends not to dive bomb the town for a joke right after the flaming Nazis have just spent the morning bombing us. It really wasn't bloody funny, let me tell you.'

'Language girl...' Walter started to admonish her, but Lilly wasn't in the mood.

'No Dad. I'm sorry but *bloody* doesn't begin to cover how I feel and probably how everyone else feels too, including Mum. He and his rich fly-boy friends need to know that they terrified people for no reason at all. It wasn't a joke, we really weren't laughing and if his idiot mates had been here that morning, hiding in shelters while the bastard Nazis bombed us relentlessly, they would have known that.'

She ran out of steam and Jimmy prayed his guilt wasn't obvious. He could feel his face flushing and he was opening his mouth to apologise when Daisy Lizzie interrupted.

'You're right Lilly, but it wasn't Jimmy's fault. He's not responsible for everything the RAF do.'

'No, I know that…' Lilly sighed. 'Sorry Jimmy. I'm not blaming you but if you do find out who did it, can you thump them for me!' She raised her hand. 'Bye, be careful and I'll see you next time.' She blew him a quick kiss and was gone. There was an uncomfortable silence while Jimmy tried to decide if he should confess that not only had he taken part but that the whole thing had been his idea so if anyone was to blame it was him. But he couldn't bear to see the disgust and shame he knew he would see on their faces so he eventually decided not to say anything and just hope they never found out.

Chapter 16

RAF Biggin Hill

It was Thursday 14 November and Jimmy crawled out of bed an hour before dawn to be greeted by a cold, miserable day with a freezing damp mist lying low over the airfield. Jimmy had spent the previous evening in the White Hart pub although he had only drunk a couple of pints, knowing he was flying the next day. But he still had a slight headache from lack of sleep although he was sure the tea and toast in the Sergeant's Mess would clear that. He tried to ignore the pain in his head, thought about the evening and a smile crossed his face. He had spent most of the evening speaking to a rather beautiful WAAF girl, Madeline Cartwright. She was the main reason he hadn't drunk too much as he'd been enjoying her company.

Jimmy washed and dressed quickly then searched his pockets, eventually finding the piece of paper he was looking for, the one with her address on. It was wrapped around his champagne cork so that had to be a good sign didn't it? Feeling much better, even though his head was still pounding, he made his way to the Sergeant's Mess.

The dispersal huts were next to the airfield, located some distance from the mess so once they'd finished breakfast they all piled into an open topped truck to be transported across the aerodrome. The tea and toast hadn't helped, he was still feeling half asleep, his head pounding, and even the sight of a pretty WAAF at the wheel didn't make him feel any better. The ground was uneven, the rocky suspension made his head pound even more and was made worse by the cacophony of the Merlin engines warming up as the fitters tested them to make sure they were airworthy. Many of the ground crew had been up all night, rectifying faults and repairing tails that had been shot up.

Jimmy climbed wearily off the truck, checked the board in the hut and saw he was Red Section, Red 2. He wished his head would stop playing up but there was nothing he could do now so he collected his Mae West, picked up his parachute and helmet and trudged out towards his aeroplane. Once there he arranged the safety harness and parachute straps, plugged the helmet leads into the radio and oxygen, checked to make sure the oxygen was flowing properly and the gun sight was working with the spare bulb in place. After that he sloped back to the hut where the other men were already gathering.

This was the worst part as far as Jimmy was concerned, he hated the waiting and couldn't resist the opportunity to reiterate one of his pet moans.

'I really don't see why we have to stay here, sitting on our arses doing nothing all day. Why shouldn't we be allowed to go on leave?' Apart from anything else he would be able to see more of the delightful Madeline.

'For goodness sake Jimmy, don't you ever stop binding?' Bob asked, raising his eyes heavenward in exasperation.

Jimmy was about to reiterate his point and explain more when Durex interrupted.

'I think we should call him *Binder* from now on as he never stops moaning!' The other pilots laughed and that was it. Jimmy forgot his complaints and laughed with the others. He was delighted to have his own nickname, one that would remain with him for the rest of the war. He was still smiling about it when Sqn Ldr Athol Forbes joined them and said he'd had a good idea. Jimmy raised an eyebrow and exchanged glances with his colleagues. 'Is this dangerous?' He asked.

Athol grinned. 'No, as some of you know I am hoping to become a writer after the war so I thought it might be a good if you wrote down your experiences while they are still fresh from the heat of battle. I can edit them and arrange to get them published. What do you think?'

Jimmy relaxed. 'Sounds good to me skipper. You can count me in.' It would give him something else to think about and his previous life as a teacher made him the perfect candidate to write up his story.[2] A few others also volunteered and then the conversation moved on to formation flying, a topic Jimmy normally loved debating but before he could really get involved the telephone rang. There was instant silence.

'Squadron scramble. Dover. Angels two zero.'

Jimmy leapt to his feet, his headache forgotten as the adrenaline coursed through him, and joined the stampede to the aircraft. Within minutes the Squadron was airborne and on its way to Dover.

****

---

[2] The book was called *Ten Fighter Boys* and was published in 1942 by Collins. Edited by Wg Cdr Athol Forbes DFC and Sqn Ldr Hubert Allen DFC

45 College Road, Maidstone/London

Frederick picked up the receiver and dialled the number Colonel Sinclair had given him. When he'd heard the gossip in the pub he'd been shocked and his first thought was that it served the boy right, a fitting punishment, but then his instincts had kicked in and he wondered if there was more to it.

'Yes!' The Colonel sounded impatient.

'It's Captain Frederick Farmer sir.'

'What can I do for you Captain?'

'I thought you might like to know. Mathew Hart has been found… dead. In a house in Liverpool with another man. I think his name was Patrick O'Brien.'

Colonel Sinclair nearly dropped the telephone. 'Patrick O'Brien you said?'

'Yes sir. Do you know him?' Frederick was so surprised he forgot who he was talking to for a moment.

'Yes, he's an Irish terrorist, wanted for several acts of sabotage in the West Midlands.' The Colonel frowned. Why was Mathew Hart with him? 'How did they die?'

'They were shot apparently.' Frederick repeated what he'd heard. 'I thought you'd want to know as soon as possible.' He hesitated. 'Do you think this has anything to do with the German spy?'

'It may do or it might be something else completely.' The Colonel was making notes while he spoke. 'Thank you for letting me know. I'll make some enquires.'

'Will you let me know if we're no longer looking?'

The Colonel frowned. 'Of course we're still looking. O'Brien isn't the spy although he might well have had something to do with bringing them into the country. The same applies to Mathew Hart. Maybe they're both dead because they've outlived their usefulness and can identify the person we're looking for?'

Frederick nodded and then remembered the Colonel couldn't see him. 'Yes of course. That makes sense.' He frowned. If the Colonel was right then they had lost their local link to the agent so there probably wasn't anything else he could do. He was about to say that when the Colonel spoke. 'There's probably not much else you can do at the moment. We'll follow up with the parents of the dead boy but I doubt they'll know anything. Thanks Captain. I'll be in touch if we need anything else.' He put the telephone down leaving Frederick listening to the dialling tone but feeling more relaxed than he had since he'd found Kristian in the greenhouse. It sounded like he was finally off the hook.

Colonel Sinclair stared at his notes and sighed. He would send his men to Liverpool to find out what they could but he was reasonably sure it would be a waste of time. He would stake his reputation that the men had been killed because of what they knew so the trail would have gone cold. Unfortunately, unlike the majority of the other agents sent by the Germans, this one appeared to be a professional.

****

Dover, Kent

The information the squadron had received stated that a number of Ju87s had just bombed Dover and were on their way back to France, but it wasn't them Jimmy was worried about. It was the Me109s that would be protecting them and they still had no idea how many of them there were. Jimmy was now flying with twenty three other planes as another Squadron had joined them, but he was sure they would still be well outnumbered. It wouldn't be the first time but he had faith in his machine, convinced it was superior to the 109s so he tried not to think about the odds.

Instructions came over the R/T and No 66 Squadron took the lead, flying over the Channel before turning back toward Dover.

'Bandits at 3 o'clock. Looks like Ju87S. Look out for 109s covering them. About fifty of them.'

Jimmy didn't need the ongoing commentary. He could see for himself. The skies were full of them swarming straight for Dover, a large bomber formation carrying thousands of tons of bombs surrounded by scores of fighters. Jimmy maintained his course and eventually the invaders spotted them and the bombers scattered. The other squadron began picking them off one by one leaving Jimmy and 66 Squadron to take care of the fighters.

Ninety aircraft filled the skies over Dover. Engines roared and screamed as the Spitfires engaged the 109s or a bomber dived to escape. Machine guns burst across the sky and one of the bombers exploded in a huge ball of fire. Above him one of their fighter escorts coughed out a stream of black smoke before plunging headfirst into the sea.

Jimmy tried to concentrate. He chose his 109, the aeroplane was below and slightly in front of him. Jimmy dived down so he could come up behind it. The fighter pilot seemed unaware of his presence and Jimmy suddenly felt a thrill of excitement. It was the enemy's time to feel the fear he'd experienced knowing there was a fighter on his tail. Jimmy flicked the gun button open on his control column and pressed the button. A stream of bullets shot out from his wing but the 109 had spotted him seconds before he fired and dived out of the way. The tracer bullets missed him by a fraction and then he was gone.

The battle was over and Jimmy had survived yet again, but there was one more battle he had to win.

****

Alor Setar, Northern Malaya

Geoffrey Maund read the message Li Kang had decoded in growing disbelief and horror. Maybe he had misread it? He started again, but there was no mistake. According to their intelligence, on 11th November the Germans had captured top secret British Cabinet papers after their raider, *Atlantis,* had come across the Blue Funnel Line *Automedon.* Having refused to stop the Germans then fired on the steamship, killing the Captain and other crew members on the bridge. The Germans sent a boarding party onto *Automedon* where they discovered a weighted bag which should have been thrown overboard. They would have been delighted with their treasure trove as the papers, addressed to Air Chief Marshal Sir Robert Brooke-Popham, Commander in Chief Far East, explained how British forces were insufficient to withstand a Japanese attack in the Far East and that the Royal Navy was unable to send a fleet in their defence. As if that wasn't damning enough the box also contained the order of battle for the defence of Singapore and the roles designated to Australia and New Zealand if Japan should attack.

Geoffrey sat back for several minutes, shock etched on his face before he finally found the enthusiasm to continue reading. Thanks to British intelligence they had quickly discovered that the Japanese were already in possession of these documents. It appeared the Germans had given the bag to a crew of a recently captured

Norwegian tanker, *Ole Jacob* who had immediately ensured that the papers were sent to Japan. Given that Britain had recently withdrawn from its Chinese garrisons at Shanghai and Tientsin, using the men to strengthen the garrison in Singapore, it didn't take a genius to work out that the Japanese would soon realise Britain was in no position to defend the Far East. Instead of preventing an attack, this had made it considerably more likely.

Geoffrey cursed loudly. What the hell was the matter with these people? That bag should have been thrown overboard the minute they encountered the German raider, and, as for withdrawing from China… that was a major mistake, sending out all the wrong signals to the Japanese. They would have considered Britain, France, the Netherlands and America much too strong to attack, however much they needed access to oil, rubber and minerals but that would have all changed now. From what Geoffrey could see the probability of an attack on Singapore and various other British bases had gone from probably unlikely to almost inevitable.

He lit a cigarette and watched the smoke curl lazily up to the ceiling before being caught by the fan and dispersed. He had been posted to the Far East in 1938 and should have been on his way home after three years, but then everything had changed. War had broken out and instead of sending out soldiers and airmen to replace those already there, more men had been sent to strengthen the garrison and those already there had remained. Geoffrey had spent lots of time regretting that Ruth had not come with him, but now he was realising that it might have been the right decision after all. Singapore was considered to be an impregnable fortress so there were no plans to evacuate which meant that if the Japanese did attack and Ruth had been there, she would have been in considerable danger, probably more so than she was in England where it seemed that the possibility of a German invasion had receded, at least until the spring.

Geoffrey turned his attention back to the message, set fire to it with his cigarette and while it smouldered in the ashtray he tried to work out if there was anything he could do to reverse the damage.

****

Yelsted, Kent

'Dead?' Charlotte stared at her father in disbelief. 'How?' She had finished training and had come home for a few days while she waited for them to find her a job which would allow her to travel freely around the area and for more details of the dead drops she would be using. Her father had just taken a telephone call and she could see her own shock mirrored in his face.

Adrian shrugged. 'Apparently he was shot with some other man, an Irishman.'

Charlotte shook her head. 'It sounds very odd to me. First he disappears without telling anyone where he's going then he's shot?' She fought back tears. With Mathew gone she had lost the last link to what happened to her sister. Now there was only the German pilot and the authorities hadn't found him yet. It seemed unlikely he was still on the run, he had either escaped or... Charlotte sighed in frustration. She had no idea what else could have happened to him unless.. Of course... Why hadn't she thought of it before? Someone had to be helping him.

'Why do you think they haven't caught the pilot yet?'

Adrian stopped thinking about Rebecca, turned his attention to Charlotte and frowned. 'I don't know, it does seem ridiculous. He bailed out of his aeroplane, he had no false papers or spare clothes or anything yet he has not only managed to elude capture, no one has even reported seeing him. Other than the parachute and Mathew's testimony, the only possible evidence that he even existed was the clothes and food stolen from the farmhouse near Sittingbourne the day after the murder.' His eyes met hers. 'You think he must be having help don't you?'

'Yes, but who?' Charlotte sighed. 'Who is going to help a German pilot? Especially one who has just killed someone.'

Adrian thought for a moment. 'Maybe he's holding them hostage?'

Charlotte considered that for several seconds. 'You can only keep people hostage for so long Dad before someone notices things aren't right. It's been weeks. If he is getting help they must be doing it voluntarily.'

There was a long silence then Adrian spoke. 'Maybe he wasn't just a pilot. Perhaps he was some sort of German agent who deliberately bailed out and had accomplices in Kent somewhere, a fifth column?'

'It's the only thing that makes sense isn't it?' Charlotte said eventually. 'Should we tell the authorities?'

Adrian sighed. 'Tell them what? We don't have any evidence, just our suspicions.'

Charlotte shook her head. 'I'm not going to just leave this Dad. I'll tell Anthony, see what he says.' At the thought of telephoning Anthony Charlotte flushed and she felt a thrill course through her body which she quickly quashed, her excitement immediately replaced by guilt. What the hell was the matter with her? How could she even think about romance when her sister was barely cold in the ground?

Adrian watched her with concern. He'd seen the brief light in her eyes and he guessed she felt more than friendship for Anthony, but then it had disappeared and he'd seen the guilt. He wanted to say something, to tell her that life went on even if she didn't want it to. But he didn't know how to explain that she should carry on with her life without making things worse.

****

Maidstone, Kent

Jeanne could hardly believe she had survived her first term at MGGS. Because of illness Jeanne hadn't started school until she was six. But she had leapt from one term in Kindergarten to two terms in Transition and then straight into the First Form. She went through the second and third form within two years, then took a common entrance exam and was given a scholarship to MGGS. At the time pupils had to pay a fee to attend the school but scholarships were free if their father earned below a certain level. However, Frederick earned more so her parents were paying £5 per term.

It had been strange adjusting to the new school, but she had settled in well and despite the headmistress's reputation for being very strict Jeanne liked her. The only thing she wasn't sure about was learning German. It seemed a very odd thing to do when above them the Germans were trying to kill them. Some of the girls suggested it was because they believed it would be useful if the invasion came, but when Jeanne had asked her father if that was the reason, he had reassured her that it had nothing to do with the invasion and was just a normal part of the curriculum, although she had sensed he wasn't that sure.

She had soon grown used to spending up to seven hours a day in the shelters, or trenches as they called them, the staff the only ones to leave them as they made their way from one class to another. Sometimes the teachers were delayed by an alert so the pupils would begin the class themselves using the trench walls as blackboards.

They often ate their dinner in the shelter, although hurrying to the trenches with a plate of food wasn't aways easy. Jeanne was sure that the Germans deliberately came when they had peas which invariably rolled off the plate as they ran for safety. Most of the food was good and often the main meal of the day to help families cope with rationing so they were encouraged to eat everything. One of Jeanne's favourites was thick soup followed by steamed pudding, another favourite was semolina. She wasn't very keen on a pale green jelly which the girls had christened slaked lime and cabbage water, but she was hungry so she ate it although she drew the line at picking it up off the ground after the alert had gone and it had slithered off the plate. Her friends weren't so fussy and assured her that it tasted better covered with cement dust. If the alert went before lunch the kitchen staff brought their dinners to them in the trenches.

The girls usually brightened up their dinner hour by putting on impromptu pantomimes, variety shows and playing card games. If bombs were heard falling the teachers would yell 'Heads forward' and the girls would lean forward to get away from the walls in case the vibration split them causing them damage to their heads.

Jeanne grew used to seeing members of staff spending their lunch hour knitting and she realised when she thought about it that they never seemed ruffled by anything, even when their Maths teacher was nearly killed by a bomb in Mill Street. The story had quickly gone around the school that the warden had yelled at her to get down but she had her best coat on so just knelt in the street instead. Somehow she was unhurt even though several other people were killed.

The shortage of paper had been the hardest to get used to. They had rough notebooks which they had to use right to the end, including the margins and when they had finished the whole book they were often told to rub it out and start again or turn the book upside down and write between the lines. The paper was very poor quality, often incorporating old rags, and had flecks of grey in the pages and it wasn't the only thing in short supply; tennis balls, batteries, paints for art and material for needlework were also hard to come by. Jeanne enjoyed helping in the school allotment where they grew vegetables which were used in the kitchen. She had also quite enjoyed being sent to forage for stinging nettles down by the railway line too but that had been stopped after they had decided that the resultant soup was inedible. Their games lessons were often spent hoeing sugar beet in the nearby farms and they had been encouraged during the holidays to help harvest apples, cherries, beans and blackcurrants while the school field had been loaned to a local farmer so he could graze his sheep there. There were also regular collections of rose-hips which were made into a syrup for babies, paper and card for repulping, bones for making glue and food scraps which were fed to chickens and pigs, and thread for embroidery kits which were sent to POWs. Because of the shortage of hop pickers stacks of hop-bines were brought into the school and the girls used their science lessons to strip them.

Every morning they lined up for their milk and buns, Devonshire Split, Chelsea or Belgian were 1d each and the highlight of her day. They each received a third of a pint of milk in a small bottle which cost 2 ½ d a week.

But the first term was almost over, it was the Friday before Christmas and the traditional carol concert had been arranged. Jeanne sat with the rest of the school in the main hall and was enjoying the carols. For the pupils from the King's Warren Girls school in Plumstead who had been evacuated to the MGGS it was the second year they had enjoyed the service. So far there had not been any air raid sirens and Jeanne had almost forgotten there was a war on. The fourth year girls were in the middle of singing *In The Bleak Midwinter* when suddenly the air raid sirens sounded. 'Everyone to the shelters, no running.' The shout went out and Jeanne sighed. Flipping Germans couldn't even let them listen to carols in peace. Like most of the girls Jeanne had become almost blasé about the air raids so she joined her friends sauntering their way to the trenches despite the frantic shouts for them to hurry.

Once they were all settled in the shelter the fourth year girls continued the concert, singing without any accompaniment and finishing with *The Holly and The Ivy*. Their voices echoed eerily around the dark damp shelter and Jeanne knew that as long as she lived she would never forget that carol service.

****

RAF Biggin Hill

The Squadron had successfully shot down twelve Ju87s with no casualties and Jimmy decided it was time to put his own battle plan into operation. Having spent an hour putting together a rota that would allow the pilots time away from the base without jeopardising operations he took his courage in both hands and presented it to the senior officers. 'You see sir, it doesn't make sense for those of us who live nearby to hang around the aerodrome when we are off duty. We may as well take the opportunity to go home and see our families and well... just have a break from it all.'

The officer read carefully through the rota and then, much to Jimmy's surprise, he nodded. 'Alright Sgt Corbin, we'll go along with your little plan, but one slip up and that'll be the end of it.'

Jimmy was over the moon. His grumbling might have earned him the nickname of 'Binder' but he was now the most popular man on the base! He hurried to the telephone and rang the number Madeline had given him.

'Hello Madeline? Its Jimmy, Jimmy Corbin... we met last night. I was wondering when you next have a night off. I thought we could meet up.'

'Hello Jimmy. I'm off in a couple of days. I could meet you in the King's Head? About 7.30?'

'Great. See you in two days then.' Jimmy replaced the receiver and did a little jig of excitement before looking around to make sure no one was looking.

Madeline replaced the receiver and smiled. She hadn't expected him to contact her quite so soon. He must like her. She went back to work, her thoughts on the handsome airman. Her smile faded slightly. It wouldn't do to get too attached, she would have to take it slowly or... She reached her desk and stared at the pile of paperwork awaiting her and shook her head. On the other hand she was entitled to some fun. Life wasn't all about work.

That day was the last time the Germans used the Ju87s in such numbers and the pilots later learned that it was that failed raid that had put the final nail in Hitler's plans for invading Britain. The following months were much quieter, Jimmy only did twelve hours flying and was able to spend more time getting to know Madeline. By the end of the year the only enemy missions to take place near them were a few reconnaissance trips which were picked up by the squadrons based near the coast. The Battle of Britain was finally over.

Part 2

1941

RSS Arkley View

Chapter 17

'South Moor', Maidstone, Kent

Daisy Irene had been feeling more nervous than usual that morning as London County Council members were coming to visit the area to see how the evacuees were adjusting to their new life. After conversations with several of the children, one of whom said that other than not seeing enough of her mother, everything was very good, they appeared to accept that in general the children were happy and well cared for.

'How did it go?' Fred had deliberately put aside his own concerns to ensure that he asked her when he arrived home. He knew how hard she had worked to ensure the children were billeted on the right people and were as comfortable as they could be under the circumstances.

'Alright I think… although some of them kept asking if an area that had to have shelters was the best place to evacuate children between the ages of 5 and 16?'

'Well, I suppose they have a point.' Fred looked thoughtful.

Daisy Irene gave a wry smile. 'I agree entirely but we didn't make that decision and that wasn't why they were here. One of them even commented that the children were in districts in the direct route of German planes. And yes, he's right but they were here to make sure we'd done our job properly, well as much as we could.'

'I'm sure you've done a perfect job, you always do. Look how happy our children are.'

Daisy Irene smiled. It meant a lot to her that Fred considered the children to be his responsibility too, especially when she knew he was so busy.

****

Liverpool

The man using the papers of Keith Burns was tall and well-built, in his late thirties with thinning hair. He had spent the morning watching the new Naval HQ where they arranged escorts for the convoys coming across the Atlantic before finally conceding defeat. He had learnt very little that he hadn't already found out by speaking to workers at the nearby docks on previous days and he was now considering his options. With Hart and O'Brien dead there was no longer a trail for anyone to follow so, in his opinion, he had done everything he possibly could in Liverpool. It was time to move onto the next phase of the operation which meant using the information he did have, following the instructions that had been originally agreed, moving elsewhere and doing what he had been ordered to do. He had considered checking with his superior first but had then decided that any unnecessary communication could lead to a failure on his part to successfully complete his mission and he couldn't risk that.

He was sure that by now the authorities would be monitoring all radio, signal and telephone signals coming out of Liverpool so his plan was to make contact with his control later that evening, once he'd moved out of the area. That way he wouldn't draw attention to himself because they were less likely to be expecting any communication from his new location. He was determined not to provide them with any clues. Yes, he'd been out of the game for a while, but he was back now and enjoying every minute.

Keith finished his cigarette, threw the butt on the pavement where he ground it out with one of his worn leather shoes. He glanced around but no one appeared to be watching him so he walked slowly into the city, his brain working overtime. Perhaps it was time to change his papers, become someone new and disappear into the background so he could do his job more efficiently? He was reasonably sure that it wasn't completely necessary yet as he was certain no one had really noticed him, but it wouldn't hurt to be one step ahead. This job was much too important to make elementary mistakes and anyway he was a professional, he had a reputation to maintain. A wry smile crossed his face to be followed almost immediately by a frown. Perhaps that should be a reputation to regain after the last mission had gone so badly wrong.

Keith shook his head. There was no point thinking about the past. It was gone and this was his chance to redeem himself. He finally made his decision. He would keep his current identity until he'd left Liverpool behind then he would burn those papers. That way his new persona would appear at the same time he arrived at his new location. If anyone had noticed him in Liverpool it would no longer matter because Keith Burns would soon vanish into thin air, his place taken by the unknown Stanley Cruickshank.

Keith allowed himself a small smile and relaxed. It was so good to be playing the game again. There had been times he thought he would never be useful again, but then this opportunity had come along and he had grasped it with both hands. He had no intention of failing the man who had shown such faith in him.

****

RAF Biggin Hill

On 10th January the RAF had carried out its first daylight bombing raid over France with a fighter escort. Jimmy had taken off with three other squadrons and headed up to 15,000 feet while three other squadrons supported the Blenheim bombers as they bombed Calais. Anti-aircraft fire had been intense, his Spitfire rocking and shuddering as shells exploded all around and white puffs of smoke appeared, forming a wall of cloud. It was Jimmy's first experience of ack ack fire and although they were five miles up it felt uncomfortably close.

'But you're alright? You're not injured at all?' Madeline sounded so worried Jimmy felt mean for mentioning it.

''Course I am. Take a bit more than a bit of ack ack to get me.' He leaned across the pub table and kissed her gently.

Madeline responded with passion until eventually Jimmy pulled back. 'Probably better get another drink in then unless…' He waited expectantly.

Madeline smiled. 'Is that the best you can do? *I was almost killed so perhaps you should come to bed with me?*'

Jimmy flushed and looked horrified. 'I didn't mean it like that…' He saw her laughing and stopped. 'You're teasing me.'

'You are so easy to tease, and I love seeing you blush.' Madeline leaned across the table and kissed him again. Jimmy forgot about being embarrassed, forgot everything except the taste of her lips on his and the rising surge of excitement coursing through his body.

'My roommate is out tonight. We could go back there if you like.' Madeline whispered.

Jimmy nearly knocked his empty glass off the table. 'Are you sure? I mean I don't want you do to anything you don't want to.' Jimmy stopped. What on earth was the matter with him? If he carried on like this she'd think he wasn't interested which was about as far from the truth as he could possibly get. 'I'd love to…'

'Come on then. What time do you have to be back?'

'It doesn't matter, as long as I'm alright to fly tomorrow.'

'I promise not to wear you out too much.' Madeline was already standing up and heading towards the door. Jimmy grinned, cleared his throat and followed. Now all he had to do was to keep himself under control until they reached her room.

****

London

Charlotte opened the back door for Anthony before climbing into the front seat and driving off. With the danger of invasion receding her role in the Auxiliaries had changed. She had been allocated to Anthony as a driver which she was happy about as she liked his company, but it was extremely boring and not what she'd been hoping for. She spent her nights in the underground praying for the all-clear and her days driving through the devastated streets.

Although the last thing she wanted was for the Nazis to invade she had been hoping that her role would be more exciting than just driving Anthony around London, even if it did involve avoiding collapsed buildings, giant bomb craters, fractured sewers and broken gas pipes.

The worst night had been 29th December. After a peaceful Christmas Day and Boxing Day the Luftwaffe had returned with a vengeance, their target the City of London. Over three hundred incendiaries had dropped around St Paul's in a minute, the night deliberately chosen because the tide was out leaving the River Thames so low that firemen were unable to cross the mud to attach their hoses to pumps. The idea had been to set London on fire. But despite numerous burning wooden structures blocking the narrow streets and firemen being unable to get access to buildings because they were locked, the city somehow survived as did St Pauls, rising out of the fires like a giant symbol of defiance. Charlotte knew she would never forget the sound of the firestorm as it spread through the streets, the frantic jangling of fire engines and the sight of bodies lying in the streets the next day.

'Are you alright Charlotte? You're very quiet?'

'Sorry, seeing St Paul's just reminded me of 29th December.' She sighed and changed the subject. 'I am enjoying driving you around but I want to do more Anthony. I'm sure there is something else I could be doing to fight back, to get revenge for Becca, especially as they still haven't found the bastard.'

Anthony didn't answer for a moment. 'I have something in mind but it will be very dangerous.' *That's why I hadn't said anything.* He could see her excited reflection in the driving mirror and gave a wry smile. 'Alright, leave it with me. I'll sort something out I promise.' He had heard about a new organisation being set up. The address was in Baker Street so he would go there after this meeting.

'You mean it?' Charlotte's eyes met his in the driving mirror. 'No one is taking any notice of us, my father and me. We have to be right. That so called pilot must have had help to get out of the country, unless he's still here of course. Surely that's important enough for them to at least investigate? Instead they just keep fobbing us off.' She clenched the wheel in frustration. 'I have to do something to get revenge for Rebecca. You do understand don't you?'

'Yes, I do.' Anthony sighed. 'I take it there's no more news then? They haven't found him yet?'

'No, it's completely ridiculous. It's like he just vanished into thin air. I don't see how he can have escaped. Someone must have helped him.' Charlotte suddenly realised that her anger and frustration had caused her to speed up and she put her foot on the brakes, slowing the car abruptly and throwing Anthony around in the back seat. He grinned. 'If you keep driving like that I'll be glad to see the back of you!'

Charlotte gave a brief laugh before her expression became solemn. 'Sorry, its thinking about Becca. It's so unfair and to think that bastard has got away with it.' She realised she was gripping the steering wheel tightly again and she forced herself to relax.

'You could be wrong you know Charlotte. They could be investigating behind the scenes, and its top secret which is why they aren't telling you anything. If you think about it, if there is a spy loose they won't want the public to know or to warn him so he escapes. That could be why they are keeping it quiet.'

Charlotte thought for a moment, then nodded. 'Yes, I suppose you could be right, but that doesn't help me, does it?'

Anthony gave a sympathetic smile. 'I do understand Charlotte but there's nothing I can do about that, any more than you can. But on the other little matter of being bored, I *will* do something I promise.' He glanced out of the window; they had reached their destination. 'I shouldn't be long.' He would speak to the man he'd come to see and then make some enquiries for Charlotte. He hated the thought of losing her, but he knew it wasn't fair to stop her using her abilities. She was wasted driving him around, that was something anyone could do. But more importantly, if she wasn't occupied there was a chance she would get herself into trouble trying to investigate her sister's death herself.

He climbed out leaving Charlotte staring moodily out of the window. It was alright for Anthony; it wasn't his sister who'd been murdered. She finally made her decision. She would give Anthony a week to find her something more interesting and useful to do or she would start using her time to find out what had really happened to Rebecca and why the authorities appeared to be covering it up.

****

RAF Biggin Hill

The next few weeks passed quickly, flying was at a minimum but Jimmy didn't mind as he was spending all his free time with Madeline. He lay on his bed thinking about her. She was the perfect girlfriend, always interested in everything he was doing and about his life in general, and very loving. He was thinking about introducing her to his parents and then maybe he could meet her parents too... Jimmy frowned as he suddenly realised that he didn't know very much about her. She didn't talk much about herself at all. He knew she had been in the WAAF since the beginning of the war and worked in London but that was it. Her job was something secret or that's what she'd said anyway. Jimmy hadn't been sure if she was joking or if her work was just boring so she didn't want to talk about it and he hadn't got the chance to ask because she'd changed the subject. She had mentioned her mother a couple of times although he'd got the impression they weren't close, but not her father and he knew she came from Richmond in London but that was all. Madeline was well spoken so he guessed her parents were quite rich and he wondered if they would object to a working class boy from Maidstone dating their daughter. Perhaps he should ask her? Or not? Maybe it was better to just enjoy himself and not rock the boat.

A couple of weeks later, on 21st February, they were ordered up on another offensive patrol, their route to Dungeness, along the south coast of England, then Cherbourg, Calais and back home. Jimmy took off and was ordered up to 30,000 feet where he was soon moaning that it was bloody freezing. They quickly formed into pairs flying in one large loose Vic formation. Jimmy's partner that day was Pickles who was known for his phenomenal eyesight. If there was anything to be seen, Pickles invariably saw it so Jimmy was feeling quite confident. The flight had been fairly uneventful and they were just off the coast of Calais when Jimmy's aircraft suddenly experienced a terrific jolt. The whole plane wobbled precariously and a pungent smell filled the cockpit. Jimmy looked in his cockpit and to his horror he could see ominous black smoke belching from his exhaust.

Jimmy swallowed nervously, the smell was cordite, a combination of the nitro glycerine and petroleum jelly that was used in ammunition. Jimmy's best guess was that a shell from an anti-aircraft battery had exploded much too close. He gazed down at the swirling waters of the Channel, five miles below and knew he couldn't land there, he had no intention of bailing out either so that left him one option. Somehow, he had to get home.

****

Liverpool

Frederick sat in the local pub and realised he would have to admit defeat. The trail had gone cold. His relief at being off the hook had been short lived. It wasn't long before the Colonel had contacted him and asked him to go to Liverpool to investigate further. Frederick allowed himself a small wry smile. Ask was probably the wrong word, he hadn't been given much of a choice, not that he'd wanted to refuse. He felt responsible for this problem and he did want to find the spy. The Colonel had provided him with forged papers to say he was a policeman which had helped considerably, persuading people to speak to him who might otherwise have been reluctant.

He had visited the lady who had rented out the farm first, but she was adamant that she hadn't seen anyone, other than the two men who had been shot on her property. Mathew and Patrick appeared to have kept their heads down once they moved in, only venturing out to get shopping and avoiding the local pub which seemed suspicious to him. What else had they been doing? Given their proximity to the docks and the Naval HQ in charge of escorting Atlantic Convoys he could only surmise that they had been spying for their German masters. Frederick felt sick. How many convoys had been attacked because of his actions? He had only been trying to protect Kristian but that wasn't an excuse. On the other hand nothing really made sense. He thought back over the lack of information and shook his head. They couldn't have been sourcing information without leaving the cottage, but all the witnesses he'd spoken to had said that the two men had barely been seen which meant the spy must have been the one who had been out gathering information. Obviously the spy hadn't been seen with the two men at all so he would have to try a different tack.

He finished his pint and headed for the door. He would start with the Liver Building and see if anyone suspicious had been seen in the vicinity. It was a long shot but it was better than sitting in the pub drowning his sorrows and feeling guilty.

****

London

Charlotte reached the building in the side street, headed up the narrow stairs and entered the door facing her as she'd been told. The room had a small table, two chairs, another door at the far end and nothing else. She glanced around, listening carefully but she couldn't hear anything so eventually she sat down and wondered if it was alright to light a cigarette. She was still thinking about it when the door at the far end opened and a tall thin man with a wispy beard and dark brown eyes walked in.

'Hello Charlotte. No don't get up. It's very nice to meet you.' He sat down. 'Do you know why you're here?'

Charlotte eyed him cautiously and chose her words carefully. 'Major Hallett said you might have some work for me.'

The man smiled. 'Yes, you could say that. I understand you speak fluent French.'

'Yes I do.' Charlotte realised he had switched to French and she had answered automatically in the same language.

He smiled. 'Good then we'll carry on talking in French if that's alright with you?'

Charlotte nodded and waited for him to explain. She was starting to feel disappointed, presumably they were looking for interpreters, hardly very exciting... She stood up. 'If you're looking for interpreters...' She began.

His smile broadened. 'What makes you think that?'

Charlotte flushed. 'Sorry... I...' She fell silent realising she was in danger of making a fool of herself, if she hadn't already. She sat down again.

'You've signed the Official Secrets Act haven't you?' He changed the subject.

Charlotte sighed. 'Yes, last year.'

'Good, well everything you agreed to then still applies. Understood?' Unlike most of the applicants he interviewed Charlotte had already been subject to a considerably deeper security check when she had been chosen to work with the Auxiliaries. For his part this was a mere formality unless she had suddenly changed her mind about doing something exciting and dangerous.

Charlotte felt the first stirrings of excitement, forgot about leaving the room and nodded again.

He sat back and looked straight into her eyes. 'We are looking for people to work for us... in France.'

Charlotte looked confused. 'France... but it's occupied... or do you mean Vichy France? Not that there's much difference...' She tailed off.

'Both, but mainly the occupied part. Your mother was French wasn't she?'

Charlotte nodded again. 'Yes. Josephine came from Paris, met my father during the war… the last one.' She fell silent. 'What kind of work?' She was reasonably sure what he meant but she wanted him to spell it out.

'The kind of information you were being trained to find out when you volunteered to work with the Auxiliaries, only this time you will be in France.'

Charlotte didn't answer for several seconds then she smiled. It was the perfect way to get revenge on Rebecca's killer. 'When do I start?'

The man laughed. 'I'm pleased you are so enthusiastic. Major Hallett said you would be. But what I am asking you to do is extremely dangerous. Your life expectancy will probably be in the region of weeks. Even less than it would have been if the Germans had invaded and you'd carried on working for the Auxiliaries.' He could see she wanted to interrupt so he raised a hand and carried on quickly. 'I would like you to go away and think about it carefully. Spend at least two days considering this. If you accept you will not be able to tell your family what you are doing… ever. It will always be a secret. Telephone this number in two days and let me know your answer.' He handed her a small piece of paper with a telephone number on. Charlotte memorised it then handed it back.

He raised an eyebrow. 'You've decided it's not for you?'

Charlotte gave a wry smile. 'I have a photographic memory. I can give you my answer now…' She didn't get any further as he stood up and shook his head.

'Take the time you've been given. It isn't something to agree to lightly, not just for you but also for your father. He's already lost one daughter.'

'All the more reason to do something to get revenge then.' Charlotte snapped before flushing. If this was some kind of test to make sure she could control her temper she'd probably failed. 'I'm sorry but if my father didn't want me to do something to help my country he would have never recommended me. I've already had this conversation with him. The world is a dangerous place. My sister was doing nothing more perilous than walking in the woods with her boyfriend. I can't let fear rule me.'

The man smiled. 'I agree. I just wanted to make sure you were completely aware of the risks. Thank you for your time and I'll leave you to see yourself out. Two days, don't forget!' He spun around and disappeared back through the door he'd entered a few moments earlier. Charlotte remained seated for a couple of minutes then stood up, walked out of the room and back down the stairs. The hardest bit would be waiting two days before ringing the number he'd given her.

****

Royal Liver Building, Pier Head, Liverpool
'There was one thing...' The Naval Control Service Officer (NSCO) Frederick had been talking to looked thoughtful.
'Yes?' Frederick tried not to get too excited.
'There was a man hanging around here, the back end of last year. Tall, middle aged, thinning hair.' He frowned. 'Said he was looking for a friend of his who was supposed to be working here.' He shrugged. 'Careless talk and all that, so no one told him anything. Figured if his mate had wanted him to know he was here he'd have told him how to contact him right?'
'Did he have a name?' Fredrick felt the hairs on the back of his neck begin to stand up.
'Now you're asking...' The man thought for a long moment then, 'Keith, Keith Burns I think.' He gave a wry smile. 'I only remember it because he seemed reluctant to tell me. Made me suspicious.'
Frederick made a note of it.
'Was he up to something?' The NSCO looked concerned.
Frederick shrugged. 'I don't know to be honest, but all information is useful.' He was about to say goodbye when some instinct made him ask another question. 'Why do you ask?'
The NSCO looked even more troubled. 'I gave instructions that no one should tell him anything but one of my men had already spoken to him. I don't think he told him very much, just confirmed that Western Approaches Command had moved to Derby House at Exchange Flags... the Exchange Buildings.' He fell silent not knowing if he should tell the policeman about the secret underground bunker that had been constructed in Rumford Street.
Frederick had seen his expression and knew there was more. 'Anything else?'

The NSCO swallowed nervously. 'I think he might have told him that it was a combined Naval and RAF Headquarters intended to protect the Atlantic convoys.' He looked even more uncomfortable. 'This Keith bloke also managed to wheedle some information about the actual building, that it was roughly 55,000 square feet with walls and ceilings constructed out of thick, reinforced concrete and that there was almost a thousand people working there, 80% of them women.'

Frederick stared at him in disbelief. 'What the hell did he tell him that for?'

The man flushed. 'He's a bit of a drinker is Jim, he doesn't know when to keep his bloody mouth shut. I gave him a right bollocking and docked his pay. I would have sacked him but we need everyone to pull together don't we? And he's a very good worker when he's not drinking…' He fell silent.

If it hadn't been for his own part in this disaster Frederick might have said more, as it was he was virtually speechless. Eventually he shook his head. 'Did you report it?'

The NSCO shook his head. 'I didn't want to get him into any more trouble…'

Frederick bit back the retort that was on the edge of his tongue, forced a smile and held out his hand. 'Well, thanks mate. If you think of anything else can you contact me on this number.' He wrote down his phone number and turned away. He would pass everything on to the Colonel and see what he could find out. Meanwhile he'd go to Derby House and see if anyone remembered seeing this man.

****

RAF Biggin Hill

The adrenaline was pumping so furiously through his body Jimmy could hardly think so he took several deep breaths to calm himself. Panic would kill him and he would never see Madeline again. Pilots were hit every day and still made it home, why not him? He scanned the instruments, oil pressure, altimeter, rev counter. Thank God… they were all functioning normally. The aircraft suddenly stopped jerking and appeared to level out, the dials and counters still looked normal. Jimmy swallowed and cleared his throat nervously. Was it going to suddenly explode?

He was still thinking about that when the CO ordered them to change direction and to increase speed so they could dodge any further ack-ack fire and then they were headed back to Biggin Hill. As the airfield finally came into view Jimmy breathed a sigh of relief which was immediately replaced by burst of elation as he landed safely and slowly taxied to a standstill. As he climbed shakily out of the cockpit he could see the aircrew running towards him. One of them nodded to the fuselage where there was a huge gaping hole.

'That one looked a bit close sir!'

'It certainly was.' Despite the horror he felt when he saw the damage and realised how close he had come to death, Jimmy somehow managed to sound calm and assured.

'Never mind, we'll have her right for you tomorrow.'

Jimmy made his way to the dispersal hut where Durex was already warming himself up by the fire with a mug of tea. 'You alright Jimmy?'

Jimmy nodded. 'Just about. The kite's a bit shot up. Anyone else run into bother?'

'Yes, apparently poor old Claude got hit the same as you. He had to land at Manston. Be back tomorrow though. Can't keep a good man down, can you?'

Betty had stepped outside for a quick cigarette and some fresh air during her break and was watching the aircraft returning home. She stared across the field at the damaged planes and shook her head. It was bad enough being bombed but it must be terrible being up there on your own and having the aeroplane shot up. When she was listening to the pilots they all sounded so calm, no sounds of panic or fear. She shivered and wondered how they really felt.

****

Derby House, Exchange Buildings, Liverpool

Frederick headed towards Derby House, his mind racing as he tried to work out the consequences of the information that had been given to the spy. The aim of Western Approaches Command was to ensure the safe and timely arrival of all the convoys and to protect them against the threats from German U-boats, aircraft and surface warships as well as the dreadful weather and sea conditions of the Atlantic. It had to be a treasure trove of information.

He arrived at the entrance and was about to give his police credentials when he changed his mind. He needed to talk to someone in charge and to do that he needed to be honest about who he was working for so instead he gave them the Colonel's name and telephone number. The guard took him into a room and indicated he sit down while he fetched a superior officer.

'Good afternoon Mr Farmer. I understand you wish to ask us some questions.' He held out his hand for Frederick to shake. 'I'm Admiral Peter Deschamps.'

Fredrick shook his hand, somehow managing to hide his surprise that he was talking to someone of such a high rank.

'What can we do for you?'

'We have a German spy on the run up here and we think that he may have tried to gain entrance to this building to garner intelligence.'

The Admiral paled. 'Does this man have a name?'

'We think it may be Keith Burns, but the description we have of him is of a tall, well built man of middle age with thinning hair.'

'It doesn't ring any bells Mr Farmer. I will ask my staff if anyone remembers him but I'm sure someone would have mentioned it. We're very security conscious here and most of our staff are women, WAAFs and Wrens, so men are inclined to stand out as we're in the minority. Even if he did get in I doubt he would have learnt much. Having been specifically recruited because of their mathematical and analytical abilities these women work as plotters in the main ops room, decode incoming signals and are radio and teleprinter operators. Some even train our naval officers in anti-submarine warfare. I doubt anyone of them would have been stupid enough to give any information away. Contrary to popular belief women seem to be much better than men at keeping secrets!' Having made his point, he continued.

'As for the building, we have a two storey Operations Room which is dominated by a large wall map which shows the positions of ships, aircrafts and U-boats across the vast expanse of the North Atlantic, but that is constantly changing so even if he were to have gained access, any intelligence would be almost immediately out of date, certainly before he could get that information back to Germany.'

Frederick felt a frisson of relief and nodded. 'I agree, in which case its more likely he just needed to know where you were based so the Luftwaffe could try and destroy the building.'

The Admiral smiled. 'They'd have a problem unless they had some massive bombs, our important rooms are located well underground and protected by thick concrete. It's unlikely the Luftwaffe would be able to cause anything but minor damage. I think you may have had a wasted journey.'

Frederick shook his head. 'No, you're aware of the problem now and I have a name which I didn't have.' He stood up and held out his hand. 'Thank you for your time Sir. Could I use one of your secure lines to speak to the Colonel before I leave?'

'Yes, of course.' The Admiral shook his hand and called the guard. 'Can you show this gentleman to one of the offices so he can use the telephone.'

Frederick followed him, his thoughts on what he'd learnt. It wasn't much but he had a name and a description and also what information the man was looking for.

****

RAF Biggin Hill

'I can't believe you were nearly killed.' Madeline sounded so scared Jimmy instinctively wrapped his arms around her and hugged her tight.

'I'm fine. I told you it would take a lot more than a bit of ack ack to finish me off.' He kissed her passionately then broke away and stared into her eyes. 'It was thinking of you that gave me the courage not to panic. I couldn't bear it if I never saw you again.' He grinned as he realised what he'd said. 'Of course, I wouldn't know about it if I was dead but, well you know what I mean.'

'I do and I'd never forgive you if you went and got yourself killed.' Madeline suddenly realised she meant it and she shivered. Falling in love had never been part of the plan.

Chapter 18

Arkley View, near Barnet

Fred had eventually mentioned his concerns to Colonel Sinclair and been reassured that they were aware that there was a German spy on the loose and if he did find anything else he should continue to report it direct to the Colonel. Fred was relieved, especially as his own instincts had been so sure that somewhere out there was another Nazi agent, one that hadn't been picked up. Knowing he was right about that made him feel much better. Now all he had to do was to try and find him. He was about to start going through the latest logs when he received orders to transfer to one of the other huts.

'You requested me sir?' He glanced around the new hut which was a replica of the one he had just left, apart from a slight extension at one end.

'You must be Fred Corben?' One of the men in civilian clothes looked up from a desk covered in a mess of files and paperwork.

Fred nodded. 'Yes sir.'

'Call me Tom, alright if I call you Fred? We're quite informal here.'

Fred nodded. 'Yes Tom, that's fine. Why have I been transferred?'

'It's very unlikely that the Krauts will invade now so we're expanding our little operation. We're going to start monitoring Abwehr radio traffic in Europe and beyond, searching for their agents and any other information. It won't be easy because their signals are very faint but we all like a challenge don't we?' He grinned. 'Let me explain our system. So far we've identified fourteen different groups and they might have more than one hundred services coming from them so we've numbered each main group and then each service. For instance Berlin is 2 and its one of the busiest so 2/153 would be Berlin and the service is linked to Madrid or Oslo or somewhere else. We then identify them by time, the number of messages and perhaps the call sign although that's not so easy because they often change their call signs.' He smiled again. 'With me so far?'

Fred nodded. This sounded far more interesting than his previous work which had dropped off considerably and now mainly consisted of checking that all the German agents who had been turned were sending what they were supposed to. The only intriguing part had been searching for the elusive spy and he could probably still do that here. 'Yes sir... Tom.'

'Good, your job is to identify new sources so you'll go through any intercepts we haven't already identified and work out where they are supposed to go, or whether we actually need them. You'll then send the information to the next hut where they'll work out what to do with it. It may be they already have that information, but if not they will classify them and let you know so you don't duplicate your effort.' He indicated a table at the far end. 'That's your desk. We've been getting some stuff ready for you as you can see!' Tom laughed and Fred realised why. The desk was piled high with logs, files and paperwork.

He grinned. 'Better get started then.' It looked like he wouldn't be home tonight, but he didn't mind. At first he'd worried about how Daisy Irene would manage if he kept having to stay out overnight, but now she had the five children to look after he knew she wouldn't miss him too much. Working through the night would also give him a chance to continue his search for the elusive agent, something he had been worrying about, but this job was perfect for that. He would see everything new, anything that was previously unidentified. The spy would eventually have to make contact with someone and then he would have something to go on. Perhaps the reason they hadn't transmitted anything to anyone in the UK was because they were receiving instructions from abroad and until they had information to send back there was no need to risk communicating. He would now be monitoring those messages too so it might be possible to find the spy that way. He sat down and reached for the first file.

****

Alor Setar, Northern Malaya

Geoffrey watched the arrival of the Australian Eighth Division, four RAAF (Royal Australian Air Force) Squadrons and eight warships and wondered how long it would be before the Japanese tried to attack Singapore. He would like to think someone had taken notice of his intelligence reports but he didn't think so and thanks to the loss of the top secret Cabinet papers the Japanese already knew the order of battle, would know exactly which elements of the Australian forces would be sent and plan accordingly.

When Geoffrey had first arrived in Malaya he'd been horrified by the situation he'd found. The Army and RAF were suspicious of each other, the Royal Navy held itself at arm's length and the civilian community treated the Armed Forces as only being there to disrupt their everyday lives and interrupt their economy. The intelligence staff he was working with were inexperienced and, although they were enthusiastic, they still had much to learn. Despite the war in Europe and his attempts to try and get the authorities to see that a Japanese attack was a very real possibility, nothing had really changed.

Geoffrey was still struggling to understand why British politicians had wasted so many years when they could have put proper defences in place. It wasn't as if the threat from the Japanese was new. Concerned about their growing power Britain had made the decision to build a naval base in Singapore in the 1920s, convinced that any attack would be naval. But over the succeeding years the politicians and military alike had realised that it would be impossible to leave a fleet of sufficient size in the Far East because they would be needed elsewhere. Even more important they had eventually accepted that a naval assault was unlikely and that any attack was more likely to come overland from the north. This meant they would need to defend the Malayan approaches and that would be impossible without a substantial air force. Geoffrey had attended several discussions by the military authorities based in Singapore and Malaya stating that they believed the best way for the Japanese to attack would be to use Indo-China as the base to land in South Thailand and North East Malaya before advancing south, but despite this nothing had really been done to strengthen their inland defences.

Although twenty seven airfields had eventually been constructed there had been no consultation between the RAF and the Army so many had been located in places that were impossible to defend by land. The number of aircraft available was also well below what was needed. Geoffrey had been there in 1940 when Commanders on the spot had ignored intelligence advice and decided that 582 aircraft would be enough, not just to defend Malaya but also Burma, Borneo and Hong Kong. However, the Chiefs of Staff in London were even more entrenched in unreality, ignoring the request and deciding that 336 would be sufficient. At Geoffrey's last count they were still waiting to reach anywhere near that number.

He was also concerned that despite his intelligence reports and those from other people about the quality of Japanese aeroplanes and the strength of their air force they had been consistently ignored. The Zero's performance was comparable to that of the Hurricane and far superior to that of the American Buffalo that the RAF were using in the Far East which was so dreadful it had been rejected for use in Europe. Geoffrey let out a long slow breath and tried to concentrate on watching the arrival of the inexperienced Commonwealth pilots. Getting angry was no use to anyone, he needed to find some way of waking them up in London before it was too late.

As he moved slightly to get a better view he felt the rustling of paper and smiled, for a moment his concerns forgotten as he thought about the letter he'd received from Ruth that morning.

My darling Geoffrey

I hate starting each letter the same way but I can't stop myself telling you how much I miss you. We seem to have survived the invasion scare although the continued bombing of London must surely be a war crime and I would love to see that fat oaf Göring hanging from a tree somewhere alongside that other megalomaniac Hitler.

Maidstone is ---------- the next part was blacked out and he guessed the censor wasn't too pleased about Ruth's description of Maidstone's defences.

Jeanne is growing into a lovely child, of all my nieces she is the nicest, she's always so pleased to see me. I don't see much of Betty -- ----- more blacked out lines *and Margaret is sulking because the young man who was staying there has gone and not written to her with his address. I think Frederick and Alice are relieved though although I don't know why as he was rather nice and very dishy, a Norwegian who had fled his country after the Nazis invaded.*

Geoffrey smiled again. It was nice to read normal news about her family although it would be much better if he could be there to see it with her. He sighed. Fat chance the way the war was going. His thoughts turned back to his own situation. He couldn't understand why they weren't quietly drawing up evacuation plans, at least for the civilians, but the top brass still seemed to think Singapore was impregnable despite the continuing dire intelligence warnings. He could only hope they were right and he was worrying about nothing.

****

Bavaria, Germany

Kristian had been granted a few days leave and he couldn't believe how wonderful it was to be back home again, to feel safe. Abteilung 5, the intelligence branch of the Luftwaffe, run by Joseph Schmid, a good friend of Herman Göring, had finally accepted he had escaped on his own and sent him back to his squadron where his commanding officer, Geschwaderkommodore Konrad Altmann, had agreed to him having some leave. Kristian had been relieved that it was only Abteilung 5 investigating him as they weren't particularly thorough. They were just pleased to have him back and to believe that one of their pilots had escaped from Britain on his own, something that was great for morale. Kristian had seen for himself the state of British air defences and number of viable British aircraft capable of flying so he guessed Schmid must have also been lying about British losses during the Battle of Britain as they didn't bear any resemblance to the true situation. The British seemed to have more aircraft now than they had over a year ago which wasn't what German propaganda was saying.

He had gone home to visit his wife and son first and for a brief moment he relived those moments, the love and delight in Ulrike's eyes as he'd walked into their family home. She'd been convinced he was dead until he'd been able to write to her when he arrived back in the country. He also couldn't believe how much Manfred had grown. He was walking now and starting to speak. It had almost broken Kristian's heart that his son had not even known him, had even cried when Ulrike had tried to put him in his father's arms, but after a little while he had relaxed and begun to accept Kristian. Unfortunately he had no idea how much longer it be before he was able to see his son again which meant Manfred would probably forget his father again.

'I bet Ulrike was pleased to see you.' Otto had read his thoughts and Kristian smiled.

'Yes, she thought I was dead, as I know you did. I wish I didn't have to keep leaving Manfred though. He didn't know who I was.'

'He's still only a baby Kristian, it will get easier as he gets older.'

'But I'm missing so much of his life and how much older is he going to get? This war could go on for bloody years, God forbid he'll have to fight it too.'

Otto sighed. 'I thought the same thing but then it finished and I thought that was it... I really hoped you wouldn't have to carry on where we left off.'

Kristian finished the glass of schnapps and watched his father do the same. 'Let's hope we're the last generation that has to fight it.' He sighed and his thoughts went back to his time in England. 'I really thought I'd had it over there. I can't quite believe I'm back here and safe, well reasonably safe anyway, if you don't count being shot at by enemy aircraft.'

Otto frowned. 'You did well to survive Kristian but you will have to be very careful.'

Kristian nodded. 'I know. I'm not being complacent. To be honest I thought it would take a lot more to convince Abteilung 5 that I had escaped on my own, without any help.'

'But you are sure they definitely believed you in the end?' Otto looked concerned.

Kristian shrugged. 'Yes, well they seemed to, but we are talking about Abteilung 5, so I have no idea. They could just be waiting for me to make a mistake, although I think that's probably unlikely. To be perfectly honest I'm more concerned that one of the other intelligence agencies may decide to start investigating.'

Otto sighed. 'Then you must do nothing to make them suspicious, nothing to encourage that to happen.'

'It's not that easy Vater. I can't just sit back and do nothing, I agreed to send information to British intelligence. If I don't do that reasonably quickly they will tell Abteilung 5 the truth and then I will be arrested.'

'The British won't expect you to do anything immediately. They will know that it's important for you to be accepted first or any information you send them is likely to be tainted.' Otto thought hard. 'How are you meant to communicate with them?'

'I've been given details of a dead drop.'

Otto nodded. 'That makes sense. I can't see them risking any of their agents making contact with you. Not until they are completely sure you are safe.'

Kristian hesitated. 'I need some help Vater.'

'What kind of help?'

'There's a spy who parachuted in the same day as I had to bail out. I need to find him. If I can send some information back about him it will get the British off my back while I settle in more.'

Otto frowned. 'It won't be easy Kristian, but I can try.'

'I'm sorry I didn't want to put this on to you, but I don't really have any access to anything.' Kristian looked embarrassed.

'I imagine your uncle knew that you would have to come to me if they were to get anything of any value so stop worrying. I can't say how long it will take though and I may not be successful. But if I can't find that I'll get something else you can send instead.'

Kristian sighed. 'Thank you. Just be careful. It's important but not worth your life.'

Ottos gave a wry smile. 'I think it's too late to worry about that, sohn.'

Kristian shook his head in frustration. 'How on earth did you manage to do this for so long? I'm already going mad with worry.'

Otto poured some more schnapps. 'When I started it wasn't that dangerous. The Nazis weren't very well organised so it was more like I was just having a chat about world affairs with my half-brother.' He eyed Kristian with concern. 'My advice, for what it's worth, is only to pass information that is critical. There's no point risking yourself and me for something that's not very important.'

Kristian shrugged. 'I'll probably leave that bit to you then as I'm not sure I would know the difference.'

Otto gave a wintery smile. 'Don't worry Kristian, I'll do my best not to get us both killed for nothing.'

****

Chatham Docks, Kent

After the bombing of 3rd December 1940 in which the Rigging House, Loco Shop and Factory were all hit with the loss of fifteen lives, the docks had remained on high alert but so far the Germans didn't seem that interested in attacking them again which was surprising considering the docks were still producing submarines and repairing damaged ships even if most of the ship building had moved north in an attempt to protect them from the bombing raids. The town of Rochester had not been so lucky though with several houses damaged in an incendiary bomb attack in January and the sea wall damaged on 21st February, but so far the docks had been able to continue their work on *HMS Umpire* without interruption.

Although John was grateful that the docks did not appear to be much of a target deep down he knew he would rather they bomb him than his wife and son. He had seen the devastation in London first hand on his way to the Admiralty to drop off some signals that he had picked up while sitting in his office one night. He had been going through some of the signals the recruits had picked up during the day when something caught his attention. As Telegraphists they were learning to pin point U-boat positions which meant the morse they normally picked up originated in the Atlantic or the Med or was a response to something from Germany, but these particular signals appeared to be coming from somewhere in the north of Britain and were being transmitted to somewhere in Germany. They had initially caught his eye because they were very short and had only been used twice. Since then that particular transmitter had gone quiet. He had double checked the traffic for the previous days but there was nothing else. It was possible the U-boat had been sunk but his instincts told him the signal didn't come from a submarine at all. The signal pattern was all wrong. John was sure there were other people around the country listening to radio traffic but he was equally certain that for some reason this was too important to ignore on the off chance that someone else had picked it up.

****

Glasgow, Scotland
Having telephoned the number and told the voice on the other end that she accepted their offer, Charlotte had been told to wait for further instructions. The next few weeks had passed very slowly and she had heard nothing. She'd tried the telephone number again but it was dead and in frustration Charlotte had been on the verge of asking Anthony to chase it up when she'd suddenly received a telephone call telling her to pack, make her way to Euston station immediately and take the train to Arisaig, a small village on the Invernesshire coast. She was not to tell anyone she was going or make any contact with her family.

After a long journey interrupted several times by bombing raids, which she had mainly endured in the dark, Charlotte arrived at Glasgow station which was teeming with people, almost as busy as London, the only difference being the strong Scots accents all around her. Charlotte glanced up at the large station clock and sighed. She had nearly an hour before her next train, she would find the canteen and have some tea and a bun. According to her instructions she would be met at Inverness Station and driven to her destination where there would be a meal waiting for her on her arrival, but that was ages away and she was starving. Charlotte found the canteen and ordered a pot of tea and a rather stale currant bun. The canteen was full of soldiers and sailors and she was one of the few civilians.

'Do you want to sit with us love?' The soldier indicated a spare seat at the rather crowded table and she smiled.

'Thanks, I was beginning to think I would have to stand.'

'No-one as pretty as you should ever have to stand...' He started before being interrupted by groans from the rest of the men around the table. He grinned. 'Sorry, best I could come up with. I wasn't expecting female company. I'm Richard by the way. Richard Coleman.'

'Charlotte Mason.' She sat down and sipped her tea. It was strong and hot, exactly how she liked it and she began to relax.

'So where are you going, Charlotte?'

'I'm visiting my uncle in Inverness. He's not been well so I'm going to look after him for a while.' The cover story had been given to her in London in case anyone asked. 'What about you lads or shouldn't I ask?'

'We're going south... can't tell you any more than that.'

Charlotte nodded and bit into her bun. As she'd suspected it wasn't very fresh but she was too hungry to worry about that. She was about to ask where Richard came from when the soldiers suddenly stood up. 'Time's up I'm afraid, we've got a train to catch. Nice to meet you.'

She watched as they made their way to the door and wondered briefly where they were going before turning her attention back to her own situation. Another half an hour and she would be on the last leg of her journey and getting ready to start her new life.

****

Arkley View, near Barnet

Fred finally found what he was looking for when he was given two messages that someone in the Royal Navy had picked up and reported. He quickly checked back in the logs and compared them with the original signals sent the previous year and knew at once that he was correct. This was the German spy operating within the UK, the one they hadn't found. Fred stared at the telephone, marshalling his thoughts, before reaching out and picking up the receiver.

'Colonel Sinclair please. Its Fred Corben, SCU 4.'

There was a brief hesitation and then the Colonel came on the line. 'Yes Corben?'

'I've found something I think you should see.'

'You can't tell me over the telephone?'

'I'd rather not sir.' Having spent so long intercepting radio signals Fred was extremely wary of saying anything important over the telephone. He heard the Colonel sigh and then 'Alright, I'll be there in a few moments.' The telephone went dead and Fred stared at it for a few seconds before shrugging and replacing it. The Colonel could hardly blame him for being cautious, he was doing what they were paying him for and it looked like he might have found the missing agent, or at least two messages from him. Not something he wanted to risk saying on the telephone.

****

RAF Exeter,

Jimmy was sad to leave Biggin Hill. He had grown used to the chaos, even if he had sometimes longed for some respite. It was also close to London so they could pile into the squadron jalopy and head for the West End pubs and clubs where people were still intent on enjoying themselves, determined not to let the enemy get the better of them, he doubted Exeter would provide the same level of entertainment. Even worse it would mean leaving Madeline behind. Yes, he could write to her but it wasn't the same. He was also sad to leave behind his beloved Spitfire Mk II, an improvement on the Mk I because it had armour plating and bullet proof windscreens thanks to Hugh Dowding, head of Fighter Command, who had allegedly stated that if bullet proofing was good enough for Chicago gangsters it was good enough for his pilots. As far as Jimmy was concerned going to the English Riviera was a step back in that they would now be flying Mk I's again. The only good thing was that Durex, Bogle, Pickles and Claude were also with him.

On their arrival the CO, Athol Forbes briefed them. 'Convoys are now our stock in trade boys.'

A groan went up and he continued. 'I know it's not the most thrilling of flying, especially after the bump, nevertheless it's essential work. These merchant boys have survived U-boats lurking in the Atlantic to make sure you get fed, the least we can do is to afford them a little protection as they continue their journey through the English Channel to London. Our role is to escort them for a set distance along the south coast until another squadron further along picks them up and relieves us of that duty. All straightforward stuff but Jerry are always looking to pick these ships off, so don't get complacent.'

There were murmurs of agreement before the CO continued. 'In addition to the convoy, we are going to be carrying out milk trains.'

Jimmy exchanged a frown with another pilot, Bobby Oxpring and whispered. 'I've a suspicion that's not going to be as pleasant as it sounds.'

'No doubt you know what a milk train is?' He waited and when no one answered he carried on. 'Right, I'll explain then. When we get the call, we take off at dawn when its semi-dark with orders to fly due west…' Forbes began.

'But that's the Atlantic?' Someone called out.

'Well done, top marks for geography!' There was some muffled laughter and the pilot blushed. 'Yes it is and you will be flying over it to see if you can hunt down any German reconnaissance planes.'

'What are German reconnaissance planes doing over the Atlantic.' Claud asked.

'Trying to spot the convoys so they can relay their positions to the U-boats who will then mount an attack before they can reach the English coast.'

'So how far are we expected to fly to find them?' Pickles asked.

'You could probably cover up to one hundred and fifty miles offshore before having to turn back. Any more questions?'

'Sir, there are rumours going around that we might do raids on France?' This was Durex.

'I've had nothing official yet, but we'll see. Right, good luck everyone.' The briefing was over.

Bogle turned to Jimmy, a grimace on his face. 'I don't like the sound of the milk trains.'

Jimmy nodded. 'Me neither.' The thought was already sending shudders down his spine and Jimmy made the decision that if he was hit he would go down with the plane, it had to be quicker than bailing out and succumbing to the freezing waters of the Atlantic and dying of hyperthermia or drowning. Either way his body would never be recovered.

****

Arkley View, near Barnet
'All it says is 'First phase finished, second phase underway.'
'And the second one?'
'No contact until two complete.'
Colonel Sinclair had listened to Fred with concern, waited until he'd finished and then sighed. 'Well done. It looks like this is the missing agent. Do you have any idea where he is operating from?'
'No sir, the signals appear to have originated from the north of the country, maybe even Scotland although I don't think it's from the islands, probably still the mainland. The operator wasn't on there long enough for the men to get a proper fix. It would seem these signals were picked up by a trainee and it was only thanks to their supervisor that we even know about them. He was checking the radio traffic when something struck him as strange about these messages. His men were supposed to be pinpointing U-boats and this didn't fit the pattern.'
Fred's mind was racing as he wondered if he'd missed anything else.
The Colonel thought for several seconds. 'Do you think it's possible we've missed any more of his transmissions?'
'I don't know sir.' Fred thought rapidly. 'It's possible, especially if they are really short. I could go back over all the radio traffic that I received before transferring to SCU 4.' Fred hesitated. 'It will take a while.'
'That's fine. You concentrate on that while I find someone else to take your place here.' Colonel Sinclair turned and left Fred wondering where on earth to start. There were thousands of messages, trying to pinpoint this one particular agent would be hard work. But the war could depend on it so the sooner he started the better.

Chapter 19

Arisaig, Scotland

Charlotte watched her new colleagues helping themselves to the free alcohol and wondered if this was yet another test. Whether it was or not she had every intention of keeping a clear head for the morning's exercises. They had spent much of the day in the classroom but tomorrow they would continue their physical training and the last thing she needed was a hangover.

'I think some of them might regret their over indulgence tomorrow don't you?' Clarisse was medium height with dark blonde curly hair, sparkling blue eyes and a sense of humour. Charlotte had been relieved to find someone else who was able to hold a conversation and make her laugh as many of the others were very uncommunicative. She knew they were not supposed to say too much about themselves but she would go mad if there was no conversation at all.

Charlotte grinned. 'My thoughts exactly Clarisse. I think I'll turn in.'

'I think I'll do the same?' Clarisse yawned. 'It's been an extremely long day.'

Charlotte nodded. 'Fun though.' They had spent their first day being introduced to the other people on the course. At least they had been given their colleagues' code names. Real names had been left at the door, along with any personal possessions and they had been instructed to speak in French all the time. Charlotte was now known as Francine. At first she had been unsure about taking another name even though she had no choice. It felt like abandoning Becca, but during the day she had gradually grown used to it and she now felt that she was, for the first time ever, an individual, not one of twins.

'There's so much to learn.' She sighed. 'I'm not sure if I'll ever remember it all.'

Clarisse smiled. 'You will. If you don't mind me saying you seem like one of the most intelligent people here.'

Charlotte stared at her in surprise then laughed. 'You are joking of course.'

Clarisse laughed. 'No, of course not. I just think that some of our number will not last long.' She indicated three men who had clearly had too much wine and were having a heated argument about French politics.

Charlotte looked concerned. 'Perhaps someone should warn them?'

Clarisse shrugged so Charlotte walked towards them and began explaining that they could be ruining their chances of remaining with the course.

'And what's it got to do with you?' Pascal, a short balding man with bad skin, leered at her. 'Why don't you do something more useful... like warming my bed.' He laughed raucously.

Charlotte glared at him, shook her head in disgust and changed her mind about helping him. The man was clearly an idiot...

'I agree Francine, I think you're right.' Victor looked concerned. 'Go to bed Pascal, stop making a fool of yourself.' He turned away ignoring Pascal's response and smiled. 'Thank you, Francine. If I survive until the morning I will owe that to you. Thank you, my friend.'

Charlotte looked closely to see if he was taking the micky but he seemed genuine. He was a nice looking man, of medium height, dark blonde hair and deep blue eyes. 'I could be completely wrong...' She began.

'Of course you're wrong, you silly cow. You just want to stop us having some fun.' Gilbert, a swarthy looking man with dark flashing eyes, interrupted.

Charlotte turned away and began walking back to Clarisse. 'Let me walk you both back to your rooms.' Victor was already by her side and although a part of her was grateful, she also resented the implication that she couldn't take care of herself.

'A few more days of training and we won't need to be escorted.' She smiled to take the sting out of her words.

Victor smiled back. 'That's probably very true but until then do you object to my escorting you both?'

Charlotte exchanged glances with Clarisse and they both nodded. 'I think we can accept, just for tonight of course!' Clarisse winked and the three made their way towards the large staircase that led to their rooms.

****

Arkley View, near Barnet

Fred stared at the latest signal from the spy and wondered what it meant. The previous message stated that there would be no contact until the second phase had been completed yet they had suddenly sent another one. Was it a trick, sent by someone different or had something changed?

'Ineffective, suggest moving direct east to have more effect.'

Fred shrugged, placed the decoded signal in an envelope and handed it to the messenger. 'Can you take this to Colonel Sinclair please.'

He watched the man leave and then turned his attention back to the other messages on his desk. It was up to the Colonel to work out what it meant although it was unlikely he would be able to forget the words that were now seared into his brain. No doubt it would go round and round his head most of the night which would annoy Daisy Irene, but hopefully not wake up the children.

He smiled. The children were already part of the family, the two older ones in particular, Mick and Sandie, were very bright and lively and very curious as to what he did, especially when he made the mistake of telling them it was secret. Jack and Lucy had blossomed under Daisy Irene's care and the highlight of their day was when she read to them at bedtime. They even had him reading to them on the odd occasion he was at home. Jack was enthusiastically learning to read and write and he could already read simple books to Lucy. Fred was very proud of them even if they weren't his. Jane was the only one he hadn't yet managed to build much of a relationship with. She was still very quiet and shy although she did now come and sit with him while he was reading but if he asked her anything she rarely spoke. He had mentioned his concerns to Daisy Irene but she had told him to persevere as Jane had been the same with her at first. He wondered briefly what would happen to Jane at the end of the war as both parents were dead. Presumably they would look for some other relatives to take her in, but if not maybe they could adopt her. That would make Daisy Irene happy and he would love to have a daughter.

****

RAF Exeter

Jimmy was sitting in the dispersal hut waiting for the day's instructions. It was always the worst time of day. Although fears of invasion seemed to have firmly receded, protecting the skies remained a dangerous job. He had been on readiness since 04.00hrs and his nerves were on edge. Some of the pilots were playing cards, others reading newspapers, some like Jimmy staring into space trying to think of anything other than what the day would bring. Eventually he reached into his pocket and pulled out the letter from Madeline and began reading it again, even though he knew it almost by heart.

My Darling Jimmy

I hope you are settling in well at your new base. Life is about the same here, bombing every night and everyone carrying on as normal during the day. At least you are away from the Blitz, well at least I assume you are.

I don't have much to tell you to be honest, the clubs are still full every night but I don't go out much now as I am no longer interested in having a good time unless it's with you. That sounds very sad doesn't it, but I've realised its very true. I miss your company and I miss you in my bed at night. I probably shouldn't have said that as no doubt the censor is reading this, but it's true and I have realised rather late in my life that life is too short not to tell the truth. Write soon and tell me what you're doing and whether you are busy. Actually, don't do that as careless talk costs lives doesn't it?

I'll try and find something interesting to talk about in my next letter, that is if you still want me to write after this abysmal attempt.

Look after yourself and please take care.

Love Madeline

Jimmy frowned, wondering what she meant about realising late in life it was important to tell the truth. She wasn't that old and what truth hadn't she told before? He shrugged. He would have to ask her next time he saw her; it was too complicated to put in a letter. Other than that one phrase he had loved her letter, it was just like talking to her and he couldn't wait to write back. He folded it up carefully, replaced it in his pocket with the champagne cork and closed his eyes, remembering the last time they had made love. If only he hadn't already written his piece for the book the Sqn Ldr was intending to publish he could have done that, but he had finished it the previous day. He had chosen to concentrate on several different incidents starting with the Elementary Training Flying School (EFTS) and ending with the Channel patrols. He only hoped it was suitable.

Outside the hut the rather tatty Spitfires that had been used and abused by several other squadrons before being sent to Exeter, had been prepared for take-off, their flying kits placed in the cockpits and the engines revved to full power to ensure they were ready.

The telephone rang and Jimmy opened his eyes, forgot about Madeline, forgot about the book and took a deep breath. The telephone operator called the flight commander over who listened to his instructions.

'There's a convoy off Dartmouth. We are to supply one section to fly over it until 09.00hrs. Scramble base.'

Green Section was despatched. Jimmy was Green Two and the three men hurried outside. Jimmy nursed his cranky old Spitfire into the sky and they headed towards Dartmouth. He reached 28,000 feet, passed through the thick cumulus clouds and a rush of sunshine filled the cockpit, the bright light bouncing off the clouds. The skies were flawless, the air pure, a perfect world and Jimmy hated the thought of an enemy aircraft intruding, ready to smash the tranquillity.

He craned his neck in all directions, trying to spot any Ju87s that might be up there but there was nothing in sight, not that he could see anyway. Jimmy licked his lips nervously. They had to be here somewhere, so where were the bastards hiding?

Eventually the CO called them up. 'Nothing doing here lads. Let's fly down and let our boys know we're here. Fly around them, we don't want to scare them into thinking we are Jerry.'

They banked earthwards, dipped through the clouds and spotted the convoy. It was an impressive sight of some twenty to thirty ships. Some of the vessels displayed battle scars acquired during the harrowing passage across the Atlantic that were either the result of a run in with German warships or their deadly cousins, the U-boats. But these were the lucky ones. They had made it. This time.

The sight of the boats beneath him made Jimmy emotional. He felt such huge respect for the men on board these ships. They weren't soldiers, they were merchant seamen. The boats were defenceless except for the machine guns mounted on their decks which were largely ineffectual against U-boats and the Germany Navy. He could only hope that when the war was over these men would be recognised for their bravery in keeping the country fed and supplied with food and arms. Jimmy passed low over the convoy as they zigzagged through the water to avoid torpedoes. Suddenly from the deck house of one of one of the smaller ships a large man emerged wearing a vest and a pair of trousers. He put a bucket on the end of a broom and then started juggling with it. Jimmy grinned and carried on. The other pilots had often talked about some of the bizarre signals the sailors used to greet the RAF.

Suddenly silvery streaks shot past the cockpit. Jimmy jumped. Christ there must be a Hun in the area. *'You bloody fool Jimmy, while you've been admiring the ships, a 109 or Ju88 has come calling.'*

The firing continued as Jimmy swivelled around trying to locate the enemy. His neck was aching, there was nothing on his tail, but the bullets kept coming. He broke out into a sweat. They could see him but he couldn't see them. If he wasn't careful this would be it, he would be in the sea. He took a deep breath to calm himself down and then decided to try and take evasive action. He was pulling the Spitfire into a tight left-hand turn when the skipper's voice came over the R/T. 'I don't believe it; the stupid bastards are firing at us!'

Jimmy stared down in disbelief and sure enough he could see two men standing on a gun platform towards the front of the convoy swivelling an enormous cannon that was pointing skywards and letting off rounds of bullets as they flew overhead.

Jimmy didn't know how he felt. However much danger they were putting him in he couldn't really blame them. They had been through hell. They hadn't crossed the Atlantic and avoided countless enemy ships and submarines to be sunk in the English Channel. They couldn't afford to take any chances and some of them had taken to shooting at anything that moved across the skies.

'Time for us to go I think.' The skipper said calmly and they climbed back up to the relative safety of the clouds. From then on they never flew directly overhead the convoys, but escorted them from a safe distance, at least until they were absolutely certain that the ships knew who they were.

****

Singapore
'I thought you should see this.' Li Kang knocked on his office door before entering and closing it quickly behind him.

Geoffrey smiled. 'Good morning Kang. Of course, come in. What have you got?'

'There's some kind of message being transmitted from Alor Setar in Northern Malaya.'

Geoffrey frowned, reached for the message and read quickly. 'You're sure this is what is says?'

'As certain as I can be. Do you think it's important?'

Geoffrey read it again. 'Inexperienced. Not expecting any more.' Then cursed. 'There shouldn't be anyone transmitting from there and this could be an account of our aircraft… or lack of them.'

Li Kang nodded. 'That was how I read it.'

'Keep a look out for anything else sent on that wavelength, however innocuous. Look for any clues as to the identity or the exact location. We have several thousand men up there. It will be like looking for a needle in a haystack.' Not to mention that most of them were part of the Commonwealth so making it public that there might be a spy up there could cause all sorts of political problems. He would have to wait until he had something more concrete.

'We've also picked up this, it was transmitted this morning.' Kang handed him a much longer message. Judging from the military language it was obviously a report to a Japanese army engineer. Geoffrey stared at in disbelief.

'Good heavens. It looks like they've got army engineers pretending to be rubber planters and mining engineers mapping paths through the jungles and plantations so they can avoid main roads.'

'Yes I saw that.' Kang hesitated. 'Something they would only need to do if they were planning on invasion.' He hesitated. 'I think it could even worse than that. I saw another report yesterday which didn't make a lot of sense but I've thought about it since then. A Japanese officer has apparently driven the length of Malaya counting the number of bridges. I couldn't understand why until I saw the follow up message which talked about amounts of construction materials.'

Geoffrey looked confused. 'I don't…' He stopped and stared aghast at him. 'You think they are estimating how much material they will need to rebuild all the bridges if we blow them up?'

Kang shrugged. 'I could be wrong but I can't see what else the message means.' He sighed. 'I really think the Japanese are planning to invade. We have to warn your people in London so they can send reinforcements quickly.'

Geoffrey didn't answer immediately, his brain going over the importance of the information they had picked up. The problem was getting anyone to believe them. 'If only it was that simple.' He saw Kang's expression and tried to explain.

'I sent numerous intelligence reports last year, warning that Japan was busy using local nationalists to stir up trouble in British and Dutch colonies. *Asia for the Asians* - that Japanese slogan has caught on right across the colonies. I told them that many leading government officials in Burma were pro Japanese, that in Malaya many Indians were sending back money to their relatives in the mother country so it could be used for anti-British purposes. The Japanese are behind a lot of it, but no one in Whitehall wants to know as for some reason they persist in seeing Japan as a friend, certainly not as a potential enemy anyway. The Japanese are fuelling insurrection right across the Far East, preparing the ground for an invasion and no one seems to care. In the Dutch East Indies they've dealt with the problem by throwing thousands of leading intellectuals into jungle concentration camps and leaving them to die. At least we're not that barbarous because their actions have played right into Japanese hands and are making things worse. From what I can see Japanese agents are everywhere, disguised as barbers, fishermen and even photographers and as well as agitating for the overthrow of western colonial powers they are also feeding back a steady stream of information to Japan. Our own intelligence is useless in comparison.' He fell silent not sure how much more he should tell Kang.

'I think I have already worked out that your intelligence agencies don't appear to work very well together.' Kang chose his words carefully.

Geoffrey snorted in derision. 'That's a bloody understatement.' He decided that Kang needed to know at least the basics or he couldn't do his job properly. 'The role of the Ministry of Economic Warfare (MEW) is to collect information from the various regional bases, like here. They concentrate on the economic factors of enemy countries as well as their seaborne troop movements and then send that information to Whitehall. Then we have the Secret Service (SIS) who also operate out here. They send everything to the Foreign Office but don't bother telling anyone else anything that they find out. The military also have two competing agencies, one belongs to the Royal

Navy and the other is a joint Army/RAF section, but they hardly speak to each other either.'

Kang remained impassive for several seconds before asking 'Do you know about Lt Col Alan Warren?'

'Who?'

'He's a marine intelligence officer working for SOE. Just opened an office in the Cathay Building, you know, the new large modern air-conditioned government building, the one in the middle of Singapore located near to the waterfront and close to the offices of the MEW.'

Geoffrey nodded. 'Yes I do, now you mention it. No one wanted to know him when he arrived either, especially as SOE is seen to be Mr Churchill's pet project and just another layer of unnecessary intelligence spying on a country that Whitehall is trying its best to ignore. You think they may be of use?'

Kang shrugged. 'You said yourself that half the problem is that no one talks to each other. Why don't we break that pattern?'

Geoffrey smiled. 'I knew there was a good reason I recruited you!' He stood up. 'No time like the present.' His face darkened. 'Especially as we have no time to waste.'

Chapter 20

Lippstadt, Westphalia

Kristian had been transferred to SKG 210 who were flying the Bf110, a Messerschmitt fighter bomber unofficially known as the Me110. The idea was for the new group to mount individual all weather attacks during day and night, either with bombs or with their formidable array of forward firing guns or even both. Kristian had completed his training in Merville, France and then waited nervously for the squadron to be made operational over the Channel. The last thing he wanted was to fly back over Britain, not after last time. But he could hardly say as much, and he was fed up with other pilots asking him the best way to avoid being captured and how to escape the country if they had to bail out. Fortunately, every time they were briefed for an operation it was scrubbed, but that didn't stop Kristian's nerves increasing. Despite the authorities playing it down they had all heard about Deputy Führer Rudolf Hess' flight to Britain the previous month and Kristian began to wonder if this strange occurrence and the number of missions being cancelled might mean some kind of peace was being discussed. He wished he could contact his father and find out what Otto knew. Unfortunately, he couldn't afford to risk it so he was left with no option but to wait in ignorance with everyone else, listen to the numerous unfounded rumours and write loving letters to Ulrike and Manfred.

Eventually the squadron had received their orders and at the end of the month they had left for Lippstadt in Westphalia. Here they spent two days practicing bombing in pairs during a very steep 70 degree dive. The idea was to fly up to 2000m, then dive, pulling out at 800m and then repeat the whole thing. As they were to work in pairs without using any signals the plan was for Kristian to mirror his number one so when he dived Kristian would follow suit. He watched carefully and when his number one levelled out Kristian pulled on his stick as well, but to his horror nothing happened, the aircraft continued to dive and the ground came rushing towards him. There was no warning from the plane, a salutary lesson that the Bf110 was no Stuka, but eventually, after several nerve wracking terrifying seconds, the aircraft responded. Unfortunately, by that time Kristian had been frightened out of his life.

Kristian was becoming convinced he wasn't ready for combat again, he was still having nightmares, not only about his parachute drop over England but now about the dive bombing as well. However, his training was over so he had no choice. On 17th June the squadron departed Lippstadt for Breslau. Although no one knew where they were going or why Kristian was sure it had something to do with the forthcoming attack on the Soviet Union, but of course he couldn't say anything so he'd joined the others in endless pointless speculation and hoped he was wrong about their final destination.

Rumours flew thick and fast as they were guided into the well camouflaged dispersal areas in the woods bordering the trees. The favourite was that they were waiting for permission to fly through Russian airspace as part of a massive pincer movement intended to trap British and French forces in the Middle East. While German and Italian troops in North Africa provided one arm of the pincer, they were part of the other arm that would fly down through Caucasus and Iraq to link up in Syria. Kristian wished they were right but sadly he was still convinced that they were about to attack the Soviet Union.

****

RAF Perranporth, Cornwall
My Darling Madeline,
Well, as you can see by the address I have moved again, and each move is taking me further from you but hopefully I will soon be back nearer home. It seems so long since we were together. I do hope you haven't found anyone else. Yes, I know that sounds very silly, especially as you write to me nearly every day. You probably don't have time to do much else so I'll stop being stupid and torturing myself. Perhaps we should make plans for the future instead or is that a bit like tempting fate?

Jimmy stopped writing and thought about the future he would like to have, one as a happily married man with children in a world that was peaceful, without war. Was that actually possible? Well not the marriage bit, but the peaceful world? Maybe after this war the lunatics would finally have had enough and they would all stop fighting. But they'd said that after the last one and this war had been declared less than twenty one years later, and if you counted the fighting between Japan and China it was even less. Jimmy sighed and wondered why he'd suddenly thought about Japan. He must have seen something somewhere, or maybe one of the other pilots had mentioned it. Perhaps someone had said that a squadron had been sent out there although he was surprised they had any aircraft and pilots to spare, even if things had quietened down a little bit. A wry smile crossed his face. Given the way the RAF seemed to keep moving him further away from Madeline he should probably be grateful they hadn't transferred him to the Far East.

****

Radzyn, south-west of Brest-Litovsk, Generalgouvernement

It gave Kristian no particular satisfaction to know his information had been correct. Flying over Britain had been bad enough but now… he shuddered and tried to fight back his nerves. On the afternoon of 21st June, they had been assembled for a short address by Geschwaderkommodore Major Storp who told them they were due to begin hostilities against the Soviet Union soon. After explaining the rules of conduct they would be flying under they were given some advice by an Intelligence Office on how to deal with the sheer size of the Soviet Union as well as the climate and prevailing weather conditions.

Around midnight they had been warned again for imminent action, given their flying clothing and emergency rations and large scale maps of the area although they were not given any targets. Kristian had lain awake the rest of the night dreading what was to come. He had not done any combat flying since his emergency parachute drop in England and after his experience of dive bombing he was terrified. He could only hope the fear would vanish once he started flying again. At 06.00hrs they were given their instructions, to attack the enemy's airfields, disrupt their supply lines, provide close support for the ground troops and fly reconnaissance deep into enemy territory.

Their first target was the Soviet airfield at Pinsk, over 150km into enemy territory, but there were no specific targets, they were told to find those on their own so Kristian assumed they were to just destroy everything and anything in their sights; aircraft, buildings, runways. It took around fifteen minutes to get into their aircraft, take off and assemble into their flying formation. At first it was like a routine training flight until they crossed the border and saw the smoke and flames billowing up from the battle grounds below as their ground troops crossed the River Bug into enemy territory.

Kristian peered nervously around expecting to see the Soviet air force or at least some flak, but all was quiet. As instructed they remained in tight formation until they reached the target, the idea being to support each other if attacked, but once over Pinsk that changed as pilots began to vie for targets. As each aircraft dived steeply and dropped their bombs explosions appeared all over the field, followed by flames and smoke which soon began to obscure visibility. Kristian was relieved that he'd survived the dive bombing raid but then, having dumped their cargo, the planes lined up, before flying low over the airfield, aiming their guns and strafing the unprotected aircraft. With so many of them flying low there was a real danger of hitting each other and Kristian began to worry more about fire from his own colleagues than the defending forces.

He eventually ran out of ammunition and headed wearily back to base, relieved that he had survived and that the terror he'd experienced the previous night appeared to have gone. His colleagues were euphoric and although Kristian tried to broach his concerns about the danger of their tactics not one was interested. The raid had been a success, aircraft, fuel supplies, hangars, workshops, all had been destroyed.

By the afternoon they were back up in the air, their target this time Volkovysk. Kristian was again carrying his two 500kg HE bombs and had a full load of ammunition. Their last instructions this time were to ensure they fired their nose guns sparingly, in short well aimed bursts or risk running out of ammunition leaving them open to attack by Soviet fighters.

****

En route to Hampshire

Thanks to her previous commando training, when she had signed up for the Auxiliaries, Charlotte had sailed through self-defence and small arms training. She had also been taught how to gather information, read maps and completed some basic infantry training, however blowing things up, sabotage, killing someone silently and laying ambushes were new but she passed all with flying colours. She had even survived the dismal weather which seemed to consist of continual rain. Charlotte smiled to herself, she had actually enjoyed living off the land for the two days they had each spent isolated and alone, attempting to make their way back from a drop in the middle of nowhere. Thanks to their training by an accomplished poacher she had fared well, and had even found an isolated farmhouse where she had managed to steal some bread and cheese without getting caught. She had made a note of where the property was and once she'd reached Arisaig again she had given one of the soldiers who were looking after them some money to give to the family. She gathered by his expression she wasn't the first person to do that and she wondered afterwards if the residents of the farmhouse were in on the whole thing. If not they would surely get fed up with people continually breaking in and stealing their food. Anyway, her conscience was clear, although she hoped she would never have to live off stinging nettles as they had discussed in one of the lectures. Her thoughts drifted to the friends she'd made and she wondered if she would see them again. Clarisse had also been extremely fit and Charlotte wondered idly where she had trained. Perhaps she too had volunteered for the Auxiliaries? She would love to have asked but she had been wary of breaking any of the unspoken rules. They were not meant to know any personal details about their colleagues.

However, it wasn't difficult to ascertain certain things. Charlotte was extremely good at picking up accents and it wasn't long before she'd managed to work out where most of the agents originated from or at least had learnt their French. Other than those who had obviously escaped from France she guessed that the rest, like her, probably had one or more French parents. Victor had a southern accent, possibly from the Toulouse area, while Clarisse was more northern, probably from around Alsace Lorraine. Charlotte found herself picking up odd bits of their accents so her own Parisian dialect had long since been softened by a variety of others, something her trainers seemed very pleased with as it would make it harder for the Germans to place her if she needed to move away from whatever location she was working in.

Charlotte glanced at her watch and then resumed looking out of the train window. She wondered where she was going. Her instructions were to take the train to Southampton where she would be met and taken to the next phase of her training. It was a shame she couldn't call in to see her father, but if she did she would have to lie to him about where she was going and she would rather not do that until she had to.

****

Alor Setar, Northern Malaya
Geoffrey finally arrived at the main base for the RAF, RAAF and Royal New Zealand Airforce (RNAF) and wondered where on earth to start looking. After Kang had shown him the decoded message he had spoken with the SOE representative in Singapore and they had decided that Geoffrey should follow up the lead himself. According to Kang there had been no other messages which meant the spy was either keeping his head down or had orders to only transmit when he had something to report. He would have to tread gently and so far his only plan was to speak to the men and see if there were any rumours circulating. If that didn't work he might have to think of something else.

****

Outside Yelsted, Kent
Adrian listened carefully, then replaced the receiver and cursed loudly. All he wanted to know was what had happened to his daughter, but everything he did seemed to lead to a dead end. He was no further forward than he had been a year ago and although time was supposed to help he wasn't aware of any improvement in his emotions. He still missed Rebecca just as much as he had done after her murder and now he was also missing Charlotte who, for all intents and purposes, had vanished off the face of the earth. He knew that wasn't true as he'd had a couple of postcards from her stating she was busy working but would be down to see him soon, that she had not managed to find out anything else about Becca's death but she would keep trying and if she did find out anything she would let him know immediately.

Adrian wondered briefly if Charlotte was about to embark on something really dangerous, he had heard enough whispers about the new organisation, SOE, to know that Charlotte who spoke fluent French and would do anything to get revenge for her sister's murder, would be an ideal candidate. He shook his head. There was no point worrying about her, it wouldn't change anything. He would concentrate on trying to find Rebecca's killer, or at the very least the traitor who had helped the German leave the country, then when she did come home he would be able to tell her that he had solved the mystery. Maybe then she would no longer feel the need to do anything dangerous. Adrian forgot his grief and anger for a moment, then gave a wry smile before shaking his head. And pigs might fly! If Charlotte had joined SOE, she would be loving the danger, she took after her father. Nothing would stop her fighting this war. He would just have to accept her decision and pray that she survived.

****

45 College Road, Maidstone

Frederick arrived back home after the weekend training exercise in which they had taken part in a pitch battle intended to be some kind of practice in case of invasion. The weather had been scorching hot, the sailors from the Royal Navy who were portraying the enemy invaders, had surrendered really quickly as soon as they realised that the Home Guard were going to ruin their pristine uniforms by throwing flour bombs at them. He was delighted to be back home, especially as the news had just arrived that the Germans had rolled into the Soviet Union. Kristian had been right after all. He wondered what had happened to his nephew and whether he had reached home safely. The Colonel hadn't mentioned receiving any intelligence, but he was hardly likely to tell him unless it was relevant. He turned his attention to Alice was sitting silently in the corner, her face pale despite the good weather they had been blessed with. The radio was on and he was aware of *In the Mood* by Glen Miller playing softly. 'You should go and get some fresh air love.' He said again.

'I can't. They are talking about evacuating all the towns now up to Canterbury, what if I go out and the Germans come?'

'It's just another invasion scare, Alice. I'm sure they aren't going to come, not now they are fighting the Russians. They've got more than enough to do.' He repeated patiently for the third time.

'Then why are their planes still bombing us?'

'They aren't Mum, it's been much quieter. I haven't even seen our own planes flying over recently.' Jeanne interjected.

'They bombed those houses near the woods yesterday.' Alice snapped. 'More people killed, how long before we get hit too?'

Jeanne's face crumpled and Frederick quickly intervened. 'You have the shelter Alice and Jeanne is right, the bombing has eased considerably.' He thought for a second before adding. 'Why don't you go and stay with your sister May for a few days? Take Jeanne with you. It will do you both good to have a break and I'm sure she'll be delighted to see you.'

Alice stared at him in surprise. 'I hadn't thought of that.' She frowned. 'But what about you? I can't leave you on your own.'

'I won't be on my own. Margaret will be here.' He grinned. 'With Margaret and her stream of boyfriends I'll never be on my own!' He winked and despite her disapproval of her middle daughter's behaviour Alice couldn't help smiling.

'We shouldn't laugh about her Frederick; she's going to get herself a reputation.'

'Maybe but we'll worry about that when the war finishes shall we? Meanwhile it's nice to see a smile on your face again love. Go on, go and speak to May, see what she says.' He watched her leave the room and smiled at Jeanne. 'Don't take too much notice of your mum love, she's just a bit overwrought. The Germans will have their work cut out fighting in Russia now, they'll give us a rest, you'll see.' Jeanne's expression cleared and he smiled and changed the subject. 'You'd like to go and have a bit of a holiday with your aunt wouldn't you Jeanne?'

Jeanne's face lit up and she nodded. 'I love going to see Auntie May. I can play with the dogs and take them for walks.'

'That you can.' He was about to say more when Alice came back looking considerably happier. 'I spoke to her and she went and asked Mr and Mrs Rice if it was alright while I was on the phone. She said they are perfectly happy for us both to stay in the servants' quarters for a short while.' Alice breathed a sigh of relief. 'I think that's a very good idea Frederick, it will do Jeanne good to get away from the constant threat of bombing.'

'That's what I thought.' *And it will do you the world of good too*, Frederick added in his mind, *it will also give me the opportunity to get on with the OB and make sure I'm ready if needed.* Despite his reassurances he was far from convinced the invasion scare was really over and he was behind in his preparations thanks to the Colonel sending him round the country after the missing agent.

Having read various newspapers Frederick was also beginning to wonder when they were going to fight back. Reading between the lines it would seem that after the last war the Army were worried the civilian population would not accept massive casualties, and as any action would result in some casualties they were not planning any offensives. The whole impetus appeared to be on defence, which was all very well in the short term, but at some point they would have to take the fight to the enemy. There was also talk about growing problems with Japan which could mean an escalation in the war. He would speak to Ruth when he got a chance and see if Geoffrey had said anything. But meanwhile he would be much happier if Alice and Jeanne were somewhere safer.

Alice's sister Mable, known as May, lived in Mortimer in Berkshire. She had gone into service as a maid with the Beresford family and after Lady Katherine Beresford married Mr Rice she had gone with her as her personal maid. The Beresford's had family houses in Berkshire, Ireland and Tenby in Wales and had travelled extensively on the continent during the 'season' and as Kathleen's maid May had also gone with them.

Jeanne clapped her hands in delight. 'I can't wait. The people in the village call Mrs Rice *the lady.*' Her face fell. 'But what about you Daddy? Can't you come with us?'

Frederick shook his head. 'Not this time Jeanne. I need to stay here but you'll have a lovely time.'

'Come on Jeanne, let's go and pack and then we can catch the train.' Alice was galvanised into action, Jeanne hurried upstairs to begin packing and Frederick smiled. He hated seeing his wife so worried and knowing what he did about his role in the event of an invasion was making things harder for him. How on earth could he just disappear underground if he didn't know they were safe. If the Germans were going to invade it would be in the summer, the Channel was too unpredictable in the winter. Despite its lack of offensive action Britain was gradually building up its resources again so this summer might be their last chance to attempt it. The knowledge that Alice and Jeanne were safe in Berkshire would put his mind at rest and allow him to concentrate on his preparations. Or it would if he could find a way of dissuading Margaret from bringing home every soldier in the area as part of her way of helping the war effort. He shook his head and grinned. He was probably being unfair, but it did seem that she spent every night at some party or other and Alice was right, she would get herself a reputation if she wasn't careful.

Frederick sighed. Even though he was her father and should be laying down the law a part of him admired her for making the most of her life. Margaret reminded him so much of Alice when she was younger and he owed everything to her, which was probably why he wasn't anything like as annoyed as his wife.

****

Beaulieu, New Forest

Charlotte glanced around as the car drove up the long driveway towards a large stately home in the distance. She had been driven through some beautiful countryside since the soldier had collected her outside Southampton Station. 'Welcome to Beaulieu, the estate of Lord Montagu.' The driver resumed his concentration on the road after the checkpoint and lapsed back into silence. It was the first and only time he'd spoken since he'd collected her. Charlotte smiled to herself and stared out of the car window. The grounds were extensive, in the distance she could just make out figures milling around near the house and she was sure she could hear intermittent gun fire. This was phase two of her training and her spirits lifted. Another step closer to getting her revenge for Becca's death.

She settled into her room, checked the time and then made her way down to a large reception room where there were several other people already seated. To her delight she spotted Victor and Clarisse and she hurried over to sit near them.

'I'm so pleased to see you both.'

'We're pleased to see you too aren't we Victor.' Clarisse's face had lit up when she saw Charlotte.

'Hello Francine, good to see you made it.' Victor was about to say more when a small wiry man entered the room, stepped in front of the rows of chairs and waited for the room to fall silent.

'Welcome to French Section, better known as F Section. While you are here you will only use your code names. You will not divulge anything personal. To do so will result in you immediately being sent back to your units or to whatever civilian jobs you have. And that applies to all the other rules. While you are her you will live your cover story, the one you are about to be given.' He waited while a soldier handed them all pieces of paper. 'You can read them after my briefing and then you must learn them by heart.' He glanced around to ensure they were all listening again before continuing.

'While you are here you will learn to be two people.' The instructor smiled at their confusion. 'In other words you will appear as one person to everyone you interact with, but in reality you will be something completely different. Your survival will depend on that ability to blend into the background and to be two people.' He indicated the room they were in and smiled. 'As you can see everything here is in French, all the newspapers are from France, you will only speak French and you will familiarise yourselves with everything in France as it is now, not how it was when you lived there or went there on holiday. Things have changed considerably since the occupation and are continually changing. There are new norms, new ways of behaving and it's important that you know these or you will draw attention to yourself. For instance, in some areas you cannot have milk with your coffee on certain days because it is rationed. If you are stupid enough to go into a café and ask for milk on that day you will immediately be under suspicion.' He ignored the shocked gasps and continued. 'We will update these things as and when we can but there is always the possibility that something will escape our attention so when you are in France you must be alert to your surroundings, to everything going on around you. Listen and watch what other people do, how they behave so you don't make mistakes.' He glanced around to make sure he had their full attention before carrying on. 'We will also teach you all about the police and security forces that you will have to watch out for and whose attentions you will have to evade. Some police are on the side of the resistance but it's always safer to assume that they are not.' He heard the rumble of disapproval and sighed. 'Yes it would make our lives so much easier if we could rely on them to help, but the reality is that we can't. I know if you are French that is hard to take but I'm sorry, it's the truth.'

He paused while the grumbling slowly faded out then continued his briefing. 'You will also have to learn how to spot and shake off surveillance and how to maintain your cover when things are not going your way. We will also teach you other aspects of the basic tradecraft of covert activity like using a dead letter box, how you can pass messages to other people in public places without being noticed, how to set up secure meetings and also how to arrange fall-back positions if things go wrong. Our teachers here are experts in their fields including a professional burglar, a research librarian, an accountant, a barrister and members of the Intelligence Corp.'

He took a breath before closing. 'Finally, while you are here we will also decide what your strengths are. Some of you will make excellent saboteurs, others will be better at gathering information or recruiting local people and some of you will have the skills necessary to be wireless operators. Every resistance cell relies on its wireless operator so we can never have enough of them. But it's a very specialised role and not everyone is suitable. Communication will form a vital part of your duties so you will be taught how to write messages, compile brief but effective reports and how to code them for transmission home. You will also learn various other skills such as blowing up safes, how to use disguises effectively, black propaganda, and various other espionage crafts including resistance to interrogation, surveillance and counter surveillance, agent handling, housebreaking, arson and blackmail. By the time we've finished with you we'll have set you up with a whole new career!' There was a ripple of laughter. He waited for it to fade before finishing. 'Make the most of your evening, it will be your last quiet one and don't forget to learn your cover story. It could save your life.'

Charlotte listened with interest. Of all the training they had done so far she had enjoyed learning morse and codes the most. Her instincts told her that this was something she could be good at. But first she had to get through the next few weeks.

****

Mortimer, Berkshire

Jeanne peaked behind the big green beige door which separated the kitchen quarters from the rest of the house and searched for the dogs, two springers and one cocker spaniel. She was really enjoying her break especially as her aunt was the housekeeper and did all the cooking. The only other servants in the house were a young girl and a daily woman who did the housework. Provided they didn't encroach on the rest of the house Jeanne could do whatever she wanted. It was considerably safer than Maidstone and a lot quieter and her mother was already looking much better.

Jeanne and Alice were getting ready to go into the village and they always took the dogs with them as there were some beautiful woods on the outskirts of the village.

'Have a nice walk dear.' May hugged her goodbye, watched while they put the dogs on leads and waved as they headed down the driveway.

'We will.' Alice moved briskly towards the gate and turned towards the village.

'Do you think we'll see Queen Wilhelmina and her lady in waiting?' Jeanne loved seeing the Queen of the Netherlands who always spoke to her, having told her that Jeanne reminded her of her own grandchildren who had been evacuated to Ottawa with their mother.

'I don't know, she may be in London making her radio broadcasts.' Alice replied with a smile.

'It must be very hard for her being on her own.' Jeanne mused.

'Well, she has her government in London and her son in law over here and no doubt she is planning for her life once she can go back home. Unfortunately, thanks to the Germans, so many people are separated.' Alice sighed.

'Do you think the war will ever be over?' Jeanne forgot her good mood.

'Of course, it will.' Alice put her arm around her daughter. 'And then you can get on with your life.'

Jeanne was about to ask more when she spotted a couple of the village children. 'Mary! Jenny!' She ran off and Alice smiled. It was so good to see Jeanne enjoying herself like the child she was and not having to be scared all the time. Alice looked up at the clear skies and closed her eyes. If only the war would hurry up and end.

****

RAF Perranporth, Cornwall

The Squadron had now been re-equipped with Spitfire Mk IIs, long range aircraft with a 30 gallon tank built into the starboard wing. It only affected flying when they went downhill as the excessive drag caused by the bulge made it difficult to keep the aircraft in a very fast dive. But that was nothing compared to the advantages it gave them as it meant they could remain in the air for much longer so could travel further into Europe. Jimmy still wasn't sure whether that was a good thing or not because it meant they could roam further afield searching for the enemy, increasing the risk to themselves.

Jimmy had been chosen to be the first in the squadron to conduct a raid into Northern France, known as a *rhubarb* for some reason he hadn't been able to fathom.

'We're going to shoot up Lannion aerodrome, its only about twenty miles in from the French coast, but it will give them something to think about.' Squadron Leader Forbes had chosen Jimmy as his number two. This was something Jimmy *was* sure about. Presumably the Squadron Leader must consider him to be reliable, so he felt it was rather a privilege to be selected.

'Yes sir, it will.' He responded.

'The success of the mission is down to the element of surprise. We can only achieve this by flying as low as possible above sea level to avoid being picked up by German radar. If we make it safely to the French coast and the airfield I will go in first, you follow as close as you can. Try and pick a target but either way, just go in once and get out fast as you can, stay in contact and good luck.'

Before long they were flying over open sea. Jimmy found flying a few feet over the water very exhilarating, reminding him briefly of the days of flying low over the Peaks of Derbyshire. For a short while he could forget the war and just enjoy flying his Spitfire. He was so low he could almost reach out and touch the waves.

Then the Channel gave way to green fields and small hamlets. It all seemed very peaceful and Jimmy hoped they had managed to avoid the radar or their reception committee would be anti-aircraft guns and the full might of the Luftwaffe. The airfield had been converted by the Germans into a fighter base and it would be much easier to shoot the aircraft while they were lined up on the ground rather than circling each other in the air.

Forbes' voice broke over the airways. 'Lannion approaching, Blue Two. Take your pick.'

'Message received and understood.' Jimmy replied before checking his air speed indicator which was tipping 300mph. He breathed in and concentrated. The faster he got there the less chance he had of getting hit. Just before Lannion they climbed up to give themselves some height from which to dive because in order to shoot objects on the ground the nose had to be pointing slightly downwards.

The CO went first, diving down and opening fire on the airfield. A neat line of earth shot up as his bullets punctured the ground and then an explosion told Jimmy that he'd scored a direct hit. Now it was Jimmy's turn. He opened up the throttle and eased the stick forward, his heart racing as the nose dropped down towards the airfield. He was vaguely aware of small figures racing in all directions as chaos enveloped them. There was no time to pick a target, Jimmy went in hard and fast and strafed the entire length of the airfield. He was flying too fast to know if he'd hit anything and it was much too dangerous to fly over again.

Jimmy glanced briefly in his mirror as the airfield receded into the distance, opened his throttle and flew back home at 330mph. Instinctively he felt for the champagne cork in his pocket and smiled as exhilaration replaced fear.

'Well done, Corbin. A good job.' Forbes soothing voice came over the R/T and then they were home and touching down gently. Jimmy had been operational for seven months now, he was no longer a sprog but an experienced fighter pilot. He was promoted to Flight Sergeant and was soon to lead his own sections. But although he had experienced every situation he had yet to bag his first kill. He still hadn't shot down an enemy aircraft.

Chapter 21

Thame Park, Oxfordshire

Thame Park had been built on the site of a former Cistercian Abbey, something that could be clearly seen by the impressive wall and gated entrance with small turrets which reminded Charlotte of a castle from the times of Robin Hood. As the car passed through the gates she almost felt like she was going back in time, through the centuries to another world. The road snaked away into the distance surrounded on either side by parkland until eventually they approached a rectangular whitewashed building that was considerably more modern than the gates she had just come through.

It was also reputed to have some of the oldest enclosed parkland in England, something she was willing to believe having just driven through it. According to her tutors she had done very well at Beaulieu, even surviving the nighttime assault by the Gestapo – the arrest by members of SOE leading to her being subject to intense questioning and having her head immersed in water until she thought she was drowning. Charlotte wondered whether she would have been quite as sanguine if captured by the real Gestapo, because as terrifying as the experience had been, she had known it wasn't real. That had made it slightly easier to stay firm even though she hadn't been sure quite how far they were prepared to go.

'Apparently this was home to some refugees from the Spanish Civil war but then someone was stabbed and that was the end of that.' Charlotte had suddenly remembered something else she had read.

Clarisse laughed. 'Better not stab anyone then!'

They climbed out of the car and made their way into the main house. They were shown to their rooms and then taken down to a large room filled with wireless transmitters and people learning how to use them.

'I'm pleased you're with me, given that most of our companions seem to be men.' Charlotte remarked eventually after a casual glance around the area set up for them to begin training.

'Given the size of these wireless transmitters I'm not surprised. Apparently they weigh around thirty pounds and also have a seventy foot flexible aerial. All of which has to fit inside a two foot suitcase. It's going to be very difficult to carry around.'

'SOE have started developing their own transmitters, something less conspicuous, it's called a paraset, or to use its proper name, a Whaddon Mk V suitcase set I believe.' One of the men had overheard their conversation. 'It's still pretty cumbersome and has other problems but it's better than those ones, and they are constantly working on improving them. I'm Pierre by the way, well that's my code name anyway.'

'Francine and Clarisse.' Charlotte introduced them. 'Have you just arrived?'

He shrugged. 'I've been here a couple of weeks now, but most of the others are new. There are two empty tables over there, complete with code books and transmitter. I'm sure the tutors will be back in soon.' He had barely finished speaking when the door opened and a couple of women came in and made their way over to Charlotte and Clarisse.

'I'm Deborah, this is Maria, we're here to teach you how to use these efficiently and to try our best to make sure you don't get caught. We'll also teach you clandestine wireless procedures, including advanced coding and cipher skills as well as teaching you the methods the enemy use to detect clandestine radio traffic and the dangers posed by direction-finding teams.'

Charlotte smiled and nodded at them, before sitting down at the nearest table. She couldn't wait to start.

****

Bavaria, Germany

Having spent the last couple of weeks flying the Bf110 over the Soviet Union as part of Operation Barbarossa, Kristian had been granted a couple of days leave so had hurried home to see his father in the hope there was some information he could pass on to the British before they grew fed up waiting for him to keep his side of the bargain. If he had time he would go to see Ulrike and Manfred later before returning to the front. Otto poured them both some schnapps which Kristian drank in one quick gulp. 'How's the eastern front?'

'Surprisingly good so far, very little opposition at all. For once the Reich's radio transmissions to the general public are quite accurate.' Kristian looked fed up. 'Having warned the British the previous year I was sure the Soviets would have been prepared and we would have been thrown back or at least have met some opposition, but I haven't seen any sign of that at all. If anything they seemed completely surprised which doesn't make any sense at all.'

Otto frowned. 'Are you sure? Maybe it's some kind of a trap?'

Kristian shrugged. 'If it is then Stalin is taking a long time to snap it shut. We're racing across the country and facing virtually no attempts to stop us. Any troops we do come across are ill prepared, have very little equipment and don't seem to have much leadership. It's very odd.'

Otto looked shocked. 'That doesn't make sense at all. Perhaps the British didn't tell Stalin?' He poured them both some more schnapps while he thought about it, trying to work out why not telling Stalin about the incoming invasion would be beneficial to the British cause, then he gave up. He couldn't think of any way it would help their fight against Hitler. He handed Kristian his glass and shook his head. 'No, I'm sure they would have done. Perhaps he just didn't take any notice.'

Kristian was in the process of drinking the second glass, he choked and then spluttered 'You're warned that Germany is going to attack your country and you do nothing?' His voice rose incredulously.

'I suppose it depends on how you see the rest of the world.' Otto was thinking furiously. 'Maybe Stalin thought it was some kind of British trap to make him fall out with Hitler, to start a war in the east and take the heat off them. Perhaps Stalin thought that if he said anything Hitler could take offence, so not wanting to rock the boat he said and did nothing?'

Kristian shrugged. 'Maybe. I can't think of any other reason he would ignore the warning unless he's stupid of course.'

Otto smiled. 'Well, there's always that. More likely he was so arrogant he didn't believe it.' He examined his son's face, the signs of strain were evident in his eyes.

'Are you alright? It's not too bad flying out there?'

Kristian shrugged again. 'To be honest it was a lot more dangerous flying over Britain but it's just the beginning isn't it. I'm not very happy about the tactics we are using, the dive bombing is bloody dangerous, the aircraft doesn't respond quickly enough. We're only surviving because there's no opposition.' He sighed. 'It's also about distances, if anything goes wrong we're probably tens of kilometres from our own lines. It was bad enough worrying about landing in

Britain, at least you knew they would just arrest you. My case was different but on the whole they treat the enemy well. Our biggest worry was ditching in the Channel. But now, we're flying over enemy territory for virtually all the time and if we are forced to ditch there the Soviets won't treat us well. No cosy POW camp for us there.' He shivered and tried to forget the fears that were with him all the time.

Otto watched his son in silence, not knowing what to say. As a Generaladmiral of the Kriegsmarine Otto had never had that fear. His demons were of drowning with his ship, the thought of being captured by enemy civilians or troops had never really featured in his nightmares.

Kristian finished the second drink and changed the subject. 'I don't suppose you have found out anything about the spy at all?' That was his second nightmare, that the British would get fed up waiting for him to provide any intelligence and turn him over to Abteilung 5.

'Nothing, I'm sorry. It's not something I can just bring into the conversation; I have to wait until someone mentions it.'

'I appreciate that.' Kristian sighed heavily. 'Sorry, I'm just worried they will run out of patience.'

Otto swirled his drink around the glass and thought whether there was anything he'd heard that Kristian could pass on that would be useful, however small. 'There is something that you could tell them.'

Kristian's eyes lit up. 'Go on.'

'I've heard that Hitler and the Oberkommando des Heeres, (OKH, the Army High Command) can't agree about their main destination. The OKH wants to go to Moscow, but Hitler wants to go southeast through Ukraine and the Donets Basin into the Caucasus. Then to swing northwest against Leningrad.' Otto shrugged. 'Not sure if it's of any help but it will give you something to tell them.'

Kristian managed a brief smile. 'It's better than nothing and it does at least sound as if I am doing something.' He breathed a sigh of relief. Now all he had to do was send the message and hopefully it would buy him some time. Then he could spend the rest of the evening with Ulrike and Manfred.

****

Liverpool

With no other leads the Colonel had suggested Frederick went back to Liverpool again, just in case he had missed something the first time, but his return trip had not uncovered anything else and he was beginning to believe that the spy had definitely left the area. It was very early morning and he was near the dockyard when he suddenly heard a noise above him. Looking up he saw the German bomber and froze. For a moment Frederick found himself staring up at the sky, unable to move and then the bombs started dropping, distant crumps turning to loud explosions as the missiles came closer. He searched the sky but could only see one aeroplane which was strange. No fighter escorts and no other bombers. Perhaps the pilot was lost? He was still thinking about it when he heard some shouts behind him.

'Better get in here mate.' The dockers were running towards the shelters and Frederick pulled himself together and joined them, his brain racing as he wondered if the spy was responsible for this latest atrocity. If so perhaps they were still in the area and then he realised that once the co-ordinates had been passed on there was no reason for the agent to remain in place and he cursed. During May nearly seventy out of one hundred and forty berths in the docks had been put out of action with many roads and rail routes through the city blocked, two main electricity generating stations had been damaged as were all the main telephone lines. The bombing had considerably reduced the amount of cargo that could be handled at the docks but then, fortunately for Liverpool and the Atlantic convoys, the Germans appeared to suddenly turn their attention to Hull and the east coast instead. Frederick was wondering why they had returned to Liverpool when it suddenly went quiet and then the all-clear sounded.

'Well, that was a quick one.' The docker who had led him to the shelter sounded relieved.

'Yeah, looks like it was only one bomber. Perhaps he got lost.' Another man joined in, repeating Frederick's earlier thought.

'Is this the first raid for a while?' Frederick asked.

The man stared at him in suspicion and Frederick pulled out his identification papers. 'Sorry, I'm investigating rumours of spy activity up here.'

The first man relaxed slightly but his companion didn't. 'Shut up Jack, don't tell him anything.' He glared at Frederick. 'You'd better go and ask your mates in the police station then hadn't you.' With his arms crossed across his chest he looked particularly angry and Frederick decided to back off.

'You're right. I'll do that. Thank for your help.' He hurried out of the shelter and headed in the direction of the police station. He didn't particularly want to speak to them but given how angry the dockers were it was probably the safest thing to do.

****

Bavaria, Germany

'Kristian!' Ulrike flung her arms around him. 'Why didn't you say you were coming home? How long have you got?'

Kristian grinned and hugged her back. 'I've only just got here and you want to get rid of me already?' He kissed her passionately before she could argue and then sighed. 'I have to go back tomorrow morning so let's make the most of our time together. I've missed you so much.'

'I've missed you too and Manfred is asleep so perhaps we could go upstairs and renew our marriage vows?'

Kristian's smile widened and he nodded. 'I was going to say I was hungry but that sounds like much more fun.'

Having spent most of the night making love, cuddling and talking about the future he was lying peacefully in bed while Ulrike made him something to eat. For the first time in ages he felt safe and happy, most of it to do with making love to Ulrike, but also he had sent his first message to British Intelligence so at least they would know he was doing something. He could hear Ulrike singing downstairs and his smile widened. He wished she would hurry up and come back to bed. For once food could wait. He wanted to feel her in his arms, to forget the war and pretend his life was back to normal.

****

Island of Salamis, Greece

Unterfeldwebel Eric Hoffer listened to their orders and felt a glimmer of satisfaction. They had been ordered to make a seaborne landing to support the operation to take Tobruk after a siege that had lasted several months. Their role would be to go in by U-Boat, destroy the British coastal supply railway that had been constructed by 16th and 17th New Zealand Railway Operating Companies and then return.

Only seven men were needed and he felt proud that he had been picked. The rest of the men would come over later, but that probably wouldn't be until the following year so the small force had been carefully chosen. There were no more details other than they were to leave immediately.

****

RAF Perranporth, Cornwall

An early morning chill hung over the airfield as Jimmy was scrambled to intercept an enemy aircraft reported at 1500 feet above Wales and heading for the southwest and presumably back to northeast France.

Heavy dew had settled on the Spits and the erks were busy wiping down the damp cockpit hoods. The night sky had begun to recede as Jimmy climbed into his cockpit, but the day promised to be dull and gloomy.

'We've got a bomber just been dropping his payload over Liverpool. We think he's probably lost. He's headed down through Wales. We think he intends to turn left along the Cornish coast somewhere and head out over the Channel. Vector 140 degrees at 1500ft.'

'Copy that.'

Red Sector took off and headed in a south-south easterly direction, the light was poor and made worse by the mist rising up from the sea. Visibility was less than 500 yards.

'Red Two. We are not going to see much up here. Take her down to 700ft. You lead the way.' Squadron Leader Forbes voice was calm over the R/T.

Jimmy followed his orders, cleared the cloud and then spotted the bomber. He was just off Start Point on Jimmy's port side.

'Red One we have a bandit at 300 degrees.'

'Copy Red two. He's all yours. I'll follow.'

Jimmy broke away and came up behind the bomber.

'Red One it's a Heinkel 111.'

'Copy. Red Two. Ready when you are.'

Jimmy hesitated, there were a lot of men on board, the bomber was flying low, between 20 and 50 ft, presumably to avoid radar. Without fighter protection he didn't stand a chance. Jimmy got him in his sights and gave him a quick burst in a starboard forward quarter attack. The CO was behind him and came in for a port forward attack, his bullets raking the machine from end to end. From then on they took it in turns to fire. Evasive action was impossible for such an unwieldy aircraft, but the rear gunner returned fire. Jimmy swung his machine from side to side to avoid the bullets and fired again. This time the gunner didn't return fire and then the 111 began to lose height, descending towards the sea. The descent slipped into a sharp dive and disappeared into the sea fret, the thick mist that sat above the sea. The event was recorded as a probable because they hadn't actually seen the aircraft's demise, but Jimmy knew without any doubt that it had crashed into the sea.

Up until then Jimmy hadn't really considered the men aboard the machines he was trying to shoot out of the sky. That they were flown by men and boys just like them had never really entered the equation. The target was always the machine, not the occupants. Somehow that made it easier.

****

64 Baker Street, London

Having passed the wireless training course with flying colours Charlotte had been sent to Ringway near Manchester to learn how to jump out of an aeroplane with a parachute. She had expected to feel frightened, but when she climbed the tower for the first jump all she'd felt was a sense of exhilaration. She'd landed safely and after a few further practice jumps she was through, considered safe enough to jump out over France. The very thought of leaping out of an aeroplane that was several thousand feet in the sky to face goodness knows what on the ground should have scared her, but it didn't. Instead she couldn't wait to start, but first she had to go to London to find out exactly what her mission was and where in France she would be working.

'Good morning Charlotte, the only people who know your true identity are here and they are a small select bunch.' The smartly dressed lady smiled encouragingly at her. 'I want to introduce you to someone. I know that you will have already been told that you will be instructed to spell certain words incorrectly when you are sending messages so we know it's definitely you, but this is an extra layer of security. This person will get to know your touch so she recognises you. That way, if you are captured and the Germans try to use your codes, we will be aware that something is wrong.'

'But what about the mistakes, aren't they enough of a warning?' Charlotte looked confused.

'Yes they should be, but sometimes there are problems with signal strength which messes up the message. It's also possible that a radio operator could be in a rush and mis sends something. We don't want to ignore important messages because of mistakes. This is an additional level of security to ensure we know it is definitely you.'

She led Charlotte into another room with several people sitting by wireless sets. She beckoned one of the women over and they headed into a small side room where she closed the door. 'Madeline Cartwright, this is Charlotte, code name Francine. Madeline will get to know your touch over the next few days so she can always recognise you. I'll leave you to get to know each other.'

****

Arkley View, near Barnet

Colonel Sinclair reread Frederick's reports on the Luftwaffe bombing raids on Liverpool and shook his head. Something didn't make sense. He'd skimmed over Frederick's explanation about having to flee the docks when some dockers appeared to threaten him after he asked a question about the bombing raids. But then he'd read the police response which appeared to suggest that the last heavy bombing raids had been in May, since then the Luftwaffe had appeared to change their attention to Hull. According to the police it was just in time because if the bombing had continued at the same rate it could have seriously affected the Atlantic convoys. So why had the Germans altered their target? The Liverpool report backed up the Prime Minister's assessment which was that the bombing of Liverpool was causing serious problems, a few more weeks and they might have succeeded where the U-Boats hadn't. If he hadn't been so sure that there was a spy operating somewhere in the area he would have put it down to luck or God or something similar, but surely the spy would have told his masters how successful the bombing was. And if he hadn't why not? He picked up the receiver and dialled Fred Corben.

'Have you come across anything new from the spy?'

Fred shook his head then remembered the Colonel couldn't see him. 'No sir, nothing at all. He's disappeared completely. The last message was the one I sent to you, the one transmitted in May.'

The Colonel sorted through the paperwork and reread the decoded signal. 'Ineffective, suggest moving direct east to have more effect.' It could be read as an instruction to move east from Liverpool to Hull or the east coast. That meant moving their campaign away from the Atlantic to the North Sea. Maybe the Germans wanted to get their ships out of the Baltic, although it didn't feel right to him. Why would the German spy tell their masters that the campaign was ineffective when plainly it wasn't? Perhaps they were no longer in Liverpool and from wherever they were it appeared that the convoys were still being successful? The Colonel sighed. Perhaps the spy had changed sides. No, that was ridiculous, there had to be a good reason for the sudden change of target although he had no idea what it was.

****

RAF Perranporth, Cornwall

Jimmy had been ordered to fly to Southend where they would rendezvous with two other fighter squadrons, 152 and 234 at 11.30hrs. Their orders were to provide protection for fifty Blenheim bombers intending to cause serious damage over Holland providing they could penetrate the German air defences.

They finally reached the Dutch coast, Jimmy's squadron and 152 keeping between 200 and 1000 feet while 234 climbed to 2000 feet with the bombers sandwiched in between, their aim to remain within four hundred yards of them to afford proper protection. A few enemy fighters made some half-hearted attempts to stop them but gave up quite quickly and they continued on to Waelsoorden. As 152 provided a defensive circle around the Blenheims Jimmy's squadron weaved about in open formation and 234 circled overhead. The operation went like clockwork, the bombers dropped their cargo, the ground was a mass of grey explosions and although the Germans filled the air with their deadly flak there was little they could do.

The squadrons prepared to return to base, 234 attached itself to the first wave of bombers and escorted them home. 66 Squadron attached itself to a further 19 and headed for the English coast. They had just passed Neuzen when a Me109 appeared from nowhere and shot past

Jimmy's starboard wing. Jimmy was initially thrown by his appearance, having not spotted him but then he was confused by the pilot's foolishness of placing himself in his sights. Having quickly recovered from his surprise Jimmy opened fire and watched as the ammunition hit the fuselage. The aircraft fell into a steep uncontrolled dive, there was no smoke coming from the aircraft so Jimmy assumed he'd hit the pilot. There was no time to check it had definitely crashed as they were escorting the bombers so Jimmy flew on. Another 'probable.'

A couple of weeks later Jimmy was detailed to fly another bomber escort when the skipper called him over. 'I'm going to stand you down for this mission Jimmy. I'll send Claude Parsons up instead.'

Jimmy shrugged and then nodded; it wasn't unusual for the line up to suddenly change so he thought little of it. The bombers did a superb job scoring a direct hit on the steelworks at Ijmuiden and the fighters gradually filtered back.

'Where's Claude?'

The other pilots looked around and then shrugged. 'He's probably landed somewhere else. I saw someone bale out as we crossed the Channel. Maybe that was Claude.' Pickles suggested.

The pilot who had baled out, Durrant, had joined the squadron earlier that year and was rescued eighty miles off the coast. Flt Sgt Claude Parsons never made it back.

Chapter 22

Bavaria, Germany

'You've got something?'

Otto could hear the relief in his son's voice. Things had slowed down on the eastern front; the army had come to a halt around Leningrad and were besieging the city. Kristian was grateful to have a few days off as he was sure the siege wouldn't last long and then they would continue to overrun the country. Kristian took the drink while Otto double checked the study door was closed before turning back and continuing.

'Yes, it's about the spy you believe is in England. You're right, there is one, although I've not been able to find out much except he's English. I was beginning to think it was a figment of the British imagination as no one had mentioned anything, but then the other day...' He stopped, deciding the background wasn't important.

'English?' Kristian was looking shocked.

'Yes, as unlikely as that sounds...' Otto shrugged. 'But on the other hand, maybe not. There are a few of them prepared to work with the Nazis. William Joyce (Lord Haw Haw) is a good example. Although he was born in New York he grew up in Galway and was even recruited as a courier for the British Army during the Irish War of Independence. He was nearly assassinated by the IRA so was sent to safety in Worcestershire then educated in Birbeck College. After being attacked with a razor in London by communists after a Conservative meeting he decided that fascism was the answer, a good example of the idiots prepared to sell out their countries to a bunch of thugs.' Otto fell silent as he realised Kristian wasn't really paying attention, then resumed his explanation. 'Being English makes it much easier for them to move around in Britain, no accent to give them away and people are less likely to be suspicious of them.'

Kristian waited impatiently. 'So, who is it then?'

Otto shook his head. 'Sorry, I don't have a name... only the fact that he's English.' He registered his son's disappointment. 'It's better than nothing Kristian and more than they already knew.' He thought hard, trying to remember everything else he'd heard but it had all seemed irrelevant although perhaps he should tell Kristian anyway. 'Presumably, like Joyce, he supported fascism so was living over here when war broke out and then volunteered his services. They obviously thought he would make a good spy so they trained him up and parachuted him back home. The only thing I did glean was that his parents are English too, well off I think and from somewhere in the south of the country. They still live there but don't know what he's doing but we seem to think they are likely to support our spy if they do find out, so maybe they have German roots or just similar views?' He frowned. 'That really is it.'

Kristian sighed. 'Well, as you say, it's better than nothing. I'll tell them that you're still trying to find out more. Anything else I can pass on?'

Otto nodded. 'Yes and this is much more important. It's the reason I asked you to come here.'

Kristian's face lit up. 'Go on.'

'The Japanese are going to attack America in December and if that's successful they are going after British interests in the Far East, Singapore, Hong Kong, Malaya, etc.'

Kristian stared at him in disbelief. 'How on earth did you find that out?'

Otto sighed. 'That megalomaniac is going to declare war on the USA after Japan's attack.'

'But that's utterly insane.' Kristian began. 'It was bad enough attacking the Soviet Union...' His face fell. 'Although, despite the setbacks it still seems to be going better than I expected.'

'Only because Stalin was too stupid and arrogant to accept all the warnings he was given that we were going to attack them. I can verify that was the reason he didn't react. He was warned, just didn't believe it. But things won't carry on this well. I wish you could get transferred elsewhere.' He saw Kristian's expression, sighed and continued. 'Once the Soviet war machine gets up and running it will be a different story. The country is teeming with resources and manpower. Hitler's only chance was to take it quickly. Another month and the autumn rains will start. You had a taste of it in July so you must have seen what its like.'

Kristian nodded. 'The sandy Russian roads turned to cloying mud which bogged down the tanks and slowed up the armoured vehicles.'

'Well, that was nothing, the autumn rains will be much worse, then winter will arrive and it will be like Napoleon all over again. The troops are not prepared for a Russian winter, they don't have the equipment or the training. Millions of our young men are going to die there for nothing unless I am very wrong.' He could only pray that Kristian wasn't one of them. Perhaps he could find some way of getting him transferred.

Kristian was listening with interest and not a little scepticism, but his father sounded so sure that Kristian decided not to question him. Instead he changed the subject. 'But declaring war on the Americans Vater? Are you absolutely sure?'

'Hitler assumes that the America First movement will keep the US out of the war and agree to a settlement of some sort, or that the Japanese will do enough damage to force some kind of armistice and, if neither of those things happen, then he is relying on his wonder weapons.'

'Wonder weapons?' Kristian was looking even more confused.

'Nuclear missiles.' Otto smiled briefly before his face darkened. The idea of Hitler getting hold of nuclear weapons was a nightmare he couldn't even begin to consider sharing with his son. 'You don't need to understand it Kristian, just pass on the message to the British. They will know exactly what to do with that information.' At least he hoped they would. He was sure the British and Americans would have their own nuclear programme although the idea of any country using them wasn't exactly comforting. He realised Kristian was speaking and he forced himself to forget everything he'd heard about nuclear oblivion and listen.

'You hope.' Kristian muttered. He saw his father's confusion. 'I just meant that they don't seem to have done much with the information about Barbarossa do they, the British I mean?'

The confusion cleared. 'Like I said earlier, they passed it on... I know that for a fact, but Stalin wasn't listening.'

Kristian thought for a moment. 'Maybe the Americans won't listen either? Didn't Roosevelt get elected on a promise of not entering the war?'

'Yes, but if the country is attacked he won't have much choice and Lindbergh and America First will vanish overnight.'

'You don't think they will agree to a settlement then?'

Otto shook his head. 'No, I'd bet my life on it.' He gave a wry smile. 'Well, I am betting my life on it.' His face darkened. 'And yours.'

Kristian smiled. 'My choice. I couldn't keep fighting for these maniacs without doing something to stop them. I'm risking my life every day anyway, I might as well risk it for something important.' He swallowed the rest his drink in one large gulp and handed his father the glass. 'I'll go and pass on the message. Take care Vater.' He gave Otto a hug goodbye before leaving the house, his thoughts on how to make sure he remembered everything his father had told him.

Otto watched him go and wondered how he could get him transferred somewhere else, not that anywhere was safe. But the Mediterranean theatre might be better, or North Africa?

****

RAF Llandow, Near Cowbridge, South Wales
Jimmy boarded the train to Cardiff, sat back on the bench seat and thought about Madeline. The RAF kept sending him further and further away from London but at least he was not going to be in the front line for a while. 53 OTU was a training squadron and he would be using his experience to train young men. He smiled to himself, it seemed hardly any time at all since he'd been one of those young boys, but now he was considered to be an old hand, simply because he'd survived this long.

He pulled out a sheet of writing paper and stared writing a letter. The sooner he gave her his address the quicker she could write to him.

The train pulled into the station and he hurried to catch the bus to the aerodrome at Llandow. On his arrival he was being shown to his sleeping quarters when he spotted a tall thin man who looked vaguely familiar.

''Pickles!'

Flg Off Pickering turned round in astonishment and waved a hand in greeting. 'Jimmy! What on earth are you doing here? Welcome to 53 OTU.'

'So, what's it like here?'

'Quiet, but it's nice to have a break to be honest and as you are a teacher you won't have any trouble with this lot.'

'What are they like?'

'Keen and green. It's quite a tough place to train, we're near Swansea and just south of the Welsh hills and mountains which can be hazardous if you don't know what you're doing. We've had a fair few accidents to be honest. It's worse when the mist and fog descent from nowhere, some of them just get completely disorientated and fly straight into the sides of hills and mountains. It's a terrible waste.'

Jimmy stared around him as he digested Pickles' words and his spirits sank. Whilst he didn't want to be risking his life every day on the front line, he wondered how long it would be before he grew bored and began to stagnate.

****

Singapore

Geoffrey had just returned from Alor Setar when Kang flew into the office. 'I think you should see this, Geoffrey.'

'Hello Kang, nice to see you too.' Geoffrey smiled.

Kang flushed and smiled back. 'Sorry, I didn't even say hello, did I?'

'It doesn't matter. What have you got for me? Something useful I hope as I didn't get anything up north.'

'It's a signal from Europe. We wouldn't normally have picked it up but I was searching the wavebands in the hope of finding something when I caught the end of a signal. To cut it short the message is warning that the Japanese are planning to attack us in December.' He held out a piece of paper.

Geoffrey snatched it out of his hand and quickly read through. Kang was right. The missive said the Japanese would attack both Britain and America in December. 'I have to get this to London.'

'That's what I thought.' Kang was heading back to the door when he remembered Geoffrey's trip to the north. 'You didn't find our spy then?'

Geoffrey shook his head. 'No. I could have searched the barracks but that would have caused all sorts of problems and I was warned off by the Commanding Officer up there. The last thing they want is to upset the troops and have mutinies.'

Kang nodded then spoke slowly. 'Well… you'll have to be careful how you send that back to London.'

Geoffrey stared at him and cursed. 'Shit. Of course. I can't send it by radio can I in case the spy picks it up.'

Kang sighed. 'By letter?'

Geoffrey thought hard. 'It's the only way to be sure it doesn't get picked up. But it will take ages.' He sighed. He had no choice. Until they found the local spy they couldn't risk using their wireless transmitters to send anything confidential. 'Finding that bastard is priority Kang.'

****

Chatham, Kent

John looked at his new orders and sighed. Gateshead and a new ship, *HMS Cleopatra* almost ready for commissioning. It looked like he would soon be back at sea, once they had carried out the sea trials successfully. The ship would be launched the following month so it was now time for him to get up there and makes sure all the wireless equipment was installed and working correctly.

The problem was what to do about Elsie and Rodney. He could hardly leave them in Kent with the danger of German bombers. Although the threat of invasion appeared to have receded now it hadn't completely vanished and he wasn't entirely happy about the way things were shaping up in the Far East although he hadn't said anything to Elsie as he didn't want to worry her. Perhaps he could persuade them to move with him. It had to be quieter in Gateshead than it was here.

****

London

Madeline saw the letter from Jimmy the minute she walked through the door and her spirits rose. Perhaps he was coming to see her...

My darling Madeline

I wanted you to be the first to know that the RAF have moved me even further away from you. I am now in South Wales, as you can see from the address. Is there any chance you can get some leave as I think it's going to be a while before I can get any time off?

I really miss you and would love to spend some time with you, even if it's only a weekend. I gather from the news, and from what I've heard from my own parents, that things are much quieter in London now so hopefully you will be able to get away.

I look forward to seeing you very soon.

Lots of love

Jimmy

Madeline threw the letter on the floor in despair before picking it up and holding it close to her heart. At least he wouldn't be in much danger for the next few months. She should be grateful for that, even if he was further away. But it would be virtually impossible for her to get any leave before Christmas as Charlotte was just about to go to France and join the other agents she had been trained to recognise. She would be needed to answer and collate all their messages and pass on any information they needed to know. It had been impressed on her just how important it was that she was there because of recognising each agent's touch so she knew there was no point in even asking. She should be pleased. This was what she had enlisted for, the reason she was here and if she hadn't met Jimmy she would have been delighted that she had done so well. But meeting him had changed everything.

****

Arkley View, near Barnet

Fred finished decoding the message that had just come in from their new spy in Germany and it made shocking reading. He stood up and headed towards the door. He would deliver this one himself.

'I thought you should see this straight away sir.'

Colonel Sinclair read the message in growing disbelief and then he stood up. 'You haven't seen this Fred.'

'Sir?'

'Just forget you saw this. I'm taking it straight to the top.' The Colonel's mind was racing as he tried to work out the permutations of what he'd read. Kristian had proved his worth. 'Our spy was right about the invasion of the Soviet Union although Stalin ignored all our warnings. This time we could be a step ahead and I have no intention of allowing intelligence like this to fall on deaf ears.'

****

RAF Tempsford, Sandy, Bedfordshire

Charlotte finished the last of the checks to make sure none of her clothes or possessions had anything that would give her away as British and shut the small suitcase. The more important case, the one containing the wireless, was already closed and had everything she would need to contact London once she landed.

Somehow, she managed to smile at Victor even though her stomach was turning cartwheels.

'It will be fine Francine.' He didn't sound very confident and knowing she wasn't the only one who was nervous somehow made her feel slightly better.

'Of course, it will.'

'At least we'll be working together.' He smiled back.

Charlotte nodded. He was right. Although they would not be living in each other's pockets they would see each other intermittently. It would be much harder to be flying in on her own, at least for the first time. 'Yes, I know. It's just nerves, I'm sure I'll be alright once we are on our way.' She fell silent and clenched her fists. This was for Rebecca, if she could keep that in her mind she would sure she would stop feeling so scared. Her thoughts turned to her father and she wondered what he would say if he could see her now. Hopefully he would be proud of her, but no doubt he would also be worried.

'We're ready for the off.' The young RAF officer put his head around the hanger door. Charlotte took a breath, exchanged glances with Victor, then picked up her suitcases and followed the officer towards the Lysander, its engine idling noisily outside the hanger as it waited for them to board. Victor followed closely behind wondering what the hell he was doing. It had all seemed like such a good idea, going back home to fight for his country but now he was about to parachute into occupied France he was having second thoughts. Knowing Charlotte was obviously feeling the same didn't really make it any better except he could tell himself that he wasn't the only one who was scared.

They climbed aboard and sat down, the aircraft began taxying along the field and then they were in the air, the airfield was falling away behind them. They were on their way to France.

****

London

'I don't understand sir?' Colonel Sinclair looked completely confused.

'It's quite simple Colonel. The President will be informed but the information will go no further. The only way the Americans will enter the war is if they are attacked. If they are warned and are able to prevent it then they will not enter the war and if that happens the conflict will drag on for years and our chances of winning will be considerably reduced. As for the Far East, if we act on this information we will not only let the Japanese know that there is a spy somewhere, but the Americans will also get wind of what is going on and then we are back to scenario one, that they won't enter the war. As useful as this intelligence is, we can't act on it.'

'But all those people will die…' Colonel Sinclair shook his head. 'It's appalling.'

'But necessary. You need to see the bigger picture I'm afraid. We're sacrificing the minority for the majority.'

'Is this the Prime Minister's decision?'

The man smiled. 'Of course not, Colonel. We can't let politicians make decisions of this magnitude. You are bound by the Official Secrets Act – you won't forget that will you?'

Colonel Sinclair stared at him for several seconds, then stood up and walked towards the door.

'Does anyone else know about this Colonel?'

Colonel Sinclair was about to say yes when he suddenly changed his mind. 'No, the message came straight through to me. I decoded it.'

'Good, the fewer people that know about this the better.' Peregrine Thompkin-Cartwright watched the Colonel go, sat back in his chair and decided that the man was probably lying to him. The brief hesitation before he had answered had made him suspicious. The problem was who else knew. The Colonel's workforce at Barnet was quite large, any one of the men who worked for him could have been responsible for intercepting the message and decoding it. To find out would be a massive task and could risk upsetting the sterling work the RSS were doing. He couldn't afford to do that. He would have to hope that the Colonel was a man of his word and would ensure that no one else spoke about this. If not he would have to take action. Meanwhile he had other things on his mind. He was due to have dinner with his daughter.

****

Bower Steet, Maidstone

'Gateshead? Why on earth would I want to move to Gateshead?' Elsie looked horrified.

John sighed. This was proving more difficult than he'd expected. He took her hands in his and smiled into her eyes. 'It will be much safer than here and you'll be with me, instead of miles away. If you stay in Maidstone we'll never see each other.'

Elise didn't look convinced. 'But it's so far away from my family and I won't know anyone there.'

'You'll soon make friends and so will Rodney and we'll be together. Don't you want that?'

'Yes of course but it won't be for long, will it? Once the ship is ready you'll go back to sea and we'll be on our own in a strange place where we don't really know anyone.'

'But that won't be for ages and meanwhile you'll be away from the bombing and the threat of invasion. If they do invade it will take them a long way to get that far north.'

'I suppose so.'

John breathed an inward sigh of relief. It sounded like she was weakening. 'Just think about it, we don't have to leave for a couple of weeks.'

'You could always go on ahead and when you have somewhere for us to live we could follow?'

John relaxed. He'd been sure she would eventually give in. 'That sounds like a good idea.' He frowned. Unless she was only pretending that she would come with him. He was about to ask her when she laughed.

'I will come with you I promise. It's just easier with Rodney to worry about if you find us somewhere first.'

John pulled her into his arms and closed his eyes. Thank goodness for that. When he did finally go back to sea he would be able to relax now knowing they were safe.

****

Outside Yelsted, Kent

Adrian replaced the receiver and sighed. Still no further forward although it seemed that the agent had moved further away from Liverpool. Even more bizarrely it seemed that the German bombing campaign in Liverpool had eased off suddenly, just when they were starting to get the upper hand and cause serious disruption to the convoys. The bombers had suddenly begun targeting the east coast instead so perhaps their agent wasn't that good after all. Or perhaps their orders had changed? He slammed his fist into his hand and cursed. He was going around in circles but he had no intention of giving up. His daughter deserved to be avenged and he intended to make sure he did exactly that, however long it took.

The trail had not gone completely cold but from the little he could find out the agent had not sent any more messages which made it much harder to trace him. Presumably his instructions were to only transmit when absolutely necessary. Anthony had been very helpful but it wasn't fair to keep pestering Charlotte's friend. He wasn't sure about the relationship between Anthony and Charlotte but it wouldn't do to cause problems. It would be best if he found an alternative source of information, someone else who was privy to signal interception. The question was who and once he had found someone suitable how could he persuade them to help?

****

London
'I am pleased you are working in London, Madeline. It makes it so much easier to meet up.' *Its just a shame your mother isn't here to see us.* Peregrine wanted to say the words out loud but his relationship with his daughter was still rather difficult and he didn't want to say anything that would prevent them getting to know each other again.

'It's very nice to have someone to buy me dinner.' Madeline grinned and raised her glass of wine to him. It still amazed her that she was sitting with her father after everything that had happened.

'How's work? You look very smart in your uniform.'

'Busy.' Madeline swirled the wine around before answering. 'You know I can't really talk about it.'

'Yes of course.' Peregrine downed the rest of his wine and wondered why he always felt so nervous around her. It was true he hadn't seen much of her over the past few years but she was his daughter, there should have been a stronger connection between them. He sighed.

'Is something wrong?'

'No, sorry. I just wish we knew each other better.'

Madeline smiled. 'It will take a little time but I'm sure it won't be too long.' She had been very wary of making contact with her father after everything that had happened but she was pleased she had now, especially as things had changed so much since she had first spoken to him. Perhaps she should tell him about Jimmy. It might make him see that she was serious about improving her relationship with him.

'I have a boyfriend.' Madeline's smile widened at his expression. 'He's a pilot, flew in the Battle of Britain, but he's in Wales at the moment, providing training to some new pilots. Perhaps you could meet him when he gets some leave.'

Peregrine nodded and forced a smile. He wasn't sure how he felt about her having a boyfriend. Part of him was delighted that she had let him into her life and was obviously intending him to be a part of it for some time, but he didn't want to lose her to another man just yet, even if he was *one of the few*.

****

Arkley View, near Barnet

Fred finished decoding the latest message from the Afrika Korps to their Special Forces based in Catania in Sicily and picked up the telephone. He had waited for confirmation before passing it on, but it appeared to have originated from Germany.

'Yes Fred?' Colonel Sinclair stopped reading the latest intelligence from the Far East and gave Fred his full attention.

'They're sending in one of the Brandenburg detachment to North Africa, should be arriving in Tripoli in two days. Looks like it's No 2 Company, its personnel are mainly those who have lived in former German African colonies, speak several dialects and are also proficient in English and Portuguese. From what I can gather they are to be used mainly for reconnaissance, to penetrate our lines and pass back information. I'll make sure we're listening in.'

Colonel Sinclair frowned. They had heard whispers about a group of German special forces who were apparently responsible for starting the war in Poland by pretending to be Polish soldiers attacking Germans at Gleiwitz but with no real information he had finally approached Otto von Klotz for more information. Thanks to him they now knew quite a lot about the Brandenburg Detachments as the

German Special Forces were known. Number 2 Company and those from No 1 Company, who specialised in Latvian, Estonian, Lithuanian, Finnish and Russian had trained at a country estate in Brandenburg and at the Army Engineering Training School where they carried out manoeuvres with live ammunition and grenades, learned how to kill silently, live off the land, parachute, handle small boats and assault craft, and to make explosives from basic commodities such as icing sugar, flour and potash. It was their use of initiative that separated them out from the main troops and the Colonel was aware that they were a force to be reckoned with. If they were being employed behind British lines they would have their work cut out finding and stopping them. 'Presumably it's all part of the latest attempt to take Tobruk?' He spoke eventually.

'It seems likely doesn't it?'

'I'll warn the authorities.' The Colonel sighed and replaced the receiver. Tobruk had been under siege for over six months and hammered constantly by Stuka's and tanks since September. He knew that a new attempt to relieve the garrison was underway. Heavy winter rains had turned the desert into a sea of thick mud and Lt. Gen. Sir Alan Cunningham's newly formed British Eighth Army had just begun Operation Crusader, an ambitious plan designed to lure Rommel's army into battle and finally relieve Tobruk. Presumably the Germans were aware of this hence their decision to use the Brandenburg men to disrupt it. His expression darkened and he reached for the telephone.

****

Somewhere over France

The parachutes opened within seconds of them leaving the aeroplane and Charlotte felt a thrill of excitement. She couldn't see anything below in the dark even though the moon was high in the sky. They floated gently down towards the ground and Charlotte searched around hoping to spot any obstacles before she flew into them. They should land in a field but it wasn't an exact science, especially in the dark and the field was bordered by trees. It wouldn't do to land in a tree. She was thinking about that when she saw shadows coming up to meet her and she realised she was almost down. For some reason she'd expected it to take longer. She assumed the correct position to land and offered up a quick prayer to Rebecca to watch over her and help her land safely.

Within seconds she was rolling around in a field, nothing was broken, the suitcases were in one piece and she felt exhilarated. Now to get rid of the parachute and search for Victor.

'Francine?'

'I'm over here.' Her eyes were adjusting to the darkness and she just could make out his shadow coming towards her. 'Are you alright?'

'Yes, perfect landing, the only time I didn't hurt myself!'

Charlotte grinned as she finished burying her parachute. Every time Victor had jumped from the tower he'd landed awkwardly although he hadn't done any damage to himself. 'A good omen then.' She lowered her voice as she suddenly spotted some lights on the edge of the field. Hopefully they were the torches of their reception committee.

'Welcome to France. The weather is quite warm for the time of the year.'

'It's warmer in the south I think.' Charlotte responded in relief. That was the coded phrase. She peered into the darkness and then he was standing in front of her, a tall good looking man with a beaming smile.

'I'm Jacques.' He held out his hand for Charlotte to shake. 'Let's get out of here before anyone sees us.'

Victor and Charlotte followed him across the field to a narrow lane where a farm truck was waiting. 'Get in the back. We'll drop you off first Victor and then get you settled Francine.' He climbed in the driving seat.

They had barely clambered aboard and sat down before the truck began to weave its way through the dark lanes.

Ten minutes later the vehicle pulled up sharply, Charlotte said a quick goodbye and wished him well then Victor climbed out. Charlotte heard a brief conversation then he was gone and the truck was back on its way. The next time she saw him would be when he had a message for her to send. In the meantime, she was to settle into her new life and try not to draw attention to herself.

****

Island of Salamis, Greece

Stabsfeldwebel Doehring stared up at the man standing in front of his desk, his face impassive. 'Go on.'

Unterfeldwebel Eric Hoffer cleared his throat, stared straight ahead and began to explain.

'Everything was going well. The seven of us had left on 12th November so after five days on the cramped vessel we were pleased to know we had finally reached our destination. U-331 approached the coast cautiously but there was no sign of the enemy so Kapitänleutnant Hans-Detrich von Tiesenhaussen immediately launched the small rubber dinghy and told us that one of his crew would help row us over and then wait and bring us back the following night when the U-Boat would return to pick us up.'

He glanced at his superior, but Stabsfeldwebel Doehring said nothing, so he carried on. 'We arrived on the shore with no difficulty and the raiding party left me with the crew member to guard the dinghy while they headed off to cut the coastal supply railway. They hadn't been gone very long when we spotted two British sentries. We kept quiet and thought they hadn't noticed us but then, suddenly, one of them saw the tracks made by the raiding party and started to follow them. We had no choice, we went after them and the crewman killed them.' Eric risked another surreptitious glance at Stabsfeldwebel Doehring but his face was still expressionless so he carried on. 'He said that he didn't know what else to do. Even if we'd tied them up they would still have been missed.' He fell silent.

'He was right, he did the right thing Hoffer, they were the enemy.'

Eric breathed out slowly and then continued. 'The raiding party spent most of the night laying the charges and then, just before dawn they reappeared and headed towards the cave where we were still hiding. They asked what had happened and we told them but there was nothing we could do but to hope that the British would not miss their sentries until the sub came back.'

'But that wasn't what happened.' Doehring prompted.

'No Herr Stabsfeldwebel. We remained hidden all day and then, just as we were getting ready to row out to the U-Boat a large, heavily armoured, search party appeared. There was no way we could win a fire fight with them so, although the sea was really rough and the swell very heavy we tried to make a run for it. But the waves were too much and eventually capsized the dingy, throwing us all into the sea. We all tried to swim for it. I was lucky, somehow I reached the submarine but it was dangerous to wait too long and once we were sure everyone had been captured it submerged.'

'You're sure everyone was caught?'

'Jawohl Herr Stabsfeldwebel. As far as I know the rest of the men were captured and U-133 only just escaped.' Eric hesitated and then asked the question he wanted to know the answer to. 'Did they succeed?'

'No, either they told the British what they had been doing or they were lucky. They appeared to have uncovered all the charges. There was no explosion.'

'I'm sorry sir. If we hadn't killed the sentries…'

'They would have discovered the rest of the men laying charges and they would have killed them so the result would have been the same.' Stabsfeldwebel Doehring sighed. 'You'll have plenty more time to get revenge Eric.'

Eric flushed. 'I didn't kill them...' He began.

Stabsfeldwebel Doehring waved a hand. 'Go and get washed and changed. You were lucky to escape so forget about the problems and get ready for the next mission.'

'Jawohl Herr Stabsfeldwebel' Eric saluted smartly and left the small office, relieved he wasn't in trouble.

Stabsfeldwebel Doehring watched the door close and sighed. He would have to keep an eye on Eric Hoffer. The man was good at the job but he would cause them trouble if he didn't concentrate properly. He was willing to give the Unterfeldwebel the benefit of the doubt this time, but he would bet his life that it was Hoffer who had killed the sentries, not the crewman. He didn't mind as it was what they had been trained for, but why lie about it?

****

London

Anthony read the signal, somehow managed to conceal his shock and raised his eyebrows. 'What are you going to do sir?'

'Absolutely nothing Anthony. We can't afford to upset things, not now.'

'But all those men…'

'Men will die whatever we do Anthony. I don't need to tell you how much we need the Americans to come into the war do I?'

'But if they find out that we knew and did nothing?'

'That won't happen Anthony. Decisions have been taken and the right people have been informed. I have done everything we need to do. I am only making you aware so you can plan accordingly.'

Anthony looked confused. 'I don't understand…'

Peregrine handed him some paperwork. 'You're off to Singapore. You will meet with a Col Warren. He'll give you your instructions.'

Anthony nodded and gave a wry smile. 'My Japanese is about to come of use then?'

'Yes, that and your other skills. The Colonel is preparing some surprises for our Japanese friends. And before you ask, no he isn't aware of the signal you just read, but he is a very intelligent man who has been preparing for just such an eventuality. Unlike most of the idiots over there he is not sitting back, assuming we can win. He's going to need you and as many people you can recruit.' He held out his hand. 'Good luck.' He had a horrible feeling it would be too little too late, but hopefully he was wrong and men like Anthony would be able to make a difference.

'Thank you, sir.' Anthony hesitated. He would have liked to write to Charlotte but as he couldn't tell her what he was doing, any more than she could tell him her own role, there was little point. He realised Jonathan was watching him and he pulled himself together. 'Goodbye sir. Hopefully I will see you soon.'

As he left the room he changed his mind. He would write to Charlotte and tell her everything he knew, a letter to be opened only in the event of his death. It was the least he could do.

****

Hebburn-on-Tyne, Durham

'Today we have been brought together in this fine ship, and she is a fine ship. But in spite of all the skill and learning that has gone into her construction, she is useless without the men to work and understand her. She is equipped with every known device that science can produce. Treat her well, learn how to use her devices and she will never let you down. We name this ship *Cleopatra* and may God bless all who go down to sea in her.' It was 5th December, the Captain had finished speaking and *HMS Cleopatra* was now in full time commission. John headed down to the radio room and continued his preparations for the sea trials which were due to start the following week. He was very impressed with his new ship, a Dido class cruiser, 5,450 tons and 512 feet long, she had ten 5.25inch guns, two four barrelled 'pompoms' as the Navy's 2 pounder gun was better known, three oerlikons (cannons) and six torpedo tubes, her top speed thirty two knots. Although most of the naval ratings had arrived at Hawthorne Leslie's Shipbuilding Yard a few weeks earlier, John had only arrived just in time for the commissioning service. He had hoped to bring Elsie and Rodney with him but there hadn't been time so they were due to travel up on their own later that week. Meanwhile he had plenty of work to do as they prepared for their first voyage.

Chapter 23

Singapore

On the night of 7th December thirty four bombers from Genzan Air Group and thirty one bombers from Mihoro Air Group took off from southern Indochina and headed towards Singapore. They had been assigned several targets in the city including RAF Tengah, RAF Seletar, Sembawang Naval Base and Keppel Harbour but thick clouds and rough winds over the South China Sea reduced visibility and caused the formations to separate. They tried several times to regroup but failed so eventually Lt Commander Niichi Nakanishi, the wing commander of the Genzan Air Group ordered them to abort their mission and return to base. Only seventeen of the remaining thirty one bombers from the Mihoro Air Group reached Singapore.

Kang raced into Geoffrey's office, relieved to find his commander still at work. 'The radar station in Mersing, Johor, Malaya has detected Japanese aircraft heading in this direction. Flight Lt Tim Vigors' request to scramble 453 Squadron so they can intercept them has been denied.'

Geoffrey stared at him in disbelief. 'Why on earth...?'

'The Air Chief Marshal, Robert Brooke-Popham, is worried that the anti-aircraft batteries might fire on them, thinking they are the enemy.'

'But Vigors is an experienced Battle of Britain pilot, he's more than used to flying at night.'

Kang shrugged. 'I think it might be more to do with the Air Chief's opinion that the Buffalo fighter is only suitable to fly during the day.'

'What about 27 Squadron in Sungai Petani? They have twelve Blenheim Mark IF night fighters.'

'I think they're being used as ground attack aircraft.' Kang fell silent.

Geoffrey stood up and hurried to the window. He could hear aircraft in the distance and he was suddenly mesmerised. Kang joined him. It was eerily quiet, the streets brightly lit and then the air raid sirens began, but the street lights remained on.

'Why the hell are the lights still on?' Geoffrey stared up at the sky then back down to the illuminated streets below.

'I have no idea. They'll have no trouble finding the city at this rate.' Kang shook his head in disbelief. 'They've only had two practice blackouts, maybe no one knows what to do.' He instinctively ducked as the first of the aircraft flew over them and onto the city, then watched as the bombs began falling and the anti-aircraft batteries began firing while from the sea the battleship *Prince of Wales* and battlecruiser, *Response* also responded, although they didn't appear to have hit any of the planes.

Geoffrey stared out of the window as the small number of bombers climbed high into the sky. He watched confused until he realised they were attempting to draw the ack ack and searchlights off the other bombers who were flying much lower. Then, in the distance he could hear the crump of bombs exploding, flames and smoke filled the air and he reached for his binoculars. 'Looks like they've hit the RAF bases at Seletar and Tengah and some places in the city.' He shook his head. 'Why the hell are the bloody lights still on?' He was to find out later that the ARP (Air Raid Precautions) HQ had not been manned and the police and power station officials could not find the employee who had the key to the switch.

Half an hour after the first air raid siren began the all-clear sounded and Geoffrey hurried down into the city. The damage was bad enough, several bombs had hit Raffles Place and it was obvious many people had been killed or injured but he knew it could have been worse. He was to learn later that sixty one people had died and a further seven hundred had been hurt. But it was the reaction from British Far East Command that really took his breath away. Despite his intelligence reports it seemed that those in charge had not believed the Japanese had any long range aircraft so were therefore incapable of striking Singapore from Indochina which was over six hundred miles away.

****

Pas-de-Calais region, France

Charlotte had spent a month settling into her new life, that of secretary to the local Mayor, her new name Estee Martin. Gérard Deshamps, who appeared to be a collaborator, but in reality was a member of a resistance group helping downed airmen to escape capture as well as passing on intelligence about troop movements and other enemy activity in the area. She had only used her wireless once and that was to confirm her safe arrival. The radio was currently hidden outside the town in the cottage of another resistance member and she had been careful to use it in a completely different location. Up until now there had been nothing to report but Gérard had just given her some details of a British airman which needed confirming before they moved him further down the line.

The airman was hidden in a place they only used for the first contact and until London verified who he was he would remain there, in isolation. He had only seen one member of the group so he could only identify her and she had worn a disguise. Charlotte smiled. Marie was very good at disguising not only her face but also her whole person, even down to the way she walked and moved. Her code name was *blackbird*, a name that gave nothing away. Marie had a northern French accent, blue eyes, long blonde hair and a trim figure. *Blackbird* had dark hair, glasses, was rather well built and spoke with a southern accent. Charlotte was not only impressed by her, she was determined to emulate her. To that end she had bought herself a dark wig and glasses and was intending to wear them when she made the long trip into the forest to use the wireless. She hurried down the stairs from Gérard's office and let herself out of the door. Her bicycle was outside and she was soon riding towards the forest. She would wait until she'd left the town before changing the bike's registration and altering her appearance. She still found it odd that her bicycle had a registration number, but the Germans had introduced them because they were fed up with the acts of sabotage being committed by people on bikes. As all cycles looked the same their ability to find the perpetrators was reduced considerably so they had sought a way to ensure they could trace them.

As she left the town Charlotte checked behind her several times, but although she passed several German patrols no one showed any interest in her.

****

Singapore
'The Japs have bombed Pearl Harbour.' The news spread through the civilians and military like wildfire and Geoffrey rushed towards his radio and switched up the sound. He shook his head in disbelief as the details of numerous casualties was relayed by the announcer in solemn tones. After the attack on Singapore last night and now this it was obvious his letter had failed to reach its destination in time or the

Americans would have been prepared and so would the authorities in Singapore. As it was neither country seem to have had any idea they were about to be attacked. He felt sick inside as he suddenly realised that if his warning hadn't reached Britain in time they would not be aware that Singapore was probably next.

'You've heard the news?' Kang rushed in, his face pale.

Geoffrey nodded. 'We have to contact London immediately. Last night's bombing raid was just the beginning. We have to make sure everyone is prepared.'

'You really think they are going to come by land?' Kang hadn't moved.

Geoffrey tried to concentrate. 'I think they are probably already preparing to do that.'

An hour later he was staring into space and wondering whether he would ever survive to go back home to Ruth. The army had assured London that they were perfectly capable of defending Singapore and to make matters worse were already issuing statements to the British soldiers that they had nothing to worry about, that the Japanese soldiers were not very good and anyway they had the *Prince of Wales* and *Repulse* in the harbour and the Japanese would never get past them. Geoffrey screwed up the piece of paper in which he had been told to stop panicking and show some backbone and cursed loudly. Whatever the idiots in charge thought he was sure things were not going to be that easy.

****

Arkley View, near Barnet

Fred paced up and down the small hut, fury on his face. What the hell were the people in charge doing? They had been given intelligence to prevent the Japanese attacks yet seemed to have done nothing about it. He stopped and reached for the telephone. Perhaps he should speak to the Colonel? Then he changed his mind. The Colonel was unlikely to tell him anything and had told him to forget the last piece of information that had passed through his hands. Perhaps he should concentrate his time on seeing if the elusive spy had sent anything recently instead.

A few hours later Fred sat back and rubbed his face in confusion. There had been a telephone call to somewhere near Maidstone from

Liverpool around the same time the spy sent the last message. The call hadn't lasted long enough for anyone to get a trace on it and hadn't been repeated, not that he could see anyway.

He searched through the logs again and found another phone call from Liverpool to London. This was to a number he recognised and he shook his head in confusion. Who was ringing the Colonel from a phone box in Liverpool? If it was anything to do with the spy why hadn't the Colonel said anything?

He searched again but there was nothing else so eventually he gave up in frustration. It wasn't for him to be checking up on the Colonel or was it? The country was at war, although most of the spies had been uncovered and were now working for them it didn't mean they had found them all. The best place for a spy to hide was in plain sight. He thought back to the night the message had come warning them of the Japanese attack, the Colonel's warning not to say anything to anyone and that he was taking it right to the top. He hesitated for a few more moments while he thought about the possible consequences of the action he was about to take then made his decision. Only one way to find out the truth. He stood up and headed towards the door. The Colonel was on the camp, he would talk to him in person.

****

Pas-de-Calais region, France
Charlotte quickly took down the cables, replaced the wireless in her suitcase and climbed back on her bike. This was the most dangerous part, taking the wireless back to the barn where she was hiding it. She would need to find a new place to send from next time or she would risk getting caught. That meant riding around the local villages on the outskirts of the woods and looking for somewhere safe to hide the wireless and also somewhere to send her next message from. The airman had checked out satisfactorily so she could pass that on to Marie and he would be moved down the line immediately. Being the wireless operator was nerve wracking enough, but having to take the airmen on trains and buses knowing they could give you away at any time would have been several times worse. At least this way she was only reliant on herself. The woods were thinning out now and she braced herself as she joined the main road. There was no one about

but she had no intention of relaxing, not while she was carrying the wireless.

****

Singapore,
Anthony had immediately reported to Colonel Warren on his arrival and been sent to join several other men who had been trained in the SOE camp during the summer to set booby traps and generally harass the enemy behind the lines. They loaded several lorries with weapons, ammunition, explosives and fuses and by the end of the day they were crossing into Johore and heading north. On arrival in Kuala Lumpur the Commander of 3 Corps directed them to head for Penang, an island two miles off the coast which was considered a good base from which to launch commando style raids on the enemy as it marched relentlessly south.

'They've taken out most of the new RAF bases in the north and instead of staying to provide air cover for 11 Division the RAF have withdrawn their remaining aeroplanes south leaving the Japanese vast quantities of supplies including bombs.'

'I thought they'd only gone as far as Ipoh?' Anthony repeated the intelligence he'd gleaned in his short sojourn in Singapore.

'They did but were only there for a couple of days before being sent back to Kuala Lumpur.' Richard G, the leader of the small party answered.

Anthony thought for a moment before asking another question. 'Is it true all the Japanese citizens in Ipoh were rounded up?'

'Yes, they weren't sure how many of them were in touch with the advancing Japs so it was safest to intern them all in a large house in the centre of town. Ironically it took a direct hit during one of the raids and there were multiple casualties. The rest were put in a lorry and sent to Kuala Lumpur.

'Not boiled alive in oil as the fifth columnists would have you believe.' One of the other men chipped in.

Anthony looked confused and Richard gave a wry smile. 'The bastards started rumours saying we'd murdered them all.'

Anthony looked horrified.

'The Japs have their own idea of morality and it doesn't seem to match ours. No doubt you've heard of the atrocities in China?'

Anthony nodded. 'Yes, Nanking was pretty well reported.'

'Well, there are rumours they've been ordered not to take prisoners as it will slow them down.' Richard face was impassive.

Anthony decided to change the subject. 'Are the Chinese working with us?'

'Yes, although we are supposed to be careful of the Communists, but we're also hoping the Malayan Communist Party will also fight with us. The main thing is to defeat the Japs, we can worry about communism afterwards.'

Anthony didn't answer. He could see all sorts of problems ahead but, Richard was right, the most important thing was to throw the Japs out.

****

Arkley View, near Barnet
Colonel Sinclair switched off the radio and sat back. For once it appeared their information had been acted on. The small Brandenburg detachment sent to disrupt Operation Crusader by blowing up the railway lines had failed. They had told their interrogators what they'd done and all the charges had been disarmed. The icing on the cake was Churchill notifying Parliament that the Garrison at Tobruk had finally been relieved. *'The enemy, who has fought with the utmost stubbornness and enterprise, has paid the price of his valour, and it may well be that the second phase of the Battle of Libya will gather more easily the fruits of the first than has been our experience ... so far.'* He hoped Churchill was right. Reports seemed to bear out the Prime Minister's words as Rommel's Afrika Corps did seem to be withdrawing westward although so far they had evaded all attempts to outflank them. He would ask Fred for an update on the location of the remainder of the Brandenburg Detachment and any further orders they had been given. That should give them some idea of what Rommel was planning. He stood up and was about to head over to the hut Fred was working in when the door suddenly flew open.

****

Landsberg am Lech,
Kristian had eventually arrived at Werl near Osnabrück and

handed over his aircraft. He was looking forward to flying the Me210 and to being in Germany again, away from the continual danger in the Soviet Union. The last few months had been hectic, Kiev had fallen and they had flown two further operations on the same day, one in support of their troops and the second one against the enemy's rail network east of Novgorod. It had taken nearly two weeks to secure the area around Kiev and their final objective had been a Soviet airbase, Lebedin, near to Kontop. On their return they had been told they were to go back to Germany to convert to Me210s. Kristian had been surprised to learn he was not the only one who was relieved. The past three months had taken their toll on all the pilots, not just him and all he could think about was seeing Ulrike and Manfred again. The Me210 had originally been brought into service in 1940 but had proved totally useless in combat conditions. Since then considerable work had been carried out although rumours were still circulating about its inadequacies. Kristian didn't really care at that moment, he was too excited to be going home, well a lot nearer home anyway. Landsberg was 50km west of Munich so he should be able to get some leave.

His first flight in the new bomber was impressive, it was much faster than its predecessor and the bomb load was carried inside. It could climb quicker and its dive was more suitable for their operational requirements. The only downside that he could see was its habit of swaying during take-off meaning he had to make constant adjustments to the rudder and throttle to keep it straight. He soon became used to flying the plane as they trained him in bombing, aerial gunnery, dive bombing and formation flying but then some new crews arrived and after a spate of minor accidents they were moved to Lechfeld which had longer runways.

Kristian stared out at the endless snow carpeting the runway and wondered when they would be able to fly again. The only good thing was that he could spend more time with Ulrike and Manfred.

****

Arkley View, near Barnet

'Fred, is something wrong?' Colonel Sinclair looked up in surprise. Fred normally telephoned him if he had found something.

'The message about the Japanese,' Fred saw no point messing about so he came straight to the point. 'You did hand it over did you?'

The Colonel's face darkened. 'I told you to forget all about that message...'

He didn't get any further before Fred interrupted. 'Yes I know and I had done until I found that someone was ringing you from Liverpool at the same time our missing spy was there. Something you didn't mention. Now I am not sure what to believe.'

'I sent someone up to Liverpool to see what he could find out.' The Colonel frowned. 'How did you pick up on his signal, he rang from a secure line in Derby House?'

Fred relaxed slightly. 'Our people are quite good sir.' He sighed. 'I'm sorry, I jumped to conclusions.'

The Colonel shook his head. 'No, I should have told you. And as to the Japanese attacks, I did pass them on, but no one seems to have acted on them.'

'Perhaps you should investigate the person you told sir?'

The Colonel was about to say no when he changed his mind. 'Maybe that's a good idea.' Their eyes met and Fred felt his anger drain away.

'I'll get back to work then sir.'

'Yes, please do. Can you keep an eye on that lot in North Africa as we seem to be having trouble outflanking them. It would be nice to sort Rommel out before the Americans get involved.'

Fred looked confused. The Colonel gave a wry smile.

'It will show that we are actually capable of defeating those bastards without American manpower. Otherwise they'll claim we can't manage without them.'

Fred grinned. 'We've survived this long. The odds were pretty much against that eighteen months ago.' His face darkened. 'And if they'd taken notice of our intelligence we might have had more success.' He shook his head, no point repeating himself. 'I'll go back to work then.'

Chapter 24

Singapore

Geoffrey read the wireless transmissions in despair. It was only two days since the Japanese had begun their attack and they had already destroyed most of the allied aircraft in Malaya. 'Are you sure they haven't found the bloody spy?'

Kang shook his head. 'No, but they are sure there is one because the Japs seem to know the correct recognition codes despite the fact that they are changed every day.'

'You need to find out where those signals are coming from Kang. I don't care if you have to listen to every bloody signal on the airwaves.'

Kang nodded and went back to what he was doing. Geoffrey continued to read the bad news coming out of the north. It seemed the defenders had held back the first wave of enemy troops to land in Kota Bharu and managed to destroy two Japanese transport ships, but the sheer numbers of attackers had soon overwhelmed them. Then the Zeros had begun bombing the airfields in northern Malaya, their accuracy had taken the allied command by surprise, but Geoffrey was sure their efficiency was more likely to be due to the presence of a spy on one of the airfields. The enemy had successfully destroyed several installations and now there were fewer than half the British aircraft remaining, they had retreated to Kuantan.

'I thought Operation Matador was supposed to stop the Japs over the border in Thailand?' Kang looked up from the transmitter briefly.

'They left it too late to implement it, then sent them to Jitra to form a defence line there. But they couldn't hold them. The heavy rain, sheer number of attacking forces.' Geoffrey shrugged. 'The bastards captured weapons, vehicles and communication equipment, not to mention over a thousand prisoners.'

'And now they are attacking Penang...' Kang was pale, memories of the Japanese assault on Nanking fresh in his mind. 'Can we hold them there?' He resisted the temptation to cross his fingers for luck.

Geoffrey shrugged. 'We have no aircraft to protect the city, I imagine it's only a matter of time before we evacuate the civilians and retreat even further south.' For a moment he thought about Ruth and wondered if he would ever see her again. Thank God she hadn't come with him. At least he didn't have to worry about her fleeing the Japs, having to endure the horrors Kang had. He placed a reassuring hand on his subordinate's shoulder. 'We're not done yet Kang. I'm probably just getting old. I'm sure we'll hold them eventually and then reinforcements will arrive and we'll turn them back.'

Kang gave a wry smile. He knew what Geoffrey was trying to do and while he appreciated his friend's attempt to put his mind at rest, he thought Geoffrey's first assessment was more accurate. The British and Americans had been caught napping, despite their attempts to warn them of the Japanese intentions.

****

London

Madeline had verified the airman's identity and then turned her attention to the other agents she was monitoring. She was not expecting to hear anything else from Charlotte until she had more airmen to verify or something else important to report. Her thoughts drifted to Jimmy and she smiled. He had flown into her life like a breath of fresh air and completely changed everything. She still couldn't believe how the short time they had spent together had made everything clear. Thanks to Jimmy she had even found her father again.

Madeline sighed as she thought back to the last meeting with her father and the elephant in the room that neither of them had yet discussed or even mentioned. She gave a wry smile at the old expression, apparently originating from a Russian poet whose name she couldn't remember, something about a man going into a museum and noticing lots of things but not the elephant. Madeline shook her head. It described their situation very well, skating around various subjects but not actually touching on the one thing that was really important. Although she now had no idea what to say if he did ask. She'd had everything planned initially, knew exactly what to say and what to ask but now she'd met Jimmy and everything had changed she was floundering, no longer knowing in which direction she should go. If only she could ask Jimmy. Madeline almost laughed out loud at the very idea except it wasn't in the slightest bit funny, then she shivered. Perhaps that was her answer. She should remain silent, say nothing and if her father brought up the subject, well she would have to deal with that, when and if it happened.

****

Penang, Malaya

Anthony and the rest of the small SOE team finally arrived in Butterworth, the ferry point for Penang, just in time for another daily raid, the previous ones had destroyed most of the British fighters on the RAF aerodrome and the Naval Base covering the town in thick black smoke from burning buildings. The roads to the harbour were packed with fleeing civilians and blocked with debris. Others had large craters which were roped off slowing their journey even more.

When they finally reached Perai they could see several Royal Naval steamers in the bay, their white ensigns flying in the breeze. For a brief moment Anthony imagined what it would have been like before the war then he was brought abruptly back to the present. A flat bottomed, rust stained, open decked paddle steamer pulled alongside the jetty and they began quickly loading the lorries. It only took around half an hour to cross the two mile Kra Straight until it reached the twelve hundred foot Swettenham Pier, the lorries drove swiftly down the ramp through crowds waiting for the return journey and along the waterfront full of fishing boats, sampans and high decked Chinese junks with large eyes painted on the bows to ward off evil spirits.

On the other side of the waterfront were various rubber and tin warehouses abandoned when the war had broken out. Eventually the lorries arrived outside the Eastern Hotel located on the hill which overlooked the island's capital, Georgetown. Anthony climbed out and stared down on the vast areas of scrub and jungle below. He could make out monkeys, butterflies, deer… and then the sound of aeroplanes broke his concentration.

'The daily raid on Butterworth.' Richard muttered as the rest of the men climbed out quickly of the lorries and began searching the sky.

Below them Anthony could also see the citizens of Georgetown pouring into the streets to watch the daily spectacle across the water. Anthony turned his attention to the approaching planes when he suddenly realised something was wrong.

'Their bomb doors are open!' He yelled but his warning was much too late. The aircraft were already diving low over the hotel and then the bombs began falling. Anthony was vaguely aware of monkeys screaming as they rushed back into the jungle to hide, before his attention was captured by the scenes in Georgetown. Bombs were crashing onto the waterfront and into Bishop Street, the busy commercial centre of the city's capital. Anthony and his companions sheltering by the hotel could clearly hear the screams of the dying below them while the ground pulsated with every explosion.

Having dropped their lethal cargo the aircraft then flew around and came in again, this time firing their machine guns into the packed streets and dropping anti-personnel mines and incendiaries. Panic ensued among the town's 170,00 strong population, some were mown down by machine gun fire, others trampled to death by the stampede of people trying to escape the death raining down upon them. Citizens who had remained indoors were trapped by falling debris and collapsing buildings, the wooden buildings and shops quickly catching fire, trapping those inside.

While Anthony, Richard and the other men remained close to the hotel the carnage below continued. Suffocating clouds of toxic smoke from the burning rubber warehouses drifted across the waterfront, unarmed ferries exploded from direct hits, machine guns raked the decks of ships leaving them covered in dead and dying, back in the city the fire station took a direct hit, its equipment completely destroyed, the police station was also targeted, its staff deserting in terror. There were bodies everywhere, in the sea, in the wreckage of shops and buildings and even in the monsoon ditches. As the death toll mounted the aeroplanes emptied their guns, turned around and flew back to Indo China. The only defence came from the small steamers off shore who fired their four inch guns at the bombers with little success. *SS Kuala* managed to bring down one bomber with its Lewis gun, but *HMS Sui Ho* was badly damaged and *HMS Kampar* only just avoided sinking. The first Japanese blitzkrieg had ensured that all civil organisation in Fortress Penang had ceased to exist.

****

Pas-de-Calais region, France

'Marie has been arrested.' Gérard rushed into the room, strain etched on his pale angular face.

Charlotte stared at him, her voice refusing to work for several seconds. She eventually cleared her throat. 'Where? I mean why? Was it one of the airmen?'

Gérard shook his head. 'I have no idea yet. A courier from one of the other networks was on another train and saw her being escorted off by a German soldier.'

'A soldier? Not the Gestapo?' Charlotte frowned.

'Does it matter?' Gérard snapped.

'No, I suppose not... what happened to the airman?'

Gérard looked confused, then shook his head. 'I don't know.'

'Surely they arrested him as well?' Charlotte persisted.

Gérard stared at her. 'You're right. I don't know. The courier didn't mention the airman.'

'Then he's still out there on his own?'

'You can't be thinking of looking for him?' Gérard looked horrified. 'That's madness.'

'We can't leave him out there.'

'Why not? He's not in any trouble is he?' Gérard snapped again. 'They'll just arrest him and send him to a POW camp.'

'But he might approach someone else, put them in danger.' Charlotte reached for her coat, scarf and hat. 'I'll go down the line and see if I can find him. Where was she arrested?'

'Arras. But I don't think you should go there. They might be waiting for someone else to come along.'

'We promised to help him Gérard and anyway, if they were after the escape line, they would have picked up the airman too or arrested Marie when she was about to hand him over. That way they would get two couriers.'

'Or it's a trap!'

'I don't think it is.' Charlotte smiled and headed for the door. 'Go and stay somewhere else for a couple of days. If it's safe I'll put the plant in the window.' She indicated the cacti that was residing on the coffee table.

'Alright, be careful.' Gérard suddenly frowned. 'How will you recognise him?'

'I saw the photo when Marie was preparing his documents.' She hurried out of the door leaving Gérard staring after her in concern.

****

Llandow, South Wales

Jimmy was relieved to have been almost immediately transferred to X Squadron which was the gunnery squadron. Formation flying had never been his favourite and trying to teach it to trainees who were not very predictable was definitely not his idea of fun. Life in the gunnery squadron was marginally less hazardous. His role was to take up trainees in the Miles Master II and teach them how to attack a drogue. This was like a huge wind sock being dragged through the sky by another aircraft at about 100mph. Jimmy didn't mind flying with the pilots but he hated it when it was his turn to pull the drogue as the pilots seemed to fire at random, bullets went everywhere and he had no idea how they managed to miss him.

Jimmy climbed out of his cockpit, spoke briefly to the student before heading back to the instructor's mess. It had been a particularly hairy experience and he was in desperate need of a decent cup of tea in lieu of something stronger.

'Bloody hell that looked a bit close for comfort!' The speaker was a big bear of a man with a shock of red hair and moustache sitting by the window.

Jimmy grinned. 'You're telling me. Bloody lunatics some of them, don't know their arse from their elbow.'

'Gerald Le Cheminant. Call me Chem, it takes less time.' He held out his hand and Jimmy shook it.'

'Jimmy, pleased to meet you. French?'

'Certainly not.' He sounded so indignant Jimmy grinned. 'I'm from Guernsey.'

'You look familiar. Were you at Biggin Hill?'

'92 Squadron.'

'I thought so. I was in 66. Bit rough for a while.'

'Certainly was. Fancy a drink?'

'After that lot I think I deserve one.' Jimmy replied. The two men requisitioned a couple of bicycles and headed into the nearest village for a few pints.

'Have you got a girl Chem?'

'She's called Eileen, lives in Twyford, near my family.' He pulled out a photo.

'Serious?' Jimmy asked.

'I'm thinking of asking her to marry me.'

'Now that is serious.' Jimmy fell silent.

'What about you?'

'Yes, her name is Madeline but I'm not thinking about marriage or anything yet.' Jimmy ignored the voice in his head calling him a liar. He had thought of nothing else lately but until he saw her again he wasn't going to rush into anything. It might just be because he was missing her.

****

Rosyth, Scotland

John smiled to himself as he listened to some of the young ratings complaining how sick they felt. Their first voyage in the North Sea had been a success but the sea had been very calm leading most of the young sailors to assume they didn't suffer from sea sickness. Unfortunately, they had soon discovered while training with the *Arethusa* further north, when the sea wasn't so accommodating, that they weren't immune and the ship had been delayed for two hours while the crew recovered. The working up period had consisted of endless drills, gunnery practice, learning to deal with any type of fire that might occur, firing torpedoes, learning the safest way to go through mine fields without any danger, known as streaming paravanes, towing the ship and various other skills needed whilst in action. John had been through this type of training several times but he didn't object to being reminded, especially as some of the drills had changed since he'd last been at sea. He wondered how Elsie was settling in. It was a shame he couldn't have been with her but he had a job to do and he was sure she would manage. He turned his attention back to the various wireless transmission sets on board and concentrated on ensuring they were working efficiently. The training would finish soon and then the real work would begin. As he listened to the crew complaining about the endless repetition and boring drills he was tempted to suggest that they should make the most of this time but he could remember what it was like to be young so he didn't. Part of him agreed with them, it had been so long since he'd been at sea he was looking forward to being back out there but then he thought about Elsie and Rodney and he was grateful for every minute he was still safe.

****

Arras, France

Charlotte arrived at the station and walked purposefully towards the platform. There were no soldiers around, she couldn't see any Gestapo agents, but there was no sign of the airman either. She couldn't afford to stand around looking lost so she made her way into the street and headed in the direction of the nearest café. She would buy a coffee and then try to work out where the airman was likely to have gone.

The café windows were steamed up and she had entered before she realised there were four German soldiers sitting near the window. Realising it would look suspicious if she turned around and walked straight back out again she tried to appear nonchalant and made her way to an empty table near the counter.

Having ordered her coffee Charlotte took out her newspaper and pretended to read, anything to avoid any eye contact with the soldiers. Her heart was pounding and she wondered briefly if coffee was such a good idea after all. She was staring down at the print, her brain racing as she tried to think where the young man could have gone when she was aware of a movement near the table.

'Good morning fraulein.'

Charlotte looked up. The soldier was tall, good looking with blue eyes and pale blonde hair and he was smiling down at her. She licked her lips nervously wondering how to respond. There was no point antagonising him but how could she fraternise with the enemy? She realised he was waiting for some kind of reply. Saying nothing wasn't an option.

'Good morning.' She smiled briefly and resumed staring down at the newspaper and hoped he would take the hint.

'I was wondering of you would like to join us?'

Obviously not. Charlotte was about to say no when she suddenly realised this could be a useful opportunity to gather some information. 'That's very kind of you.' She looked up at him again, this time giving him a genuine smile. She could feel the atmosphere in the small café changing, disapproval filling the air, but no one knew her here and she would be leaving soon. She stood up and made her way to the table where the soldier pulled back the chair for her to sit down.

'Conrad.' He introduced himself.

'Estee Martin.' She looked around and hoped her nervousness wasn't showing. This was the first time she'd had any real contact with the enemy.

'So what brings you to this café?'

'I was supposed to be meeting a friend at the station but she wasn't there so I thought I'd have a coffee and then go back and see if she had caught a later train.'

'Is she as beautiful as you Estee? If so I could come with you to look.' I'm Henrik by the way.' He held out his hand to groans and laughter from his companions. Despite her fear Charlotte found herself joining in.

'I'm sure she'll be very pleased to know you were interested.'

'Would you like something to eat?' Conrad's attention was very flattering and for a few seconds she forgot where she was. It was nice to be able to behave normally for a short while and it wasn't as if she would ever see them again.

'I'm fine thank you, but don't let me stop you.'

'Where are you from?'

'Calais.' Charlotte answered. 'What about you? Are you billeted in Arras or moving through?'

Conrad's face fell. 'We're on our way south. I can't say any more than that.'

'No, of course not.' Charlotte smiled encouragingly, sipped her coffee and wondered how long it would take her to find out what she wanted to know. There was nothing like a challenge to make her forget her fear.

Chapter 25

Singapore

Geoffrey was reading the latest reports about the Japanese attack on Penang when Kang came running in. 'We've found him! The spy I mean.' He took a breath. 'Well not us exactly, but the airmen at Alor Setah. One of the men was missing when they went into the trenches during an air raid, they went looking for him and discovered a transmitter, it was still warm apparently.'

Geoffrey dragged his attention away from the devastating report and concentrated on Kang. 'Have they got him?'

'Yes, he's been arrested. Patrick Stanley Heenan is his name. He is a captain with the Indian Army Air Liaison Unit. The British Military Police are bringing him here as we speak.'

Geoffrey nodded. 'Good, although I fear it's probably too late. Thanks to his help we have virtually no aircraft left up there and the Japs are rapidly heading this way.' He turned his attention back to Penang and his earlier depression returned. Despite the best efforts of some of the High Command he couldn't see any way out of the noose that seemed to be tightening around them and he tried to ignore the nagging feeling that their time would soon be up.

****

Pas-de-Calais region, France

Gérard shook his head in disbelief. 'You took too much of a chance.'

Charlotte shrugged. 'Isn't that what we're all doing? And it really wasn't that difficult.' She smiled as she remembered how easy it had been to find out which regiment they were with and where they were going, south to Italy and then to Greece. London had been delighted with the information. Unfortunately, she hadn't found the airman in time. She had received word that morning that he had been picked up trying to get on a train in Paris. She was surprised he'd got that far on his own. Fortunately he couldn't identify any of them and would just be put in a POW camp. Charlotte was more concerned about Marie who was still missing. Obviously she hadn't talked or the Gestapo would have been sniffing around but that didn't mean she wouldn't so they had changed all their procedures, she had even moved the wireless although she was sure Marie had no idea where it had been, but there was no point taking chances.

'I don't understand where Marie has gone.' Gérard had obviously read her thoughts.

'It's very strange.' Charlotte agreed. 'There was no sign of anyone in the station, no trap, not even any Gestapo hanging around. I didn't see anyone. Surely if they'd arrested her there would have been some sign?'

'Then why else would a soldier arrest her?'

'That doesn't make sense either Gérard. Why would a soldier arrest her? Maybe she knew him, went willingly?' She thought for a few moments. 'I'd like to speak to your contact, the one who witnessed it.'

'I'm not sure if they'll talk to you.' Gérard looked concerned.

'Tell them to meet me in the church, they can sit behind me so I can't see them. I just want to ask them some questions.'

Gérard stared at her thoughtfully but didn't answer.

Charlotte sighed and fought down her rising irritation. 'Come on Gérard, we can't go on like this. We are stuck in limbo. We can't do anything until we know what's going on in case we put anyone else at risk.'

Gérard nodded. 'Alright. You're correct, we can't go on like this.' He stood up, finished his coffee and headed for the door. 'I'll tell them you'll be in the cathedral at three o'clock, third pew from the front.'

Charlotte watched him go and sighed. Hopefully the meeting would provide some answers. If not she would have to ask London what they should do.

****

Gateshead

'I can't believe you thought we would be safer up here.' Elsie hugged Rodney tighter as the explosions grew louder. This was the third night in a row that the bombs had fallen and the third night they had spent in the shelter. The bombing campaign had started just after they had moved north and Elsie was seriously beginning to wish she'd stayed on the south coast. 'Perhaps I should take Rodney and go back home, back to Maidstone I mean.'

John had come back on leave to find Gateshead suffering their worst blitz of the war and he was horrified to think that Elsie and Rodney had been sheltering every night since they'd moved up. He would never have suggested they come north if he'd known this was going to happen. But now she was here there had to be another solution. He was about to answer when another massive explosion shook the shelter and Rodney whimpered.

John suddenly had a brainwave. Elsie didn't need to stay in the city. 'I'll find you somewhere out of the city, in a village somewhere away from the bombing. That way you'll be safe and still close to me?' He hated the pleading note in his voice but the thought of her going back to Kent was like a dagger in his heart. After Christmas he would probably be going back to sea for months and he needed to know she would be safe before he went. Despite the attacks on Gateshead it had to be better up here, away from the south coast. He just had to find a nice quiet village somewhere.

Elsie hugged Rodney tight to soothe his fears and watched John's face. She didn't want to desert him but this was the most frightened she'd been since the war had started and the Germans had begun their bombing campaign. 'Do you think you'll be able to do that? Find a little village out of the way I mean?' She waited until the explosions died away and it was relatively quiet before answering him. She could already smell the overpowering aroma of broken sewage pipes mingling with gas and she cleared her throat.

'I can try.' John's spirits rose. 'Just give me a few days to have a look around, please. I'll commandeer a bike and find somewhere I promise.'

Elsie nodded. 'Alright. A few days then. You do know it's not because I want to go back home don't you?'

John smiled and put his arm around them. 'Of course I do and I wouldn't be happy about leaving you like this, not if I was back at sea. If I can't find somewhere we're both happy with then I'll drive you back south myself!'

****

Singapore
Geoffrey stared out at the windswept Naval Base and peered through the monsoon rains trying to make out the outlines of the two

capital ships of Z-Force of the Far East Fleet, the King George V-Class battleship, *The Prince of Wales* and the Battlecruiser *Repulse*. He could see cranes and disembowelled ships in the repair docks but no sign of the ships and feeling uneasy he reached for his binoculars. Surely they were still in port? With no air cover it would be suicidal to take the ships to sea. Outside it was pouring with rain but Geoffrey barely noticed. He put the glasses down and headed out of the door. He would go and speak to Colonel Warren, find out what was going on.

Ten minutes later he bumped into the Colonel walking through the teeming rain and was about to ask him what he knew when a dispatch rider pulled up alongside them and handed the Colonel a message. Geoffrey realised he was holding his breath but before he could do anything about it the Colonel was cursing under his breath.

'Bad news sir?' Geoffrey couldn't hold on any longer.

Colonel Warren stared at him. '*The Prince of Wales* and *Repulse* have both been sunk and Admiral Sir Tom Phillips, the new commander of the Far East Fleet is missing.'

Geoffrey wondered if he'd misheard. 'I don't understand? The Japs sunk them in the Naval Base?'

'No, Phillips took Z- Force north to intercept the Japanese fleet but they were attacked by submarines and aircraft. They had no air support because of the damage done to the RAF airfields and were relying on the bad weather to provide enough cover. It didn't work.'

Geoffrey paled, shock etched on his features. 'What now?' He eventually asked.

'I think we should go to Penang and see what is going on there ourselves, if you're up for it of course?'

Geoffrey nodded. 'That sounds like a good idea. I read the earlier reports, they said it's been *bombed into impotency* whatever the hell that means?'

Colonel Warren didn't answer, he was already striding towards the station. Geoffrey took a breath and followed, his thoughts racing as he wondered what on earth he was going to find in Penang. His first shock was Singapore Railway Station, which was crammed full of people trying to find places on trains going north, away from the frequent bombing raids on the city. Meanwhile the trains coming into Singapore were full with European women and children, carrying all their possessions in bulging suitcases. As the two populations met chaos ensued. Geoffrey fought his way through to the Penang train only to find the platform packed with more than two thousand passengers, families with their relatives and servants, their animals and household goods, all trying to find places on the train while the beetle-nut chewing porters demanded larger tips. He couldn't see Colonel Warren but he guessed he was there somewhere so he continued to try and climb aboard but there were no berths and eventually he gave up. As he stepped back on the platform some army lorries arrived carrying soldiers. One look at them told Geoffrey all he needed to know, their sunburnt faces indicated they had probably just arrived in the Far East. As he watched they formed up in ranks, weapons on one shoulder, kit bags on the other and began marching into the crowds which quickly parted.

'There's no berths, not unless we pay for them, according to one of the porters.' The Colonel appeared beside him making him jump. He saw Geoffrey's expression and gave a wry smile. 'Yes, I was tempted to knock the bastard into next week, but that probably wouldn't have helped so I've contacted HQ and they've booked us on. Follow me. Oh, there's no dining car so the only way to get any food is to buy it from the vendors on the station.'

The normal service was a fast reliable twelve hours, but bombing had destroyed rolling stock, stations and track so twenty four hours later they were still on the train.

When they finally arrived in Penang they were told that the enemy was outside Kroh, just sixty miles away.

****

North Africa

Eric waved goodnight to his comrades and headed reluctantly towards his own bedspace. Once inside he slowly lay down on his bunk and stared up at the ceiling. The room seemed unnaturally quiet after the laughter and camaraderie in the Mess, the air so still he could hear his breathing. Perhaps he should have stayed longer so he wasn't the only person here, but the false bonhomie had been getting through to him. The journey back from Greece had been depressing enough, the failure weighing heavy on him, the scorn in his commander's voice wouldn't leave him, his words replaying themselves in Eric's brain as he tried to work out whether Stabsfeldwebel Doehring had guessed the idea to murder the sentries had been his, not the crewman's. He had arrived back at their camp to find the other members of the team welcoming enough, but he could see the disdain in their eyes, although most of them tried to hide it with commiserations. If only the raid had been successful he could have swaggered into the camp, instead of creeping back in, the only survivor of a failed assault which suggested he could be a coward.

Eric clenched his fists and turned over onto his side. He could no longer remember the last time he had slept without the nightmares... not since the night Karl... Eric squeezed his eyes more tightly shut. Perhaps if he thought about something nice... some happy memories instead... He focussed his attention on his childhood, on the peaceful days with his family before everything had changed and exhaustion finally took over. As he drifted into sleep his body twitched, his eyes fluttered, his legs jerked. Within seconds the farm had vanished and he was back in Belgium in 1940.

Eric glanced across at his brother Karl as they listened carefully to Leutnant Grabart's orders while pulling on their Belgian greatcoats and caps. It was their first mission with the Brandenburg Detachment and Eric wasn't sure whether it was nerves or excitement that was churning up his stomach. It had been his idea for the two brothers to volunteer for the special forces. Karl had been content to join the infantry but Eric had talked him out of it, saying they would have much more excitement doing this and they would have more opportunity to get their revenge on the British. The idea of avenging their parents had swung it and Karl had taken little persuasion to follow Eric to Germany. Both brothers were fit from their life on the farm in South Africa so had little difficulty in passing the fitness tests and their ability to speak several African dialects, as well as British and French with no German accents, had enabled them to be among the first chosen and now their talents were to be put to good use.

The plan was to prevent a repeat of the Great War in which the Belgians had deliberately flooded the Nieuport area by opening the Yser sluices and flooding the area. This had halted the German advance. Determined not to suffer a similar fate this time the Brandenburg had been ordered to seize the pump control houses on the south bank of the river at the foot of the Nieuport – Ostend road bridge. They had appropriated a Belgian Army bus and, dressed as

Belgian infantrymen, their orders were to get as close as possible to the bridge.

The bus had not been challenged as it made its way through the fighting area and into the town but once in Ostend they came under suspicion as the Belgian soldiers milling around the town noticed that the soldiers on the bus apparently didn't have any weapons.

Eric grinned at Karl and before his younger brother could move he had opened the door of the bus and was speaking to them in fluent French *'We fled the fighting with our lives, we're looking for more weapons...'* He didn't get any further.

'The Belgian Army has surrendered.'

Eric didn't have to feign surprise, he was shocked and disappointed as he'd been hoping to kill some British and if the Belgians had given up maybe they had too. *'Where are the British? Have they surrendered too?'*

'No, they're still fighting, up near Nieuport, on the far side of the Yser, only about a Company strength though.' The man fell silent and Eric breathed an inward sigh of relief. If the British were only of company strength it should make their job easier and he and Karl would be able to begin their revenge. He turned his attention back to the mission. *'What about the bridge? Has it been cut?'* There was a possibility they were too late.

'No, the charges have been laid but it's not been blown.' The soldier lost interest in the conversation and when he turned back to his comrades Eric took the opportunity to disappear back inside the bus, encouraging the driver to get moving while quickly explaining the situation to the others.

Leutnant Grabart thought quickly. *'We still need to make sure they can't blow up the bridge or flood the area. Let's go.'*

Although it wasn't a long journey to the bridge trying to get through the battle torn areas took forever and it was about seven in the evening when they finally reached their target. Almost immediately they came under fire from the British posts on the other side of the river and, worried that they would blow the bridge before they could get across, Grabart glanced at his men and picked out Eric and Karl.

'You two crawl across the bridge and cut the charges, once the bridge is safe open fire at the houses and then the rest of us will come across.'

As tracer bullets whipped along the length of the bridge Eric and Karl collected their insulated wire cutters and an MP38 then began crawling on their stomachs towards the bridge. Once they reached it Eric realised they would need to use the pavement to get to the charges so would need to know at what height the British machine gunners were firing. Eric cautiously raised a helmet on the end of the wire cutters and when it reached a foot above the ground the guns started firing. Eric swallowed nervously. They would barely have more than half an inch clearance but there was no other way. Keeping as low as possible the two men slid onto to the raised pavement and then Eric spotted the first charge, lit up by a Very light. It seemed they hadn't been noticed yet so he wasted no time in cutting the lead, rendering it harmless.

They inched forward, the next Very light exploded in the sky showering them in light and Eric and Karl froze, waiting for the magnesium flare to die. Eric held his breath, counting slowly. Eventually the light faded, the darkness became even more intense and yet again they moved slowly forward, another lead cut, another danger removed. The road neared the centre of the bridge, rising slightly, and the bullets grew even closer until the road dipped again, falling away towards the far bank of the Yser. Eric was now in full view of the British defenders, and when another Very light flared he rolled closer to the structure of the bridge, his breathing controlled while he reached for the wire cutters, felt for the lead and snipped quickly. He had cut three leads, he knew Karl had cut another three, neutralising the charges so the bridge should now be safe from the explosives which meant the rest of the Brandenburg men could make their way across, take control and prevent any counterattack. Eric nodded at Karl who immediately opened fire on the houses opposite and then all hell broke loose behind them. Eric fired magazine after magazine, he was vaguely aware of Karl throwing a succession of grenades, the air was filled with the sounds of battle, the rattle of small arms, machine gun fire and grenades, destroying the British positions and eventually forcing the defenders back from the sluice houses.

Eric ran forward, checked the pump houses for explosives and, having satisfied himself that the sluices had not been opened, took up a defensive position. He was soon joined by his exultant companions. There was no counterattack, the British had slipped away to a new *defensive line near the evacuation beaches. The danger of flooding had gone, they had won yet another victory.*

Eric felt exhilarated and he looked around for Karl to join in the celebrations with him, but there was no sign of his brother.

'Where's Karl' Eric felt the beginning of panic. He grabbed one of the other men but the soldier shrugged and shook his head. Eric ran back to the bridge, there were a few bodies scattered around but he knew instinctively they weren't Karl. He stopped still, took a deep breath and then spun around slowly, searching the edges of the pavement carefully. They were in darkness now, which obscured his view and he couldn't see anything... His heart skipped a beat, nausea rose in his throat and Eric sank slowly to his knees in horror. 'No... no, no, no...' The body was by one of the charges that had been disabled, the arms and legs were outstretched, but it was the head that caught his attention. Karl was barely recognisable, his face smashed apart by numerous bullets.

Eric woke with a start and sat up. His heart was racing, his cheeks wet from tears. The recurring nightmare always ended the same way, with him finding Karl's body. It was nearly two years now, but the pain never grew less. He eased himself back onto the pillow and stared up into the darkness, thinking about their coming mission, to disrupt the British supply lines. He closed his eyes again and repeated the oath he had made on the bridge in Belgium. The British had not only killed his parents they had now taken his brother too. They were responsible for destroying his world... all he had left was the satisfaction revenge would give him. The war had always been personal, but his brother's death had made everything a million times worse. Karl had only volunteered because of him; his brother would have been safe in South Africa if not for Eric's determination to make the British pay. Eric clenched his fists, he would not rest until he had killed as many British as possible and this new job would be the perfect opportunity.

Chapter 26

Pas-de-Calais region, France

Charlotte sat down carefully in the pew as arranged and waited patiently. It was ages since she'd last been inside a place of worship and then it had been her sister's funeral. After that she'd been too busy and, if she was honest, she hadn't felt like praying. God had let her down. He'd taken her twin and left her on her own. She still had her father but he hadn't been the same since Rebecca had died. Charlotte frowned. In fact she was sure he was keeping something from her, but she had no idea what. Maybe he knew something about Becca's death he wasn't telling her? She couldn't imagine what though. Her darling sister had been killed by the enemy and someone, somewhere had helped him leave the country. It was the only thing that made any sense. Charlotte realised she was clenching her fists and she tried to relax. There would be plenty of time after the war to look for the traitor. Maybe that was what her father was doing although why he hadn't told her she didn't know.

'Mademoiselle Martin?'

Charlotte nearly jumped out of her skin. She had been so engrossed in her thoughts she hadn't heard anyone approach. She glanced up at the young priest standing in front of her and cleared her throat.

'Oui. Je m'appelle Mademoiselle Martin.'

'Père Andre Barbeau.' He smiled, glanced around to check they were still alone then indicated that she move along the pew so he could sit down. 'I understand you have some questions for me?'

It took Charlotte a few seconds to recover, both from the surprise that the witness to Marie's arrest had been a priest and that he was making no attempt to hide his identity. She finished moving and stared at him. 'You were the one who saw Marie arrested.'

He nodded, his expression serious. 'Yes, I was getting off a train on the opposite platform when I saw the soldier approach her. I had been to Paris, to a seminar.'

'How do you know Marie?'

Père Andre expression relaxed slightly. 'She is one of my parishioners... had been for years. I knew she felt the same way as me about the occupation, so I was not surprised to know she was trying her best to do something about it.' He sighed. 'We are both working for the same thing, just in our different ways.'

'And she was definitely being arrested?' Charlotte put her curiosity about the priest aside and concentrated on the matter in hand. She was still confused about why Marie would have been arrested by a single soldier and not the Gestapo or even the police.

'I assumed so.' Père Andre frowned. 'But now I've thought about it I am not so sure.'

'What do you mean?'

He sighed. 'I think I just assumed it because I couldn't think of any other reason she would be with a German soldier...' He hesitated.

'But...?' Charlotte prompted.

'But she didn't look as if she was under duress. She looked... I don't know...normal I suppose.'

'Then why else would she be with the enemy?' Charlotte was talking to herself, but Père Andre answered.

'It occurred to me that maybe he was a friend, a boyfriend even?'

'Then why hasn't she reappeared?'

'I don't know.' He closed his eyes and thought back to the few brief moments on the platform. 'I think she may have seen me.' He said suddenly.

Charlotte stared at him in horror. 'You mean she went willingly because she knew him, but she saw you watching her and for whatever reason decided that it was too dangerous to come back. You're suggesting she was some kind of double agent?'

'I don't know. It sounds ridiculous when you say it out loud but I can't think of any other explanation.'

Charlotte didn't answer. If the priest was right they were all in trouble. But Marie? Was she really working with the Germans? And if she was why hadn't they already been arrested?

****

282 Boxley Road, Maidstone, Kent

Ruth listened to the radio broadcast in horror. She couldn't believe the Japanese had bombed Singapore, were now attacking Malaya and that they had sunk *The Prince of Wales* and *Repulse*. The attack on Pearl Harbour had been enough of a shock but at least the outcome for Britain had been a good one in that America was now in the war so they finally had a realistic chance of winning it. But this latest report from the Far East was like a kick in the teeth. How on earth could she find out if Geoffrey was alright?

'Ruth are you there?'

She looked towards the door and saw her half-brother standing there. 'I wanted to make sure you were alright after I heard the news. Have you heard anything from Geoffrey?' The concern on Frederick's face was enough to release all the pent up tension and she burst into tears.

Frederick put his arms around her. 'I'm sure he's not hurt Ruth.'

'Are you? He might have been out in his rescue boat, right in the thick of the action.'

Frederick frowned. 'I doubt he would have been at sea Ruth. The ships were sent with others to intercept the Japanese fleet in the north but they were spotted by submarines and planes and sunk.' He thought it unlikely that the rescue boats had been launched. It was more likely that they were all working hard preparing to defend Singapore. 'I'm sure you'll hear from Geoffrey once the situation settles down a bit.'

'What if they can't defend Singapore?'

Frederick laughed. 'Now you're letting your imagination and fears run away with you. Of course they'll defend Singapore. It's not like we're fighting the Germans out there. Its only the Japanese and we've had months, if not years, to prepare proper defences. The Japs won't know what's hit them.'

Ruth stared at him then gave a tearful smile. 'You're right of course. I'm being silly. I don't know what's the matter with me.' She wiped her eyes. 'How's Jeanne? Is she pleased to be back home after her little holiday?'

Frederick laughed. 'She had a great time. I'm not sure we're good enough for her now though, not being royalty. Spending time with the Queen of the Netherlands and the landed gentry definitely went to her head.'

Ruth laughed. 'She'll soon settle down. What about Betty and Margaret?'

'Betty is fine, doesn't say much but her job with the WAAF is important so she feels she's doing something useful.' He fell silent.

'And Margaret?' Ruth prompted.

Frederick sighed. 'I'm not sure where we went wrong Ruth. She seems to have a different boyfriend every night, well that's probably an exaggeration but she's going to get herself a terrible reputation.'

Ruth smiled. 'She's young Frederick. Just making the most of her life and if she's making some young men happy, men who are could be killed before they have a real chance to enjoy their lives, then is what she's doing so bad?'

Frederick sighed. 'A part of me understands that Ruth, but this is Maidstone we're talking about, not London or New York! She'll be tainted and lots of men having good memories won't help her then will it?'

'What does Alice say?'

Frederick shrugged. 'She's had a chat with her but...' He tailed off. It wasn't just the constant stream of young men traipsing through the house that was bothering him. He was still engaged on secret work for Colonel Sinclair, so their presence was a threat to the security of the country, but he couldn't mention anything about that to Margaret, or Ruth for that matter. Instead, he spent most of his time snapping at his middle daughter which wasn't very helpful.

Ruth was watching him carefully and she wondered what else he wasn't telling her. He looked tired so perhaps working full time and working as a Captain in the Home Guard was wearing him down. He wasn't a young man anymore. 'If it's disrupting your work with the Home Guard perhaps you should tell her that.'

Fredrick somehow managed not to show his shock at how close she was to the truth. 'Yes, maybe you're right. I think we're all just tired Ruth. Its over two years now and although some things have changed the war seems never ending.'

Ruth sighed. The brief lull in her concern for her husband had gone and she was close to panic again. Frederick was right, the war was expanding and now Geoffrey was in the firing line. If only she'd gone with him, at least she would know what was going on if she was living in Singapore.

****

Llandow, South Wales

Having returned from Chem's wedding and his very important role as best man Jimmy had struggled to settle down again. It had been nice to do something normal like attend a friend's wedding, he couldn't remember how long it was since he had really been able to relax. Chem had gone on honeymoon for a few days and he was missing his friend. At least he could let off steam with Chem. Although some of the students were really good, others were a nightmare to train and he sometimes found it difficult to remain calm when they were putting both him and themselves at risk. On days like that he was always relieved when he landed. But today he had spent the last hour in an old Lysander with a young Flight Lt called Greenaway. He was very keen and Jimmy was pleased with his progress and more relaxed than usual. They had just finished carrying out some routine defence exercises and after landing they had remained in the aircraft for several minutes while they discussed the training flight. Jimmy then climbed out and headed for the instructor's hut. He entered, intending to get himself a hot mug of tea but immediately sensed a strange atmosphere of gloom that reminded him poignantly of the days with the squadron. He glanced around, took a deep breath and was preparing to ask if anything was wrong when one of the men looked up.

'Have you heard?'

Jimmy swallowed nervously and shook his head. 'Heard what?'

'Pickles is dead.'

'What?' Jimmy was incredulous. He couldn't believe what he was hearing. In the days with the squadron, they had grown used to hearing that friends had been shot down or killed, but this was a training base. He shook his head as if to clear the cobwebs. 'I don't believe it. How?'

'A mid-air collision with a chap called Polton. They were doing some low level aerobatics, and... well clearly he didn't see the other chap coming.'

Jimmy slumped into a chair, everything else forgotten. Pickles was just 21 years old. He had survived the Battle of Britain only to die in a stupid training accident.

****

Pas-de-Calais

'Marie? Working with the Germans? That's ridiculous.' Gérard dismissed Charlotte's suggestion with barely a second thought, walked to his drinks cabinet and poured himself some brandy.

Charlotte waited for him to offer her some, but he didn't. Irritated, she snapped back. 'Yes, I thought so too, but we can't just discard it because we don't want to believe it.'

He swallowed the last of the brandy and let out a long sigh. 'What do you want to do then?'

'I think I should notify London.' Charlotte had thought long and hard and eventually decided she had no choice.

'What will they do?' Gérard began pacing back and forwards.

'I don't know. Presumably ask us to get some proof, unless they already have it.' She saw his confusion. 'I haven't made contact for several days, they may be waiting for me to call in.'

'Alright. Be careful Estee. Just because we haven't been arrested doesn't mean she hasn't told them everything they need to know. They could be waiting…'

'Waiting for what?' Charlotte stared at him.

'I don't know, maybe they want to find your transmitting equipment?'

Charlotte shivered. 'I hadn't thought of that.' She stood up and made her way to the door. 'It will take me about an hour to get there, make the transmission and then cycle back so if I am not back by seven you should leave.'

Gérard watched her go and then hurried upstairs. He would pack a suitcase just in case, but he would pray that they were both wrong.

****

Penang, Malaya

When Geoffrey finally reached Penang he found Georgetown virtually deserted, fires continued to rage out of control, the dead lay where they'd fallen, the only movement in the city was from soldiers looking for wounded and looters. The hospitals were full and there were temporary dressing stations in the streets manned by the wives of Volunteers, those male civilians who had volunteered to help defend the city. With the civilian authorities no longer operating dead bodies were beginning to pollute the water system and the risks of cholera and typhoid were growing. Not long after his arrival orders were given to the soldiers to start collecting the numerous bloated corpses littering every street and building and soon the streets were full of rickshaws, hand carts and stretchers taking them to be burnt on the makeshift pyres built from the remains of wooden buildings, tyres petrol and oil. Within a couple of hours the air was full of the stench of burning bodies.

Geoffrey tried to find out why no one had fired on the Japanese planes and was told that the only artillery available consisted of two six inch guns. He listened in growing anger as the young official explained that the defence plan had been abandoned back in September when the officer responsible had been transferred back to Singapore and for some reason had not been replaced.

Meanwhile a telephone link to the mainland was eventually re-established but when Colonel Warren got through to Headquarters he was told there were no plans to reinforce Penang, instead 11 Division had reformed at the Gurun Line, thirty miles from Butterworth and that they were intending to hold long enough for the Penang Garrison to be evacuated. Several hours later they were told there was little chance of 11 Division holding and they should immediately evacuate all European civilians.

****

Pas-de-Calais Region, France

Charlotte reached the deserted barn and pulled out her wireless from under the straw where she'd hidden it, then moved towards the door to where she'd hidden the wire arial before hurrying into the copse, measuring out the right amount and fastening the wire to one of the trees. Having double checked the time she was meant to be making contact Charlotte then tuned into the right frequency, connected the battery, put on her headphones, plugged in the morse key and lay out the message which she had coded earlier into the five letter groups of seemingly random combinations of letters. It was vitally important to get it right first time, as the last thing she needed was to have to send it twice, giving the enemy two opportunities to detect her. Switching on the wireless was the last thing she did because once it was turned on she was announcing her presence to the Funkabwehr, German radio intelligence.

Charlotte checked her watch again, counted down the seconds, moved the Morse key closer, then switched the set on, waiting impatiently for it to warm up. She gripped the Morse key again and began sending the message, finishing well within the five minutes they were advised was the limit to be on the air. Having quickly signed off, Charlotte replaced the radio, aerial, headset and Morse key into the metal box, placed the battery in her backpack, it would need recharging, and then stood silently listening for any signs that she had been detected. There was nothing, the woods were quiet other than the normal night time noises, insects and small creatures making their way through the undergrowth, the hoot of an owl, but no sound of engines and she began to relax slightly. Now to hide the equipment and get out of there. Just because she couldn't hear or see anything didn't mean they weren't there.

She reached the barn safely and was hiding the metal box under the straw when she heard a movement behind her.

'Hello Estee.'

Charlotte threw herself to one side, pulled out her pistol and aimed it in the direction of the voice.

'No, please don't shoot.'

Charlotte stared in disbelief. Marie was standing by the barn door and next to her was a German soldier.

****

Rosyth, Scotland

The crew of *Cleopatra* had just finished celebrating Christmas, and although the men had only been together for a short while they had been determined to enjoy it. An impromptu concert had been written with a short play and they even had costumes. It had passed off very well and then John had spent several days cycling around the area on a push bike until eventually he managed to find Elsie and Rodney somewhere else to live. This turned out to be a three storey house in a small village not far from Hadrian's Wall called Bardon Mill in Northumberland. The property was called Wool House Farm and was in the middle of nowhere. John was convinced it would not be on the path of any bombers, not even ones that had strayed off course. For the first time in ages he could really relax. Elsie loved it and Rodney was in his element. John would now be able to concentrate on his work.

After Christmas a 'buzz' had gone around that *Tirpitz* was intercepting the northern convoys and that *Cleopatra*'s first task was to help sink her. They had set sail into the angry North Sea, the ship tossing and turning, swaying wildly, climbing up high waves and falling into deep troughs, the crew gradually accustoming themselves to the violent seas and coming back from the eight day patrol considerably thinner. The first trip was a success although they never found the *Tirpitz*, but the crew had found their sea legs and John's equipment had worked perfectly despite the rough conditions.

****

Penang, Malaya

Anthony detonated the last of the bombs and watched as the remaining warehouses disintegrated. All records appeared to have disappeared so they had to rely on local knowledge to find anything that could be of use to the Japanese, anything they hadn't already destroyed by their continual bombing of the town.

Meanwhile, under the disbelieving eyes of many Asian citizens, the evacuation of over three hundred European citizens had taken place over night and they were now on the way to Kuala Lumpur by train. The members of the Chinese Cricket Club had boarded up the statue of Queen Victoria and the streets were empty of anyone other than looters.

Anthony turned his back on the waterfront and headed towards the Royal Navy launch that he'd discovered a few hours earlier. Surprisingly it was undamaged so he'd found some surviving crew from the *Repulse* and *Prince of Wales*, then they had started searching all the creeks and waterfront areas for any boats that were still sea worthy. Any they found were sunk using gunfire or grenades. As he finally made his way back to the waterfront the explosions died away and he wiped his brow in exhaustion. They had done everything they could, the garrison would be evacuated soon, in fact he could already see them heading down to the harbour. His thoughts elsewhere he was stepping onto dry land when he suddenly heard shouting, looked up and saw several enemy planes flying straight and low towards the rows of wounded lying helpless on their stretchers. Anthony held his breath but to his relief they flew on, heading for the mainland.

'The Japs have broken through!' Richard came running towards him. 'Their light tanks are heading this way. We need to get out of here now, get over to Butterworth and destroy what we can before they get here.'

The two men jumped aboard and headed towards the mainland, where they began destroying the installations around the naval base and the airfields. Behind them the light was fading fast, and soon the evacuation could be only seen by the glare of the burning oil dumps near the pier. In the distance they could hear the launches firing on what was left of the waterfront before they made their way out to sea and then all was quiet, the burning city left to the looters.

The silence was unnerving and Anthony felt uneasy. He shivered briefly before turning his attention back to his colleague. 'Where now?' He glanced down at the little ammunition he had left.

'Back to Singapore to get our new orders.' Anthony could just make out Richard's smoke blackened face in the darkness and wondered if he looked as dishevelled.

'Do you think they'll take Singapore too?'

Richard didn't answer immediately then he patted Anthony on the shoulder. 'No point speculating. We've done our job, we've destroyed anything that could be of use to the Japs, including the fast launches.'

'They seem so bloody well prepared, they'll probably have brought their own with them.' Anthony kicked the launch disconsolately. He couldn't believe they were going to lose to an enemy they should have easily defeated. It really didn't sit very well with him. He'd never run away from a fight before. He wasn't about to start now but what could a few men do against the might of the Japanese army? He looked into his backpack again and a thoughtful expression crossed his face. 'How about we stay a little longer and make their lives as difficult as we can?'

Richard frowned. 'I've virtually nothing left, I've used most of it and we've destroyed anything we could have used.'

Anthony grinned. 'I don't have much left either but… maybe we could send the others back, they could leave us what they have. Two men are harder to find than six. We could even try nicking their supplies to supplement what we do have. It's what we've been trained for after all?'

Richard shook his head in disbelief. 'You're mad. It's suicide.' He stared at Anthony for several seconds then finally shrugged, a wry smile crossing his face. 'But it's not like I've anything else to do!'

Part 3

1942

HMS Cleopatra

Cleopatra throws out smoke to shield the convoy as Euryalus elevates her forward 5.25 in (133 mm) guns to shell the Italian Fleet. Second Battle of Sirte, 22 March 1942

Chapter 27

Arkley View, near Barnet

Fred listened to the heated conversation between Colonel Sinclair and one of the senior civil servants. They were discussing Churchill's fury that he had not been aware that Singapore hadn't been fortified from the landward side. 'Apparently he told the King that he couldn't understand why no one had given orders to dig tank traps and build pill boxes hidden in the jungle. He is very concerned about the number of casualties from the continual air bombardments.' The senior civil servant said.

'Well, he could have asked.' Colonel Sinclair was watching the civil servant's face carefully.

'He said he would no more have considered Singapore having no landward defences than a battleship not having a bottom.'

The Colonel nodded. 'I have to say I agree with him. It is ridiculous.'

'Well sir, the troops were preoccupied training and building defences in Northern Malaya, the Army's role was to protect the naval base situated on the north shore of the island so they were training to fight in front of the shore not along it, years of financial limitations...' He fell quiet and the Colonel shrugged.

'None of them particularly good reasons. What it came down to was a lack of foresight and ignoring intelligence.' He was still watching the civil servant's face but there was no reaction.

'What intelligence sir? No one expected the japs to attack.'

Fred shook his head in disbelief. Obviously their intelligence had only reached the man at the top, Sir Peregrine Thompkin-Cartwright, and he had done nothing about it, for reasons best known to himself. At least the Colonel was investigating although he didn't appear to be getting very far. Unfortunately, they had not been in the habit of placing listening devices in rooms of men like Thompkin-Cartwright, although that had now been remedied. However, he had no intention of mentioning it to the Colonel, not unless it yielded results and so far nothing had been overheard that would lead them to think he was a traitor. Fred headed back to his hut. He would take a look at all the transcripts that had come in from that area. Maybe they were missing something.

****

Pas-de-Calais region, France
Charlotte let herself back into the cottage and smiled at Marie who was seated on the settee reading a book.

'Everything alright?'

Marie nodded. 'Yes. Did the message go alright?'

Charlotte smiled. 'You mean are you off our most wanted list?'

A sheepish expression appeared on Marie's face. 'I'm so sorry for causing all the trouble. I just panicked.'

'You were very lucky I didn't shoot you.'

'I know.' Marie shivered. 'I couldn't think of any other way to let you know what had happened.'

Charlotte shrugged. 'Well, it's all over now so let's forget about it. Have you planned how to move the next airman? Once we get the all-clear of course.'

'Yes, I'll take him by road, by car, it might be safer than train until we know the last one didn't say anything.' She sighed. 'I should never have abandoned him Estee, but I didn't really get time to think.'

'If you'd stopped to explain to him you would probably have all been arrested. As it is he did very well because he left the station and wasn't found until he was some distance away.' Charlotte sat down on the worn chair opposite Marie. 'How's Jacques?'

'Père Andre has taken him south to join the Maquis. He was happy to help, especially as he felt the whole mix up was his fault, which it wasn't of course.'

Charlotte shrugged. 'It's not surprising we're all jumpy and suspicious. Père Andre saw a German soldier holding your arm and, understandably, jumped to the wrong conclusion. You realised he had seen you with what appeared to be the enemy so you panicked and disappeared which made us all suspicious.'

'Jacques had managed to get all the way across Germany and back to France disguised as a German. He wasn't expecting to see me but when he did he just acted instinctively. You have no idea how shocked I was when he grabbed my arm. Then I recognised him. I was so pleased to see that he was alive I forgot everything else. We'd almost given up hope.'

'Have you told your parents yet, that their son is alive I mean?'

'Yes, and that he's gone south to carry on the fight.' Marie looked uncomfortable. 'I had to tell them that, otherwise they would have carried on worrying.'

'Well, there's not much chance of the Krauts finding him in the unoccupied zone so I'm sure it doesn't matter. I very much doubt they are still looking for him anyway. He's just one French soldier, he's not very important to them.'

'No, you're right, and they visited us when he escaped which was months ago. I doubt they'll be back.'

Charlotte smiled. 'I'm going to get some sleep. Don't worry about it anymore Marie and don't stay up too late.'

Marie grinned. 'Yes Mum!'

Charlotte threw a cushion at her before standing up and heading to bed. It had been a close call, not shooting Marie and her brother. And even after Marie had explained Charlotte had continued to have doubts but Gérard had verified Jacques' identity and that he'd been captured during the Fall of France and taken to Germany as slave labour. He had also been aware that the Germans had visited Marie's parents not long after Jacques had escaped so he was reasonably sure both Marie and Jacques were telling the truth. Charlotte had notified London and received a reply that night accepting her explanation but they had warned her to be careful and she had every intention of doing that. Whilst she wanted to believe Marie deep down she no longer really trusted her, so in future she would be careful about telling her too much.

****

Greenock, Scotland

The ship had sailed west from Rosyth heading towards America when the crew were told they were going to Greenock, apparently for a change of beer! John had mixed feelings, he was pleased to be going somewhere different after spending weeks staring at the same rocks and hills but he would miss Elsie and Rodney. He had now been promoted to Chief Petty Officer, the highest non-commissioned officer rank in the Royal Navy, and he knew they weren't just going to Scotland, they were going to Malta, but first they had important things to do. Several hours later they had steamed slowly between the snowy banks of the Clyde before dropping anchor off Greenock. Once there they began loading vast quantities of stores, the ships company worked unceasingly, ammunition was stored wherever they could find space for it, other stores were lined up everywhere, numerous torpedo warheads were stowed by the port torpedo tubes.

'We could start our own war!' Chris muttered.

John smiled at his young subordinate. Other than the sea trials this would be his first real experience of being at sea. 'Or open a new base!'

Chris laughed. 'I think I'd prefer that option.'

John smiled. 'Me too, but unfortunately I'm not in charge.'

'Where do you think we're going?'

'After Gib you mean?' John hesitated. He knew where they were going, it was part of his job to plan ahead so he could work out where the likely threats would come from, but should he tell Chris? 'No idea but given the amount of stores we're taking on, I would think it could be Malta.'

Chris paled. 'A nice safe journey then.' He said eventually.

John shrugged. 'Nowhere out there is safe Chris and imagine what it must have been like living on Malta the past couple of years.' He fell silent. Having listened to many signals from the Mediterranean since the beginning of the war he knew exactly how difficult their trip was likely to be but there was no point in worrying Chris.

****

Singapore

The massive explosion shook the building but Geoffrey hardly noticed. He guessed it was the Royal Engineers blowing up the causeway in an attempt to stop the Japs crossing from Johor into Singapore. He doubted it would slow them up for long. Despite the successful Australian attack on Japanese troops in Johor a couple of weeks earlier and the week long determined resistance by Allied troops without air support, Lt General E A Percival had finally approved the withdrawal of troops into Singapore. It was under two months since the Japanese had begun their campaign and they were now on the verge of taking Singapore. He'd spoken briefly to Colonel Warren earlier that week who had told him in confidence that they had left several men behind to disrupt the Japanese progress. The little intelligence Geoffrey had received seemed to show that despite the odds being stacked against them Warren's men were being quite effective. If they knew reinforcements were coming they might be able to hold on... but unfortunately it seemed no one was interested and now they had been ordered to leave. The only good thing was that the spy they had found had been killed by the Royal Military Police. Patrick Stanley Heenan had been sentenced to death in January but with the impending invasion nothing had been done. From the little Geoffrey had heard Heenan had become very cocky, threatening the guards and anyone else with his friends, the Japanese, so eventually the British Military Police had cut cards to see who would shoot him. After he was dead they had dumped his body in the harbour. Geoffrey knew that he should be horrified by this complete breakdown in law and order but if he was honest with himself he couldn't care less. The man had been sentenced to death legally, the police had just carried out that sentence. They couldn't leave him alive for the Japs and they certainly couldn't take him with them. Someone would have had to watch him all the time and he was taking up a space someone else could use, someone like his good friend for instance.

Geoffrey sighed and looked across at Kang. The evacuation was supposed to be for Europeans only but Geoffrey knew they would need Li Kang, his skills were too great to leave behind. 'We have our orders to evacuate. You'd better come with me Kang. We're to take all seaworthy marine craft and head south for Palembang in Sumatra.'

'I didn't think...'

'I'm not leaving you behind Kang. Apart from the fact you're my friend, you are too intelligent to abandon and the only one of my men who speaks fluent Japanese. If anyone questions that we'll ask them who they think is going to translate Japanese cyphers.' He took one further look around what was left of his office after they had spent days destroying anything that the Japanese could use and headed for the door followed closely by a bemused Kang.

By the time the two men reached harbour and climbed aboard their craft they discovered that the order had been rescinded after the Royal Navy had advised that Palembang had already fallen. 'Where are we going now?'

'We'll head for Batavia (Jakarta) in the Dutch East Indies and then hopefully through the Flores and Timor seas and eventually we should reach Darwin in Australia.'

Geoffrey and Kang exchanged glances. It was over a thousand miles to Australia, through seas alive with the Japanese. Their chances of surviving were remote to say the least.

****

London

Madeline sat at her desk staring into space before rereading Francine's latest message and the response she'd been instructed to send. If she was Francine she would be very careful around Marie. The story could be true but equally it could be an elaborate trap. If she'd been in charge she would have moved Francine somewhere else, given her a new identity and left the network to fend for itself for a while. That way, if it was some kind of trap, they would not find out any more than they already knew and Francine would be safe. Madeline had suggested they do that, but she had been overruled. She only hoped they weren't making a terrible mistake.

She reached into her pocket and pulled out Jimmy's latest letter. There was nothing else she could do about Francine so perhaps she should concentrate on her own life instead, even if it was only for a short while. Jimmy was bored training and was hoping to be transferred somewhere else. She could only hope it was somewhere closer as it had been ages since they'd been able to spend any time together and she couldn't wait to see him again.

Chapter 28

282 Boxley Road, Maidstone

A Nightingale Sang in Berkely Square was playing softly on the radio, its sentiment suiting the mood in the cottage. Frederick sipped his tea and read the newspaper with a heavy heart. After the news on 20th December the previous year that Penang had fallen and Hong Kong was under threat he had hoped things would improve. Instead, things had grown worse and now, after fierce fighting, the troops in Singapore had surrendered too. Ruth was beside herself with worry and there was nothing he could do to comfort her. She hadn't heard anything from Geoffrey since November and there was no way of telling if he was alive or dead.

Meanwhile he was as busy as ever. Colonel Sinclair had no idea where the spy had disappeared to, nor had he any explanation as to why the Germans had stopped bombing Liverpool and turned their attention to the east coast. Frederick had passed on the description of the man that had been asking questions but no one appeared to have seen him. He had then volunteered to go up to Gateshead and have a poke around himself, and he was on his way, but first he had wanted to call in and see how Ruth was coping. He also wanted to ask her help but seeing how upset she was he wasn't sure it was the right time. As he considered that he suddenly realised that asking her assistance might be a good thing. At the moment she was sitting at home worrying herself to death about her husband. Maybe what she needed was a distraction?

'I hate to ask but I was wondering if you could keep an eye on Margaret for me. I have to go up north for a little while and quite frankly I am concerned about her. She ignores Alice but she admires you so she might take some notice of you.'

Ruth frowned. Was Frederick mad? Or just totally insensitive? Here was she worrying herself to death and he wanted her to babysit his teenage daughter. She was about to say no when she had second thoughts. She liked Margaret, she didn't want her ruining her life any more than Frederick did. She couldn't do anything for Geoffrey and sitting around worrying wasn't going to help him. Perhaps guiding her niece would be a better use of her time.

Frederick was aware that he was holding his breath. He fully expected her to say no so when she suddenly nodded he almost choked in shock.

'Yes, I don't mind as long as you tell Alice. I don't want her to think I'm stepping on her toes.'

'Thank you, Ruth.' He smiled. 'I did discuss it with Alice, and she was all in favour of it.'

Ruth gave a wry smile. 'No doubt you both thought it would keep me occupied?'

Frederick was about to argue then he changed his mind. 'Well yes, that did cross our minds. You aren't offended?'

Ruth shook her head. 'No, I'll enjoy it and you're right, it will be a distraction. I can't change anything by worrying so it's best to keep busy.'

Frederick breathed a sigh of relief. 'Thank you. I know I can't promise anything but he's very resourceful Ruth. If anyone can survive, he can.' He reached towards her and put his arms around her.

Ruth hugged him back and blinked away her tears. Deep down she was sure she was never going to see her wonderful husband again, but there was no point saying that to anyone. Instead she would continue to pray she was wrong.

****

Greenock, Scotland

The captain cleared the lower deck and began his announcement. John stood with the other men, not because he needed to know where they were going, but because he wanted to show his solidarity with the captain and the men. 'Today we completed the task of taking on board hundreds of tons of valuable stores. We have received our orders from the Admiralty and we are proceeding to Malta at 1300hrs today, carrying these vital stores the island so desperately needs. We will proceed at full speed through the Mediterranean and come what may we will blast our way through to Malta. The ship must get through.'

John scanned the faces of the crew, many of them little more than boys who had never fired a shot in anger before and saw the determination there.

At 1300hrs they sailed down the Clyde with the Captain's last words ringing in their ears. 'When you shoot, shoot to kill. It's them or you.'

****

Arkley View, near Barnet
Fred stared at the message in disbelief. His instincts told him that this was from the spy, it was using the same code. But the message didn't make sense. The spy was asking about something in France which didn't fit the pattern at all. Perhaps he was wrong? This message had also come from the south of England, not the north. Fred suddenly had a horrible thought and began searching through the piles of messages he had placed in his pending tray. Peregrine Thompkin-Cartwright was located in the south. Then he smiled and shook his head at his stupidity. The senior civil servant could hardly have bailed out of a German aeroplane without someone noticing. He was being ridiculous. On the other hand if he couldn't possibly be the spy he could be the contact. They were reasonably sure that someone had helped the spy escape the security services, and who better than someone as highly placed as Thompkin-Cartwright. The problem was how to investigate without telling Colonel Sinclair. Fred had already suggested that the Colonel look into him. If only there was another way of finding information which didn't involve the Colonel. Fred was still thinking about it when he remembered the man who had been asking questions in Liverpool. If he could find him that might provide him with a way of getting closer to Thompkin-Cartwright.

****

Behind the lines, Malaya
The explosion echoed loudly around the jungle, the ground shook, trees shed their leaves and monkeys shrieked, but more importantly the railway line shattered into a thousand pieces in several places cutting off the last supply route back across the country. Anthony grinned. 'Take that you Jap bastards.' He knew it wouldn't take them very long to replace it, they appeared to have brought plenty of supplies with them but it would add a few hours onto their resupply time. He was about to move when the ground shook again, this time

almost knocking him over and in the distance he could see smoke and flames pouring upwards. A tired grin spread wearily across his face. Looked like Richard had managed to find the fuel dump then!

****

Mediterranean

The voyage had been uneventful until they passed within twenty miles of Pantelleria, the enemy base, on 11th February at 04.00hrs. John had been monitoring the ships radio constantly, but his role became even more important now they were in dangerous waters. They should reach Grand Harbour in Malta that afternoon but until they were safe in port the men were to remain on action stations. As darkness turned to daylight the seas became rough and their escort, the destroyer *HMS Fortune,* had to reduce speed. The captain decided to remain with her and approach Malta from the south, which meant they were sure to be spotted by enemy patrol aircraft. John concentrated hard, searching for any sign they had been spotted and then *Fortune* had to slow down even more thanks to the heavy sea in which she found herself.

'Alarm! Enemy aircraft approaching… estimated height 6000 feet, speed 300 miles per hour.'

'Open fire… barrage, barrage, barrage…'

The Stuka's came from all directions, shrieking wildly as they dived towards them, their machine guns chattering. They were greeted by the pounding of the 5.25 guns and the crackle of short range weapons. Tracers arced and sliced into the sky searching for the enemy, one plane stopped in mid air, wings blown apart and plunged into the swirling seas. A near miss set fire to the stowed torpedo warheads, smoke poured onto deck and men hurried towards them ignoring the danger of exploding warheads and threw them overboard, two men covered in blood narrowly escaped the carnage of the pom pom gun after it took an almost direct hit and then the *Fortune* spun to avoid a falling bomb and took water down through the funnel. To the relief of the crew on the *Cleopatra* and the *Fortune* she managed to right herself and carried on firing at the planes. In the radio room John tried to concentrate on listening to the radio signals, praying there were no subs or destroyers on their way. He was sure being stuck below was worse than being on deck as he had no idea what was happening above him. Then suddenly *Cleopatra* heaved and bucked and John knew they had been hit. 'Go and take a look.' He somehow managed to speak calmly to Chris who nodded and disappeared for several minutes. John waited patiently. The ship didn't appear to be listing in any way so hopefully...

A dishevelled Chris reappeared at the door.

'Plane dropped three bombs.' He panted. 'Two missed when we swerved to port but the third one entered the starboard side of the forecastle and tore its way through the messdecks and started a small fire.'

'Have they put it out?'

Chris nodded. 'The fire main is broken but it was enough to stop it. No casualties either and they are busy isolating the damage.' He gave a shaky smile and then instinctively ducked as a bomb landed in the water near the ship causing the swell to rise and the ship to buck again. The guns were still pounding and John turned his attention back to the transmitters. For two hours the planes continued to bomb and shoot at them, never giving their own guns a chance to cool, the ship thrown from side to side to avoid the bombs. There was no air support available from Malta because there were no spare aircraft and the island was under attack from yet another air raid.

Eventually the enemy thinned out and disappeared leaving *Cleopatra* and *Fortune* to finally enter Grand Harbour. John made his way on deck where he joined the crew as the cheers from the quayside and other ships reached them. Seventeen crewmen had died during the battle, but they had succeeded in reaching Malta and delivering the vitally needed stores.

****

South Moor, Maidstone, Kent

'Is everything alright Daisy? You're very quiet.'

Fred was still trying to think of a way of finding the man who had been asking all the questions in Liverpool, but even though he was lost in his thoughts Daisy Irene had been so uncommunicative that her silence had finally broken into his thoughts.

'Yes, I'm fine.' She sighed. 'I'm sure you have enough to think about.'

'That doesn't mean I don't have time for you. Why don't you tell me what's wrong. I might be able to help.' Fred was becoming seriously concerned. She had been so happy recently, having the children to look after had really helped her blossom. Perhaps it was that. 'Is it the children? Is there something wrong?'

'No, I was a bit worried that they would all go back to London last September but as you know their parents all decided they were safer here.' She fell silent. He knew all that, why was she repeating herself?

'Well if it's not that then what is it?' Fred prompted. 'Come on Daisy love, we don't have secrets from each other...' the irony of what he'd said didn't escape him and he smiled. 'Well only national security secrets anyway!'

Despite her concern Daisy laughed. 'No, you're right. I'm probably worrying about nothing but it's just that it's not easy to make sure all the children are alright.' She fell silent again.

'You're talking about those you've placed with other families, not the ones who are staying here?'

'Yes, quite a few of them stayed on and I'm not sure they all wanted to.'

Fred frowned. 'What aren't you telling me?'

Daisy Irene took a deep breath. 'I have my concerns about one of the children. I can't really tell you the name... but... well, the problem is it's very difficult to find out the truth about the families and the children who are billeted with them. I can't keep going round to their houses and checking and I think the children might be too scared to say anything.'

Fred thought hard for several minutes then he had an idea. 'What about the school? Can't they find out?'

Daisy Irene stared at him thoughtfully. 'I suppose I could speak to the headmistress of MGGS, she's a sensible woman.'

Fred smiled. 'Well, that's all sorted out then, isn't it? I'm very impressed.' He patted her hand.

Daisy Irene gave a wry smile. 'I have been sitting here trying to work out how to approach this and five minutes of talking to you and I have a solution or at least a partial one. Thank you.'

Fred put his arm around her and pulled her into a hug. It was nice to be back home again.

'Hello Uncle Fred, are you staying tonight?' Lucy ran towards the sofa and threw her arms around him. Jack also ran towards them although he stopped short of hugging Fred and instead held out his hand. Mick, Sandie and Jean appeared behind them and he was soon chatting to them all, even Jane who seemed less shy than last time.

'Hello children, its lovely to see you.' He cuddled Lucy, shook Jack and Mick's hand before reaching into his pocket and pulling out some lemon sherbets which he distributed amongst them. 'Don't eat them before dinner!'

Daisy Irene laughed. 'You spoil them Fred, they'll expect you to bring them something every time!'

Fred shrugged. 'It's little enough Daisy, this war is hard enough for adults, it must be so confusing for children.'

****

Sumatra

Geoffrey slumped languidly in the boat, Kang beside him, dozing in the heat, wishing they would hurry up and reach safety. It was days since they'd fled Singapore and they were almost out of fuel. He couldn't imagine how they could possibly reach Australia. They couldn't even evade the numerous Japanese patrols.

'Refueller 1186 from Seletar was loaded with diesel fuel and aviation spirit and then ordered to rendezvous with the launches at an island en route. We're not that far off now.' The helmsman spoke quietly, not wanting his voice to carry.

'What about HSL 105?' Geoffrey asked. 'They were supposed to have left Singapore before the surrender.'

The helmsman shrugged. 'HSL 105 was ordered to stay in Singapore to take the senior officers off. But the senior officers elected to stay until the end so she sailed with only half the HQ Staff aboard.'

He glanced around, the main flotilla consisted of 60ft boats of triple engine types, Pinnace 53, P54 and P36 but they had lost sight of P54 and P36 some time ago. 'P54 refuelled and then the crew were told to sink the refueller and join the pinnaces.' He continued.

Geoffrey sighed, closed his eyes and tried to sleep while they travelled slowly along the coast of Sumatra. By now they were only moving at night and keeping as close to the shore as the water allowed. The voyage was slow and dangerous, and being so close to shore they were unable to escape the heat and humidity. 'We've not seen any of the other boats at all.' Kang whispered. 'Do you think they've sunk?'

Geoffrey shrugged. 'Maybe or perhaps they've got away.' He didn't believe that deep down, but it was better to try and be optimistic.

Eventually they entered the narrow strait between Sumatra and the island of Bangks. They were only two miles from Muntok Point when they heard firing. Geoffrey ignored the orders to remain seated and standing up peered into the darkness.

'It's P54 I think. Looks like they've been spotted by a Japanese destroyer.' He didn't get time to say anything else before the shelling started. The first one landed immediately over the winch blowing the helmsman overboard. Another man had his legs severed from below the knees, several others were killed or wounded and those that did survive jumped over the side where the Japanese continued to fire on them until they decided to power through wreckage and swimmers alike, destroying them with their propellors.

Geoffrey looked away. There was nothing they could do, they were hopelessly outgunned by the Japanese and going in closer would have only made them a target too. They tried to escape but the Japanese had them in their sights and it wasn't long before they too were captured. HSL105 was attacked from the air and although they fought back several of the crew were wounded and the launch damaged. The Coxswain tried to ram one of the Japanese vessels before they were forced to surrender but failed to do any damage. This time all the surviving crewmen were taken prisoner.

Chapter 29

Bavaria

Otto paced restlessly up and down while he waited anxiously for Kristian to arrive. The latest intelligence he had learned was making him sick to his stomach, not least because the British did not appear to have acted on anything he had sent them. Both he and Kristian were risking their lives to provide vital intelligence yet it seemed it was being ignored. He had accepted that Stalin had been too arrogant to heed the warnings that their supposed ally was going to attack them, but surely the Americans would have listened and even if *they* hadn't why had the British not been prepared for the Japanese assault. Even if there was some reason for the Americans not acting to secure Pearl Harbour, surely the British didn't want to lose their colonial possessions in the Far East?

'Vater,' Kristian hurried into his father's study. 'I'm so sorry I'm late the roads are dreadful.' He smiled. 'What's so urgent?'

Ottos smiled briefly, relieved to see that Kristian looked much better than the last time he'd seen him. Obviously some weeks away from the Eastern Front had done him good. Then his face darkened. 'I have heard some very disturbing news, but I no longer trust the British to act on it. Why on earth have they let the Japanese capture Malaya?'

Kristian stared at him in consternation. 'I don't know any more than you do Vater. Perhaps there is a bigger picture that we do not have access to?'

'That is what I keep telling myself, it has to be that or…' he sighed, 'Or I have no idea what we are risking our lives for.'

'Perhaps we should just accept that we are tiny cogs in a machine and that we should just pass on whatever we can, regardless of the consequences. The alternative is to do nothing and I don't think either of us could do that.' He shrugged then turned his attention back to the reason he had been summoned. 'Well, what's this information?'

Otto turned away and began pacing again. Kristian watched in growing concern. What on earth could be worse than news of the German attack on the Soviet Union or the Japanese attack on the Americans and British in the Far East?

'Senior government and SS officials held a meeting last month at Wannsee, it's a suburb in South West Berlin.' He added. 'It was coordinated by Heydrich to agree on a final solution to the Jewish problem.'

Kristian frowned. 'I don't understand?'

'They agreed that all Jews in Europe, some eleven million or so, will be moved east to work on roads. Those who can't work will be subject to special measures.'

'Special measures? What does that mean?' Kristian still couldn't understand why Otto had summoned him.

'Special measures mean death. There was a trial of gas at Chelmno last December, they used it to kill people because they were looking for something quicker and more cost effective than shooting.'

Kristian decided he must have misheard. 'I'm sorry, you can't seriously be telling me that they are planning on murdering eleven million people?'

'That's exactly what I'm telling you.'

Kristin suddenly realised how pale his father was and he shook his head. 'You must have got hold of the wrong end of the stick. I can believe them working people to death as slave labour but mass murder on an industrial scale? No. Nobody is that mad, not even Hitler or that other lunatic Heydrich.'

'I know what I was told.' Otto clenched his fists. 'The person who told me was boasting about it, delighted that they'd finally found a *permanent* solution… their words, not mine.'

Kristian groped his way towards the nearest chair and slumped down. He had always known the Nazis were insane, but this was a step too far, even for them. 'You want me to pass this on?' He said eventually.

'Yes, for all the good it will do.' Otto resumed pacing. 'They didn't act on the other information we gave them, and to be honest I'm not sure how they can actually do anything about this, but we have to tell them. It's much too important not to.'

Kristian didn't answer. He too was furious that the intelligence they were risking their lives to pass on didn't appear to have been acted on so far, but surely they couldn't ignore this? He frowned as he digested his father's doubts. 'You're right, even if we do tell them, what can they do about it?'

'That's the big question isn't it? I have no idea, but I can't just sit on that information, do nothing…' Otto stared at his son, willing him to agree.

After a brief hesitation Kristian nodded. 'We don't have an option, we have to tell them even if they don't… or *can't* act on it.' He fell silent for a moment then another idea came to him. 'Perhaps we should pass the information onto some of the resistance groups as well, maybe they can help get some of the Jews out?'

Otto looked aghast. 'That would be much too dangerous…' He began before changing his mind, shaking his head and sighing loudly. 'How on earth are you going to do that?'

Kristian stared at him. 'I have no fucking idea, but I have to try.'

****

MGGS, Maidstone, Kent

Daisy Irene sat in the headmistress's office and outlined her concerns about the young thirteen year old girl she was worried about.

There was a brief silence while the headmistress considered what she'd said then Miss Bartels nodded. 'I agree Mrs Corben, Debbie is very quiet. I know all the evacuees adjust differently but she does seem abnormally quiet.'

'What do you think I should do? It can't be that she's having trouble getting used to being away from home. If that was the case she would have gone back home in September surely? Why would she stay if she was unhappy? It doesn't make any sense and I don't want to keep going around asking questions as I could be causing a problem where there isn't one.'

'Which is why you've come to me.' Miss Bartels smiled. 'You've done the right thing. Leave it with me. I'll have a chat with her and if that doesn't work I'll ask one of my girls to befriend her and see if we can find out that way.'

Daisy Irene stood up, thanked her again and left the room. She felt much better now. The headmistress of MGGS had a very good reputation. A passionate advocate of education for girls, she had been determined not to let the war ruin her standards. Not wearing a beret in town could lead to a serious telling off and if biscuit coloured socks were not available because of shortages she expected the girls to dye them in tea. Although most of the girls found her quite intimidating they also knew there was another side to her. She always checked areas that had been bombed before allowing children to go home, making sure their homes had not been damaged. She had been known to drive children home from school, leave them in the car and make her way through broken glass to make sure their homes were undamaged and in school she had effectively reduced Hitler and the war to an irritating nuisance. Daisy was sure that if there was a problem she would be the right person to sort it out.

Miss Bartels watched her go, her thoughts on Debbie Longmire. Perhaps it would be best to ask one of the girls to speak to her first. If she spoke to Debbie it would put her on her guard and she was unlikely to confide in the headmistress anyway. The question was who would be best suited. Who was Debbie most likely to talk to? She would watch them for a couple of days and then make a decision.

****

Maidstone, Kent

'You don't know how difficult it is to live here.' Margaret drank her tea and stared at the table. 'I could be dead tomorrow, why shouldn't I have some fun?'

'Well, there are ways to have fun that might not get you into so much trouble.' Ruth smiled.

'But I'm not doing anything wrong. I go to parties, dance with the soldiers or airmen or the men who have been exiled from their own countries and want cheering up. Then I come home.'

'Usually with a different man each night.' Ruth reminded her gently.

'No, not always…' Margaret gave a wry smile. 'Well alright, maybe. They are just so interesting. They all have so many stories to tell and they are all training to fight. Why shouldn't I help cheer them up? Dad and Mum don't understand. They're too old.'

Ruth laughed. 'I think your parents understand very well Margaret. Don't forget, your mother is the woman who pretended to be married and went on her own into a war zone to find your father. That was an incredible thing to have done then, even now it would be a considerable achievement. I think you probably take after her which is good, but I think you just need to be a little more circumspect. You don't want a reputation do you? You'll never find a nice man if you are considered to be flighty.'

Margaret pouted. 'It's not my fault if people are jealous of me.'

Ruth sighed. She wasn't getting very far, perhaps she wasn't the right person to talk to Margaret after all. Then she remembered Frederick's concern and she made another effort. 'Why don't you just stick to one young man for a few weeks, that will keep everyone happy. It doesn't have to be serious, just don't change them as often as your underwear!'

Margaret laughed but didn't answer.

Ruth searched around for something, anything she could say but she was beginning to feel old. Maybe Margaret was right. She was young, they were getting old, why should she have to conform to their outdated rules? Men were dying every day in this stupid war. She had no idea where her husband was or even if he was still alive. Had they wasted some of the time they could have spent together because of a need to please other people? 'Maybe you're right Margaret. Who knows when this war will end or how many more people will be killed? Perhaps you should just do what you think is right, what makes you happy.'

Margaret stared at her in astonishment. 'You mean that?'

Ruth sighed. 'Yes, I think I do.' *Sorry Frederick* 'But can you just try and compromise a little for your parent's sake?'

Margaret thought for a moment and then nodded. 'Yes, alright. I don't really want to upset them, so I'll be more careful who I bring home.'

Ruth reached out and squeezed her niece's hand. 'Thank you.' She removed her hand and resumed sipping her tea. She had tried, only time would tell if she'd succeeded.

****

Sumatra

Having been rescued from the water Geoffrey and Kang were finally put ashore in Muntok Harbour on Bangka Island, here they were ordered by Japanese soldiers to walk along the 656 yards of the Muntok jetty to be processed. It had started to rain and after standing for nearly two hours in the open they were finally moved into the town towards the Alhambra cinema and Customs House where they joined several hundred civilians and members of all the various forces already waiting there to be counted. Once the count had finished they were shoved towards the buildings and searched before entering, but Geoffrey and Kang had nothing left so they had no problems.

While they were being marched to the cinema, another ship, *The Mary Rose,* which had been also captured by the Japanese, was escorted into Muntok Harbour. Aboard was Mr Vivian Bowden who had previously been the Australian Trade Commissioner in Shanghai, China. He had been instructed to close the Shanghai post in September and to establish an Australian Government Commission in Singapore. By February it was obvious things were worsening so he requested that he and his staff be evacuated but was repeatedly told they were to remain at their posts. On the 11th February he was told to insist on receiving full diplomatic courtesies. Three days later he and his staff had left on a small forty foot launch, *The Mary Rose.*

'What's going on over there?' Geoffrey fought off his exhaustion, screwed up his eyes and pointed to an altercation taking place in the middle of the foyer.

Kang listened for several minutes then lowered his voice. 'It seems that the soldier lost his own kit bag at sea but found another one. Unfortunately, there was an oil can for a rifle inside and the Japanese won't believe his protestations of innocence.'

Geoffrey was about to intervene when another man entered. Geoffrey recognised the Australian Commissioner immediately and was wondering whether he should say something when Mr Bowden stepped towards the middle of the room.

After several minutes of fierce arguments, the Japanese soldier turned his attention to Mr Bowden and tried to take his gold watch and identity disc. Having worked in his family's silk business in Japan Mr Bowden was bilingual so he immediately asked to speak to a senior Japanese officer, intending to follow his official orders, explain his Diplomatic status and request proper treatment for the captives.

However, enraged by the discussion, the soldier pushed and hit Mr Bowden then, with the assistance of a second soldier, took him outside. A few moments later shots were fired. Geoffrey paled and stared at Kang in disbelief. 'For fuck's sake. He's the Australian Commissioner. Surely they haven't shot him?'

It was several hours later when Geoffrey finally heard from a witness what had happened. Mr Bowden had been forced to dig a shallow hole and collect a small bunch of flowers before being killed and pushed into the grave.

Geoffrey barely registered the next few hours, hardly noticing that they had finally been given upright chairs to sit on and that eventually, sometime after dark, the odd hurricane light had been lit. He was vaguely aware of outside latrines being dug but his main memory was of the sentries who remained with them throughout the night, yelling at them and repeatedly counting them every time someone went out to use the toilets, ensuring they had little sleep. His thoughts drifted to Ruth and he wished he had written to say goodbye. He had never dreamed it would be this bad, always sure that even if they were captured they would be treated with respect. He should have listened to Kang more closely, but instead he had assumed that it was just because Kang was Chinese that the Japanese had treated them so badly. But now he'd seen for himself. If they dared to shoot diplomats what chance did the officers or the ordinary soldiers have. After a restless night they were shouted and prodded awake before being taken to the high stone walls of the Muntok jail. Here they were separated from the civilians and the Chinese.

Geoffrey barely had time to say goodbye to Kang who was sent to join a group of about 600 Chinese workers who had been pressganged by the Japanese from streets of Hong Kong, shipped to Muntok and made to work in the local tin mines. Geoffrey's last glimpse of his friend was watching him disappear into the groups of ill and poorly treated Chinese labourers, many of whom had died where they lay in the coolie lines (huts) next to the jail. As Geoffrey watched two workers appeared to go mad, leaping onto the roof of the jail. To his disbelief one of the Japanese guards aimed his rifle and shot one of them dead – the other, faced with no choice, was ordered down. It became a daily occurrence to see two or three Chinese coolies unceremoniously carried away to their last resting place shrouded in old paper bags. Those who were about to die crawled out into the open to die unattended by the Japs or their fellow countrymen. Although Geoffrey searched every day for any sign of Kang, and even tried bribing one of the Chinese with some food, he never saw any sight of his friend.

Night after night Geoffrey huddled together in the jail with his fellow captives. The prison had been shelled and bombed several times so was in a filthy condition. The only drinking water was provided by a single tap which dripped intermittently during some hours of the day and long queues formed to fill anything that could hold water, scavenged from wherever they could find them. One man used a small tobacco tin, another half a coconut shell which he'd found on a rubbish heap. Their food came in buckets, dirty rice with a few strands of vegetables to add flavour rather than any nutrition was evenly divided to provide each person with a small handful. Rotten meat, the size of a thumbnail was much sought after, but seldom seen.

Every night the prisoners were forced to lay shoulder to shoulder on cold, sloping concrete slabs. If one person turned over, all the others were disturbed. Although his dreams were punctuated by memories of his wife his waking thoughts were concentrated on his longing for water, food and uninterrupted sleep. But things were to get worse. Not long after reaching Muntok jail, Geoffrey was woken from a restless sleep, put into trucks in darkness with several other men and taken to a field. Here, they were forced out a gunpoint. Facing them were deep trenches. This appeared to be it then. Geoffrey didn't know how he felt, he was convinced they were about to be shot and buried but given everything he had seen so far perhaps that was a good thing. He knew he should fight for life but there was nothing left. He stood still, closed his eyes, focused on Ruth and waited for the shots to ring out. But instead the Japanese began yelling at them to fill the pits, which had been dug earlier by Dutch, British and Australian soldiers in an attempt to disrupt the aerodrome and prevent its use. Geoffrey began to work, no idea if he was grateful to still be alive or not.

This was just the beginning. They were woken every day at 04.30hrs and made to work by the light of flares until 1100hrs before being returned exhausted and starving to the prison.

****

Gateshead
Frederick made his way to the station. As far as he was concerned the last week had been a complete waste of time. He had not found out anything. No one had seen anyone suspicious; no one had been asking questions. He might as well have stayed at home. He was lost in thought so failed to hear the man shouting at him until he was almost level.

'You're the man asking questions about strangers snooping around?'

Frederick nodded. 'Yes, I am.' He waited.

'I work at one of the shipyards. There was a man round here before Christmas asking questions?'

'Can you describe him?'

'He was tall, well-built, with thinning hair maybe late thirties, early forties. He wanted to know about German air raids, when they'd got bad. If anyone else had been asking questions.' He stopped and Frederick smiled.

'Thank you. Do you know where he went?'

The man shook his head. 'No, I didn't see him again and when I asked around no one else said they'd seen him so I suppose he'd got what he wanted and left.' He looked uneasy. 'I didn't tell him anything important, nothing that he couldn't have found out anywhere else. Have I done something wrong?'

Frederick shook his head. 'No, I'm sure you haven't. You definitely didn't see him with anyone else?'

'No, he walked towards the station...' He frowned. 'Only he stopped to make a phone call first.'

Frederick's face lit up. 'Can you show me the phone box?'

The man shrugged. 'Yes, of course. Is it important then?'

'Maybe. Come on show me where he telephoned from.' Frederick was already feeling better. His trip hadn't been a waste of time after all. The description fitted the man from Liverpool and, if they knew which phone box the man had used, they might be able to trace who he had telephoned. If they could find the person who was helping the spy they should be able to get them both.

Chapter 30

MGGS, Maidstone, Kent

Jeanne listened carefully to her new friend Debbie, and tried to hide her own disgust at what she was hearing. How on earth was she going to pass this information onto Miss Bartels? Apart from the nature of the secret which was so awful she couldn't bear to contemplate it, Debbie had told her in confidence, made her promise never to say anything, but if she didn't poor Debbie would continue to suffer.

'That's appalling Debbie. You can't keep putting up with it.' Jeanne spoke eventually. 'Why don't you tell Miss Bartells?'

Debbie looked horrified. 'I can't do that. They'll send me back to London or they won't believe me.'

'I'm sure they will believe you Debbie. It's hardly something you would make up. You really shouldn't have to put up with anything like that. It's not right.'

'No, I can't. But you can't tell anyone, you have to promise me.' Debbie pouted and fell silent. Jeanne could see the panic on her face and for a brief moment she wondered if her friend was making it up, then she mentally shook her head. No, she was sure it was the truth. She'd seen the expression in her friend's eyes when she'd told her.

'Well let me tell my dad then. He's with the Home Guard. I'm sure he'll know what to do.' The thought of telling her father anything so personal would be excruciatingly embarrassing but if it solved the problem for Debbie she was prepared to do it.

Debbie looked even more horrified. 'No, you can't tell anyone, you promised.'

'But if I don't...' She didn't get any further.

'You promised Jeanne. If you say anything I'll never trust you again. Please, I'm begging you not to interfere. I'll resolve it myself somehow.'

'How on earth are you going to do that?'

'Just leave it alright. Forget I told you!' Debbie stormed off leaving Jeanne staring after her in desperation. She wished she'd never agreed to do this now but when Miss Bartels had asked her she had been flattered to be asked and thought it would be a really nice way of helping someone. Now she was stuck with Debbie's horrible secret and she couldn't help her without breaking her confidence.

****

Pas de Calais

Charlotte watched the latest airman head towards the station and Marie following him from a safe distance. She would wait until he was through the barrier and then join him in the carriage. The airman would recognise her but had been told not to acknowledge her in any way. She glanced around, no one was watching her so it was probably safe to remain where she was for a little longer. She still wasn't entirely happy about Marie but London had verified her so she would have to work with her a little longer, at least until they moved her anyway. She was already growing bored with her current assignment and didn't feel she was utilised to the best of her ability. Anyone could pass on the airmen's details, collect verification and pass it back, surely there must be something more important she could do.

As she walked slowly back to the Mayor's house her thoughts drifted to Rebecca, this wasn't helping her to avenge her sister's death. She was just marking time. Perhaps she should ask for a transfer. A wry smile crossed her face. They would have no idea how she felt unless she told them. She would code a message asking to go somewhere more useful and send it that night.

****

Ayr, Scotland

Chem had been transferred to 72 Squadron based in Ayr Scotland and Jimmy was bored stiff with the monotony of the constant training. He was just thinking how much he envied Chem, especially as rumours abounded that 72 Squadron were due to go overseas, when he was called into the commander's office and told that he too was being posted to 72 Squadron. On arrival he was taken to the COs office to find that his new commander was Bobby Oxspring, a Flight Commander at 66 Squadron, a terrific pilot and the only man Jimmy knew who could detect and shoot down enemy aircraft at night. He very quickly met the rest of the crew, and they were soon experiencing a mixture of excitement and nervousness at the news they were definitely going overseas, even though they still didn't know where.

The next seven days were spent on cross country runs and route marches as they prepared for their next tour and then they moved to Ouston in Durham where they waited impatiently for their embarkation leave.

****

Arkley View, near Barnet
The Colonel read through the latest messages from Germany and sighed. It sounded so ridiculously farfetched that he was almost inclined to ignore it but so had many of the other messages from Kristian and they had all turned out to be true. He couldn't afford to ignore this one just because he couldn't conceive of any circumstances in which someone would make a decision to wipe out an entire race. However, it did sound completely outlandish. Perhaps it was some sort of trick? He shook his head. No, he couldn't see how it could benefit anyone to suggest mass murder, not even as some kind of propaganda. He would pass on the information and let other people decide whether it had any basis in reality. Then he remembered Fred's words and he hesitated. He was supposed to report everything to Peregrine Thompkin-Cartwright, but what if this really was true and his superior was some kind of double agent? There couldn't be that many people in on the plan, so it could lead the enemy to Kristian and his father. Perhaps that was the point, the Germans suspected they had a spy and were trying to find out who it was. Maybe he would forget his instructions for once, go above Thompkin-Cartwright and contact Benjamin Chalmers instead. He could pretend he had been unable to reach Peregrine. It would probably work once.

****

Malta
During the five weeks John had spent in Malta there were up to eight to ten air raids a day with continuous ones during the night. The crew had been given twenty four hours leave and some of them had chosen to go to the cinema, but a Ju88 dropped three bombs on the building which fell directly in front of the screen and killed the first two rows of the audience.

The repairs on the ship were also slowed up by the continuous bombing and John soon learned not to ignore the 'take cover' warnings as the enemy aircraft flew in at mast head height, under the barrage fire where few guns could engage them. Eventually the repairs were complete and the ship came out of dock. It was now time to rearm but as fast as they could take the ammunition on board it was being fired up at enemy bombers. John's highlight was when he picked up a signal stating that an enemy convoy was passing through the narrows and Pantelleria and *Cleopatra* and *Penelope* were sent out to sink them. Much to his disappointment the RAF got there before them and sank the convoy first but at least some old scores had been settled.

On 10th March they finally slipped their moorings and sailed away from the ravaged island, Malta's Vice Admiral's farewell words ringing in their ears. 'Goodbye and good luck! We shall miss the sound of your guns and the effectiveness of them.'

****

London

Madeline had decoded the message from Charlotte earlier and wondered what her superiors would decide to do. The new details from the latest airmen would be checked and the verification sent back as soon as possible, but it wasn't that which she was thinking about. The extra message had said that Francine was bored and wanted to go somewhere more exciting. Wireless operators were worth their weight in gold, and while Francine was doing a good job she was now more experienced and could be moved elsewhere, someone with less experience could take over her role. She was still thinking about it when the telephone rang and she reached out automatically. 'Hello?'

'Hello Madeline. I thought you might like a late meal? If you're not too tired of course?'

Madeline smiled. 'Hello Dad. Yes, that sounds like a lovely idea.' Anything to stop her thinking about how to get out of the mess she was in.

'I'll pick you up in half an hour then.'

Madeline replaced the phone and glanced in the mirror. She needed to change and put some make up on. She stared at her reflection in the mirror and wondered if this was the night they would discuss the past.

Chapter 31

Palembang, Sumatra

Somehow Geoffrey survived his captivity in Muntok and after processing the prisoners, which took about six weeks, the Japanese transported them by small boats across the Bangka Strait to the mainland of Sumatra. Having travelled up the wide Moesi River they eventually arrived in the town of Palembang. The journey lasted over twelve hours with only a handful of cold rice and sips of cold tea to keep them going.

Once in Palembang, they were first taken to a school at Bukit Besar, near the centre of the city. The civilians and soldiers were held there for several days, and then they were separated. The soldiers were imprisoned in the former Mulo and Chung Wha schools while the civilian women and children were taken to some abandoned Dutch cottages in a guarded compound surrounded by barbed wire. The civilian men were confined in the Palembang jail. In addition to the British and Australian evacuees from Singapore, many Dutch people who had lived in Sumatra were also interned in Palembang. Seized from their homes by the Japanese, these people had been brought into the prison camps in trucks. Unlike the bombed and shipwrecked evacuees, the Dutch often had significant possessions, including clothing, bedding, furniture, food and money.

The other penniless internees were sometimes able to work for the Dutch – washing clothes, cooking, chopping wood, cutting hair or minding children – for a few coins. They were then able to try to buy a little extra food from local shop-keepers who were occasionally allowed into the camp or, at great risk to both seller and purchaser, they could buy from illegal traders who came right up to the barbed wire.

****

En Route to Paris

Charlotte climbed aboard the train and hoped she'd made the right decision. Perhaps she should have remained where she was but then she remembered how bored she had become and knew that she was right to have requested a move. She hadn't expected them to send her to Paris though. They must be pleased with her work so far, either that or they were desperate. Madeline's last message had warned of several arrests and the urgent need for a new radio operator. Her new cover story and papers had come via a new agent who had just arrived in the area. In her new role she was a representative from one of the vineyards and would travel around collecting orders. It would be hard work learning everything she needed to know, or at least enough to persuade the Germans she was who she was pretending to be so she would go to a Paris vineyard first to learn everything they could teach her in a short time.

Once she was ready to begin her work she would be contacted by the leader of the local network. Charlotte assumed that was code for once the local leader had made sure she was safe. Not that she blamed him or her. She would have done the same. The hardest part was travelling to the city with her transmitter without getting caught. She had eventually decided to travel by train and send the wireless by a farm truck bringing in supplies to the city. That way it could be hidden amongst the produce. She was supposed to travel with her radio, but she had no intention of taking it by train, it was much too dangerous. If anything happened to her transmitter, they would just have to find her another one. As far as Charlotte was concerned, she was more important than her wireless.

Half an hour later she knew her decision was vindicated when two men she was sure were Gestapo and several soldiers climbed aboard and began searching luggage.

'Papers!' The man was the same height as her with a moustache, sallow cheeks, dark brooding eyes and underneath the left one there was a small crescent shaped scar.

Charlotte handed them over, a disinterested expression on her face and waited patiently.

'Where are you going?'

'Clos Monmartre, Paris.'

He frowned and she realised she would have to explain. 'It's a vineyard. I represent vineyards, helping them to sell their wine.'

He stared at her for several seconds without speaking. 'Do you have any samples then?'

Charlotte relaxed slightly and smiled. 'No not yet. I have to complete my training first.' She should have left it there, but some spirit of mischief made her carry on. 'But if you're interested, I can always contact you once I have done that. Perhaps you could give me your address.'

His mouth dropped open briefly in astonishment before he pulled out a pad, wrote quickly on the page, then tore it out before handing it over. 'I'll look forward to that.' He smiled and glanced quickly at her papers again before adding 'Mlle Durand.'

'Iris, please call me Iris.' Charlotte smiled sweetly and wondered why she was bothering to flirt with this oaf.

'Thank you, Iris. I'm Werner, Werner Fischer.' He suddenly realised the soldiers were watching him, cleared his throat and handed her papers back. 'I will look forward to seeing you. Au revoir.' He left the carriage accompanied by the soldiers and Charlotte realised she had been holding her breath. She let it out slowly, put her papers back in her bag and slowly began to relax, at least she did until she realised everyone else in the carriage was glaring at her.

****

45 College Road, Maidstone, Kent

'Is anything the matter Jeanne? You seem very distracted.' Frederick smiled kindly at his daughter. 'There's nothing wrong at school is there?'

'No everything's fine.' Jeanne answered a little too quickly and Frederick's unease deepened.

'You would tell me if something was bothering you wouldn't you?'

'Of course I would.' Jeanne snapped and then sighed. She couldn't do this anymore. 'If someone tells you something in confidence, should you ever break that... I mean tell anyone else?'

Frederick frowned. 'I suppose it depends on what the secret is.'

Jeanne looked confused. 'What do you mean?'

Frederick thought for a few seconds. 'If telling the secret will help that person, even if they don't think it will, then yes, it's sometimes possible to break a confidence.' He waited but Jeanne didn't say anymore.

Frederick tried again. 'If someone Is being hurt and is too scared to say then yes, you should definitely tell someone.'

'Even if they said you shouldn't... because you promised...?'

'Why don't you tell me what the problem is and let me decide. Then it won't be like telling anyone else because it's just me.'

Jeanne didn't really understand the logic of that but the secret had become too much for her to keep. She had to tell someone. 'It's my friend Debbie, at school. She's being hurt but is too scared to say anything.' She sighed and took a deep breath before pouring out the whole story.

****

The Mediterranean

At dawn on the following day *Cleopatra* joined 15th Cruiser Squadron and several destroyers off the coast of Benghazi. A few hours later they came under a concerted onslaught from aeroplanes of every type which continued all day, until darkness fell and torpedo bombers arrived to continue the attacks. As the darkness deepened the ships took up their positions for night cruising, while the flagship, *HMS Nadiad,* inspected the fleet before taking up her position at the back of the line. It was so dark no stars could be seen and the outline of the ships was barely visible as the crews switched from action stations to cruiser stations to allow them to get some rest. The only sounds came from the gentle throbbing and humming of the engines and ventilation fans. John concentrated on the wireless transmitters searching for any lurking U-boats but there was complete radio silence.

Suddenly an explosion shattered the air and they could see four lights flashing from the mast-head of the *Naiad*. She had been torpedoed by a U-Boat. John increased his search for the location while the remaining cruisers continued on their course and the escorting destroyers broke away to drop their depth charges and to pick up survivors. On deck the crew watched anxiously and eventually news reached them that the *Naiad* had sunk in fifteen minutes, but that two thirds of the crew had been rescued.

The following morning they had reached the approaches to Alexandria, the famous Ras el-Tin lighthouse welcoming them to Egypt. As they moored up they received the news that *Cleopatra* was now Fifteenth Squadron's flagship and they watched as the flag of fighting Rear Admiral Sir Philip Vian was hoisted to the mast-head.

****

MGGS, Maidstone, Kent

'That's dreadful Mr Farmer. Are you absolutely sure?' Miss Bartels shook her head. 'I'm sorry I shouldn't have said that. Of course, you are. It's just so dreadful. It doesn't bear thinking about.'

'Would you like me to deal with it?' Frederick still wasn't convinced he was doing the right thing. His first instinct had been to go around to the family Debbie was staying with, send her back to his house and then have a few choice words with Mr Jenkins, preferably with his fists. He had then wondered if it might be better to get the man alone and deal with him. There was a war on, bodies were a common sight. And removing threats was what he was trained for after all. But then he'd thought about it and decided that maybe the best solution would be to speak to the headmistress and let her resolve it.

A brief smile crossed her face. 'It would be very easy for me to say yes to that Mr Farmer, but it might be best to let the proper authorities deal with it.'

'Well, if you're certain?' When she nodded he stood up to leave. 'Thank you for bringing it to my attention. Will you thank Jeanne for me. I'll pretend the information came to light from somewhere else. That way she will be able to continue being friends with Debbie. She'll need friends.'

Miss Bartels watched Jeanne's father leave and sighed. She had a horrible feeling the authorities would want to cover this up. It wouldn't be very good publicity for the evacuation scheme and at the moment the only important thing was defeating the enemy. Whilst protecting the children was also important this was an isolated incident and it couldn't be allowed to taint all the good people who had opened their homes to evacuees.

****

Germany

The main subject Kristian studied during his time at the Luftkriegsschule (Air Warfare Academy) at Fürstenfeldbruck was ground tactics, but his mind wasn't really on his lessons. Instead, he was wondering if his message had reached the allies and if it had whether they were going to do anything about it. If not, he had to find another way of getting the information about the mass murder of the Jewish race out to the public in Britain and America. Unfortunately, apart from the training in Germany, he was spending so much of his time stuck in the Soviet Union that even if he could find someone to pass the information on to he didn't think they would care too much. Towards the end of the course they were taken to Berlin to listen to Hitler speaking for nearly three hours about the events that had lead up to war, the campaigns to date and how he saw the future. Unlike the rest of the audience in the Sportpalast Kristian wasn't the slightest bit interested and had trouble pretending to show enthusiasm, his only hope was that there would be some information he could pass on. Sadly, there was nothing that he could really use so he was more than grateful when the speech ended and he was on his way east again.

****

45 College Road, Maidstone, Kent

Frederick could hear shouting before he'd even walked through the front gate. 'What on earth is going on Jeanne? I can hear you girls down the street.'

Jeanne didn't answer but Debbie immediately rounded on him. 'I asked your stupid daughter not to tell anyone and she promised. I would never have said anything otherwise.'

'There's no reason to speak to her like that Debbie.' At the last second Frederick remembered that the information was supposed to have come from elsewhere and he changed direction. 'She's your friend. Whatever's happened, it's not her fault.'

Debbie's face reddened, she opened her mouth to argue, Frederick waited for the explosion then she suddenly pushed past him and ran out of the house.

'I told her that it didn't come from me. Miss Bartels told me it came from somewhere else, but she wouldn't believe me.' Jeanne looked shaken.

'She's just upset Jeanne. Don't let it worry you. I know its difficult but try and forget all about it. She'll soon calm down and realise she's being unfair.'

Jeanne eyed him doubtfully. She had to go back to school the next day and she was dreading it. What if everyone thought she'd broken a promise? She would never make any more friends.

****

En Route to Malta

Nine days later *Cleopatra,* accompanied by the remainder of the Fifteenth Cruise Squadron, and an escort of destroyers, sailed from Alexandria towards Malta. The first day was quiet, the only interruption to the peace and serenity was the odd reconnaissance plane. The weather grew worse, the sea and wind decidedly hostile and then, on 22nd March everything changed.

At 09.30hrs four Italian Savoia bombers appeared, swept in close to the water and began dropping their payload but were unsuccessful. There were six further attacks that morning but again, thanks to the barrage put up by the ships' guns, they dropped their bombs and torpedoes (known as fish) well away from the ships.

The first German plane appeared at 13.30hrs. The Ju88 flew high in the sky and dropped four red flares ahead of the convoy. This was immediately followed by more Ju88s and Italian bombers but again with no success. It wasn't until an hour later that they spotted smoke on the horizon and the lookouts reported four suspicious vessels. Admiral Vien left the cruiser *Carlisle* to protect the convoy and, with a few destroyers, headed towards the approaching ships.

As they sailed towards the enemy several bombers tried to stop them but failed. On *Cleopatra* the battle ensigns were run up the mast-heads, the ship increased its speed to thirty knots and, after ploughing through the heavy seas, they finally identified two eight inch cruisers, two six inch cruisers and further north a light destroyer screen.

They were twelve miles apart when the enemy opened fire, the first shells landing ahead of them but showering them in water, the second salvo was closer and the third was only 600 yards away. As the distance between them decreased, salvo after salvo was fired at them while overhead a spotter plane fed back instructions.

Cleopatra changed course through the heaving seas repeatedly, the ships criss-crossing each other, leaving propellor designs decorating the water. The smoke screen turned the waters black and the destroyers heaved and pitched as they turned sharply. Eventually they were within range of the enemy and opened fire. Within seconds the air was filled with black and yellow smoke. Down below John was vaguely aware of orders being yelled, the hiss of the shells as they left the gun muzzles and then the ear splitting roar as they exploded. On deck the stench of cordite caught in the throats and eyes of the sailors and then the news came that the enemy were turning away.

Cleopatra followed but a Ju88 dived through the smoke at them, dropping bombs which fortunately they fell harmlessly into the sea beside them. Eventually they ceased firing, and having judged it safe to re-join the convoy, headed back in the opposite direction. The convoy had also come under attack but none of the ships had been hit. While they waited to see what would happen next some hot tea was distributed among the crew and they began to slowly relax.

Forty minutes later John picked up more signals that the lookouts confirmed as suspicious vessels around ten miles away. One was identified as a fifteen inch gun battleship of the Littorio class. This time they would be outgunned.

Within minutes tons of high explosive and steel was heading towards them and then there was an almighty crash, the bridge had been hit. Fortunately, not by a fifteen inch shell but by a shell from one of the other heavy destroyers. The bridge disappeared under a billow of black smoke, the air full of burning clothing and other objects, while unrecognisable parts of bodies were flung onto the decks below. The after part of the bridge had become a charnel house, many of the crew dying in just a few seconds, several others were wounded but the ships' guns continued to fire. The Admiral continued to direct operations, the Captain beside him, calmly smoking his pipe. Further below John had been lucky to escape death or injury when Cleopatra's radar and wireless stations were wrecked by a 6" round fired by an Italian light cruiser. After the explosion John found himself surrounded by blown up comrades. To calm him someone gave him a lighted Players Naval Cut cigarette.[3]

---

[3] For his bravery during the attack John was awarded the DSM *'for outstanding leadership and devotion to duty throughout the action of 22nd March, and skill when nearly all the aerials had been shot away.'*

Above decks the battle continued until 18.00hrs when one of their shells hit the battleship on the quarter deck while their destroyer claimed several hits on a cruiser. Within an hour the enemy had turned away and disappeared over the horizon. They had lost fifteen men and several wounded but given the conditions they had escaped lightly. *Cleopatra* was the only ship to be seriously hit, and they left the convoy in the care of *Penelope* and her destroyers.

On arrival back at Alexandria they were greeted with sirens, whistles and hooters and it took them a while to realise that it wasn't an air raid but ships and crews cheering them as they sailed into the harbour.

****

45 College Road, Maidstone, Kent

The phone call from Gateshead had led back to Kent. Frederick couldn't get anything more specific but at least that meant he could investigate without leaving home. He would rather not leave Jeanne at the present time especially as Debbie had reacted badly once she had realised that the headmistress knew her secret and had passed it over to the authorities to investigate. Frederick guessed the girl was probably terrified which was why she'd taken it out on Jeanne, but that didn't help his daughter from worrying that everyone would blame her for breaking Debbie's confidence, even if it had been for the best.

The knocking on the front door was loud and insistent and broke into his thoughts. Irritated by the intrusion, Frederick pulled it open with some force only to find two policemen standing there.

'Can I help you?' His anger evaporated and he asked politely, assuming it must be Home Guard business.

'Can we come in sir?'

Frederick shrugged and stepped back before leading them into the kitchen. 'So how can I help?'

'Could you tell us where you have been today?'

Frederick frowned. 'Today? I've been here carrying out Home Guard work and then I came home. Why? What's going on?'

'A man has been found dead. A Mr Jenkins.'

Frederick looked shocked.

'I see you know the gentleman sir.' The older man continued.

'One of my daughter's friends, an evacuee, is billeted there.' He was thinking hard. He hadn't been in the Home Guard office because he'd been meeting with Colonel Sinclair in London but it was secret so he couldn't tell them that. He would have to hope they accepted his word.

'And your daughter reported some irregularities to you which you, in turn reported to the school. Is that correct?'

Frederick nodded. 'Yes, that's right. Where's Debbie? Is she alright?'

The policeman ignored the question. 'Perhaps you could come down to the police station with us sir. We can complete this there.'

'Why do I have to come to the police station?'

'Because we already know you weren't at the Home Guard office today. No one has seen you all day.' He sighed. 'I'm not unsympathetic sir. Given what you've been told I would probably have done the same.'

Frederick paled. ''Now just hang on a minute. What are you suggesting?'

'We don't want to make a fuss here sir.' The older policeman indicated Jeanne who was standing by the door looking shocked.

Frederick stared at his daughter. 'I haven't done anything Jeanne. I swear.'

Jeanne watched in horror as the two policemen led her father away. She had heard enough to know that this was something to do with Debbie which meant it was all her fault.

****

Clos Monmartre, Paris, France

After a brief stay with another member of the resistance where she collected her wireless and found somewhere else to hide it, Charlotte finally arrived at the vineyard. It was situated in Paris, not far from the Basilique du Sacré-Cœur de Montmartre, and she looked around with interest. The vineyard was surrounded by winding streets and museums and according to her information produced red wine and rosé. It was only a small vineyard producing around twelve hundred bottles a year, but it was a good place to start her education.

'Mlle Francine?'

Charlotte smiled at the tall, rather handsome man with a shock of dark hair and deep soulful eyes.

'Yes, that's me.'

'Bonjour. Je m'appelle Aymard.' He held out his hand and Charlotte shook it before following him into the spacious courtyard.

'What do you want to know?'

Charlotte smiled. 'Everything. I have to sound like I'm an expert. Most of the time it won't matter but there is bound to be the odd bosch who knows his wine.'

Aymard smiled back. 'Sadly, yes and they're the worst.'

Charlotte looked confused.

He hastened to explain. 'I find it hard to accept that anyone who is cultured enough to know his wine can behave like the Nazis do. I know that sounds stupid…' He shrugged.

'Actually, I agree.' Charlotte replied thoughtfully. 'I hadn't thought about it before but you're right. It's much easier to imagine the uneducated idiot believing the bosch rubbish than someone who is intelligent and cultured.'

Amyard raised an eyebrow and nodded. 'Indeed. I think you will make a very good wine expert, providing I have enough time to teach you.' He gazed into her eyes and for the first time in ages she felt her body responding to a man. As the warmth spread through her she found herself unable to look away and it was Amyard that eventually turned his attention to the wines. 'I'd better begin your education then.' The words were heavy with meaning and Charlotte blushed. Someone how she was going to have to keep her mind on work, although it had been a long time and surely she was entitled to some fun… she was risking her life after all.

Chapter 32

South Moor, Maidstone, Kent
Daisy Irene settled Debbie into the bedroom with Lucy, Sandie and Jane. It was cramped but at least she would be safe. She had been horrified to hear what was alleged to have been happening at the Jenkins house, but she'd had little time to get used to that before the news reached her that he had been found dead, a blow to the back of the head making it fairly obvious that someone had killed him.

She sat down at the kitchen table and poured out two cups of tea. She would have liked to suggest something stronger but she didn't want Miss Bartels thinking she had too much of a liking for alcohol. 'Do you think this Home Guard captain did it? Jeanne Farmer's father isn't it?'

Miss Bartels shook her head. 'No, not for a minute. If Captain Farmer had wanted to kill him he would have done so and not bothered to tell me what was going on. He handed the matter over to me and walked away. He even told Jeanne that we'd found the information from another source. I did tell the police that but for some reason they arrested him. Something to do with lying about his alibi.'

Daisy Irene frowned. 'I wonder why he did that.'

Miss Bartels shrugged. 'I have no idea but I am convinced he didn't do it.' She sipped her tea and lowered her voice. 'Captain Farmer strikes me as a very capable man. I'm sure if he had killed Mr Jenkins he would have planned it better. Either the body would not have been found or it would have happened during an air raid so it didn't look suspicious. This looks like some kind of spur of the moment thing. Someone lost their temper.'

'Perhaps they found out what he was doing to young girls.' Daisy Irene shuddered. 'I feel so guilty that I let Debbie stay there. How could I have done that?'

'How on earth could you have known what he was like, Daisy? There weren't any rumours about him, everyone was shocked. I think the killer is probably some parent who has just found out what he did to their daughter.'

'Well let's hope they soon release Captain Farmer.' Daisy Irene finished the rest of her tea and wondered how much she was to blame for this mess.

'It's not your fault Daisy.'

'I feel that it is.'

'Why? Because you felt uneasy so you decided to find out why? That was the right decision Daisy and don't tell yourself any different. We have a duty to protect the girls in our care and that's what we did.'

'I suppose you're right.'

'I know I'm right. You've done an amazing job finding homes for thousands of children, the vast majority were perfect. There was always the danger that one of the families wasn't going to be who they pretended to be. You discovered that and you rescued her. Stop blaming yourself.'

Daisy smiled. Perhaps Miss Bartels was right. If she hadn't started investigating Debbie would still be there, being abused. If Mr Jenkins was dead that was his own fault.

****

Paris

Charlotte arrived safely at the building in the centre of the city and made her way upstairs to the flat she had been told was allocated to her. She had thoroughly enjoyed being educated by Amyard, a brief smile crossed her face as she reflected just how much fun mixing work with pleasure had been. She now had considerably more confidence, at least she thought she could probably hold her own with most people as long as they didn't know too much. She'd given that some thought and decided she would stick to the truth, well her version of it. If they did question her, she would explain that she was new to the business and had only started because the man whose job it was had been taken off to Germany as part of the labour quota.

She had met the leader of the local resistance cell briefly and been given a list of people she was to visit. Andre was a short wiry man with seemingly endless energy who had listened to her account of her journey from Calais and then suddenly suggested she follow up her conversation with the Gestapo officer. He had then left without explaining why, although she had quickly realised it was obvious what he expected her to do. Charlotte was furious. How dare he treat her like a prostitute? No wonder he had disappeared so quickly. She'd put him in his place the next time she saw him... Charlotte was still thinking about how angry she was when she reached the second floor and her new flat. She pulled out her key, let herself in and stared around at the rather bare room that greeted her. She walked over to the window and stared out across the city. She could see the Basilique du Sacré-Cœur de Montmartre and she made a mental note to visit the Roman Catholic Church soon. She could do with some spiritual relaxation; the last time she'd been in a church had been when she'd met the priest to check out Marie's soldier.

Although nothing had happened she hadn't changed her mind about that situation and Charlotte still felt uneasy. She hoped London had warned her replacement, even if there wasn't a problem, it was much better to be over cautious. She resumed her gaze over the city and wondered if she dare use her transmitter here. Probably not which was a shame as the height would give her a good signal. Charlotte sighed. She would need to find somewhere else to use and keep the radio if she could. It was too late to explore the streets now, it was almost time for curfew. She would have an early night and start looking tomorrow.

****

Arkley View, near Barnet
Fred finished decoding the latest orders from Rommel to 13th Brandenburger Company waiting in Derna in Eastern Libya. The plan was for them to join Kampfgruppe Hecker which also included men from 33rd and 39th Panzerjager Battalions, 778th Engineer Landing Company and Italian 3rd San Marco Marine Battalion. The signal was quite clear. *On X+1 Kampfgruppe Hecker will land at Gabr Si. Hameida to block the Via Balbia around kilometre 136.*

Fred passed it on and hoped that this would help the Allies to finally relieve the Garrison at Tobruk. He sat back in his chair and thought about Daisy Irene. She had really opened a can of worms in her search for the truth and he was very proud of her, at least he was once he'd rescued the Home Guard Captain who had been wrongly arrested. Fred had immediately recognised the name from the Colonel's list of contacts and hastened to notify the Colonel that his man was in danger of being charged with murder.

The Colonel had acted swiftly and Captain Frederick Farmer had been released immediately. But Maidstone wasn't very big and Fred knew that the rumours would continue until they found the real culprit. It was strange going home now there were six children living in his house. He couldn't put his finger on it, but the atmosphere seemed to have changed imperceptibly. Lucy was still affectionate, but she rarely hugged him and any progress he'd made with Jane seemed to have disappeared. Maybe it wasn't surprising after everything Debbie had been through. She must have very little trust in men, but she seemed to have passed that onto the other children and that saddened him.

He had grown used to being greeted by enthusiastic children when he went home but now the atmosphere was subdued. Hopefully things would improve with time or once they caught the person who had murdered Jenkins. He couldn't bring himself to call him *Mr*. It still amazed him that no one had ever had the slightest clue what the man was like. He would have expected some rumours but there was nothing. It was all very odd.

****

Alexandria, Egypt
My dear Elsie and Rodney
I hope you are both keeping well and that the farm is as quiet as I promised you it would be. I am safe at the moment. We sustained some minor damage whilst in a bit of a fire fight with the Italians but I am unhurt so you don't need to worry about me. They did some minor repairs to the ship but they are now finished and we are already seaworthy again.

John sighed. Minor damage was a slight understatement, the bridge had been badly damaged by their encounter with the Italians and he was very lucky to be alive, many of his colleagues hadn't been so lucky but he had survived without any injuries which had allowed him to carry on with his duties and, to his surprise he had been awarded the DSM. On arrival in Alexandria Cleopatra had been immediately taken into the dockyard where repairs were begun. The guns had also needed attention and four out of the ten gun barrels had been changed. The work had been carried out quickly and they were already back at sea undertaking light patrols to break in the new guns and to enable the new members of the crew to get used to their duties.

I know you will be pleased to know that I have been awarded a DSM, I can't think why to be honest as I only did my job.

He hesitated, perhaps he shouldn't have said anything, he didn't want Elsie worrying about him but on the other hand it was nice to include some good news.

We have had lots of visitors, the first was from HRH The Duke of Gloucester. We drew up a guard of honour as he stepped on board and then the ship's company marched past him. It was a very proud moment. Sadly, he didn't stay long before leaving for an inspection of the fleet with the Commander -in- Chief Mediterranean. But a few days later we had another visit. This time it was from General Smutts, a very famous gentleman as you know. He also took the salute and march past and then gave a short but very interesting talk on the future prospects of the war in the Mediterranean. You'll be pleased to know that he forecast the defeat of the Axis powers in North Africa. The sooner the better I hope! We then had another visit, this time by Mr Casey who is the Australian Minister to England and Egypt. He complemented us on the appearance of the ship and our marching skills, we are becoming very proficient at welcoming people aboard! I think General Smutts must be right about the progress of the war as we've only had one particularly heavy air raid lately. There were several near misses but the bombs landed harmlessly in the water so there was no damage or casualties.

John frowned and wondered of the censor would object to that. Better to be safe than sorry… he crossed it out, made sure it couldn't be read and then continued

Please write soon as you know how much I love hearing about life at home when I am away from you. I'll finish now as I think that's all the news, look after yourselves.

Love to you both
Daddy

****

Libya

Eric sat quietly in the landing craft and stared around at the mixed S-boats and motor minesweepers escorting them to a landing place, 30km east of Tobruk. Once there they were to sever the Allies' Via Balbia supply route while Rommel attacked the Gazala Line and Tobruk.

The small boat had been at sea several hours now and he guessed they couldn't be too far off the coast when suddenly the radio flickered into life. Eric leaned forward, wondering why they were suddenly breaking radio silence. He didn't have to wait long to find out. The operation had been cancelled because they considered that Allied resistance was too strong. The vessels turned around and began the journey back to unload at Derna while Eric fought down his anger.

'I don't understand. Why are we going back? Surely we should be helping them overrun the Allies, not turning tail and running away.'

'Sorry Hoffer I have no idea. Like you I just follow orders.' The officer was only slightly older than Eric and he looked just as annoyed.

'Can't you pretend we didn't get the change of orders?' Eric tried again.

The officer shrugged and gave him a wry smile, only just visible in the inky blackness of the cloudy night. 'I've just announced it to the whole ship, I could have pretended before I did that perhaps and I might have got away with it. But not now. And in any case the other vessels will have been sent the same message, and are already turning round, look for yourself. If I had ignored it one of them would have tried to let us know which might have drawn attention to us and put all our lives at risk for no good reason. So in answer to your question, no. I can't pretend I didn't get it!'

Eric flushed, grateful no one could see how stupid he felt. 'Sorry sir.'

'Don't be. Its Hoffer isn't it?'

Eric nodded.

'I'm Rittmeister Gellan Biediger I admire your courage and determination, and I will be honoured to fight alongside you. But you have to use your brain too!'

Eric was about to argue when he realised the officer was right. If he had thought harder in the first place he wouldn't have encouraged Karl to enlist with him. 'I know you're right Herr Rittmeister. I will try and do that in future.'

Gellan reached out and patted him gently on the shoulder. 'This war isn't going to end that quickly Eric. I'm sure you'll have plenty of time to fight.'

After a few days stuck on guard duty Eric tried to remember the officer's words but it was difficult. How could he avenge his family when he was nowhere near the enemy. Perhaps he should leave, disappear into the dessert on his own and find some enemy soldiers to kill. He'd thought that joining the special forces would have provided plenty of action but instead he was stuck on guard duty.

'You'll be delighted to learn that we are on the move again Hoffer.'

Eric jumped and found himself staring into the amused eyes of Gellan Biediger. 'Yes Herr Rittmeister.' Eric stared ahead and then decided to take a chance. 'Can I ask where we're going?'

'We're off to Bir Hakeim. There's a fortress there, held by the so-called Free French. We're going to take it.'

Eric forgot all about deserting and smiled. 'That sounds perfect Herr Rittmeister.'

Gellan smiled to himself. He had a feeling Eric Hoffer was a soldier to watch. He had read about the mission in Belgium, the man had proved brave and resourceful, and the operation had been successful. Unfortunately, Eric had lost his brother which presumably was why he was so keen on fighting. The assault on the fortress would be completely different from the attack on the bridge in Belgium. It would be interesting to see how he performed in a real combat situation. If Eric was as good as he expected Gellan would see he was rewarded. There was plenty of opportunity for an exceptional soldier to progress through the ranks. But first he had to prove himself.

****

South Moor, Maidstone, Kent

Daisy Irene sat on the sofa knitting quietly, her thoughts on Debbie. She still couldn't understand why Debbie wanted to stay in Maidstone, after everything that had happened to her. Captain Farmer had suddenly been released without charge but because no one else had been arrested rumours abounded. But that wasn't what she was worried about. Lucy and Sandie had changed since Debbie had come to live with them, the boys had too but not as much. Jane was the worst, she had reverted back to the timid child she'd been on arrival. It was worse when Fred was home and she was sure he'd noticed the way the girls kept their distance. But she had no idea what to do about it. She understood why Debbie hated men but there had to be something she could do to change things, to show her that not every man was a threat. Unfortunately, she had no idea what. She would discuss it with Fred the next time he came home, two heads were better than one and he always talked a lot of sense.

Chapter 33

Bir Hakeim

Eric needn't have worried, he was soon in the heat of the action, struggling to maintain contact with the rapidly retreating Allied Troops as they fought their way along the old Trig el Abd camel track that led to Tobruk. Bir Hakeim was situated on the site of an old Ottoman Empire fort which had been built around an ancient Roman well. Although it was little more than a slight elevation rising above the flat desert the French defenders had fortified it well with extensive minefields containing over a hundred thousand anti-tank mines and over two thousand anti-personnel mines, three gates controlled the flow of traffic through these and was held by the original garrison of the 1st Free French Brigade.

Eric had never doubted they would succeed in taking the fort, especially as the Allies were expecting them to attack along the coast where it most heavily fortified and where they were outnumbered. Instead they were going to skirt around the French and concentrate on the thinnest part of the line. But their initial success had almost led to their downfall as they had moved so quickly that they had out stripped their supply column meaning their lorries had to travel a long way around. They had eventually encircled the fort, but the French had refused to surrender and to Eric's fury they had also discovered a battalion of poorly armed mine layers holding out near Bir-el Harmat who also refused to surrender. Rumour had it they were a Jewish Brigade, but Eric was sure that had to be some kind of enemy propaganda. There was no way a bunch of Jews could hold out against soldiers of the Reich.

Then Rommel had arrived and taken charge, the commandos had now been incorporated into the main force for the assault to be used like traditional infantry. Eric was laying in his small trench impatiently waiting for the orders to attack, his thoughts on how satisfying it would be to finally take part in some action, when a roar overhead heralded the arrival of the Luftwaffe. The noise of their bombs exploding was almost immediately joined by an extensive artillery barrage and Eric had to resist the temptation to put his hands over his ears.

By the end of the day they had overrun the first French observation post and captured a 75mm gun. Eric was sure it couldn't be much longer before the French and their allies, Jewish or otherwise, surrendered.

'What do you mean they've escaped?' Eric was devastated. Overnight the garrison had been evacuated and so had the Jewish Brigade. There was no one left to fight and Eric was furious.

Gellan shrugged. 'They've gone Eric, nothing we can do about it now expect keep pressing on.' He smiled. 'The Gazala Line is collapsing, it won't be long before we take Tobruk.' He didn't add that they had been lucky. If the French hadn't gone there was a fair chance they would have had to surrender as they were out of food, water, petrol, had very little ammunition left and had their backs to a minefield through which their supply trucks couldn't get through. It had been a close run thing.

****

London
Madeline had passed on the information from Charlotte and wondered why she kept asking about the German policy towards the Jews. It was the third time she'd asked whether they were setting up death camps. It was ridiculous. Of course they weren't doing anything so awful and she was surprised Charlotte actually believed the rumours that had obviously been started by the Jews or Poles... She took a breath, placed the coded messages back in the file and shook her head. She had a lot of admiration for what Charlotte was doing, but if she was going to believe every silly rumour she would make herself look stupid and her credibility would be called into question. But it wasn't for her to say anything. No doubt the reason their superiors hadn't answered her was because it was such a stupid question.

****

45 College Road, Maidstone, Kent
Frederick watched Jeanne surreptitiously whilst pretending to read his newspaper. He knew she was blaming herself for his arrest and even though he had tried to put her mind at rest he had a nasty feeling that she believed he might have killed Mr Jenkins.

'I didn't do it Jeanne. I give you my word. I'm not saying I didn't want to. To do something like that is despicable but I didn't do anything to him. I spoke to your headmistress, and she said she would sort it out.'

'The information did come from me then?'

'Yes. But you did the right thing Love. If you hadn't said anything Debbie would still be there so stop blaming yourself.'

'But people are saying you killed him even though the police let you go.'

'They didn't just let me go Jeanne; they exonerated me completely. Don't take any notice of stupid rumours, you know how small minded people can be.'

Jeanne nodded. What her father said made sense, but she still couldn't rid herself of the thought that if she'd said nothing her father wouldn't have been arrested.

Frederick stared back down at the newspaper and wondered who had killed Mr Jenkins. He wished the police would hurry up and arrest someone so that people stopped pointing at him and whispering when he went past. It had reached the point that when he entered the pub it went quiet as if they had all been discussing him. It was making it very hard for him to continue his enquiries into the man who had been asking questions in Gateshead.

His thoughts moved to Ruth who was still waiting to hear what had happened to Geoffrey. He had tried making enquiries on her behalf, but the War Office had only received one official list of POWs and they were from men taken in Hong Kong. Ruth was due to have her allowances stopped because it was assumed by the treasury that the men were dead. The Japanese had apparently informed the British government that a list of 280,000 men was on its way with ships carrying diplomatic staff evacuated from Japan but there was no sign of that list to date. The War Office had said there was no chance of notifying relatives by 31st July so had requested that allowances continued for another thirteen weeks. The Treasury were not happy but eventually decided that the administrative costs of transferring large numbers of men from allowances to pensions meant it was cheaper to agree to extend allowances until October 1942. The biggest problem Frederick was encountering was that they had no idea where Geoffrey had been when he went missing and as different rules applied to Malaya, Java, Singapore and Hong Kong he wasn't sure how to help Ruth with her claim.

****

Alexandria, Egypt

John decoded the latest transmission from London and sighed. It looked like their light duties were over as they were being ordered to take more stores to Malta. After the opposition they had faced last time it wasn't something he was looking forward to. He had started smoking after the bridge had been hit and although he had considered it to be a temporary thing at the time he was still smoking, not that it was a problem and, if it made him feel calmer, then what was the harm.

It appeared that two convoys would try and get through, one from the east and the other from the west. The western convoy would be escorted by battleships, aircraft carriers and destroyers, while *Cleopatra* would be part of the Fifteenth and Fourth Cruiser Squadron with *Dido*, *Euryalus*, *Hermione*, *Newcastle*, *Arethusa*, *Birmingham* and a screen of destroyers coming from the east. John handed over the signal and then returned to the radio room where he lit another cigarette and began searching the airwaves for any sign that the enemy had intercepted their orders.

****

Paris

'You want me to go and see a Gestapo Officer? Are you completely insane?' Charlotte was flushed with anger and Andre sighed.

'I'm not asking you to sleep with him Francine, just visit him as you said you would. If you don't he might get suspicious.'

Charlotte shook her head. 'I'm sure he's forgotten me by now. Its sheer madness to draw attention to myself again. You must be able to see that.' The atmosphere in Paris had deteriorated rapidly over the past few weeks. Jews over the age of six had been ordered to wear a yellow star with the word *Juif* in black inside the star, on the outside of their clothes at all times. The three badges they had to buy cost an entire month's textile ration and had to be collected at the police station where they were made to give their name and home address. This was bad enough, but the Préfet of Paris had ordered that all Jews were to be restricted to the last carriages of the Métro, but also insisted that no announcement was to be made and Charlotte had witnessed several Jews being forcibly removed from other carriages when they had no idea why. In solidarity some protesters had taken to wearing a yellow star with Zazou printed in the middle, calling themselves friends of the Jews. They were mainly young men who were influenced by jazz music and often scuffled with the Nazis in the streets. They met in cafes or basement clubs and after the Nazis ordered hair to be collected from barbers to be used to make slippers, they grew their hair long in protest.

But the biggest problem facing the city was the lack of food leading to rickets in babies and causing problems between citizens. Charlotte had soon realised that she could get extra food by leaving money under plates in certain restaurants, and she also knew the cafes where false identity cards could be bought. The only useful thing about the lack of food was that many young girls were sent out to relatives in the country to see if they could get fresh eggs. The increased traffic on the roads made travelling around easier and the trains were also more crowded which made moving the transmitter slightly easier as there were fewer checks, but she had a feeling that wouldn't last. In fact she felt as if Paris was building up for something and the last thing she needed was to come to the attention of the Gestapo.

'I disagree. The Gestapo forget nothing. He'll have made a note of your name and he will be looking for you.'

'Then if he finds me, I'll tell him I was busy or I lost the piece of paper with his address on.' Charlotte snapped.

Andre shrugged. 'I think you're making a big mistake.'

'I don't care. I have no intention of visiting the boche. He'll get completely the wrong idea and I have no intention of letting that bastard anywhere near me.'

There was silence, then Andre suddenly changed the subject and began talking about the other buildings she was due to visit. Charlotte gradually relaxed and helped draw up the itinerary. 'Once I have some information to pass on, I'll contact London.'

Andre stood up. 'Au revoir Francine. Take care.' He raised his hand briefly and was gone. Charlotte sighed. Somehow, she had a feeling that wasn't the end of the matter.

****

London
Fred walked quickly back to London Bridge station, he couldn't wait to get the next train back to Maidstone and tell Daisy Irene what he had found out. He wasn't sure what it meant but something wasn't right and he needed to discuss it with her before he went to the police. And say what? He sighed. That was the problem. He had discovered something about Debbie's parents that had changed the whole picture but in what way he didn't know. His brain had been racing ever since he'd realised but he couldn't reach a conclusion because the only one that kept nagging at him was so awful he couldn't bear to contemplate it. Unfortunately, he had no choice because as things were Daisy Irene and the children could be in danger. Even to him that sounded melodramatic, but his instincts were gnawing at him, telling him he was right. If he'd been completely sure of his facts he would have gone straight to the police but he was worried he wouldn't be believed so he needed to talk it over with his wife first. He relaxed slightly. If Daisy Irene agreed with his conclusion then he would telephone the Colonel before speaking to the police. That was the best way to make sure he was believed.

****

En route to Malta
Cleopatra had set sail on the afternoon of 13th June and soon met up with the rest of the squadron. A few hours later John received the signal that the convoy was only forty five miles ahead so the force settled down to a speed which would allow them to meet up with the convoy at daybreak. Within a short while enemy flares began dropping around them but there was no attack and while the crew assumed the enemy were concentrating on the convoy, John searched the airwaves hunting for some sign of the enemy force.

The first bomb fell at 04.35hrs on the Sunday morning and landed in the sea about a mile to starboard. Action stations were sounded but nothing else happened. The airwaves remained stubbornly silent and John couldn't pinpoint any signs of a further attack so eventually they reverted back to defence stations. An hour later they finally sighted the convoy and moved quickly to overhaul them.

'Sir this has just come in.' Chris handed John the latest message. 'The destroyer, *Heythrop* has been sunk.' John hurried up to the bridge and was talking to the captain when a Hurricane suddenly dived into the sea in front of them. He hurried back down to the radio room where Chris was already sending a request for help. 'The destroyer *Tetcott* has gone to give assistance.'

There was an anxious wait and then the airwaves came alive. Chris grinned. '*Airedale* has picked up the pilot.' John was about to answer when they heard sounds of firing on deck.

Chris ran up to take a look, quickly returning with a look of amusement on his face. 'It's alright, they spotted a mine so thought they'd have some target practice.'

John nodded, then resumed listening to the radio latest chatter before frowning. 'The *Tetcott* has just signalled that a motor vessel is on fire and needs help. It can't be from enemy attack as there hasn't been one.' He turned his attention back to the wireless but everything was still quiet. After several more minutes of silence John decided it was probably safe to go up on deck for some fresh air and a quick cigarette.

As he inhaled the nicotine he gazed out over the convoy, an impressive sight steaming along in three lines, cruisers and destroyers all around, screening the merchant ships from submarines and in position to put a protective barrage up if they came under enemy attack. Some of the merchant ships were flying barrage balloons. Everything was calm but for some reason John felt uneasy. He finished his cigarette and hurried back down to the radio room. It was much too quiet.

******

Maidstone, Kent

'Are you sure about this sir?' The policeman sounded so sceptical Colonel Sinclair had difficulty holding his temper.

He raised his voice. 'You need to get around to this address immediately or there will be another murder.'

'Yes sir, we'll go immediately.' The policeman belatedly decided it was probably safer not to question the Colonel. He quickly replaced the receiver and a few moments later they were speeding towards South Moor.

Colonel Sinclair breathed a sigh of relief, he really couldn't afford to lose one of his best men and he was convinced Fred was in danger. For a brief moment he thought back to the latest message Fred had decoded. It seemed the tide was finally turning, Hitler had cancelled the invasion of Malta and with the Allies receiving all the radio transmissions between Rommel and Berlin they could plan their next move more carefully. From the little he could gather they were going to set up a defensive line at El Alamein and then hopefully they could put an end to the Germans' war in North Africa. Once he'd sorted this domestic mess out Fred could go back to finding the two spies that Rommel had sent behind British Lines. At the moment they had very little information except that they had already been infiltrated into Egypt.

From the information they'd originally received Operation Salam had been the first attempt to enter Egypt in May, but the spies had seemingly struggled to progress through the desert thanks to numerous sand storms and shifting sand dunes. But then they had intercepted a message suggesting two agents were in place although not doing very well.

To Section 1H west of the Abwehr, Angelo. Please guarantee our existence. We are in mortal danger (or it is exceedingly urgent, according to Sandstede). Please use the wave length No 1 at 0900 Triploli time. Max and Moritz.

The Colonel allowed himself a small smile. Fortunately, Viktor Hauer, a German national at the Swedish Embassy, was working for the Allies and had immediately notified them that he had given the two agents access to the wireless he had hidden in his basement. Between them it shouldn't be too long before they were able to catch the two spies. The authorities in Egypt had pretended to kidnap Hauer so he could tell them everything he knew and then moved him to safety in Palestine. However, they had lost the two agents, so he needed Fred back on duty to help him trace their whereabouts.

****

En Route to Malta,

The afternoon wore on and although they were still on alert they were enjoying the peace. In the radio room John picked up the air chatter just minutes before the shrieking Stuka's broke their silence, diving at them in waves while torpedo bombers flew past just above sea level unleashing torpedoes. Bombs fell everywhere, somehow missing all the ships while the heavy guns fired back relentlessly, machine gun chatter filled the air and smoke drifted lazily into the sky. News reached John that both the *City of Edinburgh* and *City of Lincolnshire* had survived near misses and the last of the barrage balloons had finally been shot down in flames. Wave after wave of bombers attacked them, *Bhatan*, one of the merchant ships took a direct hit while another, *Potaro*, had a near miss and then another merchant ship dropped out of the line, damaged and unable to keep up with the convoy. The *Malines*, a naval rescue ship was left with her.

****

South Moor, Maidstone, Kent

'Fred, I wasn't expecting you.' Daisy Irene had been in the kitchen preparing dinner. She stopped what she was doing, wrapped her arms around him and hugged him. 'You have no idea how much I've missed you.'

Fred hugged her back, relieved to see she was unharmed. 'Where are the children?'

'At school of course. Why do I bore you that much you only come home to see them?' Daisy Irene joked and then realised Fred wasn't laughing. She began to feel uneasy. 'What's the matter?'

'I've just been to London, to check up on Debbie's family. I wanted to know why she was so adamant she didn't go back there despite what was happening to her here.'

Daisy Irene nodded. 'I wondered about that. You would have thought she would have jumped at the chance to get away.' She saw the expression on his face and took a deep breath. 'Do I need to sit down?'

Fred indicated the kitchen chairs and they both sat down. 'I talked to several people because I couldn't believe what I was hearing and then I spoke to the police who confirmed it.'

'Confirmed what?'

'Debbie's stepfather has been abusing her for years. It would appear to have been common knowledge among the neighbours.'

Daisy Irene paled. 'But that's ridiculous. The chances of her going from one abuser to another under the circumstances she came here must be astronomical. Her stepfather couldn't have passed her on,' she saw his confusion and explained. 'I've read that's what these people do. But in this case the evacuation committee found Debbie her billet. I can't remember who exactly…' She tailed off and shook her head. 'You're not saying one of the committee… no that's not possible.' Surely she couldn't have missed something so obscene going on right under her nose.

Fred sighed. 'It's either that or something worse.'

'What could be worse?' Daisy Irene snapped.

'Jenkins wasn't abusing her. She made it up so she could stay here.' He shrugged. 'I don't know…'

'By here, you mean with me, us?'

'Possibly?'

'But if that's true who killed Jenkins?' Daisy Irene was staring at Fred so she didn't hear the kitchen door open.

'I did.'

****

At sea

With a slight lull in the attack those who could be spared were sent to eat but they had no sooner sat down when a couple of two hundred and fifty pound bombs dropped close to the starboard side. The men hurried back to their guns while allied aircraft came to their aid, breaking up the attack formations. Eventually it began to grow dark and the assault from the high level bombing eased off, although the number of torpedoes increased. The destroyers began dropping depth charges while the *Malines* and another rescue ship, the *Antwerp,* left the convoy with the damaged merchant ship and headed for Tobruk.

Despite the numerous depth charges, the destroyer *Fortune* soon reported that they'd spotted a submarine and orders were issued that all ships were to engage the U-boats whenever possible. They were helped in their task by an enemy aircraft that kept dropping flares, illuminating the darkness. Eventually the submarine attack fizzled out but then John received a signal that the Italian Fleet had been spotted and was steaming towards them. They changed course but almost immediately he received confirmation that the RAF were now attacking the Italian Fleet which meant this was their chance to turn back and head for Malta.

'We'll need to change course again.' Chris handed John the latest signal which stated that despite repeated attempts the RAF had failed to inflict any real damage on the Italian Fleet. John was about to report this when he received another signal stating the other convoy had reached Malta safely and that as they now had no heavy ships, and the heavily armed Italian Fleet with its strong air cover was heading straight for them, they should head back to Alexandria.

****

South Moor, Maidstone, Kent

At the sound of the voice they both spun around in shock. Having been engrossed in their conversation they hadn't realised the time or heard Debbie come in.

Daisy Irene recovered quickest and somehow spoke calmly. 'What do you mean Debbie? Are you saying you killed Mr Jenkins?'

Debbie nodded. 'Yes. That's right. He wasn't interested. He said he would report me, and I would be sent back home.'

Daisy Irene swallowed nervously and tried to continue sounding calm. 'I'm sorry Debbie. I don't think I understand. What wasn't he interested in?'

Debbie looked confused. 'Me. I was sure he must be lying because you can tell can't you…? when someone likes you…, like that I mean. Anyway, I knew he liked me so I thought he was probably just shy. Some men are you know, that's what my stepfather says anyway. They need a bit of encouragement,' she smiled at Fred, 'I expect you understand... that it's hard to have to make the first move all the time… so I made it easy for him. *I* kissed *him*.' Fred was grateful she wasn't looking at him because he was sure his revulsion was clearly visible. He could feel Daisy Irene beginning to move and he guessed she was going to stand up and reach out to Debbie, perhaps hug her or take her by the hand. For a reason he couldn't immediately clarify he didn't think that was a good idea so he rested his hand on hers, hoping she would stay where she was.

Fortunately, Debbie didn't appear to have noticed Daisy Irene's movement, she was staring at the floor, too focused on her own story. She shook her head, her expression confused again. 'But he pushed me away. He said I was a slut, a whore, and he was going to report me to the evacuation committee and that you would send me back to London.' She raised her eyes again, staring intently at Fred. 'But I didn't want to go home. I like Maidstone. Everyone is so friendly, they seem to really care about you. I wasn't sure I would be happy at first but I knew I could go home if I wasn't. My stepdad said I just had to ring him and he'd come and pick me up. But I realised it was quite nice to get away from him and anyway, Gordon was so nice to me that I realised I was much better off here than in London. I just don't understand what I did wrong. I was so sure he liked me.' Debbie shook her head, oblivious of their disgust. 'He offered to buy me some new clothes you know. I heard him talking to her, his wife. He said my old things were getting too small now I was getting older, my skirts were too short and my blouses too tight and that I should have some bigger clothes. He gave her money to buy me new underwear. *And* he always brought sweets home on a Friday. You don't do any of that if you don't like someone do you?' She suddenly stopped talking, smiled in what Fred assumed she thought was a seductive way and took a step towards him. He shrank back into the kitchen chair, frantically trying to think of something, anything to distract her so he could get help. Although where he was going to get assistance from he had no idea. He was sure no one would believe the things this thirteen year old child was saying to him. Thank God Daisy Irene was with him, he would never have been able to explain this to her and if she hadn't been here, he would have forgiven her for not believing him. He didn't believe what he was hearing himself.

'You like me don't you Fred? You wouldn't push me away, would you?' She took another step towards him and, feeling sick, he automatically shrank back even further.

Debbie's expression darkened and he was frantically trying to think of something to say that would defuse the situation when he saw the knife.

****

Eastern Front

Kristian was struggling to get used to being back in the Soviet Union. The squadron had moved yet again and it had taken him some time to get his bearings despite the evening get togethers and the help from the ops room personnel. He didn't recognise most of the other flyers and most of the talk was still on the Fuhrer's Directive No 41 which indicated that they would no longer be heading for Moscow, instead the aim was to take Leningrad and link up with the Finns. Kristian knew that the plan had been to trap all Russian forces in the Great Don Bend, west of Stalingrad. But it seemed to him that the Russians had learned from their previous mistakes and had withdrawn back across the Don, leaving an empty pocket. Kristian was sure Hitler had completely misread the situation, assuming the Soviets had only withdrawn because they were beaten. He had then overruled his generals and ordered the southern sector to be split in two, 4 Panzerarmee wheeled due south, joined up with 1 Panzerarmee and headed south to the Caucasus while 6 Armee had marched onto to Stalingrad alone. Kristian was convinced this was a massive mistake but he knew he was alone in his assumptions, so he kept quiet.

****

South Moor, Maidstone, Kent

'Debbie what are you doing?' Daisy Irene somehow managed to sound calm even though her heart was racing.

'I don't understand why they keep rejecting me. Arthur said that I was very attractive and that any man would be pleased to have me.'

'Arthur?' Daisy Irene hoped that if she kept talking to her Debbie would lower the knife and they might be able to disarm her.

'Arthur…? Oh he's my stepfather. He said I could call him Arthur when we were on our own.' She sighed. 'But then he said I had to keep his friends happy too. I didn't like that. I just wanted to be with Arthur, but he said I had to be nice to them or he would be in trouble.'

'Did Arthur have lots of friends?' Daisy Irene asked, her heart went out to the young girl standing in front of them, but it was already too late to save her. Debbie had killed Gordon Jenkins because he hadn't wanted to abuse her and she had no idea what would happen to her once the police knew. She swallowed nervously. How on earth could they notify the police while she was holding a knife on them.

'Yes, although most of them didn't live very near us. We used to have to get the train. Arthur always stopped at a nice café on the way back... and we had some tea and cake.'

'And what about your mother? Did she come with you?'

Debbie stared at her in amusement and burst out laughing. 'Of course not. Arthur said it was our secret. I wasn't to tell her because she would be jealous.'

'Why didn't you want to go back home then? I mean you seemed quite happy.' Fred spoke for the first time and Daisy Irene tensed. But Debbie seemed to have forgotten her animosity towards him.

'He told me I was special.' Debbie looked confused. 'But then he said he wanted to bring Helen along too. Helen was my younger sister. He said she was old enough to come with us too, but that wasn't right was it? I was the special one not her. She wasn't meant to come with us.' She fell silent and stared down at the floor again. Fred and Daisy exchanged worried glances and Daisy raised an eyebrow at him. He hadn't mentioned anything about a sister.

Fred frowned. 'Where's Helen now? Was she evacuated somewhere else?'

Daisy Irene gasped. She had been wary about asking Debbie in case she didn't like the answer but Fred had jumped in with both feet.

Debbie shook her head. 'No, Helen had an accident at the beginning of the war.'

'An accident?' Fred was beginning to wish he hadn't said anything now.

'She fell in the river and drowned.' Debbie raised her eyes and stared at him. 'She wasn't happy so I'm sure she didn't mind very much.' She lifted the knife again. 'You do like me, don't you?'

'Yes of course he does.' Daisy Irene answered before Fred could say anything. She stood up. 'I don't know about you, but I could really do with a cup of tea. Shall I put the kettle on? Fred can you get the biscuit tin. I did some baking today and there are some fresh ones.' They had to resolve this quickly before the other children came home. Fortunately, it was the night they all stayed after school tending to the allotments, but they would be home soon.

Debbie nodded. 'That would be nice. I'm very thirsty.'

Fred started to get up but Debbie moved closer, the light glinting off the knife. 'No Fred, you stay there. Daisy can make the tea. I can get the biscuit tin.' She moved closer to him placing herself between

Fred and Daisy Irene, the knife was clenched tightly in her fist and aimed threateningly at him. Fred knew he would have to knock her out to take it away and whatever she'd done he wasn't sure he could bring himself to hit a girl. Daisy Irene cursed under her breath. She had been hoping that Debbie would let them both stand up. She picked the kettle up and nearly dropped it in shock. There were people in the back garden. One of them put his finger to his lips and she realised he was wearing a police uniform. She had barely registered that when the door burst open and several men rushed in. One grabbed the knife and pushed Debbie up against the wall. Daisy Irene groped her way to the table and flung her arms around Fred, tears streaming down her face.

Fred held her tight and then recognised the man standing in front of him.

'Are you alright Fred, Mrs Corben?'

'Yes, thank you, Colonel.' Fred eased Daisy Irene away so he could stand up, then indicated Debbie. 'I think she killed her sister too.'

Colonel Sinclair sighed. 'The police will investigate everything Fred. Just tell them what you know and suspect. You too Mrs Corben.'

'She's just a child, whatever she's done.' She wiped her eyes. 'Her stepfather is the man you should be arresting.'

'We already have, thanks to Fred who contacted me before he left London.'

Daisy Irene breathed out slowly. 'I did wonder how the police knew to come here.'

'I wasn't convinced I had made the right connections. It seemed so farfetched and repulsive but I was reasonably sure I was right so I contacted Colonel Sinclair as I didn't think the police would believe me and I was concerned about your safety, yours and the children.'

Daisy Irene shivered. 'I can't believe this poor child had to put up with that and no one did anything.'

'She's a murderer Daisy.'

'Yes I know, but surely they won't hang her?'

Fred looked at Colonel Sinclair who shook his head. 'No, she's under eighteen so she'll just be sent to prison.'

'For how long?'

'Until she's no longer considered to be a threat.'

Daisy Irene nodded. Whatever she had done Debbie was a victim and hopefully she would get some help while she was in prison.

****

En route to Alexandria

The journey back was fraught with danger as the Italian Fleet continued to attack them, their submarines sank the destroyer *Hasty* and also hit *Newcastle* who somehow remained afloat, air attacks resumed and bombers only just missed *Birmingham*. Ju88s appeared in vast numbers while the guns aboard the ships roared, filling the sky with bursting ack ack shells. Twelve Stuka's attacked the *Airedale* which received five direct hits and eventually blew up, setting off the smoke floats on her stern which smothered the sky in a pall of thick smoke making rescue attempts difficult. Having successfully sunk one ship they headed for *Cleopatra* but thanks to clever manoeuvring by the Captain all attempts to sink her missed.

The attacks continued for the next few hours eventually sinking *Hermione* until finally *Cleopatra* reached the safety of Alexandria. Here they found several of the escorting warships, they were short of ammunition and the crew exhausted after three days of almost constant battle. They hadn't succeeded in getting through to Malta, but by drawing enemy fire from both the Italian Fleet and the Axis air force they had enabled the other convoy to get through. It was a victory of sorts.

****

45 College Road, Maidstone, Kent

Jeanne sat quietly listening to her father explaining what had happened and felt bemused. Her friend Debbie had turned out to be not only a liar but a murderer too. Even worse, not only had she murdered poor Mr Jenkins who hadn't done anything despite all the awful things people had been saying, but she'd murdered her younger sister too. It didn't make any sense to Jeanne.

'It's all a bit much isn't it?' Frederick smiled at her.

'Yes, but it's over now, isn't it?'

'Yes, apart from the trial.'

Jeanne paled. 'Will I have to go to court?'

'I shouldn't think so,' he saw the horror on her face and added quickly, 'no I'm sure you won't have to. I just meant that with the trial people will start talking about it again, but once that's over they'll find something else to gossip about.'

Jeanne breathed a sigh of relief. She never wanted to see Debbie again. Her father had been arrested and people had spent weeks talking about him behind his back all because she had believed everything Debbie had said. At least now everyone knew the truth.

'You did the right thing Jeanne. You have nothing to feel guilty about.'

'Dad's right.' Margaret appeared at the kitchen door. 'It wasn't your fault. You did the right thing so you need to forget all about it now.'

Frederick smiled at Margaret. It wasn't often they agreed about anything. 'You having a night in?'

Margaret smiled. 'No, I'm off out in a minute but I wanted to let you know that I never believed any of the stuff they were saying about you.'

'I'm pleased to hear that.' He frowned. 'Where are you going tonight?'

'There's a dance at one of the halls. I'm going with some friends. I won't be late back. Night Jeanne.'

Jeanne waved as her sister disappeared out of the door and then saw her father's disapproving face. 'She's only going to dance Dad.'

'It's not that Jeanne. I'm happy for her to go out, just not every night!'

Jeanne smiled and finally began to relax. Looked like things were getting back to normal then.

****

South Moor, Maidstone, Kent

'Are you alright now?' Fred sat down on the settee, put his arms around Daisy Irene and cuddled her.

'As much as I can be. I still can't believe that today happened.'

'No, it's all been very trying, but it's over now. Debbie will be tried but she'll be sent to prison or even a hospital and she'll get help. At least poor Gordon Jenkins' family will know that he wasn't guilty of those terrible things.'

'And the rumours about Captain Farmer will stop. That poor man must have been so angry at people talking about him behind his back knowing that it was all lies.'

'And his daughter won't feel like the whole thing is her fault anymore.' Fred added.

'Goodness I'd forgotten all about that. Poor Jeanne. She must have been devastated.'

'And hopefully our children will go back to being normal again.' Fred smiled.

Daisy Irene patted his hand. It was lovely to hear him calling the children 'ours'. 'I can't wait to get back to normal.'

Fred smiled until his thoughts went to the pile of signals and telephone intercepts waiting for him to check. His normal was back to dealing with deception, finding out where the spy was, who was helping them and if there really was some double agent at the heart of the establishment. After what he'd experienced today he couldn't wait to get back to normal either.

Chapter 34

Haifa, Palestine
My darling John
I am so proud of you for being awarded the DSM. It's such an amazing honour to be married to someone so brave. Rodney doesn't really understand but I will keep telling him how brave you are so that he does eventually know how proud he should be of you. But at the same time I want to shout at you for risking your life because whatever you say about not knowing why you were given such an award I know you must have done something outstanding which means you were risking your life even more than just being on the ship in a battle. Please don't earn any other awards, they are not as important as having you back safe and sound with us again.

Anyway, I love you and I am very proud of you, but I will now talk about something else! There is so much to tell you about the farm as you didn't have much time to see it when you were here. You will be pleased to know you chose well, it is very beautiful here and, touch wood, no enemy bombers to spoil the peace and calm. Rodney absolutely loves it here, he can play outside from morning until dusk without fear of bombs dropping or some hun shooting at him. I have also made some friends in the village and I have been to some fund raising events, we raise money for Spitfires among other things. I'm surprised they don't send refugees here rather than Maidstone, its much safer but I suppose there are not enough people to take them in. Daisy Irene was swamped back in September when they sent several thousand more children to Maidstone expecting them to find families for them. It was a very hard task but she and the other members of the committee managed, much to my surprise. She now has several children herself, I'm not sure how many to be honest, but its not so bad because Fred does at least get home sometimes, unlike you. Sorry, that sounds like another moan. I just miss you very much and I would like to have another child before Rodney gets too used to being an only child or I get too old. Perhaps we could discuss that next time you are home on leave?

John smiled. He couldn't think of anything he wanted more than another child, well he would do when the war was over. He couldn't bring another child into a world that was tearing itself apart and one in which the outcome of the war was not yet resolved. He was sure they would win the war, even if it didn't look like it at the moment. But how long it would take he had no idea so Elsie would just have to wait.

****

Paris

Charlotte sat on the park bench, staring at young children playing in the small pond and listening in horror as Andre passed on the information he had received regarding a proposed round up of Jews in the city. He had his arm around her, for all intents and purposes a young couple meeting for lunch.

'Are you sure?'

'They did something similar last year, in May, persuaded foreign Jews to register on the promise of routine registration, then arrested them and shipped them off to camps in the south of the city. They were kept there while the authorities rounded up several thousand more and then they were sent to Auschwitz.' He saw her confusion. 'It's a work camp in Poland.'

'And they're doing the same again?'

'Yes, I think so. Only this time it's all Jews, not just those who were born abroad.'

'Is there anything we can do to stop them?'

Andre shook his head. 'No, we can try and get some of them to Vichy but we don't have much time.'

Charlotte sighed. 'I'll notify London but I'm not sure there is anything they can do.'

'Thanks.'

Charlotte hesitated then said what she was thinking. 'Can you get some papers for them? If so I could take some families south?'

'You're not a courier any more Francine. It's much too dangerous, you know that. We need your skills as a radio operator, we can't risk you.'

'Yes, I know but this is a one off,' he saw her intense expression and was about to argue when she continued. 'I wouldn't suggest it if I didn't know it was urgent. You can get some papers for the families and I can say I am travelling down to one of the vineyards. You could contact them so they back up my story. We just need to get them out of Paris before the round up.'

Andre sighed. He was torn between his desire to protect his radio operator and the need to rescue women and children from the camps. He hadn't said anything to Francine but judging from her reaction she too had heard the terrible rumours that had begun circulating. He had no idea if there were any truth in them… He pulled his thoughts back to the present. 'When would you be able to go?'

'As soon as possible, we don't have long, do we?' Charlotte hesitated and then decided to say what was on her mind. 'There are rumours going round that the Germans are killing them.' She continued quickly before he could say anything. 'I know it sounds ridiculous, so I asked London and they eventually confirmed that there was some evidence the Germans had set up death camps in the east.' She had asked three times before anyone had bothered to answer her and it was that hesitation that had persuaded her that the rumours were probably true and that London was just as shocked as she was.

He glanced across at her in horror. 'That's unbelievable…' He fell silent.

Charlotte shrugged. 'Is it? They don't make much secret of their hatred do they?'

'But to deliberately kill them…' Andre felt sick. 'Women and children too?'

'Yes, I think so.' Charlotte glanced around quickly before lowering her voice even though there was no one is earshot. 'No point just killing the men if you want to wipe out an entire race.'

There was a long silence then Andre finally made a decision. 'I'll sort out some papers and arrange for some families to leave.' He glanced across at her tense expression and felt concerned. 'I would say it will do you good to get out of Paris. You need a break. But I'm not sure this is the right way to get away from things.'

Charlotte gave a wry smile. 'They say a change is as good as a rest.' She carried on. 'I'm spending too much time with Germans, arrogant bastards… so sure of themselves… and not being able to do anything…' She closed her eyes for a moment, thought about Rebecca and the promise she'd made to her sister. Then she recalled the increase in sabotage which was happening because she was risking her life arranging numerous drops of weapons and materials to the resistance and realised she was doing something, even if she didn't know whether she was making a difference.

Andre read her mind. 'We couldn't carry out half the attacks without your help Francine. Your contribution is vital. That's why I am reluctant to agree.'

'I can't do nothing Andre. If I only help one family…'

'Alright, alright, I'll set it up and meet you back here in a couple of days.' He removed his arm, kissed her lightly on the cheek and walked away.

Charlotte sat there for several moments, checking every now and again to make sure Andre wasn't being followed and that she wasn't being watched, then she stood up and headed back to her apartment. She wouldn't tell London that she was going to do this, they might forbid her to get involved.

Werner Fischer leant back in the bushes and made notes in his book. He knew who the man was, although the woman was new. But she was behaving like an agent, checking constantly for anything suspicious. He would have to wait until she was almost out of sight before following. The last thing he needed was for her to notice him. He frowned. She seemed familiar for some reason, but he couldn't think why. It was only after he had followed her back to her apartment that he finally remembered where he'd met her.

****

Palembang, Sumatra

For the first few weeks there was bread available around 10.00hrs but that was soon substituted with plain rice. Lunch was between 15.00hrs and 16.00hrs, consisting of various vegetables, mainly potatoes and cucumber, chilli, sambol and rice and sometimes a vegetable soup. Camp funds, earned from working for the Dutch prisoners enabled them to buy bananas, tea and coffee. Occasionally there was pork, about half an ounce per person but fish was rarely available. At 20.00hrs they received a bowl of rice and vegetable soup which occasionally contained small pieces of meat. The camp was divided into eleven blocks and each day a different block was called first for their food. They all had tins for their soup and coffee, and two bowls for rice and vegetables. The water was chlorinated and unlike Muntok there were sufficient supplies.

After the first few days the sentries left them alone, the lights were put out around 23.00hrs and although they had tried to fix up some light it wasn't bright enough to read by, even if they'd had the energy. Geoffrey's bed consisted of four rice bags, two old thin mats and waterproof sheeting on a cement floor and he was so exhausted he was usually able to sleep for around seven hours despite the mosquitos that drove them mad, chewing up their faces and hands. So far he'd managed to avoid the various illnesses that swept through the camp but with the prevalence of flies, cockroaches and rats over running the camp most of the time he had no idea how long that would be the case.

By the summer, when the days became even hotter, he had lost over three stone since his captivity, his clothes hung off him, his hair was falling out and so were his teeth. He missed Kang and he wondered if his friend was still alive. He doubted it, not given the way the Japanese treated the Chinese, and he often thought it might have been safer to have left his friend in Singapore. The work parties were brutal, exhausting and invariably resulted in at least one man being badly assaulted. Every night he lay down and wondered why he was bothering to keep fighting but then he would think about Ruth and the determination to survive reasserted itself.

****

Arkley View, Near Barnet

Fred smiled as he read the latest intelligence report from Egypt. It appeared that both spies, Johann Eppler, Heinrich Gerd Stanstede and their small network, which included someone called Anwar el-Sadat, had been arrested on 24 July. His smile broadened as he read on, and he shook his head in disbelief. It appeared both Germans had kept diaries, started when it looked like Rommel might reach Cairo so if necessary they could prove their achievements to the Germans. Many of the entries were true although some were obviously false. The intelligence report stated that both men had actually achieved very little, had failed to make contact with their radio controller, Gefreiter Waldemar Weber, nor bothered to contact the people they were supposed to have liaised with. They had run out of money after spending most of the £3000 of forged money they had been given on enjoying themselves in the fleshpots of Cairo. Fred read on in growing amusement as it appeared that their lack of contact with Weber had been Rommel's fault who was so short of radio operators he had transferred Weber to his command and he had subsequently been captured by the South African Armoured Car Regiment.

Fred was pleased he had been able to help but the real achievement had been made back in the winter of 1941 when they had managed to break the Abwehr Enigma code. They had also broken the complicated *Chaffinch* code used by the Afrika Korps and would have picked up the two spies much earlier if they'd made regular contact.

It seemed the spies had been very helpful, preferring to save their own skins by giving sufficient information to destroy the Egyptian Fifth Column. Fred sighed and wondered where the rest of the Brandenburg Regiment were now. It was unlikely they had all left North Africa, so finding them was a priority. He put the report down and turned his attention back to the growing pile of recently intercepted signals.

****

Haifa, Palestine
Dearest Elsie and Rodney
Thank you so much for your lovely letter and I promise not to do anything too risky, honestly. As to the idea of having another child, I can't think of anything I would like more. Hopefully by the time I have some more leave the tide will have turned and we will be winning the war, the enemy forced onto the back foot. Let us pray for that moment my darling and in the meantime let me bring you up to date with where I am now.

As you can see I am in Palestine. After our forces in North Africa fell back and we lost Tobruk, Bardia and Sollom it was decided to move our ships from Alexandria away from the danger of dive bombing and the risks of the harbour being mined.

I must say how wonderful it is to see real trees and mountains for a change and we have even had a trip to the Holy Land. Our first trip was to Nazareth, yes really! Its not only the birth place of Christianity, we were able to see how native life was centuries ago, then we went to Jerusalem and saw the Wailing Wall which was equally as fascinating, if not completely different. From there we visited Tiberias on the Sea of Galilee which is apparently famous here for its health giving waters, and then Acre and it amazing mosque. When the war ends I would love to bring you here so you could see the incredible things I have seen.

Mount Carmel rises up behind the port of Haifa, a blue haze of heat in the distance and we have spent many happy hours relaxing there. It is so nice not to be permanently on action stations and to be able to enjoy a few hours doing absolutely nothing. At the top of Mount Carmel is a monastery with Franciscan Brothers who carry out their teaching and healing in Haifa and one of the monks is English. He's been here for many years apparently which has helped endear the British to the citizens of Haifa who are very friendly. They invite us into their homes or meals and we even went to a dance in an institute, a bit like one of our schools only bigger.

But it's not all fun, the crew are also busy learning new drills and exercising, fortunately I do not have to get too involved in that, most of my time spent ensuring our communications equipment is ready to cope with anything the enemy throws at us.

I hope the farm is still peaceful and that now you have made friends you are not too lonely. I miss you both so very much and I can't wait to be back home again.

John finished the letter and wished it could be sent, but most of it wouldn't get past the censor. He would save it until he got home and then Elsie could read it. He placed it in his drawer, wrote a quick letter that said very little, placed it in an envelope and lit another cigarette. He was running low, he would go down to the stores to get some more and drop off his letter in the mailroom on the way.

****

Toulouse, Vichy France

Charlotte only just managed to stop herself stumbling as she listened to Josephine in horror and disbelief. 'But I've just spent the last month risking my life bringing Jews out of the occupied zone in an attempt to save them.' She snapped.

'They started the round up yesterday. We couldn't get a message to you in time to stop you bringing any more.' Josephine sounded distraught and Charlotte immediately felt guilty for her outburst.

'I'm sorry, I'm not blaming you. I'm just furious that all our attempts to save people have been thwarted by those bosche bastards.'

'I know how you feel.' Josephine's blue eyes filled with tears and she shook her mane of grey hair. 'I've become good friends with some of them. We thought we had enough time to prepare them so we didn't hurry and we are now struggling to get them across to Spain. The patrols have increased and it's not like taking fit young men across. These are women and children.' She wiped her eyes.

'We'll need to move them tonight then.' Charlotte spoke decisively.

'But we can't. We have to set it up properly with the guides…'

'There's no time for that. If we can at least get them out of Toulouse then we can find an alternative route.' Charlotte thought hard for a moment and then it came to her. 'What about moving them to Nice?'

'But that's in completely the opposite direction?' Josephine looked confused.

'Yes, Nice is on the Italian border, if we can get them across that they would be safer. The Italians aren't interested in persecuting the Jews. Well not to the extent the Germans are anyway.'

'Are you sure?'

Charlotte shrugged. 'As sure as I can be. Trying to evacuate sixty orphans with five adults dressed as nuns was always going to be more difficult. But the disguise worked well didn't it? They weren't even questioned and if two of the children hadn't developed chicken pox and several others appearing to be sickening with it you wouldn't have had to delay their departure. But this is a much better idea. They can remain in disguise and travel by coach. If stopped and questioned they can say they are on their way to a convent and that some of the children are sick, that should stop too many questions or searches and they'll be much safer once they're in Nice. I can probably get London to arrange for one of the convents to back up the story. Can you get them some new papers?'

Josephine was looking much happier. 'Yes, it will take a few days though but now we have a plan we can keep them hidden until we're ready. We'll move them to one of the outlying farmhouses, away from prying eyes.' She frowned. 'Our biggest problem is to make sure no one finds out that they are here or that they came in by train from the occupied zone. Otherwise, they will wonder why they came here if they were supposed to be going to Nice.' She stopped. 'Leave that with me. I'll sort something out. I'll go and speak to Victor.'

Charlotte breathed a sigh of relief and glanced at her watch. 'I have to get back as well or I'll miss my train. I'll notify London that you're going to move them to Nice and ask them to arrange the convent and some help from one of the local group.'

'Have a safe journey Francine.' Josephine leant forward and hugged her before hurrying back the way they'd come. Charlotte continued in the direction of the station, her thoughts on how she was going to ask London for help hiding Jews in Nice, when she was supposed to be ingratiating herself with Germans in Paris. But first she had to survive the most dangerous part of the journey, crossing the demarcation line back into the occupied zone. At least she was on her own. It had been much more nerve wracking going the other way with several families relying on her. Somehow she had survived nearly a dozen trips and had helped over one hundred women and children escape the Nazis. The fact that some of them were now stranded in Toulouse infuriated her and she was determined to make sure they escaped. The train eased into the station, she climbed aboard and made her way to the first class carriage. She had quickly decided that a woman in her position would always travel first class as that would give her the opportunity to interest wealthy men, French and German, in the wine. It also reduced the chances of her being questioned too energetically or being suspected of anything, at least that was how it appeared.

Chapter 35

En Route to Rhodes

John read the orders again and sighed. It was a shame they were going to bombard Rhodes, but this wasn't an attack on the Greeks it was aimed at the Italians. It seemed their main targets were the flour mills as the island was known to be short of food. They had spent the day cruising around in sight of Cyprus, zig zagging madly through the calm glassy sea while the men sunbathed on deck in the brilliant sunshine. As the blood red sun finally sank into the sea the Captain had ordered action stations and they had set sail round the tip of Cyprus towards Rhodes. John sat glued to the radio listening for enemy signals, but it was very quiet. As they approached Rhodes they could see flak so he assumed the RAF were already attacking.

They drew closer to the harbour, every moment expecting to be detected, but although a searchlight caught them momentarily it petered out leaving everything in darkness again. The first salvo hit the shore, hitting the soldier's barracks, the second found the target, continuing to pulverise it while heavy batteries from the shore fired back. Huge smoke screens drifted over the harbour, as shore batteries, anti aircraft guns and Italian torpedo boats fought back.

'Submarines have been sighted off the starboard side.' The look out notified the Captain. The aft guns were still firing at the shore so, as more were spotted the forward guns changed direction. The noise was deafening, the flashes from the guns blinding, and eventually the U-Boats were seen off. Huge fires were now ablaze on the shore, the flour mills demolished, *Cleopatra*'s job was done and while the RAF and American bombers continued to bomb the airfields and harbour they turned away, ready to sail back to Haifa.

John smiled as he switched off the Italian radio station he had been listening in to. They were no longer boasting about two British Cruisers stuck in Haifa harbour, they appeared to have realised that the Fascist claim that the British had been chased out of the Mediterranean was inaccurate.

A week later *Cleopatra* sailed for Port Said. Admiral Vian's flag was struck as he left the ship and that of Admiral A J Power replaced it. John lined up on the Forecastle the following day and listened as their new Admiral said he hoped to keep up the good work carried out by his predecessor and that they should ensure they were always on alert.

'I think I prefer to be fighting.' Chris muttered as they finished yet another drill.

John grinned. 'I'll remind you of that when we're being fired on!'

'Doesn't look like it will be for a while.' Chris smiled back. 'We've sprung a leak so now we need to get some repairs done. And before you ask no, we're not going back to Alexandria because it's still under attack most of the time.'

'So where are we going?'

'Massawa in what used to be Italian Eritrea.'

'Through the Suez Canal then?' At least that would give him something to write to Elsie about, even if he couldn't actually send it.

'Yeah, I guess so.' Chris didn't look particularly interested and John hid a smile. There were few very few cargo ships in the canal, convoys being unnecessary as the area inland was under British control.

My dearest Elsie and Rodney

As you can see we are now in the Red Sea, nice and safe for once. The biggest shock is that there is no blackout here, its really strange seeing shops with lights on, even if there aren't that many.

We came here through the Suez Canal. Another new experience for me. We picked up a pilot and sailed slowly through the canal, most of the men were allowed to stay on deck while the captain pointed out places of interest. It was very peaceful, a bit like being on holiday. The funniest part was when we passed the numerous gun posts and military camps all along the canal. Several soldiers obviously thought we were coming home so they started thumbing lifts. Even funnier were those who shouted jokes at us suggesting we were running away. I was going to stay you should have heard some of the crew's replies but perhaps not!

We have just spent a couple of days in a rest camp in Asmara. It was a relief to be up in the mountains as its unbelievably hot here, around 110 degrees, but the long journey was worth it. We travelled along mountain roads with incredibly dangerous drops but the higher we went the cooler it became. Asmara is a typical Italian looking town with wide roads, some amazing churches and buildings, all architecturally stunning. Our camp was outside the town, a series of chalets, a military style dining room and canteen which quickly sold out of beer. The only drawback were the millions of flies that plagued us during the day and their even more irritating cousins the mosquitos who spent all night biting us.

John hesitated, wondering whether he should mention their trip to Karen where there had been a large battle, the British having to climb massive rocks in full view of the enemy, to take Eritrea. He eventually decided not to, there was very little to see and he was sure she wouldn't be that interested in more fighting. A slight smile crossed his face as he remembered something else he'd decided not to mention: that the brakes in their truck had packed up while they had been halfway down the perilous winding mountain roads and rather than tell the passengers the driver had decided to use the clutch to negotiate the bends. The letter joined the others in his drawer and he started again, another bland letter with no information but one that would at least get past the censor.

****

Paris

Charlotte breathed a sigh of relief as she read the latest news that Nice was now under Italian control and that the Italians had refused to hand over any Jews to the Germans. No doubt surviving Jews from all over Vichy and the occupied zone would make their way to Nice in the hope of sanctuary. At least she could relax knowing the children were safe even if she was in trouble with London. They had threatened to recall her if she broke her orders again, but she didn't care. She would never have been able to live with herself if she'd ignored her instincts and done nothing. She had heard several reports of the terrible conditions they had suffered in the Vel' d'Hive stadium, thousands of people crammed into the Vélodrome d'Hiver with no food, water or proper toilets before being sent to camps outside Paris where the children were separated from their parents who were sent somewhere else, she could only assume to Poland although she didn't know where. She had tried to find out about the children but none of her German contacts appeared to know and she couldn't keep asking questions in case they grew suspicious.

She glanced up from the newspaper to pick up her coffee and was about to sip it when something caught her eye. She made herself drink slowly, her eyes scanning the area looking for whatever it was that had caught her subconscious attention. It took a few moments but then she registered the street cleaner, slowly picking up the small amount of litter before sweeping the area around the curb. Her brain began racing. Why had he caught her attention? His clothes looked right, worn scruffy, non too clean, his face, stubble, sallow cheeks, small scar… she almost choked on her coffee and she somehow managed to stop herself staring at him. She took a deep breath and raised the newspaper until she could just see over it. The scar was crescent shaped and under his left eye. The chances of two men carrying the same scar were minimal. The last time she'd seen that scar had been on the train to Paris. The Gestapo man, Werner Fischer.

****

London

Anthony had been back in England just over a month now after a tortuous journey home via Australia. He and Richard had been lucky to escape Malaya with their lives. At the time he'd been furious that they had been ordered to leave but now he was home he could see that the orders had been sensible. If they'd stayed much longer they would have been either killed or captured and they would not have achieved very much. He was convinced Britain would take the country back from the Japanese eventually, but as it was not likely to happen very soon it was better to withdraw and regroup. Meanwhile he had been promoted to Lieutenant Colonel and was now in charge of the training for SOE agents in the Far East, his experience over the previous months invaluable for future planning.

On arrival back in Britain he had immediately tried to contact Charlotte only to find she had been sent to France and appeared to be doing a good job. Unfortunately, he could not find out when her current assignment would finish so he had decided to try and concentrate on the new job and hope it wouldn't be too long before she was back home too.

******

Sinai Peninsular
Having survived their high powered sea trials John received

Cleopatra's latest orders, that they were designated ack ack cruiser at Abu Zenima, 65 miles down the coast from Port Suez. They had been there almost a week now and would soon be moving on again.

John reread Elsie's last letter and smiled. She had written mainly to tell him that his DSM had been printed in the London Gazette on 8th September. But he sensed she was also lonely, despite her stories of fund-raising activities and arguments among the committees. She had mentioned going back to Maidstone a couple of times, not because she wanted to but because she missed her family.

John lit another cigarette and pulled out his writing paper to record more details of his life to share when he finally returned home.

My dearest Elsie and Rodney,

As you can see we are now at an even more exotic location. We are scheduled to stay here for one week which I did think was going to be rather boring as there is no swimming allowed because of the danger of sharks and ashore there is mainly sand, sand and more sand. In the distance there are snow-capped mountains which seems incongruous when we are enduring such incredible heat. As we're not allowed ashore we have been making our own amusement, tombola, some cinema shows and listening to the Royal Marine Band. We've held fancy dress parades, impromptu concerts and even dancing although that's not half as fun without our beautiful ladies to join in with us.

Why don't you invite Daisy Irene to stay for a few days or Lilly? I'm sure she'll be able to get a few days off from the Ministry of Labour and she'll probably love to get away from London.

I hope you are still enjoying the peace of the farm and I can't wait to see you both again.

Lots of love

Daddy

He would put that suggestion in the real letter as anything that stopped her returning to the dangers of Maidstone had to be a good thing.

****

Paris

Werner Fischer finished writing his latest report, sat back in his chair, lit a cigarette and watched the blue smoke wafting towards the ceiling. The smoke reminded him of Mlle Iris Durand, she was just as elusive. He was sure she was a British agent, but he had found no proof despite spending hours following her. She behaved exactly like a wine consultant, she met with numerous German and French connoisseurs, wealthy collectors, some exclusive and other not so exclusive club owners, even brothel owners and his enquiries afterwards also backed up her story. He had even watched her meet with German Military men and occasionally their wives who were ordering wine for their parties and gatherings and still had not found out anything. He knew he should leave her alone, go back to following someone else but he couldn't. He was as convinced she was a British agent as he had been the day he'd seen her consorting with Andre, he just needed to prove it. Perhaps he could bring in Andre and make him talk, but he wasn't ready to do that yet. His orders were to break up the whole cell and until he had identified at least one or two other members he wasn't in a position to do that. It would help if he could find the radio operator. The detection vans had picked the signals up several times but the operator was very good, the transmissions were never from the same place, they were always very short, barely time to get the two fixes necessary to find it and there was no discernible pattern so they couldn't anticipate when the next message would be sent.

He glanced down at the numerous reports on Mlle Durand that he'd compiled, each following on from the previous one except for a couple of brief periods where she'd gone into Vichy France and he hadn't been able to follow. But even then her papers supported her story that she was visiting their vineyards, trying to persuade them to export northwards. He had even telephoned his opposite number in Toulouse to ask him to check and he had corroborated the story that she was visiting vineyards. Werner was furious. He was sure she was lying about her business. Her trip to Vichy had coincided with the Jewish roundup and although they had managed to arrest several thousand Jews some had escaped the net and he had a feeling Mlle Durand was involved somehow. Perhaps he should bring in some help. Trying to follow her on his own was not getting him anywhere. If he used more men he could watch her around the clock, and there was less chance of her spotting him. He finished his cigarette, stubbed it out in the ashtray and stood up abruptly. On the other hand perhaps he was obsessed with her because she had made no attempt to get in touch with him. He'd been very sure she would, he was sure his instincts hadn't been wrong, there was something between them. But she hadn't bothered and although he had put her to the back of his mind until he'd seen her with Andre, a part of him had already become suspicious. It was time to increase surveillance on her. It would mean reducing the cover on Andre but that hadn't led him anywhere and she was a known contact so maybe he would find out what he wanted to know by concentrating on her instead.

****

Palembang, Sumatra
Geoffrey lay on his bed, his eyes closed and wondered how much longer he had left. Dysentery and typhoid had finally caught up with him and he knew his time was almost up. He wished he could write to Ruth, tell her how much he loved her and how sorry he was that he couldn't have stayed alive long enough to come back to her. He hoped she would remarry, find some happiness maybe… Paper and the means of writing were banned by their captors and as far as he knew no lists of Prisoners of War had been sent to Britain so he had no idea if Ruth even knew he had been captured. She might think he had died months ago, might already have mourned him and found someone else. The thought would have upset up him a few months earlier but now it made no difference. If anything it was a comfort to think of her enjoying her life. When the war eventually ended she would hopefully find out the truth, but if she didn't… well even that seemed unimportant now.

His breathing gradually became laboured and he tried to concentrate on Ruth, on their wedding day, when they thought they had so much to look forward to, a long life together. But their plans had come to nothing, fate had decreed that world events would overtake them.

'Geoffrey?' The voice seemed to come from a long way away and he made no effort to open his eyes.

'Geoffrey, can you hear me?'

The voice was very faint now and he ignored it. In the distance he could see a light and he moved slowly towards it.

'He's gone.' The camp doctor, a Captain from the Royal Army Medical Corps, moved wearily on to the next bed where the patient,

Bill Leggatt, had also died. There were times he almost envied these poor men, at least they were no longer suffering. With no drugs and no equipment his job was nigh on impossible.

Chapter 36

Arkley View, Near Barnet

'We've got another message from Germany sir.' Fred had hurried into Colonel Sinclair's hut the moment he had decoded it.

'What is it?'

'The Germans are planning to invade Vichy France.'

'Interesting.' Colonel Sinclair nodded slowly. 'Obviously things are not going their way in North Africa.'

'Will you pass it on?' Fred asked.

Colonel Sinclair stared at him then realised what he meant. 'Yes Fred. Leave it with me.'

Fred walked slowly back to his own hut in silent fury. He had hoped that his concerns about Peregrine Thompkin-Cartwright had been taken seriously, but seemingly not.

The Colonel watched him go and wondered if he could get away with going over Thompkin-Cartwright's head again although it might not be quite as important this time as that piece of knowledge would have been quite common knowledge and could have come from anywhere, even from the German's own transmissions. He would escalate this in the normal way and keep the other options for things that were more likely to lead to their spy's arrest because of the smaller distribution list.

****

London

Anthony smiled at the young woman in front of him and held out his hand. 'I'm Lt Colonel Anthony Hallett. I understand that you are Charlotte's contact.' He had finally grown tired of waiting for any information about Charlotte, so he'd decided to visit the offices in London where her radio messages were received and ask some questions. He wasn't really expecting to get any real information but he couldn't just sit back and wait any longer. If nothing else maybe he could send Charlotte a message to let her know he was still thinking of her.

Madeline smiled and shook his hand. 'Yes sir.'

'I know you can't tell me anything about her mission, but I just wanted to know that she was alright.'

'Yes sir, she's very good at what she does.' For some obscure reason she debated briefly whether she should mention the rumours Charlotte had been so insistent in knowing about, then changed her mind. He might take it as a sign that Charlotte was unable to cope with the stress. Madeline had already decided that the rumours were some kind of allied propaganda, despite the eventual confirmation by her superiors.

Anthony smiled 'Thank you Madeline. I know your messages have to be very short, but when you next speak with her can you just say I'm looking forward to her coming home.'

Madeline's smile widened. 'Yes sir. Of course.' She watched him leave and shook her head. Charlotte was a dark horse; not once had she mentioned she had a very attractive admirer. She couldn't wait to pass on his message. But now she had to get ready to meet Jimmy. It was the first opportunity she'd had to see him in such a long time, and she couldn't wait to see him again. She would love to think she had so much to tell him, but most of it was confidential so she couldn't say anything at all, and no doubt anything exciting he had experienced would be the same. They would obviously have to find another way to amuse themselves!

Anthony left the office and wondered what it was Madeline wasn't telling him. For some reason she was lying to him and it wasn't about Charlotte's performance. He had already satisfied himself that she was a very good wireless operator by speaking to her superior and had only asked to meet Madeline because he wanted to pass his message to Charlotte, but now he was glad he had spoken to her. He walked slowly across the road, settled back into the shadows and waited patiently for her to leave the office.

****

Paris

'It looks like the Germans are preparing to cross into Vichy.' Andre leaned forward over the small table and reaching out, ran his fingers through her hair.

Charlotte smiled back and gazed into his eyes, hoping that for any casual observer or otherwise that she looked like she was enjoying his touch.

'That matches the information I've received from London.' Charlotte lowered her voice. 'Shall we dance?'

They stood up, made their way onto the small dance floor and she allowed Andre to put his arms around her.

'How will we get the airmen out if they take over the south?'

Andre shrugged. 'No doubt we'll manage. We'll need to make sure our network is still operational, if not we'll need to set up a new one.'

Charlotte smiled. 'Nothing worries you, does it?'

He grinned and pulled her closer. 'It does but if the bosche are moving into the south they must be losing in North Africa. Otherwise they wouldn't need to. So that means we're winning.'

Charlotte considered his words and wondered if it was true. The war seemed to have been going on for ever, the thought of it ending… she realised he was speaking again. 'Sorry?'

'I was asking what you would do with yourself once the war is over?'

'I have no idea to be honest.' She was tempted to add *'Maybe try and find the German who killed my sister'* but it wasn't any of his business and they were ordered not to give away anything personal. She suddenly remembered Anthony and she smiled. 'Go home and find a friend I think.'

'Ah there is a man in your life?' Andre looked interested.

Charlotte smiled. 'Yes, at least he was before I came here. I'd like to find him again, see if we both feel the same.'

'He's a very lucky man Francine.'

Charlotte laughed. 'Maybe.' She allowed him to pull her closer and her smile faded as she wondered where Anthony was. Somehow, she couldn't see him sitting the war out in England which meant he could be anywhere, he could even be dead. To her surprise the thought made her feel unbearable sad.

******

45 College Road, Maidstone

Frederick was relieved the trial was finally over. Debbie had been sentenced to be detained at His Majesty's pleasure meaning she would be held until they felt she was no threat to anyone. He knew Jeanne had been dreading the trial even though the police had told her that she wouldn't be called to give evidence. Fortunately, Jeanne's role in the whole thing had not led to her being ostracised, if anything the other girls were even more friendly and some actually seemed envious of her part in the story. It would be good for her to put all this behind her and get back to normal though. He needed the spotlight to be off him as well or he couldn't chase up the man from Gateshead. He'd had to leave it alone because of the interest in the case and although he'd passed the information onto Colonel Sinclair, he would have liked to be more involved because he was responsible for this whole mess. If he hadn't helped Kristian, they might have found the spy two years ago.

****

Bavaria

Otto had just sat down to lunch when the door flew open and several armed SS men rushed in. He had no time to think, no time to reach for his gun before he was thrown to the floor, handcuffed, dragged outside and thrown in the back of a car. He was vaguely aware of his wife being pushed into a different car then the door slammed shut and he found himself seated next to a burly man with the face of a bulldog.

'What the hell is going on?' He finally managed found his voice.

'You're under arrest for treason General von Klotz, passing information to the enemy.' The man in the front seat didn't bother turning around.

'I don't know what you're talking about...' Otto spluttered but he didn't get any further before the man sitting next to him punched him violently in the stomach.

The rest of the journey passed much too quickly and before long he was being dragged inside Wittelsbacher Palace, the Gestapo Headquarters in Munich.

****

Ouston, Durham

Jimmy was furious that his leave had been cut short, but it was only by one day and he guessed it must be serious or they wouldn't have called them all back. He had spent most of the four days with Madeline although he had found time to see his parents, before making his way back north. It was strange being back in Maidstone and seeing all the bomb damage, London was even worse, but he soon grew used to it. Madeline was as beautiful as he remembered and several times he was tempted to ask her to marry him but something held him back. As he waited for the CO to begin the briefing he wondered why he had wasted another opportunity, but then it suddenly came to him. For him marriage meant being with the woman he loved. He didn't want to saddle Madeline with a child, not when everything was so uncertain. If he survived the war, he would marry her and they could settle down together. That was the time to have a family. They were both still young, there was plenty of time. He realised the CO was speaking and he concentrated his attention on him.

The CO gave them as much detail as he could. 'Sorry for the delay lads, but we've heard there's a ship ready to take us. I can't tell you where for obvious reasons, but you should pack only the barest essentials such as flying kits, some toiletries and just one change of clothing. The flight is to be divided into groups and you'll travel in separate convoys to the initial destination where you'll reform as one squadron before moving on to our final destination.'

Johnny leaned over and muttered 'Why's that then?'

'If we get torpedoed on the way, the whole squadron gets wiped out. By splitting up at least one half has the chance of getting through.'

He looked shocked. 'I wish I hadn't bothered asking!'

A series of hasty inoculations followed including one for yellow fever which sparked a lengthy debate as to their destination. Jimmy packed his essentials as ordered but also included one extra, his champagne cork.

They said their goodbyes and, together with 93 Squadron, caught the bus to the Manchester Ship Canal where they spent a grim day in the pouring rain waiting for their ship to arrive.

Eventually, at 17.00hrs pm an aging 4,500 ton unladen merchant cargo vessel called the *SS Staffordshire* appeared. Their aircraft had already been dismantled and stored into numerous crates and were quickly lifted onto the ship by huge cranes and lashed to the decks by the ship's crew.

They boarded and then set sail along the canal towards Liverpool. Here, they joined a coastal convoy and steamed up the Clyde. By Friday morning there were more than fifty ships sailing in a line, an impressive sight to the watching men who identified an aircraft carrier and several frigates and destroyers.

Jimmy managed to watch for several minutes before moaning. 'I see the officers are travelling in one of the shiny new destroyers while we're in a cramped and decrepit old merchant ship.'

Johnny laughed. 'You're only jealous because you fancy a trip on one of the warships!'

Jimmy grinned. 'True but it does seem a bit rich. We're all doing the same job after all.'

During the next few days the convoy ploughed west through dark seas. Jimmy and the rest of the crew had guessed they were probably going to Gibraltar but the ships couldn't travel in a straight line because of the German U-boats lurking below the surface, waiting for information from their reconnaissance planes. The convoy could only travel as fast as its slowest ship so instead it sailed an erratic course in the hope of confusing the enemy and took three weeks to get there.

Having explored every nook and cranny Jimmy soon started to get bored, it wasn't anything like as exciting as flying. Then one night they climbed into their bunks and drifted off to sleep only to be shaken awake by a terrific noise.

'We've been hit!"

Chaos ensued. They dived out of their beds and headed for the deck as fast as they could. Being stuck below deck on a sinking ship didn't seem like a good idea.

****

45 College Road, Maidstone

'You think the family are lying?' Colonel Sinclair frowned. 'That doesn't seem very likely.'

'No, I'm sure they aren't... well I don't think so anyway but maybe the father knows something, something he doesn't realise he knows. If that makes sense?' He realised the Colonel was looking even more confused and he gave a wry smile. 'The local boy, the one who did murder Major Mason's daughter spoke to him, when he told him that the German pilot had killed her. Maybe he said something else, something that might lead us to this man. The last information I picked up suggested the spy was in touch with someone in the Maidstone area. Unless your telephone interceptors have picked up something else since then I don't have anywhere else to start. It may be a complete waste of time but...'

'As far as the Mason's are concerned the pilot killed Rebecca. They don't know anything about any spies. You would have to be careful what you said or...' Colonel Sinclair thought for a moment then changed his mind. 'The Major has security clearance up to a certain level so I think you should tell him the truth, well some of it anyway. Just ask if the boy mentioned seeing anyone else.'

'And if he asks why?'

'Tell him we believe the German pilot wasn't the only person to have bailed out or parachuted in that night and we are looking for that person.'

'Presumably we can't tell him that the pilot wasn't responsible for his daughter's death?'

'No, because that would mean telling him about your nephew. We have to keep that secret for obvious reasons.'

'Alright. Let me talk with him and see where that leads.'

The Colonel stood up and shook his hand. 'Goodbye Frederick. I'm glad that other business has been resolved.'

'You and me both.' Frederick sighed. 'I still can't believe I was arrested for that poor sod's murder. Even if the alternative is something I would never have thought of. That poor woman and her husband. Good job you arrived when you did.'

Colonel Sinclair nodded. For a moment he was tempted to tell Frederick that the man who had nearly been killed was the man tracking the movements of the man he was tracing, but years of never letting his right hand know what his left hand was doing made the decision for him. There was no good reason for either man to know about the other, not yet anyway. If things changed then he could always revise that decision.

****

At sea

Once on deck it became clear that they hadn't been torpedoed. A gangway had broken loose in the heavy swell and was flapping all over the deck, crashing loudly against the side of the ship. A storm was in full force, waves the size of houses broke against the ship and Jimmy wondered briefly how the officers were getting on in their shiny destroyer which was smaller than the *SS Staffordshire* and so would be more at the mercy of the waves.

The men returned to bed but decided to set up their own two hour watches which helped break up the monotony and over the next few days the ships deck was often awash with keen eyed pilots searching for periscopes.

As they headed further south the weather improved, the U-boats began to take an unhealthy interest in the convoy and they wore their Mae Wests every day just in case. By the first week in November they had sighted the Spanish coast and shortly after they were sailing along the Strait of Gibraltar and into the bay. While the other ships continued through the Mediterranean the *Staffordshire* and one other ship anchored just off the Rock.

Chapter 37

London

Anthony sat in his flat and wondered if he was wasting his time. He had been following Madeline for several weeks now and there was nothing he could base his suspicions on except his instinct that she wasn't who she appeared to be. He had been through her files, everything appeared to add up which was why she had been employed by SOE, but there was something that was sending alarm bells, if only he knew what it was. He took a deep breath, picked up the files and started from the beginning. She had come to SOE's attention in 1941, been thoroughly vetted, something that had been made easier as her father was Peregrine Thompkin-Cartwright, senior civil servant in charge of several secret departments including the RSS. Anthony was about to gloss over that when he changed his mind. He turned back to the vetting information and frowned. Madeline was born in 1920 while Peregrine and his wife were living in Germany. Peregrine was a diplomat at the time, the cultural attaché in Berlin. The next few lines were blacked out and his concern deepened. Why was information on her vetting form redacted? Only people with the highest security clearance would have access to these files so why would things be hidden? More importantly perhaps from his point of view was who would know what the missing information was?

****

Wittelsbacher Palais, Munich

Otto lay on the floor of the cell, every part of him was in pain and he had no idea how much longer he could hold out. At the moment they seemed to have no idea that Kristian was involved. They only seemed to be aware of his treachery and from the little he could gather that was because of his last message, the one about German plans to move into Vichy. He had no idea how that had led to his arrest because it was quite common knowledge. He felt it much more likely that his report about the Final Solution had led to them suspecting him. Why he hadn't been arrested earlier he had no idea and he was in too much pain to really care. Except that trying to work out where he'd gone wrong was better than worrying about his wife and son.

If only he had been able to discover who the spy was in England this might not have happened, but that information had been too closely guarded even for him. He had hoped they would let him say goodbye to his wife but maybe it was better not to know what had happened to her. His guilt for putting them all at risk was already overwhelming, but what else could he have done?

His thoughts drifted to Kristian. It was ironic that his treason had saved his son's life when he'd had to bail out in England, but that very same treason would now lead to his death. If only he'd been able to warn him. At least he had managed to get Ulrike and Manfred out of reach, but because he'd only just succeeded in persuading her to go, he hadn't been able to let Kristian know where his wife and son were.

****

London

'Lt Colonel Hallett. What can I do for you?' Fred accepted the seat opposite him, stared across the desk and wondered why he had been suddenly summoned to SOE.

'I know you are really busy Mr Corben, but I need to ask you something rather important.' Anthony had spent ages trying to work out the best way to ask the question and had eventually decided to just come out and say what he wanted to know. 'What I am about to say must go no further, that will become obvious once you hear what I have to say.'

Fred nodded but didn't answer. He was beginning to feel uneasy and he was also wondering where his loyalties should lie.

'What do you think about Peregrine Thompkin-Cartwright?'

The question caught Fred by surprise, especially as he was convinced he had not been taken seriously. 'I imagine Colonel Sinclair has told you my concerns then?'

Anthony was unable to hide his shock and he made a note to speak to the Colonel as soon as he'd finished with Fred Corben. 'I'm sorry? You had concerns about him?'

It was Fred's turn to look confused. 'I assumed that was why I was here?'

'No, I can't explain at the moment, but perhaps you could tell me why you were worried.'

Fred shrugged and repeated how they had received several pieces of high level intelligence from a spy in Germany and that no action appeared to have been taken on any of them.

'And you're sure the information was passed on?' Even as he asked the question Anthony knew the answer. He had known Colonel Sinclair for years. There was no question of his loyalty.

'Yes, well as sure as I can be.'

'And the last piece of intelligence you received from Germany was…?'

'About death camps. It would seem the Nazis have set up plans to kill off all the Jews in Europe.' Even as he repeated the words, he found it difficult to believe they were true.

Anthony stared at him. 'I'm sorry?'

'I know it sounds ludicrous, but it is true apparently. Our source has never been wrong before and we've had corroboration from other sources. I did mention my concerns to the Colonel, especially as this information would have only been available to a select few which meant any leak at this end could endanger our source, but I don't know if he did anything about it. You would have to speak to him.'

'Yes, I will.' Anthony's brain was already going over the implications of Peregrine Thompkin-Cartwright being some kind of double agent when he turned his attention back to Fred. 'Is there anything else ongoing that you have concerns about? I don't know what, maybe something Thompkin-Cartwright might have had access to which hasn't been resolved?'

Fred shrugged. 'Other than the search for the spy,' he saw Anthony's confusion and quickly explained. 'No one has found him. We intercepted a couple of messages and then it went quiet. There's been nothing for ages so maybe they've caught him.' He hesitated. 'There was something a bit odd though. He sent a message from Liverpool saying the bombing wasn't working and told them to bomb the east coast instead.'

'And that was odd why?'

'The Atlantic Convoys were being seriously disrupted by the Luftwaffe, it made no sense to call them off.'

'And you never found out why?'

'No sir. There's been no messages at all since then.' He shrugged.

'Well thank you Corben.' Anthony had no idea how that piece of information fitted in, but he would bear it in mind. Fred stood up and was heading for the door when he turned back. 'Are you going to investigate Sir Peregrine Thompkin-Cartwright?'

'Yes Corben. I most certainly am.'

Fred breathed a sigh of relief. 'Good. There's something definitely not right there.'

Anthony watched him leave, sat back in his chair and went back over the conversation. He agreed with Corben. Something wasn't right.

****

Eastern Front / Bavaria

Kristian replaced the receiver in confusion. For some unfathomable reason he had suddenly had the urge to ring his father and now he couldn't understand why no one was answering the telephone. Even if his father had been out his mother should have been there or the servants. He would try telephoning Ulrike instead. Several minutes later he thanked the operator for trying and walked away, his concern rising with every step. Something was wrong. What if they had all been arrested? His heart began pounding and he could feel the panic rising. It was the only thing that made any sense. Even if his parents had been out for some reason the servants would have answered the telephone. And Ulrike was always in at this time of day so unless they had been bombed or there was an air raid going on something was wrong. The question now was whether to wait and pray they were soon released or that he was completely wrong and there was a rational reason for no one being available or to trust his instincts and make a run for it. Even as he thought the words he almost laughed out loud. He was deep in Soviet territory. Where the hell was he going to run to?

****

London

'Hello Anthony, it's good to see you.' Simon held out his arm and the two men shook hands. 'It's been ages.'

'War has that effect.' Anthony smiled. 'You're looking well sir.'

'Enough of the sir, Anthony, we've known each other too long for that.' He sat down and smiled. 'What can I do for you?'

Anthony sighed. 'I'm not sure how to put this but I think there might be a German agent operating and I think you might know who it is.'

Simon didn't answer for a moment then he reached into his pocket and pulled out his pipe. 'Alright if I smoke?'

'Yes of course.'

'You're talking about Peregrine Thompkin-Cartwright?'

Anthony raised an eyebrow. 'You know about him?'

'I didn't but I was suspicious... well one of my people suggested he might not be all he was supposed to be and I realised he was probably right, but I can't find anything out about him.'

Anthony sighed. 'The information is redacted, isn't it?'

'How did you know?'

'I was looking into his daughter, Madeline. Something wasn't right so I was trying to get a handle on her when I realised I couldn't get into her father's file.'

'So you thought you would ask me?'

'Yes, and your man, Fred Corben.'

'He's one of my best and it was he who warned me about Peregrine Thompkin-Cartwright.'

'What did you do about the last piece of information your German spy gave you?'

Simon stared at him in astonishment then shrugged. 'I went over his head, pretended I couldn't get hold of him and as it was important I needed to pass it on.'

'Do you think he knows about it now?'

Simon thought for several seconds and then nodded. 'Yes, probably.' He sighed. 'I've been worrying about our man in Germany as that was so selective it could lead the Gestapo to him.'

'Have you heard from him recently?'

'No, but he only contacts us when it's something important so that doesn't mean anything.'

Anthony was silent for a few moments. 'What about the spy, the one who parachuted in here and you never found?'

Simon raised an eyebrow again and puffed on his pipe before answering. 'That's a long story.'

'I've got all day. Maybe I could be of help.'

Simon nodded. 'You're right, we haven't got anywhere, maybe a fresh pair of eyes is needed.' He took another puff of his pipe and began telling him the whole story.

****

Eastern Front

Kristian climbed reluctantly aboard the aeroplane and after, performing all the pre-flight checks, followed the rest of the aircraft up into the sky. He didn't know whether he welcomed the distraction or whether he should use it to make his escape. At least when he was up in the air he knew who the enemy were. Back on the airfield he could be arrested at any moment. He knew if his father had been taken it was only a matter of time before they came for him. Even if his father didn't say anything he would be considered guilty because he was a close relative. His service record might save him, but he doubted it.

As usual the pre op briefing had not given very many details and Kristin tried to concentrate. He didn't want to fire on his own troops as that wouldn't help his case if he was arrested. It wasn't long before they were coming under heavy ack ack fire and despite his fears about the future Kristian was grateful when it was time to head back to the airfield. They were almost back in friendly territory when the Red Air Force suddenly appeared. Nearly twenty Polikarpov I-153 were attacking and it was virtually impossible to dodge them. Kristian forgot all about his problems and when an enemy aircraft popped up in front of him he had no hesitation in shooting it down. Eventually the planes disappeared and, as he followed his comrades back to the airfield, his fears about the future resurfaced with a vengeance.

Chapter 38

Gibraltar

Jimmy stood on deck and looked across the bay. The Rock of Gibraltar looked so close he could have reached out and touched it. They transferred to a Spanish tug and Jimmy thought they were finally going ashore but instead they were put on another troop ship with some Americans and other pilots. Again they stood on deck and stared longingly at the twinkling lights of the harbour, their only consolation that the bar was well stocked and the booze cheap and drinkable.

Two days later they were finally on solid ground and immediately taken to a secret camp on the eastern side of the rock facing the Spanish border.

'I thought this was supposed to be secret?' Jimmy muttered to himself as he watched several sinister looking German agents sitting in a hut on the Spanish side of the border watching their every move.

The next few days were spent drinking heavily and Jimmy even met David Niven who was in the army now and also liked a drink. In the afternoons they went to the flicks where they watched films like *Casablanca* which had just come out. In the evening they headed back to the camp where they played cards, smoked and drank more booze.

Jimmy was delighted when the second batch of pilots from 72 Squadron sailed into port with Chem on board and it was a rowdy reunion. Now they were all together they attended a lecture from Wing Cdr Sinclair who told them about Operation Torch, the combined sea, land and air campaign to throw the Germans out of North Africa. 'Its primary objective is to make landings in Morocco and Algeria. Those who land in Algiers will drive eastwards to Tunisia and try and locate the German stronghold of Tunis as soon as possible. They will be met there by Monty's Eighth Army which is currently south of Tunisia, fighting its way up from Egypt. As the British First Army pushes through North Africa they will secure airfields on their way for use by the RAF and we in turn will operate in support of the land forces until victory is secured. In short gentlemen its going to be a rough ride. The Germans aren't going to give up North Africa without a fierce fight.'

Chem turned towards him, lowered his voice and muttered. 'I heard the RAF boys are already having a tough time of it in Algiers. I was told pilots have to sleep in their cockpits. They're flying around the clock.'

The Wing Commander continued 'You'll all be given the requisite rations and escape packets including your 'blood' ticket.'

Jimmy frowned and glanced at Chem who shrugged. The Wing Commander was already explaining. 'Your 'blood' ticket is a small purse containing five gold coins that will come in handy if you ever have to buy your way out of trouble in enemy territory. One thing you'll quickly learn about the Arabs is that everything is negotiable.'

Jimmy listened carefully as their CO explained how important the timing was as the commandos had only six hours to capture the Maison Blanche airfield near Algiers from the Vichy French Forces. The first fighter squadron was due to arrive six hours after the initial land assault, they would not have sufficient fuel to fly elsewhere so would have to land whatever was happening on the ground. The first squadron to arrive would be 43 followed by 72 and the CO of 43 Squadron made sure he had plenty of knives and pistols on his person before he left.

The aerodrome was a huge area with over 600 aircraft and the Royal Engineers had extended the North Front runway by 500 yards out to sea to allow aeroplanes to land and take off.

Jimmy watched uneasily as army engineers unpacked the Spitfires from their packing crates and attempted to put them back together. He would have felt happier if the work was being done by RAF engineers but they hadn't arrived yet so they had no choice other than to rely on the army. To his relief it seemed his fears were groundless, the Army engineers made an excellent job of reassembling the aircraft and Jimmy felt rather guilty for doubting their abilities.

A few days later they assembled at the aerodrome in full flying gear. It had been over a year since Jimmy had last been in combat and those days felt like a distant memory. He climbed into the cockpit and took a breath. It was good to get back into an aircraft, he hadn't flown properly since they'd left Llandow, he strapped himself in, did all the checks and moved off. The rain was lashing down the window reducing visibility as he taxied down the extended runway, the Mediterranean lapping on either side. The Spit gathered power, he throttled back and she rose gracefully up in the air.

****

Yelsted, Kent

Frederick pulled up a few yards away from the house in Yelsted and turned the engine off. Despite mulling it over in his head since his conversation with Colonel Sinclair he still had no idea how to approach this without making it sound like an accusation. He tapped his fingers on the steering wheel and was praying for some inspiration when another car pulled up and a man climbed out, hurried towards the front door and knocked. Fred stared at him in disbelief and wondered if he was seeing things. The man fitted the description of the person he'd spent months chasing around England. He remained in the car, watched the front door open and a man he assumed was Major (Ret'd) Mason greet the visitor and invite him inside.

Frederick shook his head. Maybe it was a coincidence, perhaps the man just bore a superficial resemblance to the description he'd been given? Even as he tried to argue with himself he knew it wasn't true. He had been chasing this man so long he saw him in his dreams. There was no mistake. He climbed out of the car and began walking to the nearest phone box.

****

Outside Paris

Charlotte pulled down the aerial and quickly replaced everything in the suitcase. Her heart was racing as it always did during the process of transmission. From the minute she cycled out to where she'd hidden the radio she was always on high alert, her ears tuned into anything that sounded like a detector van, her eyes scanning the horizon for anything that was out of place and even when she was sure she was safe and getting ready to transmit her ears were still listening. Her message had been slightly longer this time, a request for a supply drop for one group, some answers for another, plus the information she had gleaned from her contacts about troop movements. Her own messages were short and to the point, the response from London this time slightly longer than she deemed necessary, but perhaps there was something important, she wouldn't know until she had finished decoding them. Charlotte stopped what she was doing and looked around again, everything was still quiet but for some reason she felt uneasy. Perhaps she'd been doing this too long.

She took one last look around, made her way quickly to the new location discovered earlier and hurriedly buried the wireless. She would be grateful to leave the forest tonight, something was nagging at her and as she walked back to where she'd left her bicycle she scanned her surroundings repeatedly until she heard the faint crack of a dry stick breaking and she froze.

****

Yelsted, Kent

Frederick drew his pistol and strode towards the house. The Colonel had told him to wait for support, but he was too concerned that the man would leave and then they would have to tackle him outside. Much easier to take them both prisoner inside the property.

He knocked on the door and waited for the Major to open it.

'Yes, can I help you?'

Fred pointed the pistol in his face and indicated he step back.

'I don't understand…'

'Shut up. Where's the German?' Frederick hissed.

'German, what German?' Adrian looked completely confused and for a brief moment Frederick wondered if he'd made a mistake.

'The man who just came in here.' He snapped, his pistol pointing unwaveringly at Adrian.

'He's not German…' He shook his head and indicated Frederick follow him into the sitting room. The man was sitting by the fire and he jumped up when they entered.

'Put your hands up and move over there. This place will be surrounded in a moment but if you want to take your chances with me, please do. I haven't killed anyone yet in this war and I'd quite like to break my duck.'

'I think you've made some kind of error…' Adrian began.

'And this isn't a German spy of course?' Frederick interrupted. 'He's been asking questions in some very sensitive areas. Care to explain that.'

'He's employed by me to find out how my daughter died.' Adrian snapped. 'She was murdered by some fucking Nazi pilot who bailed out of his plane in 1940 but no one ever found him so he must have had help getting out of the country. Graham here has been trying to find out who helped him. Not very successfully I might add.'

Frederick stared at him in astonishment, then focused his attention on the other man who was as white as a sheet. 'I'm really not German, I swear. My name is Graham Buckland, I used to work for the police… but I had some problems so I now work on my own.' He gabbled, licking his lips nervously.

Frederick didn't move.

'Look I can prove it. I have an identity card.'

Frederick laughed. 'Of course you have.'

'He really is who he says he is.' Adrian spoke calmly. 'Do you really think I would help anyone who killed my daughter. This man is not a German pilot or a spy I swear on my other daughter's life.' He indicated the mantlepiece where two photos had pride of place. For a moment Frederick thought they were of the same girl then he remembered that the girl who had died had been a twin.

'I think you'll find he's telling the truth.'

Frederick spun around to see another man standing there.

'Thank God Anthony. Perhaps you can talk some sense into this man.' Adrian ignored Frederick and spoke directly to the man who was now standing behind him.

'I can show you some identification, but perhaps it would be best if I tell you that I am a good friend of Colonel Sinclair.'

Outside Frederick was aware of cars pulling up. He was trying to work out what to do when another man rushed in. 'It's alright Captain Farmer, he's telling you the truth and I think Major Mason is too.'

Frederick stared at him in shock, then slowly lowered his weapon.

****

En Route to Malta

'My favourite destination, Malta!' Chris sighed as the ship finally set sail from Alexandria on 17th November. This time they were with *Orion, Arethusa, Euryalus* and *Dido* and had strong air support as well.

'From the little I can make out from the radio signals, stocks are dangerously low there so this might be the most important convoy yet.'

'Well let's hope it's the last.' Chris still didn't look very happy.

John shrugged. 'With Rommel forced back from El Alamein things are starting to go our way, but I think it's going to be a long slog. Especially now the Germans have gone into Vichy France.' He glanced at his watch. 'I imagine we'll be on Action Stations soon, they normally attack at dusk or dawn.'

Chris nodded and tried to concentrate his attention of the wireless transmitters which were ominously quiet. 'No chatter at all.'

'Perhaps they're busy having to support their retreating army in North Africa. They might not have enough planes to worry about us.'

Chris smiled. 'That's what I like about you sir, always the optimist!'

John grinned but didn't answer. He hadn't heard from Elsie for a couple of weeks but that was probably because the post was having trouble catching up with them. They had moved back to Port Said where they had welcomed Captain Stevens who was replacing Captain Grantham. John had been sorry to see him go, but the new man had not made any changes, preferring to carry on doing everything in the same way which seemed like a good omen for the future. They had then moved back to Alexandria, spent a day patrolling outside the harbour as there was trouble inside but once that had been resolved they had tied up to prepare for their latest convoy duty.

He glanced at his watch again, all was quiet outside and eventually the crew stood down to defence stations instead. John didn't relax though. They still had 'bomb alley' to get through.

****

Outside Paris

Charlotte crouched behind a tree and held her breath. At first she heard nothing and then she gradually became aware of someone creeping stealthily towards her. She eased the knife out of her skirt waistband and waited. The almost silent footsteps came steadily closer and she waited… waited until they were the other side of the tree and then she pounced.

There was a brief struggle, no noise other than the sound of breathing cut off halfway through and then silence. Charlotte eased the body to the ground and peered into the face of her stalker. There was enough light from the half-moon for her to make out his features. It was no one she recognised.

Chapter 39

En route to Tunis

The take-off had been very shaky. Jimmy was now flying the Spitfire Vb which had two cannons, four machine guns and a more powerful engine. It had been fitted with a Vokes engine air intake dust filter so it was suitable for use in the sandy conditions of North Africa but this reduced the speed slightly. They also carried 90 gallon fuel tanks which would be jettisoned when empty but which made taking off difficult because of the heavy fuel load.

Jimmy levelled out at 15,000 feet, cruised at 300mph and glanced down at the endless sea below him, littered with wrecks of naval vessels along the entire route. After several hours he reached Maison Blanche airfield, a flat featureless field bulging with various aircraft, including some Italian which he assumed must have been captured at some point. The ground crew had not yet arrived so they saw to their own aircraft and spent the rest of the day learning how to cook in preparation for the hardships ahead. Normally the airmen cooked for them and they received regular food parcels from the Ministry although Jimmy had always been convinced that the best contents had been pilfered by the time it reached them leaving them with only sardines and biscuits!

****

Paris

Charlotte let herself into her flat and tried not to think too much about the man she'd just killed. She had intended to bury him, but she'd suddenly heard more noises although she couldn't work out where they were coming from. She'd stood there for several moments trying to decide if it would be safer to just run away. If there was more than one man searching the woods, she wouldn't stand a chance. She'd remained undecided for a few more moments before making her way back through the trees. It was more important to hide the wireless and escape than bury the body. That would take her ages and she would have to dig several feet down or they would find the corpse anyway.

To her relief she hadn't seen anyone else and her journey back had been uneventful. She would have to tell Andre in the morning, it was too late now, she had only just reached home before the curfew began.

****

En route to Malta

The first attack on the *Cleopatra* came mid-morning with eight Ju88s who were quickly sent packing when a squadron of Hurricanes arrived. A second wave followed but they began dropping bombs well behind the convoy before also flying away. All was quiet until the afternoon when the spotter saw thirty enormous black planes heading towards the Italian coast. They were identified as Ju 52 transport planes and *Arethusa* decided to try and fire at them but they were too low and the guns almost hit her own forecastle so the planes were able to carry on unhindered.

The next attack was heavier, bombs fell but still didn't hit anything then torpedo bombers arrived and the ship twisted and turned as the silver streaks sped through the water, only just missing them. *Arethusa* was hit and had to fall out to put out the fire and deal with the damage.

Meanwhile the bombs continued to drop until eventually the remaining planes flew away and the convoy steamed on, this time *Cleopatra* positioned itself north of the convoy so that any attackers would assume they were the target. The ruse worked well and when they met up with the convoy the following morning they had not had any trouble.

They handed over the convoy to the Malta Squadron and then began the return journey, back through 'bomb alley' but this time at full speed. To their surprise there were no real assaults and they arrived back in Alexandria safely. To John, the lack of attacks could only mean one thing. The enemy was beginning to struggle. For the first time in ages John began to believe they really could win the war.

****

Paris

Eric arrived in the capital and quickly settled into the room he'd been given in one of the barracks. His instructions were to get used to being in France and then report to Gestapo Headquarters where he would be given a new job. He hadn't been particularly pleased to leave their base in Brindisi and move back to Langenargen on Lake Constance, but here they had been officially designated as Küstenjäger Abteilung z.b.V. 800. They now had their own headquarters, two companies equipped with landing crafts and assault boats, a third company which had French private motor yachts and a fourth company which had some explosive motor boats. They also had frogmen and a few small torpedo boats. On arrival they were told that they were preparing for a seaborne assault on Valetta and they spent their time training for that until eventually it became painfully obvious that the invasion of Malta, *Operation Herkules*, was not going to happen. It seemed to him that much of the training they had undertaken had been in vain and he was bored and frustrated so when he was told he was going to France to do something completely different he had been delighted. He had no idea why he was here but he had three weeks to acclimatise himself, lose his tan and practise both his French and English and then he would find out.

****

Eastern Front
The first snows had now fallen and Kristian was convinced that it was only because he was so far from Germany that he hadn't been arrested. He had tried to contact his parents and Ulrike several times now but there was still no answer so he could only assume that they had been arrested. If they had been killed or injured in bombing he would have heard by now as there was some post getting through so he could only assume his first instincts had been correct. The problem was what to do next. At the moment there was no leave, the Russians had launched a massive attack on Stalingrad and the squadron had been moved to Tatsinskaya, a few hundred kilometres west of the city. They were flying everyday although their efforts didn't seem to be making much difference. Rumours abounded that there were ten Russian armies tightening the noose around Stalingrad and within days they had also become a target when the Soviet air force began bombing them as well.

It was minus 38 degrees outside and when they could fly it was almost impossible to tell the difference between the enemy and their own troops spread across the frozen landscape. The other problem was finding their way back as there were few navigational aids on the ground. Kristian spent half his time worrying about surviving the missions and the other half waiting to be arrested.

****

Maison Blanche
At 11.00hrs they were told to pack and get ready to move to their forward base the following day. They were briefed with the next stage of their campaign, issued with more maps and then left to lay down on the cold concrete floor with a couple of small blankets, which was all Jimmy could find. He was extremely fed up, but for once he was too hungry and tired to moan so eventually he drifted off into a fitful sleep.

During the night he was woken briefly by the distant thud of bombs exploding and the sound of naval cannons responding. Now wide awake Jimmy tried to work out where the Luftwaffe were bombing and guessed it was probably the harbour at Algiers. The exchange continued for several minutes and, laying in the darkness, he was reminded of the day he had watched Tilbury Docks being bombed out of existence. Now, here he was, back in the thick of it again. Jimmy was still mulling that over when a loud crash shook the hangar and dust drifted down from the ceiling onto his face. Welcome to North Africa.

****

Outside Paris
Werner Fischer cursed loudly as he recognised the body of one of his men. If nothing else this proved he was right. Mlle Durand was a British agent. His man had been following her a few days previously and had obviously got too close. Death would have probably been instantaneous, the mark of a good spy. On the other hand the man was a poacher, not a trained agent so he wouldn't have expected her to jump him or to kill him. He'd let it be known that a poacher had been killed. The last thing he needed was for the British woman to go to ground. The strange thing was that she'd left the body to be found. Why hadn't she buried it? Perhaps it was time to change tactics.

****

Bone, North Africa

The CO, Bobby Oxspring, had chosen Jimmy as his Number 2 as they headed up to Bone to do some reconnaissance on the airfield and port which were attracting attention from the Luftwaffe. They took off at 10.00hrs, Jimmy finding it difficult to adjust to the loose rubble on the strip of ground masquerading as a runway. A layer of dust swirled around permanently creeping into every crevice and getting in their mouths. Tight formation flying had been scrapped and they now flew in pairs but as he flew towards Bone his Perspex hood became oiled up which reduced his visibility. He made a mental note to get it fixed on his return because it could cost him his life.

The harbour was a frenzy of activity and crammed tight with Royal Navy vessels spewing out the members and equipment of the British First Army as quickly as they could. There was no sign of enemy aircraft so they circled the aerodrome on the outskirts of town before landing. They had only just climbed out of the cockpits when they heard the drone of unfamiliar aircraft in the direction of the harbour.

They ran back to their aircraft and within minutes were searching the skies for the Ju88s who were already bombing the harbour. By the time they reached the port the bombing had stopped, the Ju88s nowhere in sight. The Wing Commander of 322, Pete Hugo, wasn't deterred. He ordered them to turn towards a place called Tabarka, just inside the Tunisian border where he was sure they would be lurking. They had only been in the air a few minutes when they spotted a lone Ju88. He didn't stand a chance against the three Spitfires and exploded in a ball of flames.

Their triumph was short lived as all day the Luftwaffe mounted continuous waves against the harbour trying to disrupt the Allied supply lines. Together with 322 Jimmy and Bobby flew sortie after sortie reminding Jimmy poignantly of the Battle of Britain and later that day the rest of their squadron arrived. By nightfall of the second day they were told to get ready to move further south, nearer the front line.

As they weren't leaving until 09.00hrs they decided to treat themselves to a night in Bone. Although the narrow streets were filled with the British First Army Jimmy managed to find a hotel and had the first decent meal and sleep in a proper bed for ages.

The following day they headed for Souk-el-Arba, less than 30 miles from the front line.

****

Paris
'I was too late, they've found the body.' Andre kept his voice low.
'Shit.' Charlotte clenched her fists, then she shrugged. 'There's nothing to say it will lead them to us is there?'
'No, probably not, although if he was following you...'
'It will depend on whether he told anyone or someone ordered him to follow me?'
'Yes.' Andre thought hard. 'We can move you on?'
'It's not that easy. It will mean setting up a new identity, it will take time.'
'Better to be safe than sorry.'
'Alright, I'll suggest it to London. Meanwhile I'll lay low.'
'How are you going to ask for a new identity then?'
Charlotte didn't answer while she thought about it. 'I'll just stick to buying and selling wine for a week or so. If there's anyone following me I should be able to spot them. If there is I'll go to ground. If not we'll get back to normal.'
Andre nodded. 'Alright. Au revoir.' He stood up and left her sitting in the café.
Charlotte glanced around nervously, but there was nothing out of place. Everything seemed normal. Perhaps they were worrying about nothing.

****

45 College Road, Maidstone
'I still can't believe I spent so much time chasing an ex-policeman.' Frederick slammed his fist into his palm and glared at Anthony who shrugged.
'It happens. At least we've ruled him out now.'
'But we don't have anyone else.'
'True.' Anthony thought for a moment then pulled out a photo. 'Have you ever seen this woman before?'
Frederick looked hard at the photo and then shook his head. 'No.'

'Do you fancy going back up to Gateshead and Liverpool to see if anyone recognises her?'

'After all this time?' Frederick sneered.

Anthony shrugged. 'She's a pretty woman. Men always notice an attractive lady.'

Despite his irritation at all the time that had been wasted Frederick found himself smiling, then his expression changed. 'You don't seriously mean you think the spy is a woman?'

'Why not? It would explain why nobody spotted any strange men hanging around. Nobody bothered to ask them about seeing any women and even if they had no one would have thought anything about it.' *That's one of the reasons Charlotte is doing so well in France.*

Frederick was silent while he considered Anthony's words. 'You could have a point. Yes, alright then. I'll give it a try. Am I reporting to you now?'

'Yes, the Colonel has plenty of other things to do.' *Like looking into Madeline's father.* 'Good luck. Let me know as soon as you find anything out.'

'I will do.' Frederick hesitated. 'Is she doing anything important… I mean for the war effort?'

'Yes, unfortunately she is.' Anthony didn't elaborate.

'Why isn't she still transmitting then?' Frederick asked the question that had been bothering him for ages. 'I know it sounds utterly ridiculous, but do you think she's changed her mind?'

Anthony shook his head. 'I doubt it. She must have done a lot of training and she risked her life parachuting into the country. She must have been pretty committed. Maybe she has someone else doing it for her?'

****

Souk-el-Arba, North Africa

The airfield was worryingly deserted when they touched down. Jimmy glanced around, half expecting some Nazis to suddenly jump out at them. 'Where is everybody? I thought the army were supposed to be here?'

'I think we're the advance party.' Chem replied grimly.

'That makes us the front line then.' Jimmy chipped in before looking up and realising there were a number of Me109s circling overhead like vultures. He swallowed nervously, pointed upwards and added. 'Do you think anyone has told them?'

The aerodrome was a bare expanse of stony ground that stretched as far as he could see, the nearby village consisted of a small huddle of low buildings with local inhabitants who ignored them. There were no accommodation blocks, mess halls or even tents. It was cold, had only just stopped raining and there were dark clouds sitting low over the airfield which was like a sea of sludge that had amazing adhesive qualities. As he wandered around it stuck to his boots and wouldn't come off. Jimmy began to worry about the effect of this on their aircraft. The airscrew would churn the mud up, throwing it back at the aircraft to clog the radiators and oil coolant meaning they could be grounded.

He was still thinking about that when other squadrons began to arrive, and an enterprising officer persuaded the French Foreign legion to loan them some tents and cooking equipment while they waited for 1st Battalion Parachute Regiment to turn up.

They finally arrived to a very warm welcome from Jimmy and the RAF, then quickly secured the airfield, a fact which made Jimmy smile as they had been standing around on a supposed unsecure aerodrome for several hours. The paratroopers dug trenches and sorted out the cookhouse so quickly it made Jimmy and his friends feel rather redundant but at least they were no longer alone. Almost more importantly the Pioneer Regiment had also arrived and began speedily putting together a makeshift runway about 30 to 40 foot wide and 400yds long by layering Sommerfeld tracking. These were large square meshes approximately six inch square and a quarter inch thick slotted together and laid on the ground in an attempt to hold the mud together so an aircraft could take off. Meanwhile Jimmy and other members of the squadrons busied themselves refilling the 90 gallon petrol tanks on their aeroplanes with 4 gallon petrol tins which took most of the day.

After a meal of watery stew they eventually settled down into their large bell tent using parachutes for pillows and covering themselves with one thin blanket each. As the dessert temperature plummeted it was soon freezing and Jimmy began to wonder how on earth he was going to fly the next day with no sleep.

He was right to worry as the next few weeks were as hectic as any Jimmy had experienced during the Battle of Britain with the Germans pouring bombers and fighters into the area, anything to hold onto North Africa. The geographical distance between them and the enemy was little different to that during the Battle of Britain, but in England they had the English Channel which at least felt like a barrier. This time they were only separated by a few short miles of sand which made them seem closer than they actually were.

Strafing had now become the favoured method of attack for both the RAF and the Germans as they sought to destroy each other's supply lines and airfields, a strategy that wasn't without risk as they had to fly low to achieve any measure of success. Jimmy could still remember being damaged by ack ack fired at him while flying at 28000 feet, so he was well aware that the danger of being hit at 8000 feet was considerably higher. But it wasn't just flying that was dangerous.

****

Gateshead

Frederick had spent days in Liverpool, but no one had recognised Madeline. He wasn't particularly surprised as it was over two years ago so eventually he had made his way to Gateshead and began a quick tour of the ship yards. After a few hours with no luck he had virtually given up and decided to go home, but first he decided he would treat himself to a couple of pints in the pub nearest to the dockyards.

'I don't suppose you remember this woman at all?' After his previous experience Frederick always made a point of showing the identification card the Colonel had given him, although he often wondered if that might be counter-productive in some cases. He had asked the same question so many times he had conditioned himself to blank looks and shaking heads so when one of the men hesitated and then nodded sheepishly, he nearly fell over in shock.

'You do?'

'Yeah, she was here about two years ago,' he flushed, 'hanging around the docks.' He lowered his voice and double checked no one was paying him any attention before indicating his empty glass and one of the vacant tables.

Frederick somehow hid his excitement, quickly ordered another pint and followed him. 'You definitely remember her?'

The man sat down, gulped some of his beer and eyed Frederick thoughtfully. 'You aren't going to speak to the missus are you?'

Frederick shook his head. 'No, we're only interested in knowing if she was here in 1940.'

He nodded slowly, drank some more beer while Frederick hid his impatience and then, 'yeah, like I said she was hanging around the docks, I thought she was a hooker so I had a chat with her, you know, like you do.'

'And she wasn't?'

'No,' his expression darkened, 'silly bint threatened to kill me if I didn't get lost.' He looked so offended Frederick had trouble hiding his amusement.

'Do you know what she was doing there then?'

The man shrugged. 'I assumed she must be waiting for some bloke, you know, a married man…' He gulped some of his beer down and then frowned. 'Are you telling me she was a spy or something?'

Frederick shrugged. 'We don't know, we're just trying to trace her movements.' He realised the man was losing interest and changed tack. 'Do you know where she went after you spoke to her?'

He thought for a moment. 'She headed further into the docks, it was dark like so I couldn't see exactly and, like I said, I assumed she was meeting someone, so I went home.'

'Thank you, you've been very helpful. I'll put you another drink on the bar.'

'Thanks.'

Frederick stood up and headed for the door. He'd got what he came for. He headed straight for the phone box and asked the operator to put him through to the number Anthony had given him. He could have waited until he was home, but this was wartime, anything could happen, and it was important that Anthony knew he was right to be suspicious of Madeline.

****

Souk-el-Arba, North Africa

'Jimmy, 153 Squadron are due to arrive. Do you want to join the reception committee to greet the new boys?' Chas Charnock put his head around the tent and Jimmy sighed, put down the letter he was reading from Madeline, dragged himself from his bed, followed Chas out to the runway and stared up at the sky.

'There they are?' Chas pointed.

Jimmy shielded his eyes from the sun and squinted into the distance. Looked like they would be there soon so he might as well stay.

'Wait!' Chas shouted suddenly.

Jimmy froze and stared intently at the incoming aircraft. As their outline became clearer he realised they were 109s.

'They aren't ours! Get down!'

It was too late, they were already under attack and any further shouts of warning were drowned out by a deafening high pitched drone as twelve 109s began to dive towards them.

Jimmy hit the deck and waited for the bullets to find him. They were out in the open and completely exposed. He covered his ears and squeezed his eyes shut but it wasn't enough to shut out the sickening thuds of bullets streaking the field, followed almost immediately by explosions as they targeted the Spitfires. The bullets were so close pellets of earth spat at his face and he was sure the next one would get him. Jimmy was terrified and, not normally a religious man, he began praying.

For some reason he opened his eyes and spotted one of the younger pilots trying to make a run for it with bullets puncturing the ground all around, somehow missing him. Jimmy watched in horror as he sprinted towards the tents and then Chas stood up and took out his pistol. 'Get down you little bastard or I'll shoot you myself!'

The boy dropped to the ground and stayed there, his life undoubtedly saved by Chas' threat. It was all over in a few moments and casualties were surprisingly light. The Spitfires had not got off so lightly though. Eight had been totally destroyed and left them completely vulnerable to further attack; an observation that wasn't lost on the Germans who returned forty five minutes for another attack. 92 Squadron did manage to get some aircraft in the air but 72 Squadron was impotent, they didn't have enough aircraft to get off the ground.

During the coming months enemy aircraft visited their airfield five or six times a day and although the first time he'd been strafed was one of the most terrifying episodes of the war Jimmy eventually became used to it.

Chapter 40

45 College Road, Maidstone

Frederick finished reading the report in the Sunday Graphic and wondered how on earth he would tell Ruth. He could only hope she hadn't read the article entitled *War Prisoners Die of Starvation*, based on the testimony of three British sailors who had escaped to Chunking from a Japanese ship. Rumours had abounded for some time about the appalling treatment of British prisoners, but as they still didn't know if Geoffrey had been taken captive or if he'd been killed in the original or subsequent fighting they had tried not to take too much notice. He had even asked Geoffrey's brothers if they could find out more, but they too had no idea about his fate. Frederick was reasonably sure that his brother-in-law was dead, but Ruth was still clinging to the fact that he would come home as soon as the war was over and he could only pray that she was right.

He glanced at his watch, folded up the newspaper and stood up. Time to get ready for his Home Guard duty.

****

Pas-de-Calais Region, France

'It's quite simple, all you have to do is to pretend to be a downed RAF pilot.' Eric repeated to himself as he ran across the empty field in the direction of the farmhouse that he had been warned was being used to hide downed enemy airmen. His job was to infiltrate the escape line, find out the route being used and pass back that information to the Gestapo. His first hurdle was to be accepted by the escape committee and that meant persuading them he was a downed pilot. They were sure the checks were thorough so the only way to get past them was to use a real identity which meant finding either a dead pilot or catching one before he made contact himself. He had spent several days waiting for the right opportunity and now he was on his way. They had found the body of an airman the previous day, he'd drowned after being shot down but more importantly he was a fighter pilot so he would have been on his own in the aircraft. The problem with using the identity of a man from a bomber crew was the danger that the other members of the team might have been rescued by the escape line and if he was faced with men he was supposed to know, his cover would be blown and that would be it. Eric was only too aware that if they suspected he was an infiltrator they would not hesitate to kill him, hence his nerves. It was one thing attacking the enemy in company with fellow soldiers, but this was different.

He finally reached the farmhouse and was stopping to catch his breath when a dog began barking.

****

Souk-el-Arba, North Africa

It wasn't until December that their replacement aircraft arrived and then there was no time to get used to them.

'Bandits at 12 o'clock.'

Jimmy squinted into the sun for as long as he could but couldn't see anything.

'I see them, there's at least ten.' Chem's voice was calm and Jimmy stared again and this time he could see them, about twenty, a text book attack out of the sun and they were coming straight for them.

'Break!' The CO commanded and they peeled away from each other.

Jimmy felt the familiar knot of fear deepening in his stomach. There was no time to think as he tried to get some height. A burst of machine gun fire shot past his cockpit, aeroplanes dived and climbed, screaming and squealing as they were pushed to the upper limits of their capabilities. Bullets pelted from their wings and whizzed across the skies. He checked his mirror, an Me109 had latched onto his tail. Jimmy reacted automatically, rolling steeply and the Hun disappeared from view. He searched for another target, swivelling round just in time to see Chem pass below him. He was closely followed by another 109 and still flying in a straight line which meant he hadn't seen it. Jimmy yelled into the R/T 'Chem you've got one right up your arse mate.'

He was too late. Chem started to react, but a line of tracer bullet raked his fuselage. Time stood still. Then his aircraft began to turn from side to side before plummeting through the low lying clouds until it disappeared from sight.

'No!' Jimmy shouted. He tried to raise him on the R/T but there was no response. Despite the danger all around Jimmy was in shock. Not Chem. Not his best friend. He was only 23, a year younger than

Jimmy and he'd been married less than a year. He wanted to go down and check if his friend had landed safely but that would have been suicidal, so feeling numb he helped chase off the remaining 109 and then they were ordered back to base.

****

Pas-de-Calais Region, France
Eric raised his arms and called out 'RAF, I'm British, please don't shoot!'

The farmer stepped closer but didn't lower his shotgun and Eric licked his lips nervously.

'How do I know you're British?' The man's English was heavily accented.

'I was told if I had to bail out I was to try and contact someone who would help me get back to England.'

'Why did you come here?' The farmer still sounded suspicious.

'One of my friends… he was shot down in 1941.' Eric glanced around. 'He said you were very helpful.'

The farmer stared at him and cursed under his breath. The pilots were told not to tell anyone how they had escaped, who had helped them, or the route they had been taken. He glanced around nervously, everything was quiet, the dog was no longer barking so if this man was a plant he was on his own and if he wasn't a British airman they would soon find out and then he would be buried in the field. He relaxed slightly, then indicated the barn behind him with the barrel of the shotgun. 'Go in there, someone will come and speak to you.'

Eric relaxed. 'Thank you so much.' He started to lower his arms but the farmer immediately raised the shotgun again and he stopped. 'I'm sorry. I'll do as you say. Go in here right?' He headed for the barn and had almost reached the door when he became aware of footsteps behind him. He started to turn and then everything went black.

****

London
Anthony sat at his desk and wondered what his next course of action should be. He didn't really have enough evidence to arrest

Madeline or her father. But all the time they remained free they could be doing damage. Of the two of them it would appear that the father was the most dangerous. Charlotte had survived in France for over a year so either she wasn't important enough for Madeline to bring down or they were using her to build up a bigger picture. That seemed unlikely as he couldn't see them letting her run this long. Her boyfriend in the RAF was no longer in the country and they'd had very little contact for the past year, other than by letter and if there had been anything important in there the censors would have picked it up. From the transcripts he'd seen the pilot was very sensible, giving no details of anything operational, concentrating on the social aspects of his life and how much he missed her, nothing of any use to the enemy. But even more interesting was that Madeline never asked anything important. Like him she kept to insignificant details of her life which didn't make much sense. Surely if she was a spy she should be trying to find out what he was doing? There was also the strange business of her redirecting the Luftwaffe bombing away from Liverpool at the height of its effectiveness. Maybe the Colonel's throw away remark about her changing her mind had some truth, especially as that had coincided with her meeting the pilot. He shook his head. No, that didn't make sense. Why would you risk your life parachuting into the country only to suddenly change your mind? Love was hardly a good enough reason, well not in his book anyway. He had to be missing something.

****

Souk-el-Arba, North Africa

Jimmy landed, his thoughts still on Chem. He saw the two aircrew who normally serviced his friend's aircraft and hurried towards them. 'Chem ran into a spot of trouble. I think he might have crash landed his kite somewhere.'

They nodded and exchanged knowing looks. Jimmy went to his bed and lay down, hoping desperately that his friend was out there alive somewhere, but the longer time went on the less chance there was. He discussed it with the others and they all agreed Chem had a chance. Jimmy returned to his tent but he couldn't stop thinking. He had known so many pilots who had died but this was different. This was personal.

'Jimmy are you ready to go?' Bobby put his head around the tent and Jimmy tried to pull himself together. They were short on pilots; he couldn't sit there moping. They carried out some further strafing, he didn't know where or really care then they returned to base and night fell. Hope was fading and he sat in his tent picking disconsolately at his sardines. It was 19.00hrs and there was still no news.

Just after 20.00hrs he heard a loud disturbance outside his tent. He went outside to see a French Foreign Legion truck pulling up. The flaps at the back opened up and a huge dishevelled figure, covered in dust, but otherwise unhurt stepped out. It was Chem.

He grinned broadly. 'Hello everyone.'

'Chem you bastard. You had us worried there for a moment.' Jimmy hugged him and tried to conceal his overwhelming emotions. He had never been so relieved to see anyone.

****

Pas-de-Calais Region, France

'He said we helped one of his friends, last year.' Victor looked troubled. Normally men were brought to him to hide, they didn't find their own way there. 'I have a bad feeling about this one Clarisse.' Victor had arrived with Francine at the end of 1941 and gradually taken over the farm, hiding downed aircrew when he could or just passing them down the line when it wasn't safe to hide them. His instincts had been honed from months of pretending to be a French farmer and something definitely wasn't right with this one.

'What do you mean?' Clarisse had been working with Victor for several months since Francine had moved on. He had been delighted to see her again and he not only trusted her skills as a radio operator, he knew she was extremely cautious. She had been in France almost as long as him and he was sure that if there was anything wrong she could be trusted to act on it.

'I can't put a finger on it. He spoke English but I couldn't detect any accent. I don't know. Maybe I am just getting paranoid.'

Clarisse shook her head. 'No, if you are concerned there's probably a good reason. I'll go and speak to him, get his details and then have him checked out.' Clarisse finished her wine and stood up. 'Meanwhile don't put anyone else with him, make sure he stays in the cellar under the barn and don't speak to him any more than necessary.' She headed towards the door. 'If I'm not back in ten minutes come and look for me.' She winked at him and he relaxed slightly. If this man was a German he wouldn't touch Clarisse, he would need her to verify his identity. They would be trying to bring down the whole line not just one or two people.

****

London
'I'll look into it.'

'You'd better. If not, I'll be paying her a visit.' The bearded man glared at his companion before sipping his pint.

'I'm sure you're mistaken. It's probably just a communication mix up.' The other man spoke forcibly, hoping to hide his unease.

'Oh come on, don't be ridiculous. She's been turned and you know it. Maybe we should be investigating you too?'

'Never!' The response was so furious that the bearded man wondered briefly if he'd over done it. This was a very important person, it wouldn't do to upset him even if his instructions had been to shake things up a bit. 'I've told you I'll look into it.' He glanced at his watch and then around the pub. 'Isn't it time you went?'

The bearded man downed the remainder of his pint, stood up, leaned forward and lowered his voice. 'I will be back if things don't improve.' He strode through the crowded pub and disappeared through the door and into the street.

Peregrine sat back in his seat and cursed under his breath. Everything had been going really well and he had been sure that no one was suspicious of him but suddenly everything appeared to be falling apart. He had chosen his side a long time ago, not that he'd really had much of a choice, not if he'd wanted to keep his daughter safe. But he hadn't counted on them using her as well. When she'd arrived back in the UK he had been delighted at first, convinced that he could now stop feeding information to them, but instead the noose had tightened and he'd been under even more pressure to co-operate. What he didn't understand was why Madeline appeared to have stopped passing information. Presumably she had come over here with the intention of working for them so what had happened? It was time he had a chat with her and found out exactly what was going on. If not they would both be in the firing line.

****

Pas-de-Calais Region, France

Victor was pacing up and down when Clarisse suddenly reappeared. 'I've changed my mind. He's already given you his name and base hasn't he?'

'Yes… but…' He didn't get any further.

'We're going to hand him over to the Germans.' Clarisse had been halfway to the barn when she'd realised that was the best solution.

Victor looked horrified. 'But if we do that, they'll know…' He stopped as he thought more carefully about her suggestion.

'What will they know?' Clarisse gave a cold smile. 'If he's German then they already suspect you, but you've handed him over so maybe they're wrong? If he's not German he can only tell them about you. He's not seen anyone else.' She shrugged. 'You locked him up and called them. If he is a genuine RAF pilot they will just take him to a POW camp. They won't hurt him.'

'He told me that his friend said I'd helped him.'

'You're French, he's speaking English. Maybe your English wasn't good enough to understand him. You didn't answer him or agree that you'd helped anyone did you? Or ask him any questions other than his name and base and that was for the benefit of the Germans wasn't it?' She shrugged. 'Or we can check him out? But to do that I have to ask him questions so then he'll have seen me and it will be obvious that you have resistance connections. If London says he's genuine we'll have to move him down the line, even if we're still not happy.'

'And what if he is genuine and London are pissed off because we handed him over?'

'We tell them why. We're in charge here, not them. It's our lives that are at risk, not theirs. He's one pilot, it's not going to affect the war. If we accept him and it turns out he is a Nazi that will stop our operation completely and that *could* have some effect on the war.'

Victor stared at her for several minutes while he thought back over her argument. Eventually he nodded. 'Alright. I agree. I'll drive into town in the morning and hand him over.' He frowned. 'Or should I go now?'

Clarisse considered it for a moment. 'It's curfew but I think you should go now. We can't afford for him them to find him here. Give me a few moments to get across the fields and then go.' She reached across and hugged him. 'Good luck Victor.'

Chapter 41

En route to Malta

A few days later *Cleopatra* sailed again for Malta but on this trip they were on their own, the ship filled with men from the Air Force, Army and Navy who were going to be stationed there. This time they didn't see any enemy planes or ships and it bore no resemblance to their first journey. They were cheered as they came into the harbour and when they went ashore they only had to mention they were from the *Cleopatra* to be treated as heroes. John was to learn later that this was the last relief of Malta. The eastern Mediterranean had been opened up again.

****

Pas-de-Calais Region, France

Clarisse decoded the message and frowned. The airman had been picked up by the Gestapo but she had decided to ask London anyway and they had verified the airman's identity. However, she still wasn't convinced. Like Victor she had been sure there was something off about him and although she couldn't work out what it was, she hadn't been prepared to take him down the line and put everyone at risk. She had made the best decision she could under the circumstances. She couldn't have left him in the cellar indefinitely and she couldn't have just killed him because she had been suspicious. That would have made her as bad as the Nazis. Despite London's assurances she was still convinced she'd made the right decision. Whether she would ever be able to prove it was another matter.

****

London

Madeline closed the front door, leant back against the door jamb and tried to stop her limbs shaking. How on earth had they found her? She was sure she'd covered her tracks well enough so they couldn't trace her. She had even stopped writing to Jimmy in case they could find her that way and anyway she daren't write to him anymore. Not only was she scared she would make him some kind of target, a way of them getting back at her for not co-operating anymore, but if they did trace him they might use his letters to find her.

She had left the blackout down when she went to work so the flat was in total darkness. She felt her way carefully towards the living room and peered cautiously down into the street through the curtains. No, she hadn't been mistaken. There was definitely someone out there.

'What's going on Madeline?'

She jumped and spun around, her right hand was already pulling out her small pistol and aiming it when her brain recognised the voice. By now her eyes had adjusted to the darkness and she could just make out the outline of a man standing in the far corner. 'You frightened the bloody life out of me, Dad. How the hell did you get in?' She took a breath and relaxed slightly. At least she wasn't in danger from her father although she would clearly need to sort out the lock on her door.

'That's not important Maddy. We need to talk.'

'What about?' She double checked the curtains were still pulled, reached for the light switch and eyed him warily.

He blinked rapidly in the sudden brightness but carried on talking anyway. 'About why you are no longer passing on information to our friends in the Third Reich.'

Madeline gasped in horror and reached for the pistol which she had already secreted back in her belt again. 'How did you...' Then she frowned. 'I don't understand? Are you working for them too?'

'I didn't have any choice, not if I wanted you to be safe.' He wondered how much more he should say and then decided that maybe he needed to be honest. The time for lying was past. Or not... Perhaps it was best to see what she had to say first.

Madeline was still looking uncomfortable. 'What do you mean?'

'I'll do a deal with you. You tell me why you've stopped working for them and I'll tell you everything.'

'I haven't... I mean...' She fell silent.

'Yes, you have. I was visited by some Irish bastard threatening me... and you, because you had disappeared, well tried to disappear. He was going to pay you a visit, but I talked him out of it. Although I don't think I've succeeded as I think he's hovering around out there.' He indicated the street.

Madeline paled and nodded. 'I was being followed. Was that him?'

'Probably... unless the British are on to you.' He had deliberately said the British so he didn't give anything away but as he said the words his heart skipped a beat. If the security services were suspicious of Madeline they might well be checking up on him too. He could only hope it was the bearded Irishman creeping around and not someone more professional. 'Did you actually see anyone?'

'No, I just felt like someone was watching me. I've felt it for a couple of weeks.' She was the colour of chalk. 'Do you think they are on to me?' She groped her way to a chair and slumped down.

Peregrine watched her for several seconds before following suit and sitting opposite her. 'You have stopped spying though, haven't you?'

She nodded.

'Why? You risked everything to come over here. Why have you stopped?'

Madeline sat back and focused her gaze on his. 'It sounds stupid...' She fell silent.

Peregrine sighed and waited.

Madeline looked away and stared down at the rather worn carpet. 'I fell in love.'

****

Paris

Charlotte was delighted to finally return to normal. Despite Andre's assurances that the man she'd killed had definitely been a poacher she had still decided to take the opportunity to lie low. After she'd killed him and they'd decided to put everything on hold until they knew they were safe, her imagination had run riot and she had even prepared herself to prepare to go home, but then Andre had come around to the apartment with the good news.

'You're quite sure? Its not a German trap?'

Andre had grinned. 'Not unless they've been employing him for years. My contact says he lives in one of the villages, poaches regularly and then sells his produce in Paris. He's probably been richer since the bosche have been here, but he's been doing it for years. I didn't just ask one person Francine, I asked several and they all agreed.'

'Then we can get back to business?'

'Yes, and I have just the thing.'
Charlotte smiled. 'Go on then.'

****

Souk-el-Arba, North Africa

It was the last day of the patrol and Jimmy was flying with Pete, Robbie and Johnnie when they jumped two 109Fs. At one time Jimmy would have been wary about any new enemy model but by now he was convinced the Spitfire could handle anything. There were flying at 8000 feet when they spotted them and as Pete was nearest he went in first. After firing several rounds at the 109, all of which missed, he pulled away, leaving the way clear for Jimmy who went in close.

For some reason the German fighter tried to out fly him which seemed eminently foolhardy to Jimmy who knew he had the speed to stay with him. He opened the throttle and stuck to him, lining him up, flicking the gun button up on his joystick and pressing the tit. A quick two second burst of machine gun fire spat out from his wings and the bullets struck the 109s engine and its fuselage in a perfect deflection shot. Glycol bled profusely from its nose and black smoke streamed copiously from its wounds. The aircraft dived at an angle of about 40 degrees and slid vertically all the way towards the ground. Jimmy watched as his first kill fell from the sky and felt nothing but a sense of achievement and success. He had finally broken his duck.

The rest of December was wet, the rain falling in sheets, the airfield becoming a sea of sludge while deep muddy pools confined them to long periods of doing nothing. As Christmas approached both the Germans and British stepped up their attacks and after carrying out a dawn patrol on Christmas Eve the weather deteriorated even more, turning their airfield into a quagmire, so much so that they were grounded. But for once Jimmy didn't mind as they toasted Christmas by drinking their way through forty eight halves of beer, six bottles of whisky and two bottles of gin. Christmas Day was just as bad weather wise, but as they had managed to acquire some more alcohol from the NAAFI which had been set up in the village, they didn't mind too much.

On 30th December eight 109s flew in low, bombing the camp and damaging three planes in the process, but their orders were to stay on the ground. By New Years Eve Jimmy and everyone else were exhausted. Other than the past few days they had been fighting non stop since November, some still didn't have a proper bed to sleep in and their food on New Year's Eve was a tin of sardines. Then one of the men took the initiative, disappeared into the village and returned with a large roasted turkey.

Jimmy never did find out where it came from but six of them disappeared into their tent and quietly devoured it with ample quantities of cheap red plonk. For the first time in ages they forgot about the war and he even forgot about Madeline who still hadn't written to him.

****

Arkley View, Near Barnet
Fred stared down at the decoded message and took a deep breath. He knew it was ridiculous to be upset over the death of a man he'd never met but that wasn't how it felt to him. The intelligence from Germany had been of such importance that he had been overwhelmed with admiration for the man who was risking his life to help them win the war. Unfortunately, it was almost certain that he was dead, his family too as the Gestapo rarely accepted that any members of the family were innocent. He could only hope that the poor man had not suffered too much, but even that was unlikely. He had never been particularly religious, but he found himself saying a prayer for the soul of the best German spy they'd had, before standing up and walking slowly to the door. This was a message best passed on in person.

****

Malta
My dearest Elsie and Rodney
As you can see we are now in Malta and it seems that the island is finally safe. There are still air raids, but they are few and far between. Fortunately, these cause very little damage which is good because Malta is already badly scarred, beautiful churches pulverised into heaps of rubble, houses, shops, warehouses flattened, the dockyards littered with skeleton buildings, the harbour full of sunken ships. It's so tragic to see what the bastard Huns and Italians have done here, but the people are not cowered or defeated. They are amazing and the

men we brought out from home have done a fantastic job of chasing off the enemy, so much so that they normally just drop their bombs in the sea and head back to Italy. The citizens are currently preparing spring crops, rations are very short here and we don't have much that we can give them, but it doesn't stop them clearing wreckage and repairing the dry docks.

John thought back to the last convoy they had escorted in. The only scare had been from a Dornier which had ignored the convoy and flown towards Africa instead. He smiled, this time they had been going to intercept an Italian convoy. It was a chance to get their own back so he and the rest of the crew were disappointed not to get anywhere near the Italian ships. He had heard the radio chatter and knew before the crew that the ships had been warned by their escorting aircraft. It was still disappointing though to hear that the ships had scuttled back to the mainland as quickly as they could. It was soon obvious that they would be too close to the coast for comfort so they had been ordered back to Malta. He picked up his pen, lit another cigarette and began writing again

Well, another Christmas gone and over a year since I've seen you. Because of the strict rationing I was not expecting much food on Christmas Day but they have done us proud, we even had roast turkey, roast potatoes, stuffing and cauliflower as well as Christmas pudding with sauce and fruit and nuts. They have even made Christmas cake. It wasn't the same without you but things have definitely taken a turn for the better. Lord Gort VC, the Governor of Malta paid us a visit on 30th, the ship and her company spent the 29th rushing around getting ready to welcome him. Another inspection over and another day closer to seeing you both again. The enemy is on the run at last and the war will soon be over I'm sure and then I will be back home and we can talk about an addition to the family. I miss you both so much.

He sat back in his chair and wondered how much longer it would be before the war ended and he could give Elsie his real letters, not the bland ones he wrote for the censor. Yes, things were improving and there was now a light at the end of the long dark tunnel, but, as Churchill had said on 10th November: '*This Is Not The End. It Is Not Even The Beginning Of The End. But It Is, Perhaps, The End Of The Beginning.*'

Part 4

1943

RAF Pilots scrambling from their dugouts in North Africa

Chapter 42

London

'I have an idea.' Peregrine eyed Madeline thoughtfully. She had moved into his flat temporarily while he tried to work out what to do. Unfortunately, he only had two options. He could find them both some new papers which wouldn't be difficult, but they couldn't remain in Great Britain, that would be much too dangerous. He could try and get them out of the country, but he didn't know where to go. Ireland was out of the question as was America, Australia or Canada. In any case if he tried to leave that would cause even more problems. That left him with option two which wasn't without risk, but did at least offer some kind of solution, not to mention the chance to at least tell his daughter some of the truth.

Madeline looked up from the book she was pretending to read. She had told her employers that she was ill to avoid having to leave her father's flat. She hoped Charlotte hadn't sent any messages although someone else would deal with them if she had, but for some reason she felt very close to Charlotte, almost as if she was a sister. 'Go on…'

Peregrine hesitated and then made his suggestion. 'I could talk to someone in the security services, and we could offer to work for them instead.' He held his breath.

Madeline paled. 'Provide the Germans with false information you mean?'

'Yes. Why? Would you object to doing that?'

Madeline shook her head. 'No, to be honest I wouldn't. I would very much like to do that.' She took a breath. 'It wasn't just that I fell in love… the reason I stopped. That was the start of it, but then I started to realise that the Nazis were wrong… about everything, but in particular about the Jews. You know the work I am doing, and my agent suddenly began asking questions about something called the Final Solution.' She wasn't watching her father so she missed the change in his expression. She carried on. 'I thought she was being ridiculous, listening to some propaganda made up to discredit the Germans and as no one answered her to start with I couldn't understand why she kept asking. But then they did reply…' She shuddered and stared up at him. 'Did you know that was what they were planning?'

Peregrine gazed back at her and wondered where to start.

****

Ghardimaou rest camp, North Africa

'Well, it's nice to know that everyone else knows how good we are!' Jimmy joked as 72 Squadron received the news that they had been awarded the mantle of highest scoring squadron in North Africa with 31 confirmed kills. He was recovering from a bout of what had been diagnosed as dysentery, but was really caused by drinking Chas's cheap booze which came from petrol cans which he hadn't bothered to wash out thus delivering them all with a lethal dose of petrol and alcohol. Jimmy would have liked to blame his friend, but he was still in hospital in Bone, having been shot down. In any case Jimmy knew it was his own fault and that, even if they had known it would make them ill, they would probably still have drunk it. Meanwhile it was probably safer to agree with the doctor that it was dysentery!

The rest camp was near the airbase and situated in an olive grove at the foot of some hills and was very peaceful. Jimmy felt like he was a million miles away from the fighting and he was determined to enjoy his break from the front line, spending his days with some rifle practice and long walks in the hills. He had been feeling shaky and unnecessarily jumpy and knew that these were the classic signs of fatigue that caught up with them all at one time or another and had differing effects on them. One of his friends had even taxied down the runway and then come to a sudden halt. When they had rushed down to see what the problem was they found him staring down at the controls, unable to move. He had a few days off and then returned as if nothing had happened. Jimmy knew he was exhausted, but the problem was deeper than that. He was worrying about Madeline. He still hadn't heard anything from her since before Christmas and although he knew it took the post a while to reach them he had the strangest feeling that something wasn't right. He had written to her three times since her last letter, and he was starting to feel annoyed that there was nothing from her. Maybe she had found someone else and didn't know how to tell him?

After a few days he insisted he was well enough to return to the squadron, determined to join in the celebration over their award. He also wanted to find out if other people's mail was coming through properly. To his delight Chas had discharged himself from hospital and for a brief time Jimmy forgot to worry about Madeline and listened enraptured as Chas wasted no time in telling him what had happened. 'I was pretty lucky to be honest. The plane crashed near Djebel Abiod, which I knew was in enemy territory. I managed to crawl from the wreckage and while I was trying to work out what to do I was found by a local Arab. I gave him one of my gold sovereigns and he agreed to take me to British lines. You have no idea how relieved I was but we'd only gone a short distance when I realised the bastard was going the wrong way so I pulled out my pistol and shot the ground in front of him. I can tell you he changed direction pretty quickly after that and led me straight to a British army patrol.'

Jimmy shook his head in amazement and wondered if he'd have had as much presence of mind if it had happened to him. 'Well done mate. I think we should go into Constantine and celebrate in style.'

Chas grinned. 'Great idea Jimmy old boy, but there's one snag. We've got no money.'

'We could tell the CO that one of the tents went up in flames in the strafing and we could go into town and use our blood money to replace it.' Chem's idea was met with plenty of scepticism, especially from Jimmy. But he was persuaded to go along with it and to his astonishment it worked. They headed into town, beginning their search for canvas in the first bar they came to. Here, they converted their blood ticket into beer money, a not inconsiderate sum of Algerian francs. It crossed Jimmy's mind that this would mean that none of them could afford to land in enemy territory, but at that moment the war seemed miles away, Madeline's silence was forgotten and the drink flowed freely. For some time afterwards there was a very attractive French barmaid from Constantine wearing rather large earrings made out of gold sovereigns.

****

Paris

Eric stood to attention and waited for Kriminalkommissar Fischer to tell him he was going back to Germany in disgrace. His first solo mission had been a complete disaster. He had been sure the farmer believed him, but instead he had spent a night in a cellar and then been arrested by the Gestapo. Not his finest hour.

'Not a great success Eric?'

'No Herr Kriminalkommissar.' Eric stared straight ahead. 'I'm sorry I…'

'It doesn't matter, it's done and hopefully you will have learned from this.'

'Yes Herr Kriminalkommissar.' Eric wasn't exactly sure what he was supposed to have learnt as he had no idea why they hadn't believed him.

'Good because I have another job for you. You will repeat the exercise, only this time you will be successful.' He handed him some documents. 'Memorise these and then we'll find you some suitable clothes and get you ready.'

Eric's eyes lit up. 'You're going to trust me…'

Werner smiled. 'Of course, Eric. That was just a practice run. This is the real thing. You understand me don't you?'

'Yes Herr Kriminalkommissar.'

'Good, you have a couple of hours then we'll send you out to do your work for the Fatherland.'

Eric smiled and relaxed. 'Thank you, Herr Kriminalkommissar. I won't let you down.'

Werner smiled. 'I'm sure you won't.'

****

London

'We have a problem.' Peregrine sat down in the back seat of the Bentley and glanced across at the person sitting next to him. The partition between the driver and the back seat was closed, the driver watching ahead, keeping guard.

'What kind of problem?'

Peregrine quickly explained about Madeline. 'I need to bring her into the operation and you need to call off Lt Colonel Hallet and Colonel Sinclair. Otherwise, they are going to ruin everything.'

There was a short silence. 'Yes, I've been watching developments and I agree. Why did you take so long to suggest bringing her on board?'

Peregrine sighed. 'I think you know the answer to that but if you want to hear it out loud... I wasn't sure we could trust her. I wasn't happy using her, but it was the safer option for all of us, but now she's stopped sending the bastards anything which has made them suspicious.'

'They've sent the Irishman?'

'Yes, he paid me a visit and has been following Madeline. I've moved her into my flat but that's only a short term measure. If we don't act quickly they'll either kill her or try and take her back to Germany.'

'I think the latter is more likely. Your intelligence is too important for them to lose so she's more valuable alive.'

Peregrine nodded. 'I agree but that's much too dangerous now.'

'Does she know about you?'

Peregrine shook his head. 'No, at least I don't think so.' The expression on Madeline's face when she had believed he supported the Final Solution still cut deep into his heart... that she could think anything so heinous about her own father... That he hadn't been able to deny it was still eating away at him and one of the reasons he knew now was the time to bring her into the operation. At least then he could finally be honest with her, well he could tell her most things anyway, not everything… that would have to wait until later. He turned his attention back to the other person. 'She thinks I'm a Nazi supporter, that's what they told her and my actions since she's been here have borne that out.' He gave a wry smile. 'If not, I'd probably have been dead long ago!'

'It must be quite difficult now that she's had her eyes opened then…, thinking you support such appalling things.'

Peregrine frowned as he digested her words then the penny dropped and he let out a deep sigh. 'It was you who authorised her reply to that agent wasn't it…? The one about the Final Solution?'

'Yes. It was time. I'm not going to apologise Peregrine. Surely you would prefer her to know the truth about the people she was working for?'

'Yes, but…' He realised there was no 'but' and fell silent.

'Do you think it will help for her to know I'm still alive?'

The question caught him by surprise. 'I don't know.' He thought hard. 'No, it might have the opposite effect. Knowing I used her… lied to her… will be bad enough but now she's seen through the bastards she may accept that… in time. But knowing we *both* deliberately used her, *both* lied to her might send her back the other way. We have no idea what happened to her while she was in Germany or how strong their hold over her is. We can't risk blowing everything now.'

He gazed at her in the darkness and waited. There was a long silence. 'Unfortunately, I agree. I was just hoping you might think it was time for me to reappear. Looks like I'll have to wait a bit longer then.' He could hear the catch in her voice, and he reached out and took her hand.

'I've missed you so much Johanna.'

She fought back her tears, smiled and squeezed his hand. 'It's been a long time since anyone has called me that. Its Joanna now.' She let out a long slow breath. 'I can't believe we ever thought this was a good idea, Peregrine.'

'I'm not sure we did think about it Johanna, we just went along with the plan and it took on a life of its own.'

'I miss her so much, at least you've been able to see her over the past couple of years.' He could just make out her silhouette and realised she was wiping her eyes.

'And spent all the time lying to her, watching what I was saying, feeding her rubbish to send to her Nazi masters.' Feeling guilty, his tone was rougher than he'd intended and he immediately regretted it. He had been the driving force behind this whole thing and yet she had suffered the most. That had never been his intention but he couldn't change the past only the present. Johanna was right, at least he'd had the benefit of his daughter's company, even if he had needed to be careful.

'Still better than for her to think you're dead.' Johanna snapped. She took a breath. 'Do you think she'll ever forgive us?'

Peregrine pulled her into his arms and hugged her close. 'Let's hope so, with time. Especially now she's heard the truth about the Final Solution.'

'I hope you're right.' Joanna pulled back into her protective shell, the one that had kept her free of emotion and allowed her to carry out this whole plan throughout the past ten years. 'You'd better go. I'll arrange the meeting for you. I think its best you see them both together on your own. Once you've decided on a strategy you can bring Madeline in. I would suggest not telling her too much yet. The truth is better left unsaid at the moment.'

Peregrine frowned. 'I don't understand? I thought I was going to come clean...'

'No. Just tell her that, like her, you've changed your allegiance. There's no reason for her to know anything else.'

Peregrine was about to argue but he realised she was right. It was much too dangerous to tell Madeline anything like the truth. It could backfire. If she believed her father was changing sides to protect her she would be grateful and less likely to betray them.

'Alright. Make it quick, I have a feeling we're running out of time. Goodnight Darling.' He climbed out of the car and shut the door quietly behind him.

'Goodnight my love.' Johanna watched him walk away then tapped on the partition glass. As the driver started the engine and the car pulled away she eased back into the comfortable leather seat and closed her eyes. They had given up so much for their country, made choices that had led to pathways that entailed so many sacrifices. None of them had been particularly intentional. As Peregrine had said, the plan had taken on a life of its own, one decision following on naturally from another, not really their choices but those decisions had moulded their daughter into the person she was now, someone who had chosen to work for a brutal enemy and in whom she had no trust. At the time she hadn't questioned the decisions they'd made, but now she wasn't sure. Why hadn't they said no? Then she remembered how it had all started and she straightened up, opened her eyes and gazed out at the darkened streets, the obligatory blackouts blocking any light, but not hiding the numerous bomb craters or the scarred and jagged remains of buildings. No, they had seen the future back in 1933 and they had done the right thing. Time would prove them right and if Madeline couldn't see that then she would have to find a way of living with it.

****

Malta

John picked up his pencil and began writing his new diary. Up until now he'd had to rely on his letters, but he had decided to start the new year by keeping a proper record for the future, something he would be able to share with Rodney and any other children they might have in the years to come.

Cleopatra had set sail on 22nd January for Zuara, an enemy strongpoint. We were accompanied by another Dido class cruiser, Eurylus, and the destroyers, Jervis, Kelvin, Nubian and Javelin. Our main targets were the harbour and the town, which was well fortified. We arrived at the harbour and began our attack. This lit several fires ashore and was then followed by a massive explosion which sounded like an ammunition dump going up. The destroyers moved in closer for a better look while Cleopatra steamed past the harbour entrance. I was up on deck and couldn't believe that the harbour was almost completely empty of ships. I then turned my attention to the town and realised what had happened. Zuara has one lighthouse at the harbour entrance and a large minaret on the mosque in the town. In the darkness we had mistaken the minaret for the lighthouse and fired on the town instead of the harbour. This was extremely fortuitous because if we'd fired at the empty harbour we would have wasted our shells. Instead we had made a considerable mess of the town as we had been ordered to do and fortunately we had not sustained any damage or casualties. I have just heard that the day after our *bombardment the Eighth Army entered the town meeting little opposition.*

John smiled to himself. Things were going very well in Libya, the air attacks on Malta had decreased considerably and the island was finally beginning to return to normal. He was about to write some more when he was interrupted by Chris.

'We're off to Alexandria, looks like we're back on convoy duty.'

John put the diary in his desk and stood up. 'Well at least it should be safer than it was at the beginning.'

****

Souk-el-Khemis, North Africa

Having arrived back at the camp minus their gold and any canvas Jimmy was relieved the CO didn't appear to notice. The weather had deteriorated even more, lashing the airfield with heavy rains which suspended all flying and eventually they decided to move camp to somewhere that was more suitable to build runways on.

Souk-el-Khemis was about fifteen miles away, closer to the frontline with a fast draining sandier soil. Four new runways were quickly installed, Euston, Paddington, Marylebone and Kings Cross, and 111 and 93 Squadrons were already ensconced. They quickly settled down, the facilities were much better, as was the food, a fact Jimmy gleefully included in his diary, having enjoyed a steak and kidney pudding after months of dried biscuits and pickled fish. They had set up camp in a disused railway station which was considerably more comfortable than the tents they had been living in. The only downside were the stray pigs from the farm next door foraging for food. The weather hadn't improved however, and the constant rain and storms continued to hamper operations, becoming more of a hazard and claiming more lives than the Germans.

****

London

'It would have been a lot easier if we'd known from the beginning.' Colonel Sinclair glared at Peregrine.

'But it was good to know we were right.' Fred interjected. 'Although we could have saved a lot of time if you'd told us who the spy was and told us to leave her alone!' He sighed. 'But I understand why you didn't.'

'We've been told that your daughter has no idea that you are a double agent, she believes you have been working for the Germans?' Anthony interrupted.

'Yes, and that's how it has to stay. We don't know how she'll react if she knows the whole story...' He fell silent realising they didn't know the whole thing and that it wasn't in his remit to tell them anything more than they needed to know. 'She believes I have changed sides to protect her and she has agreed to work with you too which means she has to send them some information asap or they will become even more suspicious than they already are.'

'What kind of information?' Fred frowned. 'We need time to find something that's not going to compromise any ongoing allied operations. We can't just make something up.'

'It would also have to be something Madeleine would have access to. Other than information she could get from you that restricts it to her work with SOE.' Colonel Sinclair mused.

Anthony frowned, his thoughts immediately with Charlotte. 'You can't seriously be suggesting betraying one of our agents?' He exchanged glances with Fred who was looking equally horrified.

'No, of course not.' Colonel Sinclair snapped at him. 'Don't be so bloody ridiculous. The Minister and I will find something we can leak, something that doesn't involve betraying our own people to the Nazis. But that's our problem. We just wanted you both to know that the spy was now known to us and that she is now going to work with us. Fred, I will tell you when we've worked out a plan and then you will monitor all radio traffic from Madeline as she resumes transmissions.' He saw the Minister's expression and resisted the temptation to snap at him. 'It's a precaution, we can't just take your word for it!' He turned back to Fred. 'Obviously, you will keep this conversation to yourself?'

'Yes sir.' Fred waited for more instructions, but as it soon became obvious there weren't any he stood up and left the room.

Colonel Sinclair looked at Anthony. 'Thank you for all your hard work. A fresh pair of eyes was all we needed in the end. Now you're up to date you can get back to doing something else. I believe they are looking for people with your experience to help make some plans for Italy.' He smiled and carried on before Anthony could interrupt. 'No, not the military aspect, some little surprises from our friends in Italy. I gather we have quite a few so that will be right up your street!'

Anthony smiled back and nodded. 'Thank you, Simon. If anything comes up I think you can use I'll be in touch.' He headed out of the room leaving the two men to decide on how best to utilise their latest asset.

Chapter 43

Paris

'Is he definitely genuine?' Charlotte eyed Andre cautiously. 'Clarisse said they had someone trying to infiltrate them at the end of last year.'

'I thought London verified that one, even though she turned him over to the Gestapo?' His tone was disapproving and Charlotte frowned.

'It's up to us, not London whether we take them and Clarisse was sure he was a German plant.' She wondered if she should add that she'd asked London to follow it up and check whether the pilot had ever turned up in a POW camp. The last she'd heard, he hadn't. But there was no time arguing over something that had happened in the past, she needed to focus on the present, so she decided not to say anything. 'This one has been verified then and you're all happy with him?' She repeated.

Andre nodded. 'He had his papers, managed to get out of the Lancaster with them and he was checked out further down the line, we already had another member of the crew so when he turned up we put them together and they recognised each other. They've been hanging around a while now and they're getting restless.'

Charlotte shrugged. 'It takes time to do everything we need to do, they should have been told that. This is not a game.' She sighed. 'Alright. Do you want me to take both of them?' When Andre nodded in relief she continued. 'I'll collect them both at the station then, normal place and take them south. Let me have their details and descriptions. I'll leave it to you to prepare them for their journey.'

Andre quickly described the two men and gave Charlotte the names on their false papers. She memorised the details and left to make arrangements, her thoughts on Victor and Clarisse. She would have liked to meet up with one of them and get a description of the German, but Victor had already come to the attention of the Gestapo so perhaps it was safer not to contact them for a while.

****

Algiers, Algeria
'The new Spits are ready!'

Jimmy looked up and was about to rush outside when Chem grinned. 'No, we've got to go to Gib to collect them.' They had been waiting for the Spitfire Mk IXs for a while and this was a good excuse to escape the dreadful weather.

A few hours later they had arrived in Algiers to be told the aeroplanes weren't ready and they would have to wait there until further notice. Algiers was a pretty town and they soon settled into a school that had been requisitioned for the RAF before finding a good pub. An American bar became their favourite place followed by the local casino. Their stay turned into one long round of late mornings, liquid lunches, time at the poker tables or watching films at the local flicks. They were beginning to grow bored with their time off when they were finally told their Spits were ready and they flew off to Gibraltar.

****

London
'Madeline is handling radio traffic for agents in France. I suggest we hand over something about the escape lines or resistance.'

Peregrine stared at him in horror. 'Are you serious?'

'I can't think of anything else. I've spent days trying to work out what information we could send. We can't risk making something up because Madeline has been out of touch for so long. It has to be genuine and useful.'

'But to hand over our own people?' He shook his head. 'I don't think I can be party to that.'

Simon looked shocked. 'Of course not. What do you take me for? I was thinking of handing over some information about one of the communist cells, not SOE.' He shrugged. 'There's going to be an almighty struggle for France at the end of this war and we can't let the Commies take control. This way we can kill two birds with one stone.'

Peregrine breathed a sigh of relief. 'Well why the hell didn't you say so!' He snapped.

'Just double checking whose side you're on Minister.'

Peregrine flushed. 'This whole fucking mess was your idea, Simon. You've known *whose side* I was on since the beginning! And for your information, if Johanna hadn't agreed to go along with it, I most certainly would have told you where to stick your games! We've lost years with our daughter and God knows what brainwashing or damage they've done to her.'

'Probably best to keep my involvement to yourself Peregrine. You're the only one who knows that, well you and Johanna.' Colonel Sinclair saw the furious expression on Peregrine's face and sighed. 'It's not been easy for me to play this straight down the line. I've had to lie to people I admire and trust and pretend not to know anything. I've used people too, but the end game was always more important and now we've reached the point where all our plans have finally put us in control, in a position to take advantage of the wheels we put in motion so many years ago. We can't waste that opportunity or our sacrifices have been for nothing.'

Peregrine glared at him, then reached for a cigarette, lit it and inhaled deeply. 'Your sacrifices have been nothing compared to ours, but I take your point. What do you want me to tell Madeline?'

****

Paris

Charlotte recognised the two men from Andre's description and walked swiftly towards them, dropping her newspaper as she passed. The taller of the two men bent down, picked it up and handed it back to her.

'Ici vous êtes miss.' The French was lousy but at least he had tried.

'Merci beaucoup.' Charlotte smiled, took the paper and carried on walking towards the barrier. After a brief moment the two men followed. Charlotte passed through with no problem and she made her way quickly to one of the carriages where she sat down and began reading the paper. Out of the corner of her eye she watched the two men board the carriage and sit on the opposite side, where they could watch her without making it too obvious.

Charlotte appeared to be scanning the words but her eyes were really on the two men and also whether anyone was paying undue attention to them. As far as she could see everything was normal, there were roughly the same number of soldiers wandering around the station, a couple of Gestapo agents hovering by the barrier, which again was normal. There was no heightened sense of tension, nothing seemed out of place, but for some reason she still felt vaguely uneasy. Charlotte relaxed back into her seat, stared out of the window again and wondered what was putting her on edge. Perhaps she had been over here too long and was beginning to jump at shadows. Even as the words crossed her mind she knew it wasn't that. It had everything to do with the Gestapo man. She hadn't seen him for a few weeks but that didn't mean he wasn't having someone else watching her although she was sure she wasn't being followed. If she'd had the slightest inkling of that she would never had agreed to take the two pilots south. The whistle blew, the train eased out of the station and she let out her breath. Her eyes met those of the taller man and he smiled before looking away.

Charlotte frowned. He didn't seem in the least bit nervous. She'd taken several pilots down the line, not to mention the Jewish families and they were all so terrified, she'd had to remind them to relax so they didn't draw attention to themselves. Perhaps it had been a mistake not speaking to Victor or Clarisse before agreeing to do this.

****

Suez

The ship had been docked in Alexandria for the past couple of weeks, members of the crew who had completed their time were drafted back to their home depots and as new crewmen arrived to take their place, the usual drills were carried out to enable them to fit into the ship's routine, some took place in the harbour, but others needed the ship to be at sea. They finally shipped out for some night exercises with two destroyers, but the wind was soon at gale force, hampering any attempt to do anything constructive and then they developed a problem with the starboard engine which meant they had to return to harbour. However, the high winds and volatile sea made it impossible to tie up to a buoy so eventually they had no option but to drop both anchors.

The following day they set off again for Port Said before entering the canal for the third time within three months. They made good time and reached Suez before 18.00hrs. The following day they took part in numerous exercises playing the target for torpedo bombers. John had considered himself an expert on surviving enemy attacks, but tactics had moved on and even he was relieved that the 'enemy' were only firing dummy torpedoes.

****

London

'Are you sure this is what they want me to do?' Madeline didn't sound convinced.

'Yes, the network is communist so the leak will benefit France in the long term.'

Madeline raised an eyebrow and then shrugged. 'Alright. I'll send the information immediately. Hopefully that will get them off my back.'

'It should keep them busy for a while and then we'll find you other things to send.' He hesitated and changed the subject. 'Why have you stopped writing to your pilot?'

'Because I can't lie to him anymore and I can't tell him the truth either. I was also concerned that I might make him a target with the Germans. I love him too much to do that to him.'

'I'm sorry.' He wished he could tell her the truth about her mother, but he couldn't risk ruining things. Furious as he was with Simon, he knew the man was right. If they blew it now, everything they had worked for, everything they had sacrificed would be for nothing. He still wasn't entirely sure it had been worth it, only time would tell, meanwhile he had to keep playing the game.

****

Souk-el-Khemis, North Africa

Having stopped off in Algiers again and spent the night in Hussein Bay stables on a hard concrete floor with damp blankets they were finally on their way back to the air base. But, as they approached their old airfield at Souk-el-Arba they ran into an enormous electrical storm. Hailstones the size of golf balls pelted the hood of Jimmy's cockpit threatening to smash the Perspex. Lightning flashed and forked across the black clouds and crashed around the aircraft while torrential rain teemed down the sides of the aeroplane. Jimmy gripped the control column, but it seemed to make little difference as the Spitfire rocked and bumped through the storm, the airwaves were silent as they all fought to control their aircrafts.

Finally, Jimmy spotted Euston runway and a sense of relief swept over him but visibility was diabolical and he quickly considered his options. Eventually he decided that he couldn't stay up there forever, one lightning strike and he would be dead, so he eased back the throttle and began to descend. The Spitfire swung wildly as the high winds buffeted it, visibility distorted by the teeming rain but finally he made contact with the ground with a hard jolt. Jimmy knew immediately that something was wrong, but his problems were only just beginning.

The undercarriage seemed to be dragging in the mud and the machine careered along the runway. Jimmy struggled with the controls, trying to prevent the plane skidding into the quagmire that surrounded him but he needn't have bothered as the runway was completely waterlogged. The aircraft was moving at 60 mph, the wheels continuing to drag in the deep mud and slush, Jimmy fought with the controls, but it made no difference. The wheels trapped themselves in the mud and then the inevitable happened. The whole aircraft tipped over onto its brand new nose and came to an abrupt halt.

The rain beating down on the cockpit let Jimmy know he was still alive and in one piece. The straps had saved him from falling forward and smashing his head on the instrument panel. Jimmy reacted instinctively, calling up his number two and telling him not to land. One brand new smashed up Spitfire was enough.

Jimmy carefully undid the buckle, slid the hood back, eased himself out of the aeroplane and jumped onto the ground where he stood surveying the mangled machine.

'Are you alright sir?' One of the erks had braved the rain.

'I'm fine but that isn't!' The brief euphoria he'd felt at still being alive was replaced with a murderous rage. They'd waited months for these new models and he'd damaged his, possibly even written it off on its maiden voyage. He was furious with himself, the weather and the whole bloody war. 'It's totally fucked up isn't it?'

'It's not the worst sir. Two made it successfully at Waterloo, five came down at Paddington and four are still missing. We have heard nothing from Sgt Passmore and Sgt Hussey.'

Jimmy returned to the mess, kicking out at a pig seeking shelter, and lay on his bed, waiting for news. Eventually news came through that Sgt Hussey had crash landed at Ghardimaou, but was unhurt, two more landed safely at Tingley Bay but Sgt Passmore had spun in as he landed and was killed instantly. The weather was definitely becoming more deadly than the enemy.

******

Arkley View, Near Barnet
Having been warned the spy was going to send a message Fred decoded it quickly and then felt sick. He read it again and shook his head in fury. No, he hadn't made a mistake. She was turning over an escape line to the Gestapo. He thought back to the meeting and Lt Colonel Hallett's fury that they would even consider selling out SOE agents to the enemy then he strode out of the hut and made his way to Colonel Sinclair's hut.

'She's made contact… *sir.*' The hesitation and emphasis on the title was marked and Colonel Sinclair stared at him.
'Something wrong Fred?'
'You've given up the resistance to the Gestapo?' He could barely make himself sound civil.
'No, we've given up the communists to the enemy.'
Fred looked confused. He glanced down at the piece of paper and re read it.
'I can assure you Fred that we haven't given up SOE, it's the communists we've betrayed.'
'I thought we were all supposed to be on the same side.'
'We are…' He began, 'Well… actually we aren't.' Colonel Sinclair sighed. 'Sit down Fred and let me bring you up to date with the planning for the future.'

****

Toulouse
The train finally arrived in Toulouse and Charlotte alighted onto the platform. The journey had been long and tiring and she was totally exhausted, not just from double checking they weren't being followed and that they were safe in the various houses they stopped at overnight, but also from her own thoughts which were driving her mad, questioning everything and everyone. In all her previous journeys she had never felt like this and several times she had almost

decided to leave the two men to travel the rest of the way on their own. But her own sense of duty refused to let her abandon them.

She walked briskly towards the barrier and her heart began racing. Standing by the soldiers was Werner Fischer. Charlotte turned back towards the two pilots, her first thought to distance them from her but neither of them was watching her, they were staring at the barrier but, unlike her, they didn't seem terrified. She tried to catch their attention but it was pointless they weren't watching her at all, so she used the emergency signal. She dropped her newspaper and as she bent forward to retrieve it she glanced back, expecting to see them melt back into the crowd. Instead, the taller of the two, the man using the papers of Martine Devreaux, smiled at her and gave a half salute.

****

Soviet Union

Kristian felt the bullets tear through the fuselage and knew with utter certainty he'd been hit. He had seconds to decide what to do, go down with the aircraft or jump out. The last time he'd jumped out he had set a chain of events into motion, but he had survived so…

The parachute floated gently down to earth, in the distance he heard the aeroplane crash, saw the flash of bright light as it exploded and was grateful he had decided to bail out after all. But that would have been quick, he could only pray that he would not regret not remaining with his plane. He was still thinking about that when he realised he was nearly down, he bent his knees and then it was all over, he was rolling down the snow covered hill, the bitter cold catching him by surprise.

He finally stopped falling, climbed quickly up, undid the straps, pulled the parachute towards him and began burying it. There was no sound at all and he wondered where he was and whether he would ever be able to find his own lines. He pulled out his compass and waited for it to settle before heading west. He had been flying over the south of Stalingrad so he was definitely in enemy territory. Somehow, he had to get around to the other side of the city before the Russian armies forced the German army even further back.

Kristian stared all around him and sighed. He was alone in the vast wastelands of the Soviet Union, in a country that hated Germans, something he could hardly blame them for. He had no food, or proper winter clothes and his only weapon was a pistol so he was virtually unarmed. The only thing he had in abundance was snow so he wouldn't be thirsty. On the other hand there was little chance of the Gestapo finding him. He gave a grim smile and looked around again. Perhaps he should go the other way?

****

London

'What on earth's the matter Madeline?' Peregrine looked up from his desk in astonishment as she rushed into his office.

Madeline shut the door loudly behind her and glared at him. 'What the fuck have you done?'

Peregrine was looking totally confused. 'I'm sorry, I don't…'

'Charlotte has been arrested.' She realised he had no idea what she was talking about so she elaborated. 'Charlotte, my main agent in France. SOE, she's been arrested by the Gestapo. How could you betray her?'

'I didn't know what you're talking about. You have to believe me.'

'You gave me that message to send; to my German handlers. You told me it was safe.''

Peregrine shook his head. 'That was a communist resistance cell, not SOE. I swear it on my life.'

Madeline was still glaring at him. 'Then why has she been arrested and the whole escape line brought down?'

Peregrine stared at her his face darkening with anger. 'I don't know but I intend to find out.'

'You really didn't know?' Madeline eyed him warily.

'I swear I was told the message was to lead the Nazis to a communist cell. I would never have agreed to any transmission betraying our own people. I'm telling the truth Madeline, you have to believe me.'

****

Soviet Union

'He's definitely crashed?' SS Major Arnold Schmidt sounded furious.

'His plane was last seen diving towards the ground. He may have parachuted out, but my men were too busy trying to kill Soviet pilots to watch him.' The Squadron Leader sounded just as irritated. 'If he survived he will try and make his way back here. What his chances of success are I have no idea, but I would say they are pretty slim. Normally a bail out over enemy territory means time up. You either get shot, if you're lucky or get taken prisoner and I don't need to remind you that we're not very popular over here and as the Soviets haven't signed any agreements they don't treat us too well.' He hadn't been able to resist the dig about the Soviets not signing any protocols because he was sick of being told by the SS that they could treat the Soviets however they wanted because of it. 'So, unless you want to go and look for him yourself, I would say you have no chance of seeing or hearing from him again as he's probably dead.' The Squadron Leader took a breath. 'I hope it wasn't too important?'

Major Schmidt clenched his fists and cursed under his breath. He had arrived just after von Klotz had taken off and the Squadron Leader had refused to call him back. He had been relishing the thought of getting his own back on the man who'd nearly killed him three years earlier when he'd been a young trainee pilot hiding in the Oberleutnant's aircraft in Magdeburg. He had never been so scared as he had been on that evening and he'd wanted to report the pilot for doing acrobatics but that would only have caused him problems so he'd done nothing. Since then he'd done well for himself but he'd never forgotten that evening and now he'd lost the opportunity to get his revenge.

****

London

'What the hell have you done Simon?' Peregrine stormed into Colonel Sinclair's office, slamming the door hard behind him.

Simon removed his glasses and stared in confusion at Peregrine. 'What on earth are you talking about?'

'You betrayed an SOE escape line.'

'I'm sorry I really don't…

'Madeline's message!' Peregrine snapped.

'It had nothing to do with SOE, I told you it was a communist cell…'

'Then why has everyone on the SOE escape line been arrested?' Peregrine interrupted.

'I have no idea. Coincidence… It has to be.' Simon's brain was racing as he went over the preparations they had made. They had been so careful to make sure none of their own people were affected it wasn't possible they had got it wrong. If Fred hadn't decoded the message he might have believed Madeline had played them for fools but he'd seen the signal with his own eyes, it had been the one they'd agreed on and that definitely had nothing to do with SOE. 'I really don't know what's going on except that it must have been an unfortunate coincidence.'

'I don't believe in them.' Peregrine stormed out of the room leaving Simon staring in bemusement after him. If only they still had their contact in Germany he could have tried to find out what had happened, but according to the signal Fred had intercepted he had been arrested.

Chapter 44

North Africa

The spring months had been long drawn out affairs, adverse weather meaning that many missions were cancelled leaving them with little to do other than carry out tests on the aircraft. Jimmy had been relieved to find that his Spitfire could be repaired, the spectacular flip over hadn't caused much damage and all it had needed to get it airworthy was a new airscrew. They had continued their raids on German targets but the Wing Commander had lost interest in strafing after he'd had a narrow escape over Beja when a 1inch shell shot up through the floor of his cockpit and out through the roof only just missing him.

As the weather improved they became more active and soon they were so close to the front line they could hear the bombing and gunfire. As the patrols moved to Cape Rosa the rain had been replaced by scorching heat. Patrols were frequent, two aircraft always on a constant state of readiness, parked on the runway, the pilot seated in the cockpit as the sun beat down mercilessly, waiting for the Very pistol to fire into the air, signalling they should take off.

Jimmy sat in the cockpit as the two planes climbed to 8000 feet and headed towards Tunis. They scoured the sky but there was no sign of the enemy, so they turned back to Souk-el-Khemis. It was a perfect flying day, visibility excellent and Jimmy spotted the Me109G immediately. He speeded up, got him in his sights, pressed the gun button and orange white tracer bullets streamed from his wings. They hit the fuselage, the nose dipped downwards and the aircraft fell into a steep dive. Jimmy knew it was seconds before he crashed into the ground and he pulled away. Waiting to confirm a kill was a dangerous distraction.

****

London

Anthony listened to Madeline, the shock and horror apparent on his face. 'You're sure?'

'That she has been arrested and the escape line completely compromised, yes. About the Colonel and my father's involvement, no. They both swear the message I was given to send had nothing to do with Charlotte and that its some kind of unfortunate coincidence.'

Anthony could feel the blood boiling slowly inside of him. He stood up, walked over to the window and lit a cigarette with trembling hands.

Madeline watched him, unsure whether to say anything else, not that she could think of anything to say. After her initial shock she was inclined to believe her father had not known anything about it and she couldn't think of a good reason for the Colonel to betray Charlotte so she had eventually decided to accept their view of events.

'I'm going to France, to find out what happened.'

Madeline stared at him in shock, intent on talking him out of such a reckless course. 'That's insanity, how is that going to help? You'll never be able to find out anything…,' then she suddenly stopped as an idea came to her. 'Take me with you?'

Anthony spun around and glared at her. 'Why would I do that?'

'Because the Germans think I am one of them. We can make up some cover story… I don't know exactly what yet, but I think we are more likely to find out the truth if you take me with you.'

Anthony inhaled deeply as he thought carefully about what she was suggesting. 'They'll never let you go.'

Madeline shrugged. 'Then we won't tell them.'

It made sense, unless of course she really was still a German agent in which case he would be in a lot of trouble. But he couldn't think why they would want him, or what she had to gain by going to France. If she was still working with the Germans she was of more use on this side of the channel, especially with her contacts. 'We tell no one.' He walked back to the desk and stubbed out his cigarette in the ashtray. 'Why are you doing this Madeline? You could stay here; be nice and safe?'

'I owe it to Charlotte and my other agents.' She sighed. 'I feel guilty about the little intelligence I did send them. This is my way of making amends.' *And I want to find out what really happened to my mother.*

****

North Africa

They returned to the airfield, wandered into the Mess where Daniels was filling out his logbook and began discussing Jimmy's kill, only to be interrupted by the familiar sound of grunting and shuffling.

'For Christ sake, those bloody animals.' Daniels pulled out his revolver and fired. The pig gave a short indignant squeal, keeled over, twitched and then went still.

Jimmy stared in disbelief. 'Bloody hell Danny, you shot it! What did you go and do that for?'

Danny blanched. 'I don't know. I didn't think I'd hit it. I was just messing about.'

Word quickly spread and several men gathered in the mess debating what to do with the carcass which was now attracting flies.

'You have to do the decent thing. Tell the owner you shot it by mistake.' Jimmy urged.

'Tell him you thought it was a spy.' Chem chipped in.

'Shut up Chem.' Jimmy struggled to keep a straight face. He was about to say more when there was a knock at the door. Fully expecting to see an angry farmer brandishing a rifle Jimmy tentatively opened the door. Perhaps he could say it attacked them and they shot it in self-defence…

'I thought I might be able to help you boys out.' A young airman stood there. 'I used to be a butcher.'

He was ushered quickly into the room and the door was closed behind him. He looked down at the pig and grinned. 'No problem as long as I get a piece.'

In no time at all he had butchered the meat into a range of joints and that night they sat down to a huge meal of succulent pork.

'Where's Daniels?' Jimmy asked in between mouthfuls.

'Don't know, perhaps he feels guilty.' Chem began when the door suddenly opened and Daniels walked in followed closely by the farmer and his wife. Daniels showed them to the table, piled some meat onto two plates and placed them in front of the farmer and his wife. They thanked him and tucked in. Jimmy and Chem exchanged glances, then grinned as Daniels muttered. 'It seemed only fair. It was their pig after all.'

****

84 Avenue Foch, Paris

Charlotte lay on the floor of her cell and wished she could die. She had no idea why she kept waking up every day only to face more pain. She no longer knew how long she'd been a prisoner or even if she'd told them anything useful, so she had stopped speaking completely.

At first she had stuck to her cover story and even when it was obvious they didn't believe it she had stuck to it a bit longer, hoping she had given the others enough time to escape. Then she had begun making things up, giving them names of collaborators and pretending they were resistance workers. It gave her a respite from the pain as they disappeared to presumably check out what she'd told them and a certain amount of satisfaction. But eventually the pain was so bad that she couldn't really remember what she'd told them so she decided it was best to say nothing, at least that way she knew she wasn't giving them anything useful.

'Sorry 'Becca, I haven't avenged you have I?' Her words were little more than a croak, her throat dry and sore from dehydration and from not having spoken for days. 'If I survive the war I'll keep trying.' She stopped trying to speak and wondered why she wanted to carry on. She couldn't take much more pain, she would never forgive herself if she told them anything important although that was probably unlikely now, given the length of time she'd been in custody.

The door flew open, interrupting her thoughts and two men rushed in, dragged her along the floor and out into the corridor. 'Please God, what do I have to do to die?'

****

Tunis, North Africa

The attack on Tunis, the final stronghold of the Germans, began in earnest on 6th May. Jimmy began by escorting a group of bombers on their mission to attack the city which was surrounded by orange groves. But intelligence reports said this was where German tanks and aircraft were hidden so they dived onto the long lines of trees and began strafing. The resulting explosions proved their intelligence was correct. They returned to base to refuel and then took off for the second sortie which yielded little more than some minor flak. On the third sortie they ran into some 109s 7000 feet over Tunis. These pilots were inexperienced making Jimmy's job much easier. 72 Squadron destroyed five aircraft and damaged three for no loss. On their fourth sortie they damaged a further aeroplane before returning home.

Jimmy was exhausted. They had spent months sitting around doing nothing and becoming demoralised and critical of the seemingly inadequate tactics, but they had been proved wrong. Monty had taken his time and delayed his offensive until he could be sure of success. The sheer scale of the attack was overwhelming, and Jimmy felt like a tiny cog in a massive unstoppable military machine.

It came as no surprise on 8th May that Tunis had fallen and Jimmy's job now became one of shooting up the road between Tunis and Bizerta to prevent the Germans from evacuating the area. Tebourba had also been captured and when Jimmy took off at 18.18hrs he noted in his diary that he was reversing Dunkirk. The following day he took off to patrol the area and came across a line of enemy lorries at Zaghouan. He lined them up in his sights and dived down towards them. There was surprisingly little flak as he opened fire and strafed the column of vehicles and men. They flew onto the port at Carthage where enemy ships were waiting to collect German soldiers. The flak was intense, the skies full of Me109s and 190s.

Jimmy picked out a motor torpedo boat, flew towards it and opened fire. As he flew away the boat exploded and an enormous ball of fire shot up into the air, deafening him.

By the middle of the month the RAF dominated the skies and a sweep over Tunis and El Aouina airfield showed large numbers of damaged aircraft. Enemy activity in the air was scant and eventually it was clear that the Germans were defeated. Jimmy had now moved to La Sebala and with little fighting left they decided to borrow a jeep, scrounge some whisky and visit the city they had spent so long patrolling over.

The damage to the city was immense, entire streets had disappeared leaving behind dusty piles of rubble and a few pocked marked buildings that had somehow survived. As they rounded the corner of a street on the outskirts of the city they were confronted by a huge compound hemmed in by thick curls of barbed wire that stretched as far as the eye could see. Inside, row upon row of defeated German soldiers, unkempt and crushed, sat crossed legged in the heat and dust in eerie silence, their faces expressionless, their uniforms ripped and filthy. This was the enemy, the people who had killed his friends, bombed innocent women and children, people who had wanted to invade his homeland. Jimmy took a swig from his whisky bottle and said to no one in particular. 'I don't know whether I should hate them or feel pity for them.'

****

84 Avenue Foch, Paris

Charlotte had been left alone for some time now, no interrogations, no torture and she had slowly recovered her strength. She no longer had a cell to herself but not daring to trust anyone she had barely spoken to her new companion, a young woman who introduced herself as Daniele. Fortunately Daniele appeared to feel the same so the two girls had come to an unspoken agreement to only discuss things that couldn't be of any use to the Nazis.

To start with, each time they heard footsteps in the corridor they had both frozen, expecting the guards to take them for more interrogations but as time passed and they appeared to have been forgotten they slowly ignored the noises outside the cell and concentrated on regaining their health.

'Do you think they'll shoot us?' Daniele eventually voiced the question Charlotte had been asking herself for weeks.

'I don't know. Maybe they'll release us?' Charlotte somehow managed a wry smile. 'With an apology for arresting us by mistake.'

Daniele smiled back. 'That would be something wouldn't it? But somehow I don't think so.'

'No apology then, just throw us out?' Charlotte sighed, closed her eyes and fell silent as she thought how desperately she had longed to die when they'd first arrested her but now, now she wanted to live, to survive and go home, to see Anthony, if he was still alive of course. 'Do you have a boyfriend?'

It was the first time she had asked anything remotely personal and Daniele stared at her suspiciously.

Charlotte sighed. 'Sorry, you don't have to answer. I was just thinking about someone I was very fond of and wondering if I'll ever see him again.'

'Yes, I have a boyfriend but we didn't really… you know… the war kept getting in the way.' Danielle suddenly answered.

Charlotte smiled. 'I'm very pleased to say I behaved disgracefully so at least I won't die a virgin!' She smiled at Daniele's expression. 'I used to laugh when men used the old chat up line about going to war and not wanting to die without making love, but now I understand.'

'You think we're going to die then?'

'I don't think they're going to release us so yes, I imagine that will be their solution. The Nazis are nothing if not practical, we're eating rations while we're alive.'

'So why haven't they done it already?'

Charlotte shrugged. 'I don't know. Maybe they want to give us some hope and then take it away.'

Daniele nodded. 'That sounds like the truth. Maybe they want to hear us say how much we want to live.'

'Do you? Want to live I mean?' Charlotte asked. 'I'm not sure I want to, not that much anyway. Maybe I've done everything I was sent here to do.' She realised that could sound like a confession of sorts so she smiled and added. 'I was reading some spiritualist literature, it talks about us being spirits taking bodies to experience things and to learn from those experiences. Then when we've done everything we're chosen to do, we go back to spirit and start again.'

Daniele looked interested. 'We choose to do things… you mean we aren't just born here randomly?'

'Not according to some of the books I read.'

'Do you believe it?'

Charlotte shrugged. 'It makes a lot more sense than anything else.'

Daniele thought for a moment. 'If you're right then the Nazis chose to start a war and kill people. Why would they want to do that?'

'I don't know, I've been trying to work that out too.' Charlotte sighed. 'Maybe good things will come out of this war.'

'Like what?'

Charlotte shrugged. 'I have no idea but then I suppose we wouldn't have that knowledge would we or it wouldn't work. I mean if we knew everything already there would be no point being here and we wouldn't learn anything from our experiences, would we?'

Daniele considered her words carefully. 'You do think they will learn something then?'

Charlotte shrugged again. 'I suppose so, perhaps they will learn that hating people for being another race is pointless as we're all the same underneath, a spirit who have taken life in a body.'

There was a long silence and Charlotte smiled to herself. If the Gestapo were really listening to them or Daniele was a plant that should give them something to think about.

'Then dying isn't so bad, is it?' Daniele suddenly smiled. 'I mean it's not the end of life, it's the beginning. We are going home so we can carry on living. And when we come back again the world will be a better place because all this will have taught people so many lessons.'

Charlotte stared across the cell as she considered Daniele's thoughts and then wondered if she was dying. She could swear there was a light around Daniele that hadn't been there earlier.

****

London

Anthony finished writing the letter, sat back, lit a cigarette and began reading it through. There was probably little chance of Charlotte still being alive and even if she was, she was unlikely to survive the war, but if she did and he didn't, he wanted to make sure she knew everything he knew at this moment, before he left the country. He had made all the preparations and he and Madeline were due to fly to France the following day. He knew it was madness, but he needed to make some attempt to find out what had happened. The idea of writing to Charlotte had only occurred to him that morning when he was trying to work out how to make sure the reason for his actions weren't misconstrued. If Simon had betrayed them all then someone needed to know.

He finished reading, placed the letter in an envelope and wrote Charlotte's name on it. He would leave this with Adrian with instructions to open it if he had definite proof of his daughter's death.

****

Ravensbrück Concentration Camp, Northern Germany

The guards shoved them inside the truck and when it was full they slammed the doors shut leaving them in darkness. There was no noise other than some sobbing and groaning and then one of the women spoke.

'Are they going to shoot us?'

'I doubt it, they won't want to waste bullets on us.'

'Then where are we going?' Another woman joined in.

'To a camp probably.'

'A camp?' Charlotte asked, forgetting her decision to remain silent.

'Concentration camp, Germany and Poland is full of them. Where have you been?' There was some sarcastic laughter and Charlotte felt Daniele move closer to her.

'I've heard about the camps but why do you think that's where we're going?'

'Because that's what they do with women they arrest, especially those they think are probably resistance or SOE, but they can't prove it. It's a way of killing us slowly, a bullet is much too quick.'

Charlotte felt Daniele's hand in hers and she squeezed it. 'We'll be alright Daniele, remember what we talked about.' She murmured. 'Dying isn't the end it's the beginning. If it's our destiny then we will learn everything we can from it.'

She felt Daniele nod her head and she wished she felt as calm as she sounded. Her conversation about spiritualism had been mainly to see if the bastards had been listening or whether Daniele was a spy. She was now sure Daniele wasn't, as there was little point sending her to a camp with them. She had been a prisoner much too long now for anything she knew to be of any use to them so they would have taken Daniele away and used her somewhere else.

A short while later the doors opened, dogs barked and guards prodded them with rifle butts until they were all were herded onto railway trucks. It was airless, crowded and the smell of their unwashed bodies filled the small space. Charlotte and Daniele somehow managed to stay together as the doors slammed shut and eventually the train moved slowly out of the station.

Charlotte closed her eyes and finally fell into a restless sleep. When she woke she had no idea how long they had been on the train but the smell was worse and the light from the slats on the side of the truck indicated there was at least one dead body on the floor. Charlotte wanted to close her eyes again but she couldn't as the train suddenly halted and then the doors were flung open. After hours of near darkness the bright light blinded her but as her vision returned she gazed around in terror. More guards, dogs barking and snapping as thousands of people poured off the train.

Charlotte stumbled out and into hell.

****

Tunis, North Africa
It was early June when Jimmy found out that he was to be recommended as a flight commander in the Coastal Defence Squadron. The irony didn't escape him as it was the Coastal Defence Squadron he had initially applied for before he'd volunteered for his second choice, Fighter Squadron.

'Flying Officer Corbin, you have notched up 450 operational flying hours which is an impressive record for any man and one you should be proud of. You are more than ready to be given command of your own squadron here in North Africa, if you wish. The other alternative is that you could return to England and take over a squadron there. Do you have any preference as to where you'd like to go?'

Jimmy had already given this some considerable thought. If he stayed in North Africa he would be part of the push up into Sicily and Italy and then into France or Germany. He didn't want to be part of the rear party entering through the *soft belly* of Europe. He wanted to lead from the front which meant being back in England so that when the time came to launch an invasion of France he would be there in the centre of the action. 'Sir, I would like to return to Britain and take up a squadron there. If you wouldn't mind?'

****

Algiers
On 6th July John watched the hot Mediterranean sun rise with its usual splendour and then glanced around at the numerous Allied craft anchored in the bay. Their break would be short, he'd just decoded the latest signals from the Allied Commander and he made the most of his Players Naval Cut cigarette, who knew when he would next have time to stand on deck and smoke in peace.

Later that day he watched the first units of the Allied Fleet move out, battleships, aircraft carriers, cruisers and destroyer were heading towards Sicily. He knew from their numerous encounters that the

Italian fleet was formidable, and he doubted they would have an easy ride.

Three days later he was surprised that they had met with so little opposition and then, despite the gales bombarding the coast the airborne troops went ashore on the south east of the island, followed quickly by the landing craft.

Cleopatra and the rest of the battle fleet continued to patrol the coast expecting the Italian Fleet to attack them at any minute but the only ship that had been attacked was the hospital ship, *Talambra* which was being bombed by enemy aircraft. She finally took a direct hit and a destroyer came along side to rescue the survivors, medical assistants and nurses, clinging to rafts and wreckage just before she sank.

Cleopatra and *Euryalus* now moved inshore to patrol the area between Catania and Messina and eventually they too came under attack from aircraft. Both light and heavy anti-aircraft guns began firing and the aeroplanes flew off but before long they were back again. Bombs crashed ahead and astern but missed the ships and eventually the aircraft flew away and silence returned. The cruisers remained patrolling the coast until dawn and then returned to the Battle Fleet where the day passed uneventfully until the evening when John reported the imminent arrival of boats heading towards them at full speed. Two enemy cruisers were later sighted by British Motor Torpedo Boats (MTB) but they were soon gone and the night passed peacefully.

****

Yelsted, Kent
Adrian looked at the letter Anthony had given him for Charlotte and wondered what was so important. At first he'd assume it was just a goodbye letter in case he didn't come home, but when Anthony had told him that he should only open it if he had definite proof of Charlotte's death, he'd realised there was something more. He was tempted to open it now but how could he explain to his daughter that he'd opened her private letter. On the other hand Charlotte was missing, presumed dead, so perhaps that was enough? But she could still be alive. Anthony obviously thought so or he wouldn't be risking his life to go to France and look for her. And if she wasn't dead and

he opened it he could cause her death. Adrian shook his head. What on earth was the matter with him, he was never superstitious. But then he'd never lost one daughter to a murderer before and now Charlotte had been arrested and was missing. He stared at the letter for several more minutes before finally making his decision.

****

45 College Road Maidstone
Jeanne watched as the latest maid disappeared up the road and sighed heavily. Rene had left to join the Women's Army leaving the room over the garage vacant again. It hadn't been that long since the previous maid, Joyce had left. She had liked Joyce and Rene but presumably they thought they could serve the country better by joining up rather than being a maid. She couldn't blame them, she was sure their wages of 7s and 6d per week were much less than they could earn in the army. Although they wouldn't have Wednesday afternoons and Sundays off to visit their families. More importantly though it meant she might have more freedom as it was part of their job to look after her. Her mother seemed to have recovered from her nerves now and was very busy outside the home, involved with the Conservative Association, the Mother's Union and the Women's Institute, so it was good they still had their cleaning woman or she might have had to do more. At least the bombing had stopped now and most of the evacuees had gone back to London, so maybe the war would soon be over.

****

Off Sicily
Two days later John picked up a submarine on the radar. It hadn't seen *Cleopatra,* but the alarm went out, submarine to port and the destroyers began the attack with a star shell to illuminate her in the darkness. She began to crash dive but it was too late, the destroyers began dropping depth charges and as dawn lit up the sky she took a direct hit, broke the surface and *HMS Echo* managed to save a few survivors before she sank beneath the waves.

Five days later, after repeated orders to refuel in Malta had been changed at the last minute, the crew were making for the bathrooms when the ship suddenly shuddered and rocked. There had been a massive explosion on the starboard side. They had been torpedoed. A huge cloud of black smoke interlaced with red flashes of flames billowed high above them. The steel plates on the bulkheads buckled, oil gushed high above the bridge before cascading back down again onto the deck, the lighting failed and the ship began listing heavily.

For a few seconds the crew were shocked and stunned, then their training kicked in, repair parties checked damage, men set to rescuing those trapped below and the rest of the crew waited on deck for further orders. With *Euryalus* protecting them they were able to make their way to Malta at a speed of ten knots.

John checked the radio room, there was little in the way of damage. 'Go and check on the damage.' He turned his attention to the radio and began tapping a request for help.

Chris dragged himself out of his shock and headed out of the radio room, but he didn't get very far. The torpedo had hit the ship between the forward engine room and boiler room, and it was obvious there were no survivors among the twisted and buckled steel. He made his way up on deck where he spoke to one of the crew. 'I need a damage report for the radio room.'

'The ratings in the flats have been injured by the blast and from burning oil, some of which has burst through the upper deck vents and injured the men working the guns.' The crew member shouted back above the chaos. Chris took another quick glance around and hurried back downstairs where he began outlining what he'd seen.

'Jesus...' John was horrified.

'Apparently it could have been worse.' Chris was pale in the half light. He took a breath and repeated what the crewman had told him. 'The engine room branch managed to get control of the fires below quite quickly, despite being in shock those in the next engine room remained on their station and the ship was almost immediately under way again. They don't know what damage we've sustained under the water line, we'll have to wait until we get to Malta to find out.' He took another breath and continued. 'The upper deck's a bloody mess, the plates are buckled, one leg of the tripod mast has been wrenched out of the deck and we've lost the motor boat. It was blasted from its moorings and lost over the side.'

John finished sending and turned back to him 'What about the injured?'

'They've been dealt with the first aid parties, they wiped the oil and fuel off and covered them in anti-burn jelly. The medical officers are working flat out with help from the cooks. The lights are working again thanks to the torpedo party, there are men clearing the deck to stabilise the ship.' He fell silent, his face still showing the shock of what he'd seen.

The funeral was at 10.30hrs. Twenty-one ratings and one Engineer Officer were missing, presumed killed, and a further twenty four ratings were injured – one very seriously. Despite medical attention, the Royal Marine bandsman died from his injuries and was also buried at sea that day. John stood to attention as the last of the bodies was dispatched overboard and waited while the Captain finished the service, his thoughts with his colleagues and his own survival.

Somehow, he had made it through again, but the war was far from over. How much longer would his luck hold out?

Epilogue

1955

Jimmy's medals

Jimmy's DFC

Chapter 45

Maidstone, Kent

Jimmy sat quietly and thought about the past few years. He couldn't believe he was finally going to be married. His love life had been unsuccessful to say the least. Madeline had disappeared without a trace. Having not heard from her since the end of 1942 he had wasted no time in trying to find her when he returned to England in the summer of 1943. Maidstone had seemed small and parochial, the house on Bower Street claustrophobic after being in the RAF. But he had used his leave to try and find the love of his life, but there was no trace of her. If he hadn't still had her letters he would have begun to wonder if he'd imagined her. That wasn't his only disappointment, instead of being posted to an operational squadron so he could lead the assault on France, he was sent to RAF Eshott in Northumberland to become an instructor at an operational training unit. The most interesting event while he'd been there was to see his name in the *Daily Telegraph*, recipient of the Distinguished Flying Cross for his services in North Africa. Bobby Oxspring had mentioned he was going to put his name forward, but with the disappointment over not getting a front line squadron and Madeline disappearing, Jimmy had forgotten all about it. Lilly had attended Buckingham Palace with him while George VI presented him with the medal. It was an intensely moving ceremony and Jimmy felt very proud to be singled out and awarded such a prestigious medal.

After that he had returned to Northumberland, but it was a world away from North Africa and he was soon bored, a feeling that intensified when he wasn't given a squadron to help liberate Europe. Instead, he was posted to 11 Armament Practice Camp at Fairwood Common near Swansea and, although he had never given up hope that Madeline might get back in touch, he finally came to accept that she had gone from his life. He dated a few other girls, but none had any effect on him until he met Joan, a slim attractive Flying Officer at Fairwood. After several dates he finally realised that he was over Madeline. He would always wonder what had happened to her, but he no longer spent every waking hour thinking about her.

When the war ended so did Jimmy's service as a volunteer reservist in the RAF. It didn't take him to long to decide that rather than return to teaching he wanted to stay in, so he applied for a commission. To his delight he had been accepted but then he'd told Joan and she'd said she didn't want to be married to a pilot so in January 1946 he had resigned his commission and become plain Jimmy Corbin once again. A few months later Joan told him she had found someone else. After the initial shock wore off Jimmy came to the conclusion that he was never going to be married. He had wasted the opportunity to ask Madeline and she'd disappeared and then he'd given up the RAF for Joan, but she had still left him.

Then everything had changed. Jeanne had come into his life. His best friend, Alf McDermott, was supposed to have been meeting a girl on a blind date at the Queen's Head pub, Jimmy's local. But he had been unable to make it so had asked Jimmy to go in his place and apologise. Jimmy had turned up expecting to meet the girl, apologise and then leave but he had taken one look at her, a tall slim graceful girl with her hair piled on her head in the fashion of the day, and suddenly Jimmy was head over heels in love. He hurried over to her and within minutes Madeline and Joan had been relegated to the long and distant past where they belonged. Determined not to lose out this time Jimmy had wasted little time in taking his courage in both hands and proposed. To his delight she had accepted, the next six months had flown by and they were getting married the following day. He couldn't wait.

****

Maidstone, Kent

Kristian lay on the bed and stared up at the ceiling. It was so strange being back in Maidstone after all those years. Coming back there had reminded him of things he thought were long forgotten. But he could still remember everything about that time, especially that poor girl's death. He wondered if the boy who'd done it had ever been caught. Or the spy? He frowned. For some reason he had forgotten that part. From what he could remember a spy had also apparently parachuted in the same night he had been shot down and had then disappeared because they had asked his father to try and find out who it was. Kristian sighed. There were so many things he wanted to ask his uncle. Over the years he had made a mental list of all the things that were puzzling him and he couldn't wait to get some answers.

He turned over and sighed. If only his parents had survived his father might have had some of the answers. But even worse was the loss of Ulrike and Manfred. He had searched everywhere after his release from the Soviet Union, but the trail was cold then and he was left with the conclusion that not only had the Gestapo arrested and killed his parents they had done the same to his wife. However, they were not known to kill children, so he had hung on to the hope that his son had somehow survived, maybe had even been adopted by another family. Sadly the chances of finding him were virtually nil. Most records had been lost during the bombing of Berlin or destroyed deliberately. If there was anything left it would be in the east and he daren't risk going back into Soviet run territory. He could never cope with more years of captivity. He had only just survived the years he had spent in their gulags. He would have to accept they were gone and try and start a new life, which was why he'd come to England.

****

Yelsted, Kent

Adrian watched Charlotte getting ready to go to work at the hotel for the wedding the following day and felt uneasy. She had changed so much he hardly recognised her. Not physically, she had soon regained her weight and strength after she'd arrived home, but mentally she was a different person. Not that he didn't understand why, he'd seen the newsreel of the camps and to think his daughter had somehow survived such horror and brutality still amazed him and he thanked God every day for her survival. He thought back to the letter Anthony had left for her and, not for the first time, wondered what it had said. Charlotte had never told him and even though he had searched for it when she wasn't there, he had never found it. He should have taken his opportunity and opened it back in 1943.

He also wondered where Anthony was, especially as it was thanks to him that Charlotte had come home. Anthony had apparently searched Europe for Charlotte after the end of the war and eventually found her in a refugee camp, but almost immediately after bringing her home he had disappeared and he had never found out why. It was years since they'd heard from him. Even now Adrian didn't understand why Charlotte hadn't told the authorities in the refugee camp who she was and asked them to arrange her passage home.

Adrian had tried asking her, but Charlotte had just shrugged and said she didn't know. He knew he should be grateful his daughter was back home when so many had died, but she was such a different person now, so brittle and on edge that he couldn't stop worrying about her.

Charlotte watched her father out of the corner of her eye and wished she could explain everything to him. She knew he was worried but first she had something to do and until she'd finished that she couldn't tell him anything or she was sure he would try and stop her. Her eyes narrowed. She could hardly believe she was finally going to avenge Rebecca. It had taken so many years to find out the truth, the name of the pilot who had bailed out over Kent, the people who had helped him escape the country and the lies that had been told to cover up his existence. But she'd got there eventually and now she would confront him. There had been so many times she believed he had died but then her prayers had suddenly been answered. She had learned quite quickly that his parents had been killed by the Gestapo, for treason, but that they had not arrested the pilot because he had been in the Soviet Union and they had left it too late. Well tomorrow he would meet his destiny and so would those who had helped him escape. It would be a breach of the Official Secrets Act that she had signed, but she didn't care. The only thing that was important was to keep her promise to Rebecca.

****

Maidstone, Kent

Jeanne sat down in front of her dressing table, gazed into the mirror and smiled at her reflection. She would be Mrs Jimmy Corbin tomorrow and she was so excited she could barely breathe. She would never sleep tonight, she was much too excited and she wondered if Jimmy felt the same.

Jimmy was a war hero, a Spitfire pilot who had fought the Nazis and been awarded a DFC. He was so brave and funny and she couldn't understand what he saw in her. She had spent the war hiding in the Anderson shelter or visiting her aunt in Mortimer, Berkshire with her mother to get away from the bombing. At least her father had been in the Home Guard, and he'd fought in the First World War too, so he wasn't overwhelmed by her future husband.

Jeanne's smile widened. Her parents both loved Jimmy thank goodness, it would have been awful if they hadn't approved, something they had both feared because he was older than her. But they needn't have worried. Jimmy's credentials as a teacher, first Collier Road School and now Maidstone Technical School where he'd not only been a pupil himself, but a laboratory assistant while training to be a teacher, had been more than enough for them to ignore the age gap.

'Hope you're ready for bed Jeanne, you've got a busy day ahead.'

'Yes Mum. Just about to turn the light out.' Jeanne shook her head. She would be a married woman tomorrow and her mother was still treating her like a child!

****

Maidstone, Kent

Anthony arrived at the hotel, quickly booked in and headed up to his room. He had hoped to get there much earlier so he could speak to Frederick before the wedding, but he had been held up in Dover.

He had made all the other arrangements so everything would happen at the reception. That was rather unfortunate but couldn't be changed now. Hopefully it wouldn't ruin the day for Jimmy and Jeanne, but this was much too important to wait any longer. If everything went as he expected he would be in considerable trouble, breaching the Official Secrets Act wasn't something to be done lightly, especially as the death penalty applied in cases of treason. But he was convinced he was doing the right thing and that what was about to happen wasn't treason, although some people might see it differently. The time for secrecy was over, in his opinion anyway. If he didn't make everything public, dealt with this in private, through the chain of command, there was a real danger it would get swept under the carpet. Too many people would be embarrassed by what was going to happen, but he didn't care. He owed it to all those who had died to see justice served and if it meant the end of his career, arrest and prison, even death, he no longer cared.

His thoughts turned to Charlotte. He had been convinced he'd seen her on the ferry coming across the Channel, but he hadn't been able to get close enough to be sure and when the ferry finally docked he was too busy to look for her. But he was sure everything was going to plan and soon he would see her again. But first he had to make sure the final pieces of the jigsaw puzzle were in place.

****

London

'I'm really not sure this is a good idea, Madeline.' Peregrine glanced at Johanna for support, but she was staring down at her nails and saying nothing.

'Its really important we put all this behind us and the wedding is the only place where they will all be at the same time. Anthony has spent a lot of time arranging this, there's no going back now.'

'But it's *his* wedding Madeline. Surely you could at least wait until after the ceremony. Or is this some kind of revenge for him marrying someone else?'

Madeline frowned. 'I'm not a complete idiot Dad, nor am I that insensitive. I don't want to ruin Jimmy's wedding, I wish him nothing but happiness, he deserves it. I don't love him anymore, not in the way you are thinking of anyway and I truly want him to be happy with Jeanne. She seems a lovely girl and perfect for him. If I could do it another way I would. Unfortunately, this was the perfect opportunity because they will all be there and none of them will be suspicious. But of course, it's not going to be during the actual wedding. I'll be waiting until the reception.'

'I'm surprised you know where the reception is being held?' Peregrine started before realising what a stupid remark it was, given how their daughter had spent the war and the work she was still doing.

'I think Madeline is right.' Johanna raised her eyes to him and suddenly interjected. 'It's time all this came out into the open.' She turned to Madeline. 'Do you want us to be there too?'

'Yes.' Madeline gave a cold smile. 'Like the Colonel, you're where it all started.'

Chapter 46

'Well Mrs Corbin. How do you feel?'

'I feel wonderful Mr Corbin.' Jeanne kissed him passionately. 'At least we can relax now.' Jimmy opened the back door of the Alf's car, and she climbed in. Once seated he closed the door and walked around the other side. Like Jeanne he was glad the formal ceremony was over and that now, after all his concerns that he was somehow jinxed in love, he was finally married. He felt in his top pocket and smiled, he had been unable to resist bringing the champagne cork with him.

'What's that?'

Jimmy grinned. 'If I tell you you'll laugh.'

'No I won't. I promise!'

Jimmy repeated the story of the champagne cork and Jeanne listened with a rapt expression on her face. 'I suppose I should be glad you didn't bring the propellor as well!'

Jimmy laughed. 'It sounds ridiculous, but I genuinely feel it has kept me safe throughout the war.'

'But we're not at war now Darling.' Jeanne held out her hand. 'Why don't you put it in my handbag, it will be more comfortable for you.' She saw his hesitation. 'I won't lose it I promise.'

'Alright, just see you don't!' He handed it over and watched as she placed it carefully inside.

'There you are, perfectly safe.'

Jimmy leant towards her, his lips on hers and Jeanne forgot all about her bag, the reception, everything except the feel of him against her.

A few minutes later they arrived at the Royal Star Hotel, the car stopped and they moved reluctantly apart.

'This way Mr and Mrs Corbin.' Alf hurried to open the door, Jimmy helped her out and they walked into the hotel. Alf closed the door and then frowned.

'Jeanne…!' The driver stared after them in frustration. 'You've forgotten your bag…' He watched the doors close behind them, then shrugged, picked up the bag and headed towards the hotel. He would leave it with the hotel staff, she could collect it later.

****

John escorted Elsie and the children into the large reception room and they made his way to the table with their names on. 'Sit down children, dinner will be a little while so be on your best behaviour alright?' He smiled at Rodney and Sally, lit one of his favourite Players Navy Cut cigarettes and thought back to his own wedding. It all seemed such a long while ago now, even the war seemed an age away. Life in the Ministry of Labour was nothing like as exciting but at least he was no longer away from his family as much. He glanced around the room, raised his hand briefly to Jimmy and then turned back to the door to see who else was arriving.

****

Frederick handed Ruth a glass of champagne and made sure she was comfortable.

'You fuss too much Frederick.'

He smiled. 'I'm so pleased you decided to come to the wedding.'

Ruth sighed. 'I keep telling myself I can't mourn Geoffrey for ever, but its not true. I think if I'd been told when he had died instead of waiting until the end of the war, expecting him to come home and then finding out he'd died in 1942.' She sipped her drink and shook her head. 'I'm sorry. I know you don't want to keep hearing this.'

'You know you can always talk to me Ruth.'

'But not on your daughter's wedding day. Go and see to your other guests, I'm fine I promise.' She watched him go then stared down at her drink and thought back to her own wedding, a day filled with such promise until the war destroyed it all. She had been out to Sumatra in the hope of trying to find out something about her husband's final months, but it hadn't helped. If anything it had made things worse knowing how he had suffered and how no one seemed to care about punishing those who were guilty. Japan seemed to have escaped any real censure. Some of the top men were executed but the rest went home and continued with their lives as if nothing had happened and that was what she couldn't forgive. If those who had treated her husband and the other POWs had been penalised in some way she might have been able to get over it, but the thought they had escaped any real punishment was eating away at her.

Frederick wandered over to Betty and Margaret who were sitting with Margaret's husband Keith Sharp. 'Hello girls, can you go and talk to your Aunty Ruth, I think she's feeling a bit sad.'

They exchanged glances and he sighed. 'Yes, I know what you think but this must be very difficult for her. We're all here with our husbands and wives and Geoffrey isn't here.'

'She's not the only one to lose someone in the war…' Margaret began…

'But she spent the whole war thinking he was alive only to find out months after it finished that he'd died years earlier.' Frederick interrupted.

'You're right.' Margaret flushed. 'I'll make sure she's alright Dad. You go and enjoy yourself. Its Jeanne's wedding, two down only Betty to go!' She winked at him and made her way over to Ruth.

****

Jeanne sipped her wine and raised the glass to the numerous guests trickling into the large reception room. 'I'm so pleased all our friends were able to come. It…' She fell silent, an expression of surprise on her face.

Jimmy glanced at her, waiting for her to finish, but she was staring at the double doors at the far end of the room, the surprise turning to bemusement. Jimmy turned his face to see who she was looking at and saw a tall blonde-haired man in conversation with a darker haired man entering the room. Once inside the tall blonde man stopped and began slowly scanning the room.

'Obviously he's one of yours as I don't recognise him…' Jimmy began before he realised she wasn't paying attention.

Jeanne stood up and he watched as she walked slowly towards the blonde haired man. 'You're Olaf aren't you?'

The man smiled at her. 'Hello Jeanne. You have grown up since the last time we met. I am so sorry to gate crash your wedding.'

'Don't be silly. Its amazing to see you again.' Jeanne stopped and glanced around for Margaret before remembering her sister was married now so she might not be too pleased to see him. She turned back but Olaf was no longer paying her any attention. He was smiling at her father.

'Kristian? Frederick stared at him in total disbelief. 'Is it really you?'

'Yes it is. I found him in Berlin.' The darker haired man smiled at him. 'You asked me to look and I told you if he was still alive I'd find him.'

Frederick shook his hand, 'Thank you so much Anthony. I can't believe it.' He turned back to Kristian, stepped towards him and engulfed him in a hug. 'I am so pleased you survived the war.' He fought back a sudden surge of emotion. 'And your father?'

Kristian shook his head. 'No, the Gestapo arrested him and my mother. They would have taken me too, but I was in the Soviet Union. Sadly, Ulrike and Manfred are also gone.' He suddenly realised they were the centre of attention and not everyone was looking happy.

Frederick was seemingly unaware of the animosity around him. He ignored the growing anger and announced proudly, 'this is my nephew Kristian and yes, he's German, but he spent the war spying for us and sending us valuable information.'

'No, he's not, he's a murdering bastard. He killed my sister.'

****

Jeanne spun around in shock and saw one of the waitresses pointing a pistol at Olaf or Kristian, whatever his name was. Frederick saw her at the same time and moved in front of Kristian who was staring at her in shock. It was the lady who had been so kind to him on the ship.

'No, he didn't kill anyone, I swear it.' Frederick swallowed nervously and tried to keep her attention. He was aware of Anthony moving slowly around them and he knew he needed to keep talking. 'You must be Charlotte. Rebecca was your twin sister?'

'And this bastard dropped out of his plane after bombing us and strangled her. She was just walking in the woods, she wasn't a threat...' Her voice broke, Charlotte raised the pistol and her finger tightened on the trigger. 'Get out of the way or I'll shoot you too. I've waited a long time for this.'

'Charlotte, he's telling the truth. This man had nothing to do with your sister's death, but he did see the man who did it.'

Kristian stepped out from behind Frederick. 'She was with a young man, they were arguing. I think he wouldn't take no for an answer, so he hit her. I don't think he meant to kill her...' Kristian couldn't think of anything else to say.

Charlotte glared at him. 'How do I know you're telling the truth?'

'I am, I would never have come back to this country if I had killed her.'

'Then why didn't you tell someone what you'd seen?'

'He did. He told me and I believed him.' Frederick interjected, ignoring the collective gasp that echoed around the room. 'Kristian's father was a spy for us, long before the war started, and he gave Kristian my address in case he ever needed it. Well, that night he did. He was shot down and he came to me. He wanted to tell the police about the man who killed your sister, but we didn't think they would believe him. I talked him out of telling the police, so if you want to blame anyone blame me.' Frederick remembered much too late that this was all top secret and he was now liable to be arrested for breaching the Official Secrets Act.

Charlotte's eyes narrowed. 'So, you helped him escape?'

Frederick pulled his attention back to the present and was about to answer when Fred Corben interrupted. 'Did you help the spy escape too?' Fred was standing close to him, fury on his face.

Frederick looked at him in surprise and was about to answer when another voice spoke. 'No, he didn't help the spy escape because no one knew who it was. They were all looking for a man, not a woman.'

Frederick stared at her in disbelief, and he didn't seem to be the only one. Charlotte had spun around and was now aiming her pistol at Madeline instead. 'You were spying for the Nazis?'

'I was briefly but I stopped after only sending a couple of messages.' She looked at Fred who reluctantly nodded.

'Yes, she only sent two messages and then she went quiet. We didn't know why.'

'No wonder you stopped writing to me. Wasn't I giving you enough information?' Jimmy had only been vaguely interested in the accusations flying around until Madeline had stepped out of the shadows. He had been so shocked it had taken him a few moments to speak.

'Hello Jimmy. No, you didn't give me anything. If you think back to our conversations you'll remember that I never asked you about anything important. By the time I met you I was having second thoughts and you finally changed my mind completely.'

'How did he do that?' Jeanne spoke before Jimmy could answer.

Madeline smiled. 'He didn't do anything. I fell in love with him. I was stupid enough to think I could marry him and disappear, but my masters had other ideas. They threatened to take me back to Germany but that would have compromised everything so we came up with another plan, to make them trust me again. That's where you came in Charlotte.' She glanced at Anthony who continued.

'There's a lot we can't tell you but suffice to say that Madeline could not have done more than she did to ensure the Nazis lost the war. Unlike some other people.' Anthony suddenly pulled out a pistol and aimed it at the man who had just arrived. 'If you want someone to blame for your arrest Charlotte then that's him. He told Madeline that she was betraying a communist network, but he had already betrayed you to his Nazi masters, her message was confirmation it was safe to pick you up. He betrayed Kristian and his father, and he also knew who had killed your sister. He tried to cover that up, not to protect Kristian but to protect his own involvement in helping Madeline go to ground. Frederick gave him the perfect opportunity to have everyone wasting their time, running around looking for a pilot he'd already helped escape the country. Once he'd found out about your father Kristian, he was able to let his superiors know they had a British agent in their inner circle. Otto became a dead man.'

Colonel Sinclair began to back towards the door, but Charlotte was too quick for him. 'I don't think so Colonel.' She gave him a cold smile then spoke to Anthony. 'I didn't think you were going to make it.'

'Sorry, I had something else to do.' He pointed towards the door as Madeline's parents entered. 'This is Johanna and Peregrine Thompkin-Cartwright. Sinclair persuaded them to leave their daughter in Germany so she could be trained as a spy for Germany. She believed her mother was dead and that the British Secret Service had killed her. She was told her father had gone back to England to spy for Germany and she would do the same when she was older. Peregrine was in fact a double agent sending the Germans the information Colonel Sinclair was giving him, but of course Colonel Sinclair was also a double agent so much of what Peregrine was sending was extremely important intelligence, at least it was until the middle of 1941. It wasn't until 1943 that all the pieces came together thanks to Madeline's bravery in deciding she would no longer spy for the Nazis.' He smiled at Colonel Sinclair who was sweating and eyeing Charlotte cautiously. 'There's no need to rush away Simon. Charlotte is a very good shot by the way, she won't miss.'

Everyone was staring at the Colonel, but it was Fred that finally spoke. 'You're a German agent?'

'No.' Anthony answered before anyone could say anything. 'Actually, Colonel Sinclair is working for the Soviets and has been for many years, hence the fact that he was actually helping the Nazis until they invaded the Soviet Union in 1941.'

There was a collective gasp from those near enough to hear the conversation. 'The Soviets?' Fred eventually managed.

'Yes. The real reason he persuaded Peregrine to leave his daughter in Germany, was not so she could spy for the Nazis, but so that he could use her information to give to the Soviets. The last thing he expected was for her to turn up here in the middle of the war.'

'But why didn't Stalin take notice of his warning about Operation Barbarossa?'

'Because he was too arrogant. He received warnings from several people but still took no notice. And by the time the Japanese attacked Pearl Harbour it suited the Soviets to help us to defeat Hitler, so for a short while our interests were aligned which made it easier for him.' Anthony glanced at his watch. 'And just in case you were considering denying this Simon I've someone else I want you to meet.'

As he spoke a middle aged woman and a young man walked slowly through the doors, their eyes darting around searching for the man they had told would be there. He smiled at Kristian. 'I think you've been looking for each other?'

Kristian had been watching them walk towards him and he paled, his eyes met Anthony's who nodded. Kristian returned his gaze to the two people and he finally stuttered, 'Ulrike? Manfred?'

'They were in the east, it's taken me quite a lot of bargaining to get them out so...' Anthony stopped and smiled. Kristian and Ulrike were hugging, tears falling down both their faces. 'When Frederick asked me to try and find you I thought I would also look for your wife and child.' He realised they weren't paying him any attention so he spoke to Jimmy and Jeanne instead. 'I'm really sorry to have interrupted your wedding, but it was the only place we knew everyone would be and we needed to make sure no one wriggled out of their crimes.' He glanced back at Colonel Sinclair and gave a cold smile.

'By the way Simon, Ulrike has been working for the Stasi. Its mainly thanks to her that we have more than enough proof to charge you with treason, so don't bother wasting everyone's time by lying. With her evidence and that of Peregrine, Johanna and Madeline you'll be swinging from a rope before very soon. I hope it was worth it.'

Simon smiled as he allowed the two policemen to place handcuffs on him. It was a shock to be caught, especially as he'd had no idea anyone even suspected him. But the game wasn't over yet. He wasn't the only person hidden in plain sight that they needed to worry about, perhaps he could make some kind of deal.

Chapter 47

Jimmy was still in shock that Madeline had been a spy. Thank goodness he'd spent most of the time they were together training pilots so he didn't need to worry about having given anything away. He glanced at Jeanne, suddenly worrying about how she would react to Madeline attending his wedding, but instead she was watching the Colonel being arrested.

Anthony patted him on the back. 'Go and enjoy your wedding... oh, your wife left this in the car. Your best man gave it to me.' He handed Jeanne's handbag to Jimmy. Jimmy thanked him and was already walking back to his wife, wondering how he could explain about Madeline, when he suddenly remembered the champagne cork. He looked inside, shook his head and smiled. It was still there. Everything was going to be just fine.

****

Anthony watched Jimmy walking back to Jeanne then noticed Fred standing aloof, watching the Colonel being escorted from the hotel, his face expressionless and walked over to him. 'I'm really sorry Fred. I know this must have been a shock. I wanted to bring you in on it, but we were concerned you might be too close to Sinclair.'

Fred ignored the implication that he might have betrayed them to Sinclair and asked the question he most wanted an answer to. 'How long have you been suspicious of him?'

'Back in 1943 after Charlotte was arrested. Madeline has been working with me ever since and once we rescued Charlotte from Ravensbrück we all worked together. Did you ever suspect him?'

Fred shrugged. 'I began to wonder after some of the really good intelligence we were supplying didn't seem to have been getting the right results, but it appeared to be the minister who was the spy ... if there was one and it wasn't just a series of random events. I would never have suspected him of being a Russian spy though.' He shook his head. 'I'm so sorry I didn't see it.'

'If you had no one would have believed you Fred. He was much too clever for that; he would probably have found some way of making it look like that you were spying for Germany. He would not have wanted to suggest a Soviet spy for obvious reasons. Given the amount of power he had you could have ended up being executed for treason, so don't blame yourself.'

'Was he responsible for many deaths?' Fred was finding it hard to leave it alone. 'I was supposed to be helping the war effort not aiding the enemy, even if it was by ignorance.'

'Forget about it, Fred, that's an order. You did sterling work, broke up numerous German missions, helped break the Army codes that enabled Monty to win El Alamein amongst other things and saved God knows how many people. You have absolutely nothing to reproach yourself for.' Anthony saw he wasn't getting through, and he wondered how he could make this man see that he was a hero, not a failure. Then he had a brain wave. 'In fact you should be very proud of yourself. Just think how furious Sinclair must have been when he discovered just how good you were at your job. He had to pass most of your information on or people would have become suspicious. He was working against himself; he would have hated it!' He smiled and patted Fred on the back. 'You did a wonderful job Fred. Go and celebrate your nephew in law's wedding and congratulate yourself on everything you did to save Britain!'

Fred considered his words for a few moments then he nodded. 'I suppose you're right. Thank you, Lt Colonel Hallett.'

'Anthony please.'

Fred smiled. 'Anthony. I'm just glad you got him in the end.' He was about to say more when Daisy Irene took his arm.

'Come on Fred, whatever was going on has finished now. We have a wedding to celebrate!'

Anthony smiled at Madeline who winked. It had taken her a while to persuade Mr Corben's wife to intervene but the quicker they returned to normal the sooner she could leave. She would rather not be arrested if possible, so she was only staying in case Jimmy wanted to speak to her. She didn't think he would, but she felt she owed it to him to explain why she had just disappeared.

****

'I'm so sorry about Madeline turning up…' Jimmy didn't get any further.

Jeanne interrupted. 'I think she's the least of it. I can't believe we had a German pilot hiding in our house during the war. Not to mention that my father was working for a Russian spy!'

'So was my uncle.' Jimmy grinned. 'This has been some wedding!' He was about to say more when Frederick appeared looking apologetic.

'I'm so sorry Love, but he was my nephew, son of my half-brother, someone I knew was helping us so I couldn't leave him to get arrested. At that time he would never have been believed.' Frederick put his arm around her and looked at Jimmy. 'I'm so sorry this has ruined your wedding.'

Jeanne glanced at Jimmy who shrugged and smiled back at her. Jeanne grinned and turned to her father. 'You don't have to apologise. Apart from the fact you had no idea any of this was going to happen, we don't think it's been ruined at all. Its been totally unique and we'll always remember it. After all, no one else can boast of a major Russian spy being arrested at their wedding or meeting a German cousin who was also spying for Britain and who was hiding in their house during the war. We should be able to dine out on this for years!'

****

Madeline watched Jimmy and Jeanne laughing with her father and smiled. She glanced across at her parents and moved towards then. They headed out of the door and headed to their car. It was time they went home.

Out of the corner of her eye Madeline was vaguely aware of the Colonel climbing into the back of a car, and then suddenly shots rang out. Instinctively she threw herself to the ground and reached for her weapon, but she remembered too late that wasn't armed. Anthony came flying out of the hotel, Charlotte close behind, more shots followed, the Colonel fell to the floor, blood pouring from his chest.

Madeline forgot the danger and rushed over to him. He couldn't die, not yet, not until he'd been tried and found guilty. He opened his eyes and smiled at her. 'Sorry Madeline. Looks like I won't be in court after all.'

'Noooo….' Her voice echoed around the now silent car park and she sat back on her heels, staring down as the man who was responsible for so many deaths passed peacefully away.

The End

Jimmy and Jeanne on their wedding day March 1955

Hunting Shadows
A Family's War

The REAL family

The name Corbin arrived in England with the Norman Conquest of 1066. There is no record of the name in England before this. We know from the Battle Roll (a list of all those who served with William the Conqueror, that was kept at Battle Abbey in Sussex) that during William's invasion of England, the following four Corbins were present: Philip Corbin, Nicholas Corbin, Robert Corbin, Margaret Corbin.

Surnames were first introduced into general use in England by the Norman barons soon after 1066 in order that they could control and administer personal tax collection. Our name was recorded as 'Corbin' in the Domesday Book of 1086 in both Warwickshire and Kent.

We are very likely to be direct descendants of one Robert Corbyn, who is recorded to have established Corbyn Hall at Kingswinford in Staffordshire, England around 1080. The next mention of the Corbin name is Robert's great-grandson, who gave land to the Abbey of Talesworth, between 1154-1161, in the reign of Henry II, of England – a great act of charity. The name has had several spellings over its history, Corbin, Corben, Corban, and Corbyn.

The Corbin family lived in Staffordshire at Kingswinford, just west of Birmingham, for around 380 years until around 1460ish, then moved to Halls End at Polesworth, Warwickshire where they lived until 1652.

The oldest descendent we are sure of is William Corbin (1380-1430). He was our 16th great grandfather. William was born and died in Staffordshire, probably at Kingswinford. He married Margery Blunt in 1398. His son, John (1398-1460), married twice, Katherine in 1416 and then Elizabeth Everden in 1430. His grandson, Lord Thomas Corbyn, also lived at Kingswinford and married Joanne Holbach, a wealthy heiress, in 1500.

Thomas's son, Lord Nicolas (1475-1553), our 13th great grandfather, married Johanna Sturry, who was the heir to William

Sturry. They had three children Richard, Alice and Leonard. This inheritance included the Polesworth estate.

Nicolas, who lived until he was 78, moved the family to Halls End to establish the family in the Polesworth estate, a distance of 35 miles from Corbyn Hall and to the east of Birmingham.

Nicolas's son, Lord Richard (1490-1535) had five children. He married his wife at the age of fifty eight. The eldest son, Lord Thomas, inherited the estate, land and titles.

Lord Nicolas' grandson, Richard (1525-1587), our 11th great grandfather, was the second son and therefore inherited no titles. He moved his family away from Halls End to Langton Matravers in Dorset in 1572. Our ancestors remained in Dorset until around the 1830s.

Alexander Corbin (1726- August 1762), our 5th great grandfather, died in military service aged 36. He was on the militia list for Dorset, which appears to have been a volunteer military unit. He was a stonecutter by trade. This was the time of the Seven Year's War (1756-1763), a global conflict involving all five of the great powers in Europe at the time. In August 1762 the British took Havana and western Cuba. The militia were rarely deployed overseas, and I can't find where he was killed.

James Corben (1773-1831) our 3rd great grandfather moved to Ramsgate after the family had been in Dorset for 260 years and eight generations.

His son, Thomas Corben (1816-1879), our great great grandfather, lived in Church Place, Ramsgate and was a coachman.

William Corben (1842-1915), Thomas's second son, our great grandfather, was living and working as one of three 'assistant servants' at Henry Hill's butcher shop on King Street at the age of 18 years old. Ten years later he was a butcher, married to Ann and was living in 16 Brunswick Street, Ramsgate. This was to be the family home for the next 30 years.

Walter, our grandfather moved from Ramsgate to Maidstone in about 1900.

Corbin or Corben?

William was born a **Corbin**, however in the 1871 census he and his family are recorded as *Corben* including his son Frederick.

Frederick's birth is registered as **Corbin,** as is his baptism and his marriage registration to Edith Thorpe. However, his death is registered as *Corben* and his service record shows his name as *Corben.*

Frederick was born a **Corbin** but his son Frederick W T, who married Daisy Irene (Dad's sister) was a ***Corben*** all his life. In the family bible William and his entire family, including Walter, are written as *Corben.* But Walter entered his name and his family's as **Corbin**.

Despite the various family legends, especially the one that says there was family argument, I think it no more complicated than misspellings in handwritten documents.

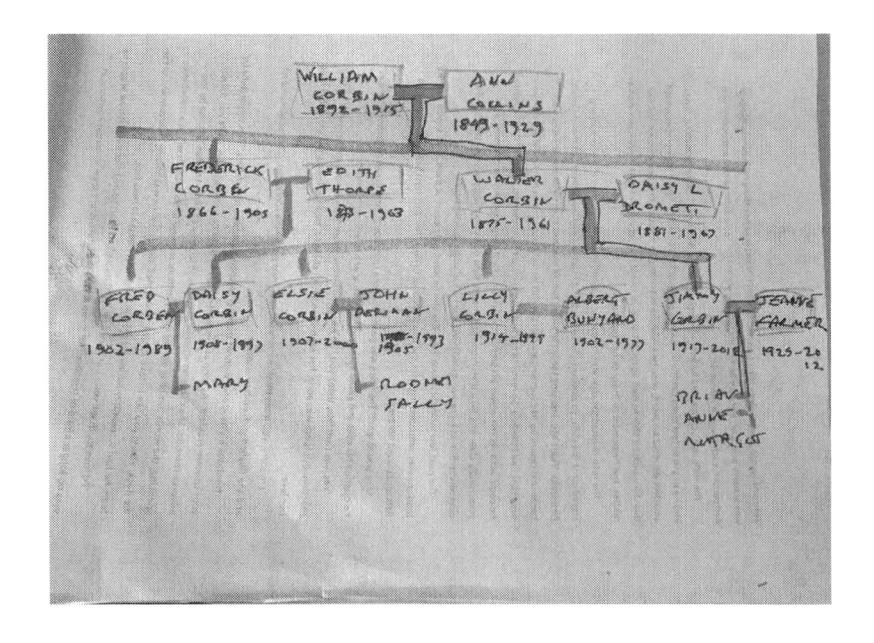

Jimmy Corbin (my dad)

Sergeant Pilot Jimmy Corbin with newly awarded 'wings' 1940.

The book follows my dad's story closely using extracts from his book *Last of the Ten Fighter Boys*.

Walter and Daisy Issie Corbin in Margate

The Corbin's lived in 133 Bower Street after Walter and Daisy Lizzie married in 1905. Walter was a builder and plumber, highly skilled in lead work. He was very strong and was known by his first name in all the pubs nearby to Bower Street. Once for a bet he climbed up the chimney of the Style and Wynch brewery carrying 3/4 ton of lead.

Jimmy Corbin was an only son with three elder sisters, Elsie, Daisy and Lilly – so he was spoilt.

Lilly, Jimmy Corbin's youngest sister in the back garden of 133 Bower Street

    He did well at school and went to a teacher training college in Highbury. He joined the volunteer reserve of the RAF in 1938 and learnt to fly at Rochester. He was mobilised as war broke out in 1939 and flew spitfires operationally in the Battle of Britain with 66 squadron and then with 72 squadron in North Africa. He accumulated over 1000 hours of operational flying and was posted to South Wales where he was 2IC of the fighter gunnery school for the rest of the war.
    He was awarded the DFC for bravery in North Africa and he tells his story in two books. *The Ten Fighter Boys* was written during the Battle of Britain and the *Last of the Ten Fighter Boys* was written later

in life. Dad was best-selling author for a week in Waterstone's in Maidstone knocking Harry Potter into second place!

Extract from London Gazette dated 27 July 1943

Distinguished Flying Cross

Flying Officer William James Corbin, Royal Air Force Volunteer Reserve, No 72 Squadron

This officer has taken part in a large number of sorties, commencing operations during the Battle of Britain, later participating in operations in occupied Europe and continuing through the North Africa Campaign. He has also taken part in many low level machine-gun attacks on enemy airfields and been responsible for the destruction of at least 2 hostile aircraft and a number of enemy transports, including 2 petrol lorries, by cannon fire. Throughout his long operational career Flying Officer Corbin has displayed keenness, courage and determination worthy of the highest praise.

After the war, Dad went back to teaching, took up golf and lived a full life. He married Mum in 1955 and they were a great couple. Well known, popular and respected in the golf club, where both were captain, the rugby club and cricket club bars.

Dad met Mum as described in the book and all the details of their wedding are correct, well nearly all…

The Corbin's at Jimmy and Jeanne's wedding. L-R Lilly, Sally, Elsie, Walter, Daisy Issie, Fred, Jeanne, Mary, Jimmy, Daisy and John at All Saints church, Maidstone, 1955.

Mum and Dad had three children, myself, Anne, who lives in Vancouver and has three offspring. Daniel and Megan, who coincidentally both get married this year, and Thomas, and Margot who lives in Mayfield with her partner Steven.

I married Belinda Tan Bee Gek in Singapore in 1989 and we have two children of whom we are immensely proud. Andrew is due to marry Ciara next year and works in insurance. His real passion is cooking. Dr Emma PhD has just joined a biotech start up and lives in Newcastle with her partner Liam.

Dad was a very social person and loved a drink. He was popular, well liked, funny, cheeky and loved putting people on edge. On 16 September 2010 Dad was honoured by being only the 13th person in history to be granted the freedom of the borough of Maidstone- unfortunately he never got to drive sheep down the high street!

Fred Corben (my uncle)

Fred Corben

Uncle Fred was my dad's sister Daisy's husband, and they were first cousins. He was born in 1902. The Victorian age had ended just the year before and Edward VII had just ascended the throne. Fred passed away when he was 77, surviving four monarchs and 25 years of Elizabeth II. He lived through a lot of change.

Frederick Corben (my great uncle)

His father was Frederick William Corbin (1866-1905), who was our Grandfather's older brother by nine years. Born in Ramsgate and baptized in St George's church, he lived his early years at 16 Brunswick Street at the family home.

He had three brothers, one of whom, George, died very young, and two sisters.

Frederick W. Corben with wife Edith Annie Thorpe

Fred's mother was Edith Annie Thorp who was seven years younger than Frederick. A local girl, born and baptised at St Luke's in Ramsgate from two local families, she married Frederick at age 22 and gave birth to Fred in 1902. She died aged 89 in Durham.

On 2nd April 1885 at the age of 18, Frederick joined the Navy where he served as a blacksmith until 8 September 1904. Service number 132312, he was described as having a fresh complexion, grey blue eyes, 5'9" tall with light brown hair. He served as a stoker until 1888, was promoted to leading and then chief stoker seven years later:

There is a note in his service history that whilst on board the Sappho he was invalided to the Navy hospital at Chatham. His service record shows his name as Corben despite his birth and death being registered as Corbin.

It seems he left the Navy in September 1904 in good health, however, four months later he was in the Medway Poor Law Union workhouse and was taken from there to a lunatic asylum where he died – causes unknown.

Uncle Fred

Uncle Fred had a tough life. His father died when he was only three years old and seven months later his mother had remarried a Tom Copeland who worked in Naval pensions. When he was six his half-brother Lionel was born and he was seven when his half-sister Olivia was born. He often said he did not care for his stepfather.

When Fred was 12 he 'joined' the Navy and his mother moved to Co Durham whilst he was left to board in a very tough naval school.

His service history shows his 1st service date being 7th January 1917 when he was 15 years old. His first ship was HMS Ganges. His service lasted until 4th November 1925. Just before he was discharged, Fred, like his father before him was invalided from the Navy hospital at Chatham. It seems this precipitated his discharge. He appears not to have participated in any significant Naval action. His first job after the navy was with the GPO at Berwick on Sea, presumably he went up there to live with his mother after leaving the Navy. He was paid 31s/week. He worked for the GPO for 35 years mostly as a senior accountant.

Fred worked for the RSS during WW2. His wife Daisy always talked about Fred being collected by a 'staff car' - unusual for a man who wasn't of senior rank. He was also paid about double the normal pay for his rank. RSS almost paid for their house in the duration of the war. They would have needed had to recruit exceptionally accurate people for code breaking. Its likely someone senior remembered him from his naval work which led to him being recruited. He was 37 when

WW2 broke out. Mary, their daughter has passed away but her husband Graham is doing well and lives in Hampshire.

Fred was always very quiet, reserved and correct. He drove all his life never having an accident.

> Telephones:
> BARNET 6500 (4 Lines)
> MILL HILL 4271 (4 Lines)
>
> P.O. BOX 25
> BARNET
> HERTS.
>
> It is with great pleasure that I forward to you the attached certificate in recognition of the valued and devoted service which you have voluntarily rendered to our Organisation during the War.
>
> This certificate is signed by Sir Herbert Creedy who, during the War years when your work was of the utmost value, was the head of the Department to which we were responsible.
>
> I would like to add my personal thanks for all you have done and for the many hours of hard work and personal self sacrifice you have contributed.
>
> Colonel,
> Controller,
> Radio Security Service.

Letter to Fred from the Controller of the RSS - note address is PO Box 25, Barnet.

CENTRAL CHANCERY OF
THE ORDERS OF KNIGHTHOOD.
ST JAMES'S PALACE. S.W.1.

Sir,

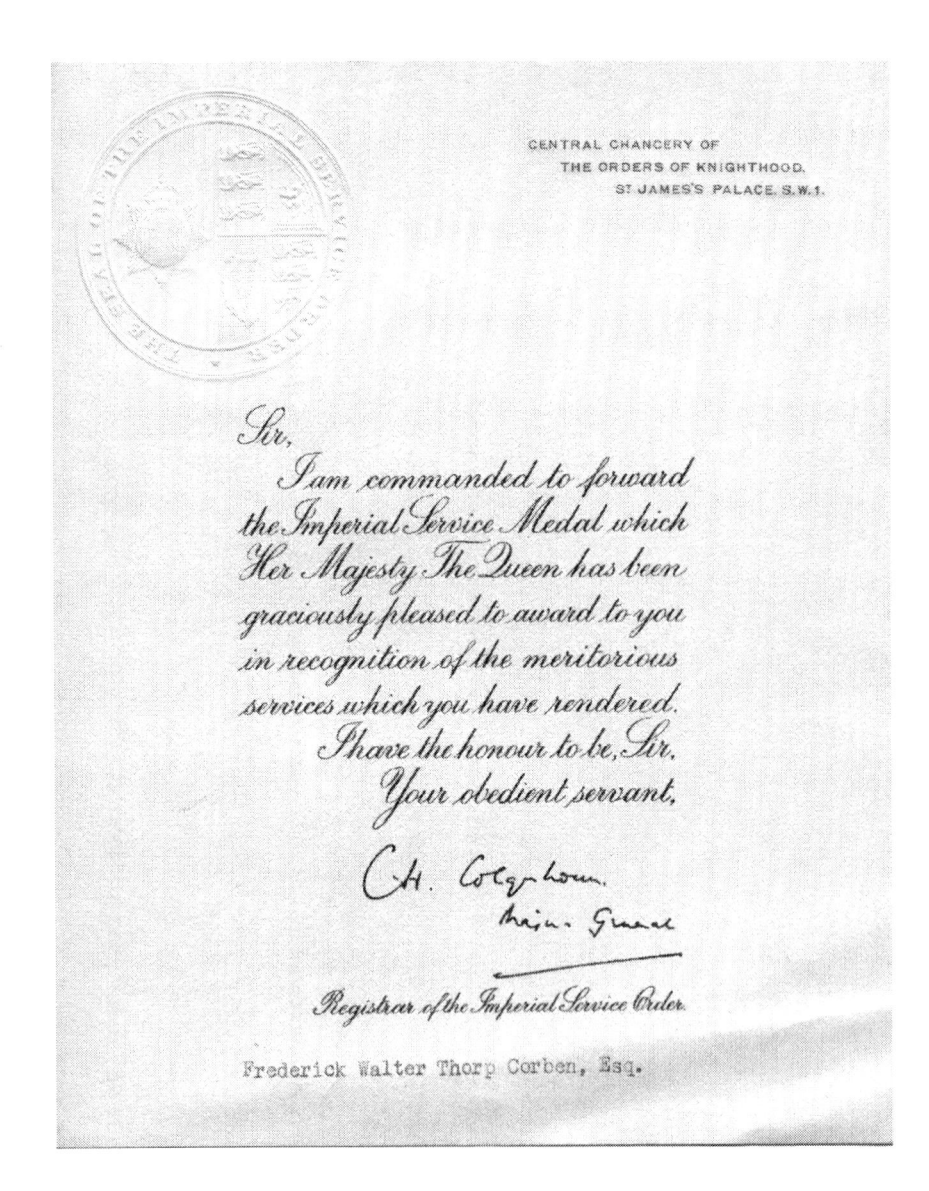

I am commanded to forward the Imperial Service Medal which Her Majesty The Queen has been graciously pleased to award to you in recognition of the meritorious services which you have rendered.

I have the honour to be, Sir,

Your obedient servant,

C.H. Colquhoun.
Major General

Registrar of the Imperial Service Order.

Frederick Walter Thorp Corben, Esq.

Citation for Fred's Empire Service Medal

I WISH TO MARK BY THIS PERSONAL MESSAGE
my appreciation of the service you have rendered to your
Country in 1939.
In the early days of the War you opened your door to strangers
who were in need of shelter, & offered to share your home with
them.
I know that to this unselfish task you have sacrificed much
of your own comfort, & that it could not have been achieved
without the loyal co-operation of all in your household.
By your sympathy you have earned the gratitude of those to
whom you have shown hospitality, & by your readiness to
serve you have helped the State in a work of great value.

Elizabeth R

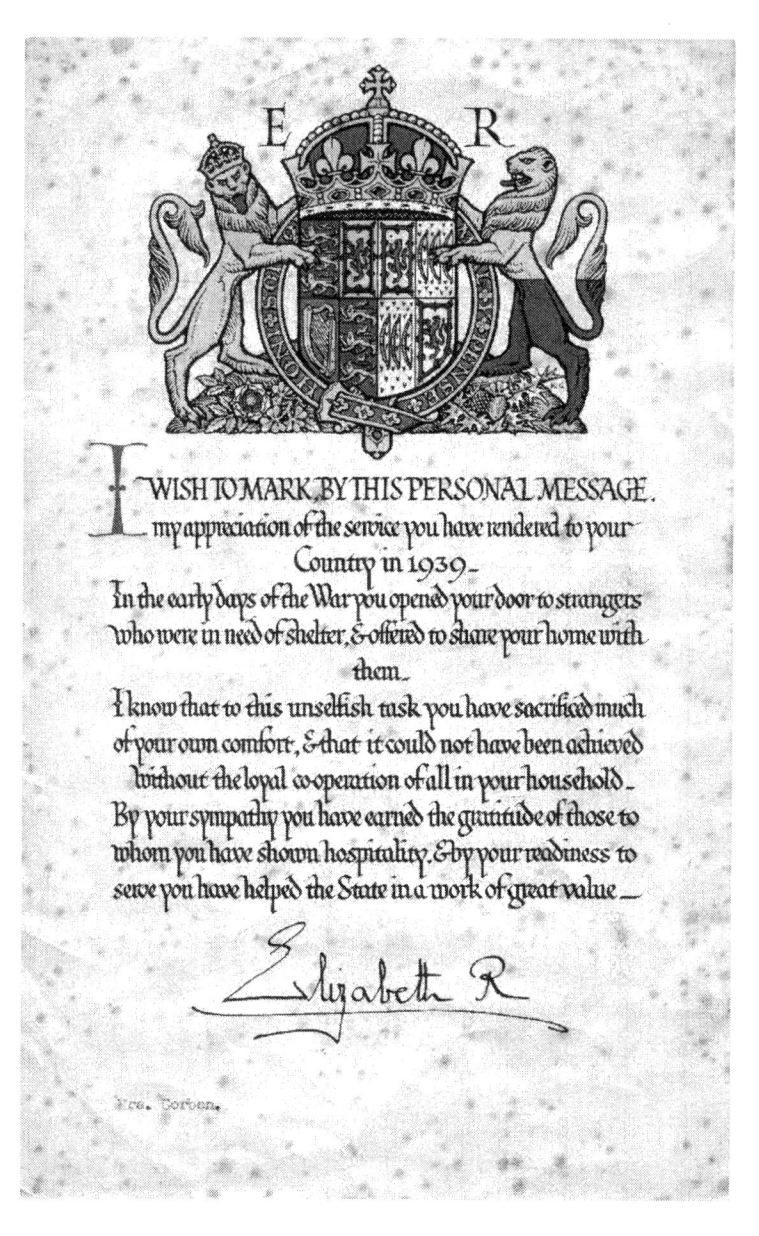

Letter from Buckingham Palace in appreciation of Fred and Daisy's work with evacuees

In the years when
Civilisation was menaced with destruction
F. W. J. Corben
who served 1940 - 1942
gave generously of his time, powers and technical skill in essential service to his Country.

Herbert Creedy

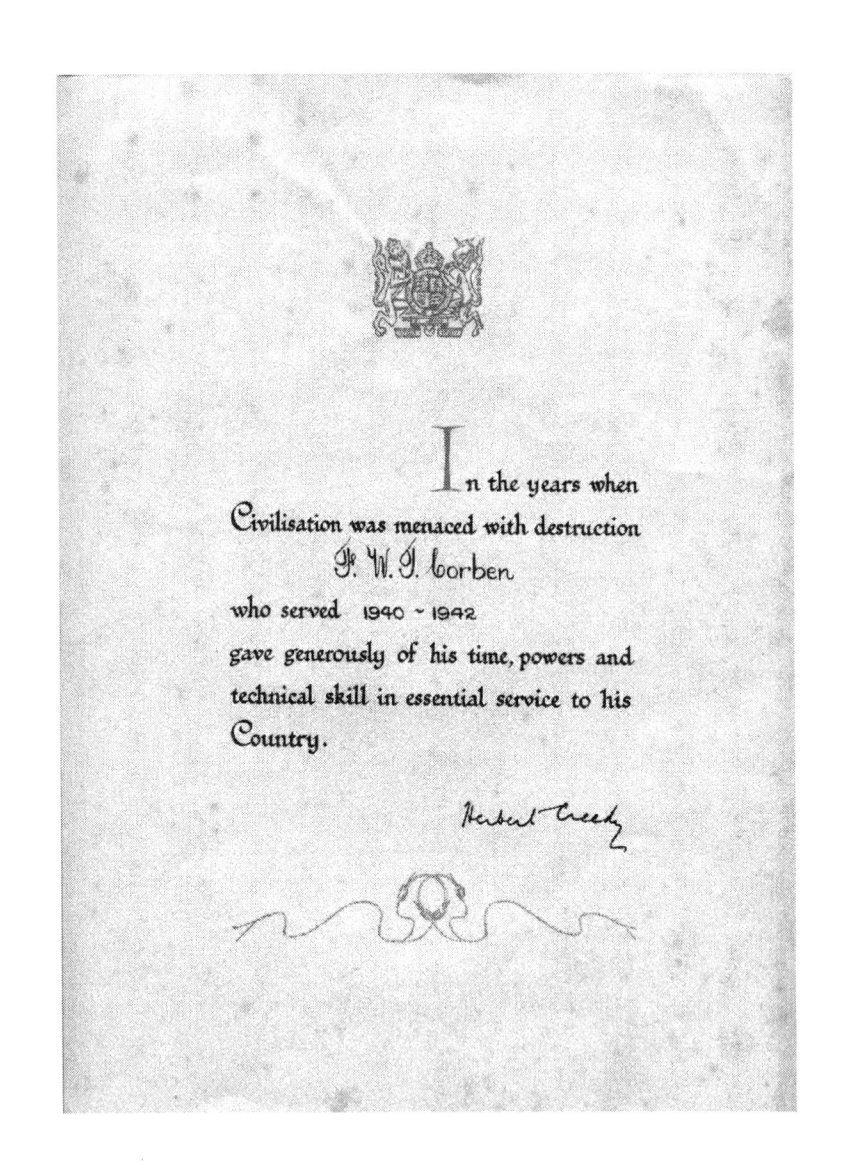

Letter from Sir Herbert Creedy, permanent secretary to the War Office in recognition of Fred's work with the RSS

John Perriman (my uncle)

Dad's eldest sister, Elsie (1907-2006) married John Perriman (1905-1993) in 1934 and they had two children who are my only living cousins Rodney and Sally.

Rodney married Pamela Leale on 28th July, 1962. They have two children, Alex, who lives In Germany, and Nancy, who married Richard Brenchley in 1997 and they have two sons, Jude and Luke.

Sally married John Barfoot in 1960 and had two daughters.

Uncle John was in the Navy 25 years, from 1921, when he was 16, to 1946. He was awarded the DSM, Atlantic and Mediterranean stars, the RN Long Service and Good Conduct medal. He was a telegraphist and was temporarily commissioned in February 1943 to the quasi-permanent rank of Temporary Acting Commissioned Telegraphist.

John Perriman with wife Daisy and her sister Lilly

Uncle John's father

Uncle John's father was Jonathan James Perriman (1877-1940) who married Olivia Louisa Banfield (1885-1952). They had three children John, Daisy Elizabeth (1903-1984) and Lillian (1910-1976).

Daisy Elizabeth was in Quebec, Canada for a year from 1933-4 working as a cook. She travelled out on the Montclare and back on the Empress of Britain.

Jonathan attested to the Royal Army Medical Corps in 1915. His regimental number was 2658 and he was a corporal. Jonathan's character was recorded throughout his service as VG occasionally G. He was living at 276 Queens Road, Maidstone, which is very close to Bower Street, at the time. He had a younger sister, three older brothers and an elder sister.

He also had a tough life. At the age of three he was living in a house without his father, Charles Perriman (1843-1907) who was a barge man so, presumably, was often away. His mother, Elizabeth Reeves (1841-1925), was working in a paper factory to support the family who were boarding with another family. Ten years later he was living in a household headed by his brother, Charles, 21, who was a bricklayer. Jonathan is listed as a bricklayer's labourer at the age of 14.. His trade was listed as Shop Boy at the start of his service.

Coincidently, after WW1, Jonathan was always ill and it was thought that he had been poisoned by gas. He was survived by his wife by 18 years who left her entire estate of £702 9s 2d to Uncle John.

Charles' absence from the family home can be explained two ways. Firstly, he was a bargeman, often with only himself plus a teenager on board. His barge was called 'Sarah Anne.' Also by the time he was fifty years old he was registered as a patient in Broadmoor Asylum at Sandhurst, which was for criminal lunatics, where his occupation was listed as bargeman. Johnathan would have been 16.

Charles was tried in Maidstone Assizes Court for Felonious Injury, which I think we know now as attempted murder.

He was found guilty by the jury on 12 December 1889 and held over in Maidstone before being sent, on the jury's recommendation to Broadmoor on 24 April 1890. Charles was released from Broadmoor in 1901 and died in 1907 when he was hit by a train between Cuxton and Strood.

Uncle John

The book follows the story of John's life on the *Cleopatra* closely using diaries and notes from the time.

Cleopatra went out to Gibraltar early in 1942, and on 9 February she sailed for Malta, where she was immediately damaged by a bomb from a Junkers 88s. After repair, she was transferred to Alexandria in early March to join the 15th Cruiser Squadron. She was Admiral Philip Vian's flagship during the Second Battle of Sirte, when his group of four light cruisers and 17 destroyers held off an Italian force which included the battleship Littorio, two heavy cruisers, a light cruiser and 10 destroyers, which had all been sent to intercept their convoy to Malta.

During the engagement, Cleopatra's radar and wireless stations were wrecked by a 6" round fired by an Italian light cruiser. After the explosion Uncle John found himself surrounded by blown up comrades. To calm him someone gave him a lighted cigarette and so started an 80 a day habit.

It was for his actions during this engagement that he was awarded the DSM 'for outstanding leadership and devotion to duty throughout the action of 22nd March, and skill when nearly all the aerials had been shot away.'

His award was gazetted on 8 September, 1942.

By this time John was a Chief Petty Officer – which is the highest non-commissioned officer in the Royal Navy.

In 1945 *Cleopatra* went out to the East Indies, where she was the first ship into the newly recaptured base at Singapore in September.

Uncle John finished WW2 in Hamburg as a member of the team responsible for decommissioning German ships after VE Day. He was de-mobbed in 1946. Always a keen sportsman John was playing football the day before his de-mob when he broke his leg. He arrived home at Featherby Road, Gillingham in the back of a 3-ton truck with several large German radio sets!

Rare Photo of Corbin Family. L-R. Jimmy, Fred, Elsie, Lilly, Bert, Daisy, Jeanne. My guess is that John took the photo

Frederick Farmer (my grandfather)

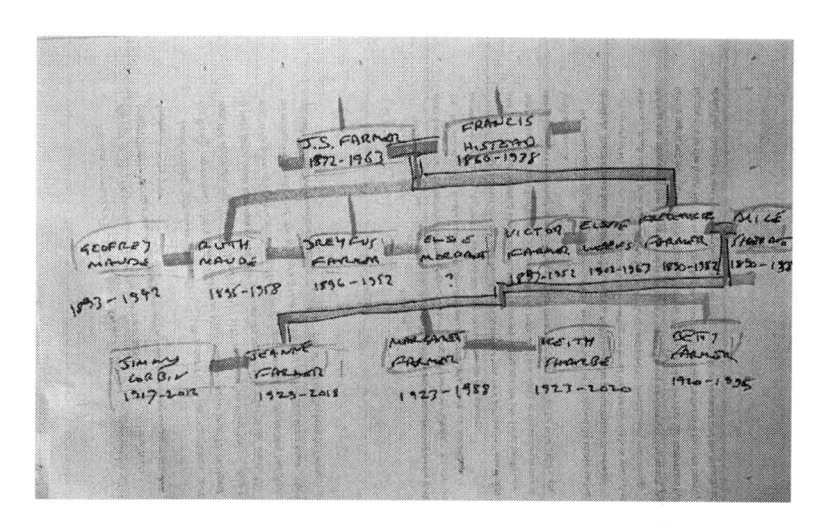

My maternal grandfather, Frederick Farmer, was born on 11th March 1890 in Crowborough Sussex and the family later moved to Tunbridge Wells.

His mother was Frances Elizabeth Selina Histed – his birth certificate shows Frances of Crowborough as his mother and Fredrich Klotz of Germany as his father.

Family legend and Mum's notes on family history suggest that Frederick Farmer (1890-1982), our maternal grandfather, was born out of wedlock. This is true. He was born three years before James Samuel Farmer and Frances Histed were married.

Mum's notes also suggest that her elder sister Betty destroyed Frederick's original birth certificate as she believed that the matters surrounding his birth should be kept secret. For many years, none of the siblings or progeny were told about it at all.

I remember being told that before marrying James Samuel, Frances had an affair with a high-ranking Prussian officer serving in the Prussian embassy in London. Mum's notes say his name was Freidrich Klotz. The family were all poor, agricultural labourers. Any notion of Frances crossing paths with anyone from London, let alone a high raking German diplomat seems highly unlikely.

Frances Farmer (ne Klotz, ne Histead) at 72 Boxley Road, Maidstone

I have obtained a copy of Frederick's original birth certificate from Somerset House (the one Aunty Betty destroyed):

This has the following details:

Frederick was born on 11/3/1890. His father was Edward Klotz whose profession is recorded as a house decorator (journey man) and his mother was Frances Klotz, maiden name Histed. The birth was registered on 12/4/1890 and it looks like registration of the birth was done by Frances on her own. Klotz may not have been there or he may not have existed?

I have also found the marriage details for James Samuel and Frances from 1893 in which she is named as Frances Klotz, not Histed, which was her maiden name.

I can find no record of Frances marrying or divorcing Klotz.

What is certain is that Frances had a child, Frederick, three years before marrying James Samuel. Edward and Frances may have been married or he may never have existed. However, she subsequently married James Samuel, as Frances Klotz and Frederick was raised as their firstborn. However, at the same time, James Samuel Farmer came into possession of the Cock Horse Inn. Where James Samuel got the money to buy a pub when both his father and grandfather were agricultural labourers is unclear…

Frances had three children with Samuel: Victor, Ruth and Dreyfus. Victor married Elsie Weekes, they had no children. Dreyfus married Daisy Merchant and had two children, James (a lecturer) and Gerald (an assistant teacher) who inherited all James Samuel's estate between them.

James Samuel Farmer

Dreyfus Farmer, Frederick's stepbrother

Victor Farmer in the Locomotive, the pub he bought in Ashford with money "embezzled" from Charles Arkcoll and Sons

The Farmer family in 1912. Back row Frederick, Ruth, Victor. Front James Samuel, Frances, Dreyfus

Frederick attested for WW1 on the 9th September 1914 at 57a Farringdon Road in the City of London, the headquarters of the 6th London Regiment. He gave his address as Detling, near Maidstone in Kent and signed in front of a witness that the answers he had given to the questions he had been asked were true. He was in fact living in digs in Maidstone working as a clerk at Charles Arcoll's. Detling was where his mother, and stepfather lived in the Cock Horse Inn which he owned.

3129 Private Frederick Farmer joined the 6th (City of London) Battalion the London Regiment (City of London Rifles) which was raised in 1859 and at the outbreak of the Great War, the battalion, known as the 'Cast Iron 6th' was in the 2nd London Brigade, 1st London Division. At the end of August, a duplicate or second line battalion was formed, and the two battalions were named 1/6th and 2/6th. In November, 1914 the 1/6th was transferred to 4th London Brigade, 2nd London Division, later 140th Brigade, 47th Division with which it remained till January 1918.

Frederick in France early 1915. Second from left

Frederick initially joined the 2/6th Battalion, a reserve battalion formed to accommodate the flood of new recruits, and was subsequently transferred to the 1/6th (the original 6th Battalion, as it had been titled before August 1914) on the 28th February 1915. This posting to the 1/6th Battalion occurred just under three weeks before the battalion set sail for France and so Frederick was an original member of the battalion when it set sail for France.

Training was in Sussex and then Watford. They sailed to Le Harve on the night of 17/18 March, 1915 and they took responsibility for holding a section of the front line for the first time in April. Their first major action was at Loos that September. Subsequently they saw action on the Somme, and at Messines, Third Ypres and Cambrai.

Frederick received a gunshot wound on the 1st September 1915. The bullet entered near his wrist and exited near his elbow. The family in Detling received a telegram on 13th September confirming his admission into Le Petit Trianon hospital in Versailles.

This is where my grandmother, Alice Sherratt, travelled to visit Frederick in September 1915. She assumed the name Farmer by pretending to be his wife whereas they did not get married until 1917 – so a passport obtained on false premises! This was 1915, women rarely travelled on their own and certainly not into a country at war. It was extremely brave to travel into a country at war to visit a wounded man. Alice told my mother that she travelled with some gold sovereigns sewn into the lining of her corset in case of emergency. She must have been a very determined lady to go to such lengths for the man she loved.

Frederick was sent back to UK on 7th October 1915 by No2 Hospital Ship Astona and was in hospital in Aberdeen from 9 October 1915 until 2 March 1916 from where he went to Southwold to be discharged.

According to the roll, Frederick enlisted on the 9th September 1914 and was discharged on the 24th August 1916 as no longer physically fit for war service (the meaning behind paragraph 392 (xvi) of King's Regulations). He was discharged as a result of sickness rather than wounds, and the roll entry confirms that he served overseas. Frederick's silver war badge was impressed with the number 97278.

He and Alice were married on 22nd December 1917 in Detling Church. They lived in King Edward Road Maidstone where Betty, Margaret Mary and Jeanne Ursula were born.

Frederick Farmer's three daughters, Jeanne, Margaret and Betty

In 1940 Frederick became Captain of the Maidstone Home Guard. People with Frederick's experience were asked to join the Auxiliary Units, often known as Churchill's Secret Army, set up to continue fighting in the event of a Nazi invasion. Their members were only known by cover names. Having signed the Official Secrets Act many of these brave volunteers took their secret to their grave.

Officers of Maidstone Home Guard A Company. Frederick is second from left front row

He was awarded a pension for life of 8s/week and two in service payments of 16s and 12s. Frederick remained a member of the Old Comrades Association of the City of London Rifles until his death in 1982.

Alice and Frederick Farmer

Frederick in full Masons regalia. He was a member of several lodges.

Geoffrey Richard Gwynydd Maund

Frederick's step-sister, Ruth Farmer, married the swashbuckling Geoffrey Maund who was handsome, brave and debonair. He was in the Navy and the Flying Corps in the 1914-18 war and dabbled in all the dangerous sports possible.

Ruth Maund (née Farmer)

Jeanne Corbin: 'The album of photographs and cuttings are wonderful to read through – especially the motorcycle racing episodes – he ended up doing something in the Far East equally dashing. I never met him but he must have been quite a man.'

In a letter from Geoffrey Maund to Ruth 'This was taken by my boy. 6:30 outside my bungalow.'

'It doesn't appear that he and Ruth ever had a home, other than some rooms for a while in Albion Place, Sittingbourne Road, where Betty remembered visiting them for James Samuel was not in favour of the match and Ruth was forced to live at home in the pub as a housekeeper, cook and bottle washer for the rest of her life. She too was quite a daring lady in her time and was the first woman in Maidstone to own and ride a motorcycle and wear leathers with trousers; quite shocking. She swore like a trooper and although small and delicately made had a huge persona. I don't believe James Samuel allowed her to work outside the pub, or later in his home, but she stole whatever she could from her father – 'the old bugger' – her words.'

Geoffrey Maund was in the RAF Air Sea Rescue Service, but rumours have persisted that this was just a cover for other activities more suited to his experience and temperament.

Jeanne Corbin (née Farmer) Mum

Jeanne at Stone Bay, Broadstairs

Mum was a child during the war and the book follows her life closely, the only fictional part of Jeanne's story is the evacuee story.

Mum was born in 1929, the third of three daughters. She was schooled as her mother was (and as my sisters were) at Brunswick House County Primary and then at Maidstone Girls Grammar School – mostly during WW2.

Jeanne at the tennis club at the top of Postley Road. August 1954

She matriculated before taking the civil service exams leading her to work at Scotland Yard until marrying Dad in 1955. Three kids later she went back to work as an usher in the courts of Maidstone. She was a school governor, lead her old girl's association and was Bearsted ladies golf club captain. She survived Dad but dementia set in soon after, and after fighting off several bouts of cancer left us in 2016. She was bright, intelligent, very social, fun and displayed the old-fashioned virtues of never complaining, helping others and being the rock around which our family was built.

Brian Corbin

Brian Corbin attended Maidstone Grammar School and graduated from Southampton University with a BSc in engineering. His career was marked by the successful delivery of major infrastructure projects worldwide and significant groundbreaking first of a kinds. Now retired, he lives in south London and is deeply involved in trying to reduce his golf handicap despite being diagnosed with Parkinson's 20 years ago.

Printed in Great Britain
by Amazon